A history of religion and politics in Turkey:
A Century of Contradictions

I0160728

Tatavla Publishing
Türkiye Series - 1

Tatavla Publishing
Türkiye Series - 1

A history of religion and politics in Turkey:
A Century of Contradictions
by Racho Donef

First Edition, Paperback 2022, Sydney
ISBN: 978-0-9874239-3-1

Cover and design: Cemil Gündoğan

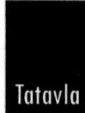

Tatavla

A history of religion and politics in Turkey:

A Century of Contradictions

RACHO DONEF

Tatavla Publishing
Sydney

TABLES

ACKNOWLEDGMENTS

A doctoral thesis is in theory an individual effort, and for the most part it is. However, in practice the active assistance of the supervisors renders it a collective effort. I am indebted to Professor Marion Maddox and Dr Banu Şenay for their great efforts to keep me on track, as I often waivered from the target. They provided me with invaluable feedback on various drafts. I could not complete the thesis on which the present book is based without their support.

Contents

PART C

PREFACE

This study was originally prepared as a thesis for the requirement of a doctorate in philosophy degree in the field of political science, with the title of "Religion or Secular Politics in The Turkish Republic: laicism and secularism". Some changes were required to the present book as a thesis is intended for a very narrow readership and it was necessary to update some of the content to some extent reflect the latest developments in the Turkish political process (see Postscript). These developments post-completion have not altered the basic findings of the thesis. Though, there is no question that the pace of Islamisation remained stable, i.e. on course to alter the secular aspects of the Turkish society. There were also many developments occurring in the political scene as the 2023 elections are approaching. However, these developments related to the political process are not the focus of this study.

Furthermore, given the requirements in relation to the size of a doctoral thesis are stringent, additional material that could not be used for the thesis were added to the present, hopefully, without affecting the main arguments of this study.

SYNOPSIS

This study focuses on the interaction between religion and politics in Turkey. The problematic examined is whether, in the context of Turkish history and politics, these two fields of human endeavour are autonomous from each other. The secondary question examined is whether Turkey can be described as a secular/laic state.

As the Turkish society throughout the Republic's history underwent radical transformations, first transitioning to a secular society and then to a "post-secular" one, the nature and effect of these changes is an important area of social inquiry. The current political and social *milieu* and group conflicts in Turkey can only be understood in the larger context of the Republic's history. The study examines the foundation principles of Turkey, including various competing narratives, and whether these principles have been properly applied and sustained.

It is my contention that in contemporary Turkey the fields of religion and politics are indistinguishable, nationalism acting as a conduit. This is not necessarily a unique situation. These boundaries are porous in other societies as well. Turkey is a particularly intriguing society through which to study the interaction between the two fields because no Muslim majority country went to the length the Kemalists did, to achieve laicism and secularisation.

I also argue that laicism has not been very successful, although the early Republican Kemalist state made enormous efforts to implement secularisation as part of westernisation and modernisation, the three-pillar strategy. The process of secularisation was followed by the process of de-secularisation as the tight grip of Kemalism loosened and the power of the Islamists grew. I argue that, while the de-secularisation process has been underway for some time, the secular has not disappeared but co-exists with the non-secular in a hybrid form: "practical secularity" (as opposed to ideological secularity).

Finally, I also argue that the Republican system established the founder Mustafa Kemal's hegemony. This Kemalist hegemony was gradually replaced by the hegemony of Islamist Recep Tayyip Erdoğan and his Justice and Development Party (*Adalet ve Kalkınma Partisi*). All the signs indicate that this hegemony is also in the process, or at least at risk, of being dismantled and AKP is riddled with scandals, mismanagement, blatant favouritism, and disregard to the plight of the population.

The Kemalist and the Islamist narratives are examined in light of a variety of primary and secondary sources in several languages to construct a cohesive and analytical account of the Republic, tying it to the theoretical material related to the themes of the study.

PART A

CHAPTER 1: INTRODUCTION

Preamble

At first glance, the scope of the study appears to be wide, covering as it does a century of historical context. Yet, I only outline and analyse the political context which is relevant to the title of the study. Eric Zürcher's comprehensive review of Turkish Republic's History consists of 429 pages.[1] The biography on Mustafa Kemal alone by Andrew Mango contains over 660 pages.[2] My study is not as ambitious and the scope of the study is more limited than it appears. However, I endeavoured to trace the most important stages in the Turkish political history in the last hundred years or so. Selecting only a period in the history of the Republic for this subject matter would not have been satisfactory. To understand the deeper context in which Turkish socio-political processes operate, even the immediate imperial past needs to be considered to some extent.

Sources

Any researcher working on religion and politics in Turkey will in no time ascertain that there is no shortage of material related to these themes both in English and Turkish. This study also uses sources in other languages, primarily in French.[3] On the basis of the authors' ideological position, the Turkish sources can be classified roughly as Kemalists, Islamists, and left-leaning secularists. Historically, Kemalist sources tended to label Islamists or those opposing the three pillars of westernisation, secularisation, modernisation project as "backward" (*gerici*). Primary Kemalist sources in the early Republican period, consisting mainly of memoirs of politicians and high-level administrators, reflect this thinking. Secondary sources of the same ilk in later years maintained this tendency of polemicism against recalcitrants. The parliamentary proceedings of the early period (1920-1930), including the "secret proceedings", provide a more objective, first hand, source.

---

1. Zürcher, Erik, *Turkey*, London, 2004.
2. Andrew Mango. *Atatürk*, New York, 2000.
3. Occasionally, sources in Greek, Italian and Spanish are also used. Unless otherwise indicated, all translation, from the identified languages are my own.

This is counter-balanced with a review of Islamist writings. The Islamist sources used in the study vary. Their point of view depends on whether they supported Necmettin Erbakan and various iterations of *Millî Görüş* (National Perspective)[4], headed by him, Recep Tayyip Erdoğan and the Justice and Development Party (*Adalet ve Kalkınma Partisi*/AKP) in later years, or Fethullah Gülen. Considerable space has been dedicated in the study of two prominent Islamic thinkers of the early years: Bediüzzaman Said Nursî (1877–1960) and Necip Fazıl Kısakürek (1904-1983). Both have been influential in setting the agenda for opposition to the Kemalist project and inspired generations of Islamists, including those who sought to re-transform Turkish society, to reverse the three pillars of Kemalist reforms.

Secondary foreign sources include both research of academics but also of think tanks. Think tanks have stated or concealed objectives to pursue, depending on their source of funding, and caution is exercised in utilising these sources. Nevertheless, the same can be said for academic scholarship. It has to be expected that research tends to reflect the bias of the proponent whether ideological or due to expediency. Either way, motivated reasoning is often in play. Furthermore, current western scholarship goes to great lengths not to be seen criticising aspects of Islam, especially under the influence of Edward Said's Orientalism, and therefore many of these studies fall short. In contrast, Kemalist scholars go to great length to criticise Islamists, overlooking Kemal's contradictory discourse on Islam. At the same time, there is a plethora of studies of think tanks, which pursue a veiled anti-Islamic agenda, and portray Mustafa Kemal as anti-Islamic in order to promote Turkey as a model for other Muslim-majority countries to emulate.

The field of study is therefore riddled with contradictions and paradoxes both because the theoretical terrain related to such concepts as religion, politics, Islamism, secularism and modernism contain their own incongruities and because of the promotion of various ideological agendas. A student of politics and religion in Turkey needs to weed out the exaggerations, the propaganda, the bias in the sources to reach a balanced conclusion. This is by no means a straightforward process. In this endeavour, a number of primary sources such as British Diplomatic cables, Wikileaks cables, newspapers, journal articles and party program pamphlets were utilised, in addition to those mentioned above.

---

4. Also translated as National Viewpoint or Outlook.

Study arguments

The present is about the interplay of politics and religion in Turkey. The title suggests that these two fields can be separated, but the boundaries between them are amorphous. The stated objective of laicism by the early Republican regime did not translate to laicisation i.e. separation of religion and politics, but it remained a forceful state narrative until Erdoğan came to power. I argue that the entire project of laicism project was flawed in execution. Separation of religion and politics did not occur; instead, the management of "religion", i.e. Sunni Islam, became a state project. As Taha Parla and Andrew Davison contend "[t]hrough these reforms, the removal of religious influence from within the state was to be achieved by subordinating religion to the state, rather than simply their separation".[5]

There was a separation of the two spheres only as a rhetorical construct with its commensurate narrative, for a good part of the Republic's history. There are two key reasons for this problematical implementation of laicism. Firstly, from the beginning, the Republican founders, i.e. the Republicans, because of political expediency, chose to be in the business of management of religion by controlling and defining it. Anti-clericalism, which was fervently expressed by the Republicans, is not considered a sufficient condition for laicism. The stated objective of laicism was therefore stillborn. The powerful institution of *Diyanet İşleri Başkanlığı* (Presidency of Religious Affairs/Diyanet), established in 1923, throughout the Republic's history implemented government policies, though at times putting forward its own views. Diyanet has never been an autonomous institution but a tool of the government of the day. Seeking to monopolise the "religious market", it has played a significant role in shaping the way Islam is practised, both at home and outside Turkey where significant communities of Turkish migrants live.

The second reason for the failure to implement laicism was the ideological undercurrents and opposition to state policies within the society. These ideological currents expressed themselves through a variety of religious formations: *tarikats* (Sufi orders) as representatives of folk-Islam (or exilic Islam), especially the Nakshibendi tarikat, *cemaats* (religious communities, e.g., Nursî, Gülen) and *Millî Görüş*, a religio-political movement. These formations competed for the meaning and proper role of their version of Islam in Turkish society while Diyanet continued to shape the official Islam.

---

5. Taha Parla and Andrew Davison, *Corporatist ideology on Kemalist Turkey*, Syracuse, New York, 2004, p. 118.

The emergence of Islamic political parties from the 1960s onwards, and the integration and absorption of Islamic social movement in these parties, have contributed to the eventual demise of the narrative of laicism. However, I also argue that the differences between the two sides, the Kemalists and the Islamists, were/are not as divergent as promoted by both parties.

My core argument is that there is no observable distinction between institutional religion and politics in contemporary Turkey, noting that nationalism played an agglutinative role in connecting the two fields. By institutional religion, I refer to organisations with structure, ecclesiastical and administrative hierarchy and established dogmas, rather than to religion as lived out by individuals. There are a variety of approaches to the study of religion, as discussed in the following chapter.

To be sure, Mustafa Kemal and his cohort saw "religion" as something antithetical to the "secular". Although they used this concept ("religion") to suit political needs, their approach was to control the associated practices via Diyanet, singling out Sunni Islam as the dominant form to harness and shape Islam in Turkey and maintaining a monopoly over other interpretations of Islam. In the process, they needed to navigate strategies to address Alevis, who are not Sunni, and the religious orders (*tarikats*) which were popular among the subaltern. They chose to eliminate tarikats. With Alevism, they chose a *laisse-faire* attitude, once they encouraged academics to make a connection between an alleged primordial Turkic religion, shamanism, and a constructed Alevism.

I will be analysing laicism as a *portmanteau* concept incorporating the notion of secularism. While laicism was not comprehensively implemented, early Republicans had substantial success in applying secularist ideology to secularise the Turkish society. The secularisation process they chose was to remove Islam from the public square and introduce radical changes into the legal system. Removing Islamic symbols from the public sphere went hand in hand with a de-Ottomanisation of cities. Biray Kirli Kolluoğlu argues that as "part of the process of the construction of Turkish nationalism in the 1920s", the Republicans embarked upon "destruction of Ottoman spaces and the redefinition and reconstruction of new cityscapes and public spaces".[6] The Republicans sought to de-Islamise and de-Ottomanise Turkish society.

Despite considerable opposition, Kemalists were able to pursue secularisation as part of their three pillars strategy (modernisation and westernisation being the other two). This was challenged by the emerging political

---

6. Biray Kirli Kolluoglu, 'Forgetting the Smyrna Fire', *History Workshop Journal*, Issue 60, Autumn 2005, p. 27.

Islam and eventually the dismantling of the secular edifice – de-secularisation process – was/is undertaken by AKP.

Turkish political history is often seen as a continuous conflict between the Islamists and the laicists/secularists.[7] Jenny White notes that "Turkish society appears to be divided into secular and Muslim positions".[8] Certainly, when for the first time the Islamist parties emerged in the 1960s, the laicist establishment tried to shut them down for fear of undermining what they claimed to be the laic foundations of the state. In turn, the Islamist parties used a discourse hostile to laicism, which seemed to represent a wide gap between the two views. However, both sides exaggerated their position to suit their respective political and ideological agendas. The differences were not as pronounced. The laicists, at least in the early years, used an anti-theocratic language but at the same time, they defined Turkishness as a synthesis of nationalism and Islamic religion and promoted the notion of "the acceptable citizen" (makbul vatandaş). İhsan Yılmaz calls this ideal citizen, "Homo LASTus", a concept similar to WASP, composed of the acronym in Turkish, i.e. Laicist, Atatürkist, Sunni Muslim and Turkish.[9]

Parties espousing Islam as their primary drive, starting from Necmettin Erbakan in 1969, employed a nationalist discourse as well as an Islamic one. Erbakan was competing with other nationalist parties (all except the Turkish Worker's Party/Türkiye İşçi Partisi which did not display nationalism). This is not to suggest that Islam was not a component of nationalism already. Erbakan's parties also synthesised religion with nationalism, much like Mustafa Kemal, but starting from a different point. Mustafa Kemal started with nationalism as a base and added religion; Islamists started with religion and added nationalism. The gap was only seen as wide because both sides exaggerated their position and emphasised different aspects of the synthesis.

Undeniably, there were some differences. The nationalism of Mustafa Kemal, "proto-Kemalism" as I call it, that is Kemal's Kemalism defined the basis of the Turkish nation as essentially pre-Islamic and went to great length to encourage academics to manufacture an idealistic past originating in Central Asia. On the other hand, Erbakan's first Party, National Order (Millî Nizâm Partisi), articulating principles of an ideology known as Millî Görüş, saw the history of the Turkish nation as approximately 1,000

---

7. For instance see Zeyno Baran, *Torn Country*, Stanford, 2010, p. 12; Elliot Ackerman, 'Atatürk Versus Erdoğan: Turkey's Long Struggle', *The New Yorker*, 16 July 2016.

8. Jenny White, *Muslim Nationalism and the New Turks*, Princeton and Oxford, 2013, pp. 10-11.

9. İhsan Yılmaz, *Kemalizm'den Erdoğanizm'e*, İstanbul, 2015, pp. 9-10.

years old; essentially, starting from the arrival of Seljuk (*Selçuk*) tribes in Anatolia. In time, the Kemalist establishment, post-Kemal, also shifted its position from the anti-Ottoman rhetoric of the first years, thereby minimising the differences between the two versions of nationalism.

Eventually, Erdoğan used the scaffolding established by other Islamists to gain power in 2002. Between 2002 and 2018 many changes to de-secularise the public sphere were introduced - gradually at first, at an increased pace later. These changes have profoundly affected the state and civil society. Erdoğan started as a leader of an Islamist party, the AKP, which he called moderate. The initial absence of nationalism in his language supports this claim. Gradually, this gave way to yet another synthesis of nationalism and religion; a synthesis not a great deal different to the original, since it still excluded non-Sunnis and Kurds. The only difference, between the "acceptable citizen", as constructed in the early years, is that it was no longer required to be Kemalist or Atatürkist. A new nationalism of reduced Kemalist content emerged, though in the last stages of 2017 and early 2018, Erdoğan rediscovered Kemalism - a version of Kemalism, say "pseudo-Kemalism". This was Kemalism simply for the purposes of the elections in 2018: to divert votes from the far-right parties, which still held on to a nationalist version of Kemalism.

In the process of establishing his rule, Erdoğan strengthened Diyanet, which became even more involved in the diaspora affairs as a long arm of the state. His party now controlled political discourse through a whole set of institutions and mechanisms (Diyanet, Constitutional Court, the military, education, media) and shaped public life to reflect its perspective, much like Mustafa Kemal once did.

Turkey under Erdoğan provided a striking example of the mutual interrelatedness of religion and politics with the state no longer promoting Kemalist ideology or laicism. The foundation myths are no longer useful as the governing party now produces different kind of discourse, for instance martyrdom, using Islamic motives. The original project to manage, control and define Islam through the monopoly of one party and ideology has transformed the state to a near monopoly of another party, which still constructs and defines Islam, nationalism and civic life.

Though it is only peripheral to the problematic examined, one other aspect of the Turkish Republic is the extent of the dominance of the state. The Kemalist regime has often been described as "hegemonic" by many scholars (see Parla and Davison),[10] given its domination of nearly

10. Parla and Davison, *op. cit.*, p. 35.

all aspects of life. However, dominance alone is not hegemony; hegemony requires consent:

> For Gramsci, hegemony is based on a combination of consent and dominion. In essence, the subordinate classes are consenting to be dominated. 'Organic Intellectuals', become the educators of the masses spreading the word of the ruling class and thus achieving the consent of the masses.[11]

This hegemony is achieved by "internalization by members of society" consciously or subconsciously.[12] The system of governance the Kemalist built fit the Gramscian theorem. It is therefore hypothesis that Turkey under Kemal was a hegemonic system, and, in time, this hegemony shifted from Kemalist Republican/secularists to Islamists. The Kemalists held a genuine belief in their radical agenda to pursue their three-pillar strategy but they were unable to carry it out through democratic means.

Finally, another incidental field in the study of this kind is, inevitably, a review of Kemalist historiography. Especially until the 1980s, the Kemalists nearly monopolised the narrative related to the creation of the Republic. This study seeks to balance this by utilising non-Kemalist, including Islamist sources, often overlooked primary sources and secondary sources of later periods when the Kemalist taboos were gradually becoming insignificant and disregardable. The narrative constructed by the Kemalists and official historians is no longer the dominant one. Post-1983, after neo-liberal Turgut Özal came to power, non-Kemalist Turkish historians (Islamists and leftists) in a more liberal environment, were able to challenge the official version, question, review and revise Republican history.

Study outline

Part A consists of the introductory chapter (Chapter 1) and Chapter 2, which deals with the theoretical concepts related to the theme of the study: religion, politics, secularism, Kemalism, Alevism and political Islam. In Chapter 2.1 it is pointed out that the definition of religion proved to be a challenging task and different points of view on the subject are juxtaposed. The task becomes harder when a separation line between the two fields is traced, only to discover such a separation line to be moveable. In Chapter

---

11. John D'Attoma, Hegemony or Dominance? A Gramscian Analysis of US Ascendancy, January 2011, https://www.researchgate.net/publication/284284551, [Accessed on 24 April 2019], p. 13.
12. Parla and Davison, *op. cit.*, p. 35.

2.2 it is argued that in the Turkish context secularism has to be separated from laicism, in order to evaluate its applicability in Turkey. Chapter 2.3 reviews political Islam as a relatively novel concept. Chapter 2.4 focuses on Alevism as a system occupying space beyond state sanctioned Islam. In Chapter 2.5 it is contended that Kemalism is a multi-layered and flexible, if somewhat incoherent, ideology. Its multiple layers are examined to demonstrate its flexibility and adaptability as an ideology to suit changing requirements.

Part B deals with a period spanning from 1920 to 1960. The first two chapters are dedicated to the period in which Kemal dominated politics until his death in 1938. The remaining chapters deal with the post Kemal period. Chapter 3 reviews the period leading up to the proclamation of the Republic (1920-1923). I label this era pre-Kemalist, as Kemal's attitude towards Islam is supportive, as well as exploitative, in order to form and maintain alliances to further his agenda. Once the Republic was proclaimed, Kemal changed his tack and put measures in place to control Islamic institutions. Chapter 4 argues that while Kemal was pursuing this radical agenda, paradoxically, he also ensured the designation of Islam as one of the core components of Turkish identity. Chapter 5 reviews Kemalism in the absence of Kemal and the slow dilution of the Kemalist ideology in light of pressure by Islamists, including two prominent intellectuals, Necip Fazıl Kısakürek and Beddiüzaman Said Nursî.

Part C examines the transformation of the Turkish society from a relatively secular one to a society where the visible Islam expanded its space. Chapter 6 reviews what I call the pre- post-secular period. What Turkish historians call the Second Republic, initiated after the 1960 coup, is a period in which Kemalists still dominated the political, social and cultural landscape and tried to control political Islam. After the 1980 coup, the control of political Islam took the form of accommodating it in part, in order to limit its expansion in the public sphere but also to ensure Kemalists stayed in power. Chapter 7 analyses the Gülen movement which proved to be a catalyst for the ascendancy of political Islam in the domination of Turkish politics over nearly two decades. This is further reviewed in Chapter 8, where the intensification of a de-secularisation process is noted. In the Epilogue (Chapter 9) it is posited that seemingly dichotomous concepts and categories converge in the context of Turkish politics: religion and politics, the sacred and the profane, Kemalism and Islamism. In relation to the main themes of the study it is concluded that religion and politics are interrelated, laicism as a project failed and that the secular space has retreated, but that both Islam and the secular co-habit in a new form. Finally, the Postscript includes a brief update on recent political development, which, as I argue, do not alter the main arguments of the study..

CHAPTER 2: THEORETICAL CONSIDERATIONS

2.1 RELIGION AND POLITICS

At the outset, it is important to state that this study is not about "religion" *per se*. It is rather a study of the interaction between religion and politics in Turkey, a country which from 1923 onwards promulgated an ideology and practice of laicisation. The study title, "Religious or Secular Politics in The Turkish Republic", suggests that these two official domains, religion and politics, can be separated, but the boundaries between the two fields are not clearly demarcated. Laicisation was meant to separate the two fields and lead to secularisation of the Turkish society. Myron J Aronoff notes that

> Religion and Politics have been inextricably interrelated since the dawn of human culture and civilization. Yet the scholarly tradition has tended to reify the dichotomous analytics distinctions made to distinguish between the two dimensions of human activity.[13]

A related theme to explore is whether a Muslim-majority society can be secular, when many scholars and Islamists argue that Islam at its inception was a temporal as well as spiritual system.[14] In the Ottoman Empire after the reclamation of the office of the Caliphate, the Sultan as Caliph also combined these roles. However, in time with the creation of the office of the Şeyhülislâm, the Sultan divested from the spiritual role by transferring this authority to the Şeyhülislâm (*Shayk-al-Islām*). While the *Sadrazam* (Prime Minister) looked after administrative affairs, the Şeyhülislâm managed "religious affairs". Nevertheless, as Gazi Erdem notes: "The Şeyhülislâm had both political and religious authority, as the Ottoman state provided the means and independence for the Şeyhülislâm to organise and administer Islamic affairs."[15] The Republic inherited this opaque triumvirate, which was partly reformed only during the Ittihadist period.

We must also bear in mind that the experiment with secularisation imposed from above faced many stumbling blocks, opposition from below and militant Islam, in other Muslim countries, *inter alia* Afghanistan (both

---

13. Myron J Aronoff, "Introduction" in Myron J Aronoff, (ed.), *Religion and Politics*, New Brunswick and London, 1984, p. 1.
14. For instance, Gareth Jenkins. *Political Islam in Turkey*, Basingstoke, 2008, p. 2.
15. Gazi Erdem, Religious Services in Turkey: From the Office of Şeyhülislâm to the Diyanet, *The Muslim World*, Vol. 98, No. 2-3, p. 201.

under Amānullāh Khān and the Soviet era), Iran under the Shah and Egypt in various periods.

Though, as stated, this study is not directly about religion as such, a discussion about religion is unavoidable. Yet, before we even embark upon the study we encounter a number of definitional problems. Indeed, what is "religion"? This is not a simple question. Many scholars have attempted to define religion and perhaps no definition is satisfactory. No single definition would capture cross-cultural, cross-historical and lived experiences of what modern English speakers refer to as "religion". However, my focus is not lived in religion but institutional religion, as described in the introduction.

If religion cannot be defined, at least not satisfactorily, then how can its interaction with the political sphere be evaluated? Also, how do we define secularisation, or laicisation (*laiklik*), to cite the preferred Kemalist expression, in order to measure its effect on political and social life? These are significant questions, which need to be tackled before the specific circumstances of Turkey can be assessed.

The concepts of the sacred and the profane are a useful starting point. The sacred/profane distinction was first delineated by Émile Durkheim in 1912 in his *Elementary Forms of the Religious Life*:

> All known religious beliefs, whether simple or complex, present one common characteristic: they presuppose a classification of all the things, real and ideal, of which men [sic] think, into two classes or opposed groups, generally designated by two distinct terms which are translated well enough by the words profane and sacred (profane, sacré). This division of the world into two domains, the one containing all that is sacred, the other all that is profane, is the distinctive trait of religious thought; . . . by sacred things one must not simply understand those personal beings which are called gods or spirits; a rock, a tree, a spring, a pebble, a piece of wood, a house, in a word, anything can be sacred. A rite can have this character; . . . The circle of sacred objects cannot be determined, then, once for all. Its extent varies infinitely . . . .[16]

In 1959, Mircea Eliade systematised the distinction between the sacred and the profane further, though he made no reference to Durkheim. Eliade argued that the concept of the sacred first appeared in Rudolf Otto's *Das Heilige* (The Sacred), published in 1917, and persisted in 1959. According to Eliade, "[t]he sacred always manifests itself as a reality of a wholly dif-

---

16. Émile Durkheim, *Elementary Forms of the Religious Life*, trans. Joseph Ward Swain, London, 1915.

ferent order from "natural realities" and can be defined as the opposite of the profane.[17]

In order "to designate the act of manifestation of the sacred", Eliade employed the term "hierophany" and used the example of a sacred stone. A stone that it is the same as any other stone in its constituent qualities may be regarded as sacred in the process of hierophany. For instance, the Black Stone (*al-Ḥajar al-Aswad*) in *Kaaba* is revered by Muslims as an Islamic relic which, according to Muslim tradition, dates back to the time of Adam and Eve. To others, looking at it from the profane point of view, the stone may be indistinguishable from any other black stone but to those that venerate it "its immediate reality is transmuted into a supernatural reality".[18] The same can be said of *Kaaba* itself, which has been reconstructed and rebuilt many times to the point of not having much in common with the original, pre-Islamic structure, except it occupies the same space.

This is the most elementary manifestation of the sacred, which can graduate to what Eliade calls "supreme hierophany", for example "the incarnation of God in Jesus Christ"[19], or to provide an example pertinent to Islam, Prophet Muhammad's ascent to heaven in the Night Journey to meet the prophets. Though "for those who have religious experience . . . The cosmos in its entirety can become hierophany", Eliade concludes that there are two modalities of experience, the sacred and the profane, which is divided by the abyss.[20]

In Eliade's study therefore, there is a clearly established boundary between the sacred (religious experience) and the profane (secular experience). This is in line with Durkheim's definition "of religion based on the distinction between sacred and profane: 'a religion is a unified system of beliefs and practices relative to *sacred things*, that is to say, things set apart and forbidden'".[21] William Arnal and Russell T. McCutcheon, interpreting Durkheim's definition, contend that

> the content of each of the categories if we follow Durkheim, essentially [is] arbitrary. Anything can be sacred in a given society, provided only that it is not profane, and vice versa. A visitor to New York's Metropolitan Museum of Art, for example, will find in the collection a medieval reliquary containing a (supposed) tooth of Mary Magdalene.[22]

17. Mircea Eliade, *The Sacred & the Profane*, New York, 1959, pp. 8 and 10.
18. Eliade, p. 11.
19. *Ibid.*, p. 11.
20. *Ibid.*, pp. 12 and 14.
21. William Arnal and Russell T McCutcheon, *The Sacred is the Profane*, Oxford, 2013, p. 21.
22. *Ibid.*, p. 21.

The relic can be regarded both as sacred and profane, depending on each individual's perception of reality. The point Arnal and McCutcheon are making is the arbitrary nature of these qualities and experiences. They could have also cited that the various relics of Prophet Muhammad such as his beard (*Sakal-ı Şerif*) located in Topkapı Museum, as examples from the Islamic world to demonstrate the universality of this arbitrariness. A sacred object may fall out of favour and become profane or a place of pilgrimage may no longer viewed as such. The pilgrimage of Santiago de Compostela, which was significant in the sixteenth century, waned in significance in modern times; yet it became popular again in recent times, as a kind of both sacred and profane undertaking. There are people who follow the established course as a "religious" experience, while cyclists follow the route as a sporting activity. Thus, the sacred is indistinguishable from the profane, except in the minds of the participants.[23]

Clearly, the sacred does not have to be an object. As Ann Taves points out:

> [I]n the case of the shrine at Lourdes ... most Catholics do not consider the water holy special in its own right, but by virtue of its association with an alleged appearance of the Virgin Mary to Bernadette Soubrious. The primary thing that was set apart, in other words, was not an object (the water), but an event (a series of visionary experiences).[24]

Experiences of apparitions of the Virgin Mary turned profane spaces into sacred only for a short period. Thus, the profane can become sacred and vice versa for intermittent periods. Nonetheless, in Eliade the chasm between these realms of experiences (the sacred and the profane) is vast and discernible.

Subsequent scholarship elaborated further and argued the gulf not to be so unambiguous or wide. The Santiago de Compostela example demonstrates that perhaps there is no abyss after all. The clear boundaries in Eliade are blurred in Arnal and McCutcheon's *The Sacred is the Profane*. As the title suggests, their study is antithetical to Eliade's and the dichotomy between the two concepts is not self-evident: "One person's "sacred", as it turns out, is someone else's "profane".[25] Furthermore, sacralisation can happen to any object irrespective of whether it is connected to a "religious" ex-

23. Miguel Farias *et al* conducted a study to determine the respective motivations of atheists and religious pilgrims: Miguel Farias *et al*. 'Atheists on the Santiago Way: Examining Motivations to Go On Pilgrimage', *Sociology of Religion*, Vol. 80, No. 1, 9 January 2019, Pages 28–44.
24. Ann Taves, *Religious Experience*, Princeton and Oxford, 2009, p. 31.
25. Arnal and McCutcheon, *op. cit.*, p. 23.

perience. For instance, many visitors to *Şişli Atatürk Müzesi* (Şişli Atatürk Museum) would realise that objects used by Mustafa Kemal are treated as sacred objects, while a photograph hanging on the wall shows a cloud formed in such a way as to depict Mustafa Kemal.

This experience, may not readily be interpreted as "religious". Nevertheless, Taves's concept of "specialness" - as a "net that captures most of what people have in mind when they refer to 'sacred,' 'magical,' 'spiritual,' 'mystical,' or 'religious'"[26] - is applicable to this experience.[27] Specialness can be interpreted as "religious" because the image brings together a mundane element - cloud - and invests it with a connection to either a visionary experience (the representation of Kemal) or perhaps a unified system of beliefs and practices (Kemalism), that take on an aspect of set-apartness, in Durkheim's terms, due to being manifested in the sky. This experience could be described as "hierophany" in Eliade's terms.

Arnal and McCutcheon complicate the theoretical terrain further by investigating "the claim made at [a] German conference that the binary pair of church and state, or that the very designation "religion" itself was invented by Christian theologians", and come to the conclusion that religion is a product of the Enlightenment.[28] Their study alters the conceptual framework of the study of religion and politics.

The idea that "religion" is a relatively new construct is a challenging one; hitherto religion has been described as universal, ever-existing and ubiquitous. Many scholars attempted to define religion by approaching it from different dimensions. For instance, anthropologist Clifford Geertz defined religion as a cultural system and philologist F. Max Müller as primitive intuition and adoration of God, to cite only two. Religion as a cultural system retains its potency but it is not sufficient.

Similarly to Arnal and McCutcheon, Talal Asad also views

> 'religion' as modern concept not because it is reified but because it has been linked to its Siamese twin 'secularism' It is this simultaneous birth of religion and secularism that merits attention.[29]

A paradox is also emerging, in that the secular state defines religion and the sacred in order to dissociate itself from it in the process of secular-

26. Taves, *op. cit.*, p. 12.
27. Other "apparitions" of Mustafa Kemal Atatürk have also been reported; e.g., 'Atatürk Silüeti Nerelerde Görülür?', [Where is Atatürk's silhouette seen?], https://www.lavitasarim.com/ataturk-silueti-nerelerde-gorulur/, [accessed on 14 January 2022].
28. *Ibid.*, pp. 10, 19.
29. Talal Asad, "Reading a Modern Classic" *History of Religions*, Vol. 40, No. 3, 2001, p. 221.

isation. The dichotomy emerged in a particular period in Europe and the newly defined "religion" was supposed to be confined to the private sphere:

> Historians of seventeenth- and eighteenth-century Europe have begun to recount how the constitutions of the modern state required the forcible redefinition of religion as belief, and of religious belief, sentiment, and identity as personal matters that belong to the newly emerging space of private (as opposed to public) life.[30]

The dualities of the sacred and the profane, religion and secularism, private and public spheres appear to be a product of a certain geopolitical region, era and particular historical processes, such as colonialism, which have influenced the way people think and behave in the constructed spaces. Arnal and McCutcheon in their study explored the concepts of the sacred and the profane, and the notion that established religion to be a relatively new construct. Having done so, they point out the fluidity of the concepts in question:

> As scholars of social classification, we see no reason to assume, as do many of the people that we happen to read, that the categories 'religion' and 'politics', or 'sacred' and 'secular', refer to actual qualities in the real world, requiring us to align ourselves with one or the other.[31]

Furthermore, they wondered, "is it important for us to distinguish between a political activity and a religious activity? Even if the two *could* be separated, why bother?[32] Their question is somewhat dispiriting to encounter at the beginning of a study of this nature, but, thankfully, they come to the conclusion that

> [we] don't see why we cannot understand such distinctions as church/state, private/public, and sacred/secular as nothing more or less than socio-rhetorical devices that have stayed on our minds because they have continued to prove so useful to a variety of groups over the past several hundred years, all of which have tried to regulate - to divide and rule - their highly competitive economies of signification.[33]

The key therefore is to treat these concepts as "socio-rhetorical devices". This is a useful notion. We can still "bother"; lack of definitional certainty should not be, and has not been, an impediment to scholarly inquiry. Part of the process is to point out the definitional difficulties.

It would have been beneficial for Arnal and McCucheon's ground-break-

---

30. Talad Asad, *Genealogies of Religion*, Baltimore and London, 1993, p. 205.
31. Arnal and McCutcheon, *op. cit.*, p. 132.
32. *Ibid.*, p. 25.
33. *Ibid.*, 132-33.

ing work to have drawn additional examples from the non-Christian world. In essence, their study is particularly of the Christian experience, western Christian at that. This presents difficulty in the application of their analysis to the Islamic world, and particularly Turkey. In contrast, Brent Nongbri, working in similar theoretical terrain, overcomes this handicap, casts a wider net and cites examples from beyond Christian Europe to support his argument:

> [t]erms and concepts corresponding to religion do not appear in the literature of non-Western cultures until after those cultures first encountered Europe and Christians. They have pointed out that the names of supposedly venerable old religions can often be traced back only to the relatively recent past ('Hinduism', for example, to 1787 and 'Buddhism' to 1801). And when the names do derive from ancient words, we find that the early occurrences of those words are best understood as verbal activities rather than conceptual entities; thus the ancient Greek term ioudaismos was not 'the religion of Judaism' but the activity of Judaizing, that is, following the practices associated with the Judean ethnicity; the Arabic Islam was not 'the religion of Islam' but 'submitting to authority'.[34]

This is an important point. As it was stated in the introductory remarks, the relationship between the state and Islam and the relationship between the state and Christianity may be dissimilar. "The summary of Islamicist Jacques Waardenburg is apt":

> The calls of prophets in the course of history to make people turn or return to almighty God were not only incentives to monotheism. They also carried messages about the right way of life to be followed by each person in the community concerned and in society at large. In other words, these calls imposed not only what we would consider a strictly 'religious' belief and practice, but also rules of what we would today call

---

34. Brent Nongbri, *Before Religion*, New Haven and London, 2013, p. 2. Nogbri also surveys ancient languages and concludes the term "religion" which has been wrongly translated in Greek and two other ancient languages, Hebrew and Aramaic, do not have a term which corresponds with the modern understanding of the term "religion" at all. Nongbri also looks at Arabic and modern translations of the Quran. The Arabic term *dīn* has been translated as "religion" and "faith" in early printed translations, though experts in Arabic frequently point out that *dīn* does not really correspond to modern ideas of religion". The term *dīn* took the meaning of "religion" as the interaction between English and Arabic increased (see pp. 5, 26, 27, 35 and 39). Another example is cited by Oliver Roy, in that "the great French sinologist Marcel Granet, in the time of Jesuit missionaries, wrote a book entitled *The Religion of the Chinese People*, whereas the word "religion" has no exact equivalent in Chinese and the phrase "school of thought" (*jiao*) is more appropriate" (Olivier Roy, *Holy Ignorance*, Oxford, 2013, p. 27).

social order, law, ethics or morality, with corresponding prescriptions and prohibitions.[35]

Consequently, the Islamic "religion" at its inception incorporated elements other than just spiritual, in which the sacred and profane are not easily distinguishable. Yet, the issue of what "religion" is, still remains outstanding. Arthur L. Greil's quotation has articulated this problem wonderfully: "It seems safe to assert that no consensus on a definition of religion has been reached and that no consensus is likely to be reached in the foreseeable future".[36] Taves notes that the terms "religion," "religious," and "religions" are Western folk concepts, that their meaning is unstable and contested, and that they cannot be defined so as to specify anything uniquely.[37]

This is a significant quandary. Jonathan Z. Smith has contended "that *there* is *no data* for *religion*. *Religion* is *solely* the *creation* of the *scholar's study*. It is *created* for the *scholar's analytic purposes* by *his [sic] imaginative acts* of *comparison* and *generalization".[38]* A number of scholars approach the field of religion, or politics for that matter, as mental categories of scholarly construct to be used as analytical tools. As Satlow notes "These categories have no independent existence; they need not indicate anything 'real'".[39] Asad theorised that the category of religion is an invention of a western scholar. But as it is inevitable to refer to "religion", whether western construct or not, many scholars handle this problem by using scare quotes as Smith does in "Religion, Religions, Religious";[40] the present study uses the same method.

There are many different approaches to the study of the construct of religion. Cécile Laborde enumerates three basic approaches. the first approach is "criticizing religion", a perspective of being critical and sceptical of the category of religion, as a product of western imperialism. It sees religion only as colonial project. This is very limited and ideologically coloured framework.

The second approach "upholding religion" questions the first approach. Within the "upholding religion" approach there is an anthropological ob-

35. Jacques Waardenburg cited in Nongbri, *op. cit.*, p. 44.
36. Arthur L. Greil cited in Michael Bergunder, 'What is Religion? The Unexplained Subject Matter of Religious Studies', *Method and Theory in the Study of Religion*, No. 26, 2014, p. 247.
37. Taves, *op. cit.*, p. 25.
38. Jonathan Z. Smith, *Imagining Religion*, Chicago, 1982), p. xi.
39. Michael Satlow, 'Disappearing Categories: Using categories in the study of religion', *Method & Theory in the Study of Religion*, No. 17, 2005, p. 293.
40. Michael L. Satlow, 'Defining Judaism: Accounting for "Religions" in the Study of Religion', *Journal of the American Academy of Religion*, Vol. 74, No. 4, December, 2006, p. 838.

jection and what Labord calls a normative objection. The anthropological objection claims that it is just not correct or helpful to say that religion only functions as a term associated with western imperialist and neo-colonialist projects. Satlow notes the claims that religion is a "Western Christian category . . . are exaggerated. Many societies have terms and concepts that *in some way* are analogous to modern Western notions of religion."[41] The normative objection is that questioning or denying the existence of religion would have consequences for "religious freedom".[42] The concern is that scholars' work might be employed by states to deny certain groups' beliefs (for instance, Scientology).

While the anthropological argument has merits, the normative objection is not a convincing argument. States that want to deny certain religious interpretations will construct their own arguments, irrespective of the current scholarship and/or definitional handicaps. For instance, in Turkey Alevism is denied access to state resources on the ground that if such access were to be granted it would endanger unity. As Marcus Dressler points out, *Diyanet* tended to present Alevi worship places, cemevis, as *cultural* and not *religious* spaces and therefore denied funding them. The former president of Diyanet Ali *Bardakoğlu remarked:*

> We can't be against the Alevi cemevis, their traditional cultures, their supplications, their cem rituals - they are valuable, too. However, I do not think that it would contribute to the unity . . . of our society if we were to include them - that is these particularities beyond the common share [of Islam] - into the legal structure and make them part of the Directorate's services.[43]

Laborde's third approach is the "disaggregation strategy", the acceptance that "as religion is indeed not a thing but a term of art (it has different meanings in different contexts), different dimensions of it will be appropriated in different ways in different disciplines."[44] This is similar to Arnal and McCutcheon's approach to "religion", as described above, and seems to be the most sensible one to adopt. To paraphrase, religion is in the eye of the beholder.

Nevertheless, for the purposes of this study it is imperative to select a

---

41. Michael. L. Satlow. 'Disappearing Categories', 288.
42. Cécile Laborde, 'Three approaches to the study of religion', *The Immanent Frame*, 5 February 2014, https://tif.ssrc.org/2014/02/05/three-approaches-to-the-study-of-religion/ [Accessed 24 March 2018].
43. Markus Dressler, "Making Religion through Secularist Legal Discourse: The Case of Turkish Alevism" in Markus Dressler and Arvind-Pal S. Mandair (eds.), *Secularism and Religion-Making*, Oxford, 2011, p. 192.
44. Cécile Laborde, *op. cit.*

definition that seems to fit the various phenomena peculiar to the Turkish context. I examine Naomi Goldenberg's theory "thinking of religions as vestigial states". Goldenberg suggests that this approach is "one way of demystifying and deconstructing the category of religion" and that

> [v]estigial states tend to behave as once and future states. They are always somewhat restive and are generally eager to take on whatever social, cultural and/or managerial functions the recognized state cedes to them. For example, presently in contemporary nation states, categories of custom and law pertaining to the 'family' are considered proper spheres for 'religious' authority. In contrast, economic policies and most forms of violence are currently placed outside of religious control.[45]

As the study progresses it becomes evident that Goldenberg's theory is applicable to the Turkish political context and Islamic movements, for instance, to the Gülenist Movement.

A distinct approach is employed by some scholars in the United States to the study of religion, namely the "religious market" theory. This theory is applied especially in the United States context in which both evangelical churches, but also various forms of Judaism compete for influence. Economic analysis is used to compare different paradigms for understanding the marketplace for religions and religious ideas.[46] This theory in Laborde's schema can be classified as the "upholding religion" approach.

> The core proposition in the religious market approach is the notion that vigorous competition between religious denominations has a positive effect on religious involvement.... Proponents argue that the continued vitality of religious beliefs and practices in the United States can plausibly be explained by the sheer diversity of American faith-based organizations, strong pluralistic competition among religious institutions, freedom of religion, and the constitutional division of church and state.[47]

Carmel Chiswick's approach, incorporating systems in which there is an official religious establishment, may have some application to Turkey. She writes:

> Religious groups compete with each other for followers. This is explicit

---

45. Naomi Goldenberg, 'An Argument for Thinking of Religions as Vestigial States', 12 March 2012, https://criticalreligion.org/2012/03/12/an-argument-for-thinking-of-religions-as-vestigial-states, [Accessed on 7 March 2020].
46. Carmel U. Chiswick, 'Competition vs. Monopoly in the Religious Marketplace: Judaism in the United States and Israel', IZA Discussion Paper, No. 7188, January 2013, p. 1.
47. Pippa Norris and Ronald Inglehart, *Sacred and Secular*, Cambridge, 2004, p. 12.

in a country with religious pluralism, but even in countries with an official religious establishment, there are always non-believers as well as dissenters and dissenting religions.[48]

Is the competitive religious market theory fully applicable to Turkey given that the majority of the population would describe themselves as Muslims? The competing ideas are mainly of Sunni origin. Such religious formations as *tarikats* and *cemaats* offer divergent views of Islam. Some, like *Milli Görüş*, were involved in politics from the beginning of their formation; others, such as the Nakshibendi tarikat, evolved and eventually became explicitly involved in politics to compete and promote their own versions of Islam.

> Establishing an 'official' state religion is analogous to granting a monopoly to a business enterprise. Monopoly is justified by a desire to control the market, often in the belief that competition is inefficient and wasteful of resources. Similarly, governments establish an official religion in the belief that it will bind citizens into a single society and buttress their loyalty to the nation.[49]

By establishing Diyanet, as a controlling and management mechanism, the regime tried to do just that. Diyanet was to monopolise the market of religion, if we follow this conceptual framework. By selecting solely to be representative of Sunni Islam in exclusion of Alevism and forms of popular Islam, Diyanet was well positioned to exercise its monopoly on Sunni Islam and "religious life". The exclusion of other expressions of religious view did not stop other formations to compete, but the state mechanism actively discouraged (i.e., the Nursî cemaat) or forbade them from functioning at all (i.e., the tarikats).

The Republic closed down all Sufi orders in 1925 and banned their *tekkes* and *zaviyes* (lodges). Thus, the states strove to maintain a monopoly of a particular version of Sunni Islam, though with the re-emergence of tarikats, this monopoly could not be maintained. The Sufi Sunni tarikats, outside the state control, at least since the 1980s, have been able to compete for "clients" and "poach" members from Diyanet-run mosques.

The discipline of economics is not equipped to deal with such a field as "religion". The ideological tendency to view market-based mechanism as a *panacea* is problematic enough in the field of economics, let alone in the multi-layered category of religion. However, aspects of religious market theory are useful in analysing competing views of religion and the efforts

---

48. Chiswick, *op. cit.*, p. 1.
49. *Ibid.*, p. 2.

to recruit followers. Norris and Inglehart note that "[t]he theory fits the American case, but the problem is that it fails to work elsewhere."[50] One aspect of the theory is that religion thrives in a competitive environment, but not when there is monopoly; the lack of competition is expected to have the opposite effect. Yet, Ireland and the United States, with different religious markets, i.e. monopoly vs. competitive market, both have a high level of religiosity.[51] There are therefore other factors in play, but the theory has some applicability even in countries with different cultures and social contexts.

Religion and Secularism

No study of religion and politics in Turkey is complete without discussion of secularism and secularisation. Religion and secularism are so closely related that, in the words of Asad "any discipline that seeks to understand 'religion' must also try to understand its other".[52] A key principle in Kemalism was laicism (*laiklik*), a concept close to secularism. Laicism and secularism "share meaning" but should not be equated[53] (this is discussed further in the following chapter). The founders of the Republic claimed that they were establishing a laic state. The importance they assigned to this goal is demonstrated by the inclusion of laicism in the 1937 Constitution. In the interim, the original clause in the Constitution stating Islam as the religion of the state was removed. *Cumhuriyet Halk Partisi* (The Republican Peoples' Party/CHP) established by Mustafa Kemal, in its six arrow (*Altı Ok*) emblem represented the six principles of Kemalist ideology: republicanism, laicism, nationalism, populism, statism and revolutionism.

The claim has been propagated by post-Kemal Kemalism - that is Kemalism after the death of Mustafa Kemal. It is argued in this study that the claim to establish a laic state and initiation of the process to transform society into a secular one is fallacious. This is not to deny the genuine desire for reforms to transform Turkish society from an eastern to western one, but laicisation was a stillborn project.

In examining secularisation, one significant question to ask is how to evaluate it. In other words, how do we know whether secularisation has increased or decreased, assuming it is present, and how can we measure it? What sort of criteria should we use? Is attendance at temples a sufficient

---

50. Norris and Inglehart, *op. cit.*, p. 24.
51. *Ibid.*, *op. cit.*, p. 34.
52. Asad Talal, *Formation of the Secular*, Stanford, California, 2003, p. 22.
53. Parla and Davison, *op. cit.*, p. 14.

marker? Examining Britain in 1970, Vernon Pratt suggested that the dwindling numbers of churchgoers is not a sufficient marker of secularisation.[54] Pratt's study includes a survey of research, which considered this question in trying to determine objective criteria:

> Harvey Cox attempts an answer in his study of 'The Secular City'. One feature he regards as important is what he calls the 'anonymity' of modern life. A great many of the relationships with which a modern urban dweller has to be involved are in a sense 'impersonal'.[55]

Cox suggested that anonymity, as well as mobility, as characteristics of "the secular-urban style". The processes of secularisation and urbanisation are therefore connected[56] and anonymity is a significant factor in the formation of the secular.[57] In Turkey, a *mahalle* (neighbourhood) is not conducive to anonymity; relative anonymity may be present in affluent suburbs but not in working class neighbourhoods or suburbs or in the disappearing squatter towns (*gecekondu*) in urban centres. Şerif Mardin developed a concept of neighbourhood pressure (*mahalle baskısı*). "With this term, Mardin sought to capture the unofficial, local, communal pressure on individuals to conform to religious-conservative norms in their everyday lives."[58] Consequently, urbanisation, which does not guarantee anonymity, is not a sufficient indicator of secularisation either. In any case, anonymity is difficult to maintain in a technological environment of increasingly intrusive social media platforms and communication devices with tracking capabilities.

There are inherent difficulties in objectively measuring secularity to assess the extent of its presence. As Norris and Inglehart put it, "[w]e simply do not have the massive longitudinal database that would be required to demonstrate beyond any doubt whether secularization is or is not taking place."[59] It may be a futile project, but paradoxically there is no shortage of studies trying to determine it, including the present.

How do we distinguish a secular from a non-secular society? How does secularity manifest itself? According to Bryan Wilson in Religion in Secular Society, as cited by Pratt, "a secular society is one where 'the sense of the

---

54. Vernon Pratt, *Religion and Secularisation*, London and Basingstoke, 1970, p. 1.
55. *Ibid.*, p. 1.
56. *Ibid.*, p. 2.
57. Harvey Cox, *The Secular City*, Princeton and Oxford, 2013, p. 72.
58. Ates Altinordu, 'The Debate on "Neighborhood Pressure" in Turkey', *International Perspectives*, Vol. 37, No. 2, February 2009, http://www.asanet.org/sites/default/files/savvy/footnotes/feb09/intl_persp.html, [Accessed on 31 March 2018].
59. Norris and Inglehart, *op. cit.*, p. 36.

sacred, the sense of the sanctity of life, and deep religiosity are . . . absent'"[60] and secularisation is "the process whereby religious thinking, practice and institutions lose social significance".[61] Wilson's study in the 1960s, still operating within the framework of the dichotomy between the sacred and the profane, posits the established idea that secularisation means the reduction of influence of religion in public life.

Yet, there is another aspect of the "sacred world". In the 1950s, Geoffrey Gorer surveyed over 10,000 English people.[62] The analysis of the responses led him to conclude

> that about a quarter of the population, which must include a good number of those who neglect the institutions of religion, hold 'a view of the universe which can most properly be designated as magical' . . . and the wide spread appeal of superstition among the (largely non-church- or chapel-going) working class has been noted by several writers.[63]

Therefore, neglecting to attend religious institutions is not a satisfactory indicator either, as the community may partake, engage or believe in experiences such as magic, though Durkheim makes a distinction between religion and magic. In Durkheimian dichotomy, magic is profane. In Taves's view, Durkheim's efforts to distinguish "magic" and "religion" were tortured and unhelpful.[64] Durkheim pointed out that "magic is full of religion and religion full of magic" and wondered whether it is impossible to separate them. He nevertheless concluded that there is a demarcation line and that is the existence of church in religion. In his system, the existence of "one single moral community called a Church" is central to the definition of religion and "[t]here is no Church of magic".[65] Magic is not exclusive to a particular culture; it has a universal appeal and practice. Lucy Garnett writing around the same time as Durkheim, unaware of Durkheim's dichotomy, equated magic and religion in the Islamic context in general, and in the tarikats function in particular:

> Considering that the existence of magic and witchcraft, and the power of the Evil Eye are stated as absolute facts in the Koran, it is not surprising that in Mohammedan countries superstitious beliefs and practices play so great a part in the social life of the people.[66]

60. Pratt, *op. cit.*, p. 3.
61. *Ibid.*, p. 3.
62. Geofrey Gorer, *Exploring English Character*, New York, 1955, p. 9.
63. Pratt, *op. cit.*, p. 8.
64. *Taves, op. cit.*, p. 26.
65. Durkheim, *op. cit.*, pp. 40-44.
66. Lucy M. J. Garnett, *Mysticism and Magic in Turkey*, New York, 1912, p. 136.

This is definitely a second order definition and classification of religion and magic. "Superstition" is an unstable term, as Taves pointed out, and its scope and definition would be relative to the culture in which it is operating. Garnett suggested that Sufi dervishes were involved in witchcraft and sorcery:

> By the populace the Dervishes are held to be experts in the magic of the old Paganism, belief in which is thus sanctioned by their Holy Book. They are indeed, credited with the faculty not only of healing mental and bodily diseases, but also of counteracting the effects of witchcraft and sorcery, of interpreting dreams, recovering lost or stolen property, and even of restoring to wives the waning affection of their husbands.[67]

I would definitely classify this view as a product of Orientalist perspective - despite my reservations about the tendency to apply this label to discard many studies related to the "Middle East". Garnet saw aspects of mysticism of the Sufi dervishes as being engaged in magic. Interestingly, her account of wandering dervishes and dervish involvement in selling talismans and magic charms was not much different from the views of the early Republican deputies, who expressed similar views (see Chapter 4.0). The discussion above, related to the themes of "magic" and "superstition", therefore constitute a useful analytical platform in the review of the early Republican period as its parliamentary deputies held strong views on these concepts.

Having reviewed different criteria employed to define and understand what secularisation entails, Pratt suggested "secularisation of the mind". This is in line with Cox's view of "profanity", which refers "to secular man's [sic] wholly terrestrial horizon, the disappearance of any supramundane reality defining his life". Cox is saying that we no longer think in terms of "the Supernatural". Our worldview has changed, our conceptual framework altered:

> I have said that the origins of the intellectual aspect of secularisation are to be found in the scientific revolution of the seventeenth century. My argument will be that the development of science has given rise to a conceptual framework importantly different from that in which 'traditional Christianity' flourished.[68]

The implication is that in Cox's view, secularisation in the Christian context is a product of scientific development, rather than political processes, as suggested by Asad and others. A more recent formulation of a

---

67. *Ibid.*, p. 138.
68. Pratt, *op. cit.*, pp. 6 and 11.

similar idea can be found in Charles Taylor's *A Secular Age*, with the concept of "immanent frame". This is another challenging concept, which Taylor does not exactly define in his book:

> [W]e come to understand our lives as taking place within a self-sufficient immanent order; or better, a constellation of orders, cosmic, social and moral. . . . these orders are understood as impersonal. . . . The immanent order can thus slough off the transcendent. But it doesn't necessarily do so. What I have been describing as the immanent frame is common to all of us in the modern West, or at least that is what I am trying to portray.[69]

There is a duality of the immanent, which excludes the beyond (gods, spirits etc.), and the transcendent ("religion"). Taylor believes we live in a vast impersonal immanent order, which is unprecedented. In the medieval ages, he argues, it would have been incomprehensible to view the world, the cosmos, anything but reflecting the divine. Partly because of science, we have now moved into the immanent frame.[70] "Thus, whilst adhering to their own comprehensive doctrines, [even] religious people who live in secular societies are also surrounded by the immanent frame."[71] The immanent frame is the dominant form and "they must translate their concerns into non-theological language for the public square [which is marked by] secularity."[72]

Religion and Politics

The topic of politics is vast though it is only the politics of secularism and laicism that is of concern in this study. As Elizabeth Shakman Hurd notes, "secularism is one of the most important organizing principles of modern politics".[73] Secularism and laicism therefore occupy a significant portion of politics and it has evidently done so in the case of the Turkish Republic. This is discussed in Chapter 2.2, while Chapter 2.3 discusses political Islam specifically.

69. Charles Taylor, *A Secular Age*, Cambridge, Massachusetts, and London, 2007, pp. 543-544.
70. https://www.youtube.com/watch?v=f2L6_wHLFSI, [Accessed on 2 April 2018].
71. David Cheetham, 'Ritualising the Secular? Interreligious meetings in the 'Immanent Frame'', *The Heythrop Journal*, 15 February 2017, p. 7.
72. Ted Troxell, Belief in the Immanent Frame, Religion at the Margins, 6 November 2010, http://religionatthemargins.com/2010/11/belief-in-the-immanent-frame/, [Accessed on 2 April 2018].
73. Elizabeth Shakman Hurd, *The Politics of Secularism in International Relations*, Princeton, 2008, p. 23.

The effort to delineate political Islam raises an additional issue; in the endless effort in the social sciences to define terms and concepts used to describe socio-political processes, the term "politics" is also required to be clarified. Politics is usually defined as "the art of governance" or the process for dealing "with the affairs of the state".[74] This definition is not satisfactory because it ties politics to parliamentary processes, party politics and public administration. I use the term politics in the sense of a suite of efforts to influence socio-political processes and outcomes, without necessarily going through the established structures. For instance, social media campaigns by *GetUp!*[75] or the *ad hoc* campaign #*MeToo*, or *Black Lives Matter* movement in 2020 are political, aiming as they do to sway public opinion. We therefore cannot limit the scope of politics to government affairs and public administration.

The main concern of the study is interaction between religion and politics and many scholars pointed out, for instance Erin Wilson, that the fields "are not separated by the public/private divide, but interact and influence one another".[76] This issue is discussed throughout the study.

While empirical evidence points to the failure of separation of the two fields in Turkey, the dominant theoretical material in this field, some of which are cited in this study, suggests it is a futile effort to separate the two fields in the first place, whether in Islam or Christianity. A well-established scholarship points out the porous lines between religion and politics. For instance, Talal Asad notes:

> In a sense what many would anachronistically call 'religion' was always involved the world of power. If the secularization study no longer carries the conviction it once did, this is because the categories of 'politics' and 'religion' turn out to implicate each other more profoundly than we thought.[77]

Timothy Fitzgerald also argues that there is a "mutually parasitic relationship between "religion" and other categories such as the secular state, "politics," "society" and other secular discursive domains" and concluded that "religion" is not a standalone category. Fitzgerald's contention is that the boundaries between such rhetorically-constructed fields are porous.[78]

---

74. Kasomo Daniel, 'An examination of co-existence of religion and politics', *International Journal of Sociology and Anthropology*, Vol. 1, No. 7, November 2009, p. 124.
75. An Australian pressure group which pursues issues it identifies as "progressive."
76. Erin K. Wilson, *After Secularism*, Houndsmill, Basingstoke, Hampshire, 2012, p. 6.
77. Talal Asad. *Formations of the Secular*, Stanford, California, 2003, p. 200.
78. Timothy Fitzgerald, 'Religion is not a standalone category', *The Immanent Frame*, 29 October 2008, https://tif.ssrc.org/2008/10/29/religion-is-not-a-standalone-category/ [Accessed on 3 March 2019].

David U.B. Liu, following Fitzgerald's attack on religion and politics as supposedly autonomous categories, uses the terms "religiopolitics" and "religiopolitical" "to refuse both categories" but without assigning "substantive meaning".[79] Liu's terminology solidifies the scholarly consensus of the difficulty of separating the two domains.

---

79. David U.B. Liu, "The Ancestral, the Religiopolitical: in Stack, Goldenberg and Fitzgerald, op. cit., pp. 143-44.

2.2 LAICITY AND SECULARISM IN TURKEY

In Turkey, secularism has been expressed by the term *laiklik* (laicity), to denote the policy of the state dissociating itself from the influence of religion. Traditionally, the term *seküler* (secular) has not been used. This term became wider in use as the influence of French decreased and English became more widely spoken in Turkey. In more recent times, the term *seküler* and *laiklik* have been used synonymously.[80] James W. Warhola and Egemen B. Bezici point to the ambiguity of the terms, which makes it difficult to delineate between the two concepts:

> The meaning of 'secular republic' has varied over time, however, and has certainly varied in interpretation by the relevant actors in Turkish political life, including popular perceptions of what secularism should mean. The word itself is ambiguous and may carry a wide array of meanings; the Turkish word, 'laiklik', is as intrinsically ambiguous.[81]

Yet, many researchers argue that there are indeed differences between the two concepts. Sociologist Niyazi Berkes thought that "[w]hile the underlying emphasis in the word "secularism" is on the idea of worldliness, the term "laicism" emphasises the distinction of the laity from the clergy".[82] This distinction as a starting point is useful but not sufficient.

Undoubtedly, the provenance of the concept of *laiklik* is France. Political scientist Baskın Oran makes the point that the French anti-clerical thinking of the French Revolution had influenced Kemalist laicism. Oran explains that the terms *laïcité* and *laïcism* come from Latin *laicus* (of the people) and argues that laicism is an attribute of the state. The term *secularité* (secularism) also comes from Latin, *Soeculum*, that is to say, contemporary, and it is used in Anglophone and Germanophone countries. Secularism is an attribute of society. Oran makes a distinction between France, on the one hand, and the Protestant-majority countries on the other, in that the Protestant countries "do not need laicism", because the society is already secular.[83] Though this is arguable, the distinction between laicism and secularism is valid.

---

80. For instance, Volkan Ertit, 'Birbirinin Yerine Kullanılan İki Farklı Kavram: Sekülerleşme ve Laiklik', *Akademik İncelemeler Dergisi*, Vol. 9, No. 1, 2014, *passim*.

81. James W. Warhola and Egemen B. Bezici, 'Religion and State in Contemporary Turkey: Recent Developments in "Laiklik', *Journal of Church and State and State*, November 2010, p. 1.

82. Niyazi Berkes, *The Development of Secularism in Turkey*, London, 1964, p. 5.

83. Baskın Oran, 'État et religion en Turquie', *multitudes altyazı*, Vol. 8, No. 9, October 2005, p. 12.

According to Oran, laicism gained momentum in France when the democratic process was in good shape and lost ground when it was weak, for example during the Vichy regime. In the case of France, Oran associates laicism with a well-functioning democracy. He argues that the opposite can be observed in Turkey where laicity was imposed by an authoritarian regime. When a democratic transition in Turkey promoted the freedom of cultural expression but also the development of an Islamic political action, this mutation was denounced by the westernised elites who supported a military intervention that claimed to restore the laic order. The pattern is "forced *laicité*, democracy, Islam, *laicisant* military coup!"[84]

There are two important elements in Oran's argument: that laicism is a state policy and practice, while secularism or secularisation is a process to be observed in civil society. Thus, the distinction between the two concepts is crystallised. Other scholars, such as Umut Azak, see *laiklik* as a form of secularism, though with its own peculiarities.[85] In other words, secularism incorporates laicism. In turn, Warhola and Bezici describe laicité as "active secularism" as opposed to a politically "passive secularism," on the part of the state, as is claimed to prevail in the United States. They contend that the term *laicité* in the Turkish context "was initially instituted to convey a certain disposition of civil authority to religion in which the state itself actively embraced and fostered a nonreligious worldview in the public realms (such as partisan politics, public education, media, *etc.*)."[86]

Volkan Ertit, specialising in secularism, asserts that "Turkish academics and media have preferred to use the terms of laic, laicité or laicization to express what the term secularization asserts". In Ertit's interpretation, secularisation incorporates the idea of the progress of time, separation of spheres, albeit in the realm of the church, but also the attenuation of influence of religion in public life. [87] Ertit makes a distinction between laicism as a political term that defines relationship between the state and religion, while the term secularisation refers to the "bumpy", i.e. ever changing, relationship between religion and the community. Laicism is described as a political principle and project, which is in line with Oran's thinking as described above.

At the 1931 Congress of *Cumhuriyet Halk Fırkası* (CHF - CHP's forerunner), the principle of laicism was included in the party program. In this program CHF declared that religion was only a matter of conscience

84. *Ibid.*, 13.
85. Umut Azak, *Islam and Secularism in Turkey*, London, 2010, p. 8.
86. Warhola and Bezici, *op. cit.*, p. 2.
87. Ertit, *op. cit.*, p. 105-06.

(*vicdan*) and that accordingly, it would separate religious thinking from state and worldly affairs and politics.[88] This separation of religion from state matters is the basic principle of laicism but does not sufficiently cover the concept. At the 1947 CHP Conference, Seyhan Deputy Sinan Tekelioğlu said that seeing laicism only as separation of worldly matters from religious matters was deficient and that laicism should also be about "not bestowing privileges upon any extant religions". Tekelioğlu thought that "Turkish Christians and Turkish Jews" were receiving such privileges by not reporting to Diyanet and maintaining autonomy.[89] Although the proposition that the state discriminated in favour of Christians and Jews at the expense of Sunni Muslims was not valid, Tekelioğlu pointed to a second principle for true laicism, the state's equal distance from all religious and ethnic minorities.

Mustafa Kemal himself expressed the view that "[l]aicism is not only the separation of religious and state affairs. Laicism is to guarantee all citizens' freedom of conscience, worship and religion" and "religion and sect cannot be used as a political tool".[90]

Former professor of law Kemal Gözler identifies two main principles of laicism: religious freedom and separation of state and religious affairs. In relation to the latter, he adds five related criteria:

1) the state should not have an official religion;
2) the state should be neutral in its approach to all religions;
3) the state should have equal treatment to all members of different religions;
4) state and religious institutions should function separately; and,
5) state laws should not be obliged to follow canon laws.[91]

Ertit connects the use of the term "secularisation" with industrial capitalism and urbanisation, as well as modernisation.[92] This suggests that secularisation is a process imposed by social and economic forces, as opposed to laicism, which, as noted, is imposed by political forces. Olivier Roy suggested that secularisation is not anti-religious or anti-clerical: peo-

88. Hüseyin Kara, 'Tek Parti Dönemi Din Politikası (1923-1946)', *Mehmet Akif Ersoy Üniversitesi Sosyal Bilimler Enstitüsü Dergisi*, Vol. 9, No. 19, June 2017, p. 130.
89. Cemil Kocak, '1947 Kurultayında CHP'de laiklik tartışması başlarken'. Star, 18 April 2015, https://www.star.com.tr/yazar/1947-kurultayinda-chpde-laiklik-tartisma-si-baslarken-yazi-1021790/ [Accessed on 18 February 2020].
90. Şayan Ulusan, "Atatürk Dönemi Din Uygulamaları (1923-1938)", *Cappadocia Journal of History and Social Sciences*, Vol. 11, October 2018, p. 309.
91. Kemal Gözler, *Türk Anayasa Hukuku*, Bursa, 2000, pp. 3-7.
92. Ertit, *op. cit.*, p. 106-7.

ple merely stop worshipping and stop talking about religion. *Laïcité*, on the contrary, is explicit; it is a political choice that defines the place of religion in an authoritarian, legal manner. *Laïcité* is decreed by the state, which then organizes the public sphere.[93]

Ertit further suggests that secularisation does not mean to become irreligious or to lose faith; it is not a term measuring the increase or decrease of religious faith. An individual can believe in religion and a creator but live a secular life. Ertit borrows a definition by Grace Davie to press his point, "believing without belonging". The term refers to the degree of influence of religion on daily life and not the number or strength of faith on any religion.[94]

One of the aims of those who were the principal instigators of the French Revolution was to ensure the people worshipped the state, not a religion. After the French Revolution the state brutally suppressed and even assassinated any clergy seen as supporters of the *Ancien Régime*. Ertit also notes that Mustafa Kemal and the intellectuals of the nascent Republic, who were influenced by the French thought and state structure, adopted a similar attitude: acting as social engineers, they wanted to redesign Turkish society.[95] This authoritarian tendency is highlighted by many researchers studying this period in Turkish history. One such researcher, Sinem Gürbey, suggests "[s]imply put, the Turkish conception of secularism, laiklik, came to be regarded as authoritarian, hostile to religion, or assertive, aiming to eliminate the influence of religion on the public sphere in a coercive manner.[96]

Davison argues that "the Turkish experience can be defined not as secularism, which assumes a non-religious, religion free-state, but as laicism, which connotes the transfer of some fields, such as education and governance to lay control." *Laiklik*, according to Davison, "did not entail ending state interest in religion", as it was based on religious policy which reflected a specific interpretation of Islam".[97] Davison's examination, which is to a large extent within the scope of inquiry of the present study, implies failure of laicism in Turkey.

Gürbey, like many other scholars, some of whom were cited above, challenge the assumption "that religion is an objectively identifiable con-

---

93. Olivier Roy, *Secularism Confronts Islam*, New York, 2007, p. viii.

94. Ertit, *op. cit.*, p. 108.

95. Ertit, *op. cit.*, pp, 109-110.

96. *Sinem Gürbey, 'Islam, Nation-State, and the Military: A Discussion of Secularism in Turkey', Comparative Studies of South Asia, Africa and the Middle East, Vol. 29, No. 3, 2009, p. 371.*

97. Azak, *op. cit.*, p. 8.

cept and that as such it can be separated from the realm of the secular and become an object of state power":

> In the case of Turkey, secularism, on the one hand, produced a particular conception of religion marked as univocal, archaic, backward, antimodern, and aiming to capture state power, which, in turn, justified the necessity of a secular state in the first place. On the other hand, secularism also involved the construction of an 'enlightened' conception of religion based on a particular Sunni interpretation of Islam.[98]

The difficulty in defining "religion" objectively, as suggested by Gürbey, is fairly evident; but it is not "religion" the Republican "laic state" was interested in defining - at least not in the beginning. It was its outward practice and its influence in daily life that the Republic wanted to curb, shape and control, if not eradicate. Often what is regarded as manifestation of religion can be manifestation of cultural practices. However, this distinction may be moot. Often, in the western conception of religion, religious and cultural practices are seen as two distinct realms of life which influence one another. This distinction is harder to delineate in Muslim societies, or at least in Turkey, which is the subject of this study. Along these lines, Berkes thought that in a Muslim-majority country:

> [t]he basic conflict in secularism is not necessarily between religion and the world, as was the case in Christian experience. The conflict is often between the forces of tradition, which tend to promote the domination of religion and sacred law, and the forces of change.[99]

Yet, to the Republicans in post-1923 Turkey, the difference was of no importance. They equated culture with civilisation [*medeniyet*] and civilisation with western civilisation. Closely related was the idea of modernisation. The Kemalists were very assured of themselves and their ideology, and defined themselves as the "enlightened", i.e. *aydın*, and those opposing laicism as "backward", i.e. *gerici*. As the "enlightened", they knew better and set on a course to alter the worldview of the citizens and "secularise their minds".

According to Mardin, Atatürk had a dual aim in mind after the proclamation of the Republic: imposition of laic regulations and cultural westernisation. "Mardin holds that the fez and *shalwar* (şalvar), whose definitive legitimacy is based on religious values, were forbidden in line with this

---

98. *Gürbey, op. cit., p. 371.*
99. Berkes, *op. cit.*, p. 6.

understanding."[100] Specifically, the prohibition of the *fez* under the "Hat Law" (*Şapka İktisası Hakkında Kanun*) was ironic, because the *fez* was introduced in the nineteenth century by the reformist Sultan (Mahmud II), whom Anık calls "a significant name in Ottoman modernization". Among his reforms,

> a more European style of dress began to be adopted within the official/bureaucratic realm in which the fez was approved as the official headgear of the empire by an imperial declaration. Therefore, the fez, which was prohibited under Hat Law in 1925, was itself a product of modernization activities in the Ottoman Empire.[101]

The irony was lost on the fervent supporters of the Hat Law as well as on its opponents. The masses that opposed the prohibition of the *fez* had no idea of the provenance of the *fez*; seemingly neither did the state which prohibited the use of it. Perhaps it did not matter. Whether or not the *fez* was once a product of a modernisation project, a century later it came to be associated with tradition, it became one of the symbols of Islamism. In Mardin's analysis the *fez* is a religious sign; this is commensurate with Taves's Durkheimian view that ordinary, mundane objects become invested with significance that connects them to a religious system. This is also an example of modernisation being an unending process, which has an ultimate objective only in the eye of the proponent; what is modern today will be old-fashioned tomorrow. Also, it is noteworthy that a profane object such as the *fez* became sacred and profane again, to demonstrate the instability of the dichotomy.

Mustafa Kemal and his colleagues expressly wanted to laicise the state, secularise society and modernise cultural practices and civic society. Yet, there were clashing objectives and contradictory practices in the way they embarked upon to create a secular society. The Republicans wanted to establish a homogenous nation-state based on Turkish identity only. As White noted, "Ankara . . . viewed Muslims as Turks, and non-Muslim outsiders, regardless of their willingness to assimilate.[102] Essentially, a laic state for Muslim Turks was the objective.

Gürbey points out the *Memurin Kanunu* (Law on Government Employees) enacted in 1926, which made being Turkish, that is, Muslim, a precondition for becoming a government employee, hence institutionalis-

---

100. Mehmet Anık, 'Two Axes Revolving Around the Discussions of Secularism in Turkey', *insan & toplum*, Vol. 2, No. 4, 2012, p. 20.
101. *Loc. cit.*
102. Jenny White, *Muslim Nationalism and the New Turks*, Princeton and Oxford, 2013, p. 31.

ing the dominance of one "religious" group over the state,[103] and equating religion with nationality. *Gürbey also points out the* population exchange with Greece in 1923, as the case in point. The agreement used religion as surrogate for ethnicity and exchanged Christians with Muslims. There were Greek-speaking Muslims in Greece and Turkish-speaking Christians in Turkey, who were deemed to be Turkish and Greek respectively and they were subjected to the population exchange.

Nevertheless, the population exchange as a pertinent example of weak laicism is not convincing, as the Greek state was also complicit and it was an international agreement (the Lausanne Treaty), with many international participants and constraints. The implementation of *Varlık Vergisi* (Wealth Tax) in 1942, discussed in Chapter 5.1, is a much more suitable example of weak laicism than the population exchange. Two fundamental principles of laicism were identified above: the state and institutional religion do not interfere in each other's spheres, and the state keeps equal distance from different religions and people. During the Second World War, as well as at other times, one of these basic principles of laicism was ignored. The state did not keep equal distance; in fact, it actively discriminated on the basis of stated or designated religious affiliation and ethnicity.

Process of secularisation

To assess the extent of laicity and secularisation in Turkish society, the present study is to examine laicism and secularism as two closely related yet distinct fields. The early chapters outline the stated objective of laicity by the Republic, the process undertaken for laicisation and its successes or failures. The later chapters examine the process of secularisation and assess its extent in Turkish society. Berkes's assessment of the secularisation process conveniently describes one evaluative criterion:

> To understand the process of secularization in a non-Christian society, one must examine the extent of domination of religious rules over all areas of life and discover whether or not this domination is either implemented or supported by the state.[104]

We need to bear in mind Asad's often-quoted observation that the "secular" is an epistemic category; "secularism" a political doctrine;[105] and "sec-

---

103. *Gürbey, op. cit., p. 374.*
104. Berkes, *op. cit.,* p. 6.
105. Talal Asad, *Formations of the Secular: Christianity, Islam, Modernity,* p. 1.

ularisation" a historical process.[106]

While in Turkey the state favours Sunni Islam, this is hardly a unique situation; in neighbouring Greece the state favours the Orthodox creed of the Church of Greece to such an extent that even the Old Calendar Church of the same creed (Παλαιοημερολογήτες) was not recognised until relatively recently.

The secularisation process is not universal. Its application would vary according to prevailing socio-political conditions. In his 1994 study José Casanova identified three definitions of secularisation[107], which he reiterated in his 2006 study: "secularization as the decline of religious beliefs and practices in modern societies", "secularization as the privatization of religion" and "secularization as the differentiation of the secular spheres (state, economy, science), usually understood as 'emancipation'" from religious institutions and norms.[108] These three processes may overlap. Kemalists vigorously pursued the latter two processes, enforcing the privatisation of religion through different means and "emancipation" through the principle of laicism.

Similar to the secularisation processes, "secularity" also has a number of permutations: Taylor identifies three types of secularity:

> One understanding of secularity . . . is in terms of public spaces. These have been allegedly emptied of God, or of any reference to ultimate reality. . . . the considerations we act on are internal to the 'rationality' of each sphere . . . In [the] second meaning, secularity consists in the falling off of religious belief and practice, in people turning away from God, and no longer going to Church. . . . The shift to secularity in [the third] sense consists, among other things, of a move from a society where belief in God is unchallenged and indeed, unproblematic, to one in which it is understood to be one option among others.[109]

While in Casanova's definition of the secularisation process the state has a role, especially in the second and third processes, in Taylor's spectrum of secularity it requires involvement and influence of other forces and fields such as science as competitors to religious explanation. Although the state can forcibly empty the public space of God (North Korea, Albania under Enver Hodja, Pol Pot's Cambodia), outside such extreme cases science,

---

106. Talal Asad, 'Thinking about the secular body, pain, and liberal politics', *Cultural Anthropology*, Vol. 26, No. 4, 2011, p. 660.

107. José Casanova, *Public Religions in the Modern World*, Chicago, 1994, p. 211.

108. José Casanova, 'Rethinking Secularization: A Global Comparative Perspective', The *Hedgehog* Review, Vol. 8, Spring & Summer 2006, p. 7.

109. Charles Taylor, *A Secular Age*, Cambridge, Massachusetts, and London, 2007, pp. 2-3.

the arts, education and technology may influence the spectrum. Kemalists pursued this option by pushing religion to a "private" space, so defined.

Secularity is a spectrum, not an absolute, neatly fitting into a dichotomy. Even in countries where the Sharia is the law of the land there are still secular activities. For instance, as Tayfun Atay argues, football is an activity that finds life in a secular grounding.[110] Except for very strict interpretations of the Sharia, in the instances of temporary states such as the Taliban's first administration in Afghanistan and the so-called "Islamic Caliphate's" territories, football is played in all Muslim majority countries, though women are excluded from participating in some.

Modernism

Closely related to the concepts of laicism and secularism, as they apply to Turkey, is the idea of modernism. Mehmet Anık contends that in a broader sense laicism

> is directly related to modernization because it also encapsulates the replacement of spiritual and religious values as well as those life styles based on these values with modern earthly ideals and objectives and the transformation experienced in practical terms.[111]

Alev Çınar argued that the modernism of the early Republican years "took shape by maintaining a distance both from excessive Westernism, on the one hand, and from stagnant Islamism on the other, thereby creating a unique in-between, hybrid modernity à la *Turca*."[112] Modernism is peripheral to this study, but it formed part of early Republican discourse. Mustafa Kemal and his cohorts saw the three pillars, modernisation, westernisation and secularisation as one combined desirable outcome.

Like many social constructs, modernity does not have a universally accepted fixed meaning, rather its context depends always on the proponent's agenda. Çınar contends that

> Modernity may refer to a lifestyle, a culture, a discourse, a historical epoch, a movement, a project, a mind-set, an intellectual trend, to capitalism, industrialization, democracy, constitutionalism, or secularism. Sometimes it is generalized to mean all of these at once, running the risk of overloading the term to the point of analytical uselessness, and

110. Tayfun Atay, *Parti, Cemaat, Tarikat*, Istanbul, 2017, p. 71.
111. Anık, *op. cit.*, p. 10.
112. Alev Çınar, *Modernity, Islam, and Secularism in Turkey*, Minneapolis, London, 2005, pp. 14-15.

sometimes one of its narrower meanings is privileged over others at the cost of oversimplifying the term and overlooking its other unexpected manifestations.[113]

In broad terms, in Mustafa Kemal's period, modernisation referred to a process of westernisation. This process included the cognate notions of secularism/laicism. In its narrower sense, it was about lifestyle. Mustafa Kemal made a great effort to establish western style high culture institutions in the country, as well as imposing laws to influence the dominant culture. He ensured to be seen in western style clothes and dancing at formal balls, women and men mixing freely, disregarding the prevailing cultural attitudes of the day.

Writing in 2005, before AKP's Islamist project, Çınar noted:

> For many, being modern is a deeply cherished ideal that is held very much as a religion, with its own shrines, rituals, sacred spaces, and mantras. Indeed, for some, routinely going to a Western classical music concert at the Atatürk Cultural Center (Atatürk Kültür Merkezi, or AKM) in Taksim Square in Istanbul has a meaning far beyond the immediate function of experiencing musical pleasure: it is a reaffirmation of a modern and European lifestyle. Perhaps because of this devotion and to preserve the sanctity of the AKM Concert Hall as a sacred site of modernity, which is identified with secularism, the presence of patrons with Islamic attire is met with extreme annoyance and is certainly unwelcome.[114]

It would be wrong to see modernisation as a unique Republican project. Ahmet Çiğdem, with some exaggeration, notes that the project to combine modernisation with religiosity in Turkey is 300 years old.[115] At least during the Tanzimat period, Sultan Mahmut introduced reforms to modernise the Empire. Mardin noted that Turkish society in the nineteenth century was interacting with Europe and, whether or not the Palace forced modernisation, the idea of modernity was already present by the time the Republic promoted it.[116]

113. *Ibid.*, p. 1.
114. *Ibid.*, p. 4.
115. Ahmet Çiğdem, "İslamcılık ve Türkiye Üzerine Bazı Notlar" in Bora, Tanıl and Gültenkingil Murat, (Eds.) İslamcılık, İstanbul, 2005. p. 33.
116. Şerif Mardin, 'The Just and the Unjust', *Daedalus*, Summer, 1991, p. 116.

2.3 POLITICAL ISLAM/ISLAMISM

The terms "political Islam" and more frequently "Islamism", or "Islamists, are used throughout the study. It is therefore essential to discuss the meaning ascribed to these concepts. As with the complications tackled in Chapter 1.1 with the definition of religion, commensurate difficulties attend the precise definition of political Islam, or its corollary Islamism. Given the appropriation of Islam as an ideological tool for political action and the spectrum of activities associated with the terms, we may not be able to define it satisfactorily to encapsulate the wide array of these activities. Furthermore, these terms mean different things to different people, whether lay people or scholars. These unclear terminologies, such as political Islam and Islamism, are neologisms registered only recently in Arabic:

> In fact, the modern Arabic term for Islamism, islamiyya, has been adapted to this usage by contemporary Muslim writers and intellectuals when writing about political Islam. In its classical and modern standard sense, islamiyya refers to things pertaining to Islam or to the status of being Muslim - in which case it is merely an adjective. Thus, even in Arabic, Islamism it is not a classical Islamic religious or political term, such as Sharia, ibadat (religious duties), or jihad.[117]

The Turkish term *İslâmcılık* (Islamism) is also relatively novel, having registered in the Turkish language only in the post-Republican era. In fact, Çiğdem uses the term "Republican Islamism" (*Cumhuriyet İslâmcılığı*) to emphasise the period of emergence of the term in Turkey parallel to the Republic.[118]

Goldenberg suggests that "[t]erms such as political Islam and Islamism are invented to cordon off appropriate forms of Islam from those that are considered dangerous to public order as defined by ruling governments."[119] Political Islam therefore, in Goldenberg's view is a construct with negative connotations.

Why "Political Islam" in the first place? After all, there are no such terms as political Christianity or political Buddhism. Yet, there is such a thing as "Political Hinduism", "Engaged Buddhism", and in both Judaism

---

117. Richard C. Martin and Abbas Barzegar, "Introduction: The Debate About Islamism in the Public Sphere" in Richard C. Martin and Abbas Barzegar, (eds.), *Contested Perspectives on Political Islam,* Stanford, 2010, p. 10.
118. Çiğdem, *op. cit.,* p. 26.
119. Naomi R. Goldenberg, "The Category of Religion in the Technology of Governance" in Trevor Stack, Naomi R. Goldenberg and Timothy Fitzgerald, *Religion as a Category of Governance and Sovereignty*, Leiden and Boston, 2015, p. 282.

and Christianity the categories of religion and politics often intermingle. This fusion in Christianity with politics is expressed through, *inter alia*, Religious or Christian Right in the United States or such organisations as *Opus Dei* within the Catholic Church. Even from the left of the spectrum, Christianity expressed dissatisfaction with the existing political system through liberation theology in Latin America. In Judaism, both orthodox and ultra-orthodox non-secular parties are represented in the *Knesset* and play a significant role in the political process. Political Islam is therefore not unique.

Some analysts use the terms political Islam and Islamism interchangeably. For instance, Graham E. Fuller, from the Rand Corporation, notes the use of the terms as synonymous and describes an Islamist as

> one who believes that Islam as a body of faith has something important to say about how politics and society should be ordered in the contemporary Muslim World and who seeks to implement this idea in some fashion.[120]

Similarly, the term Islamism is used in this study for politically motivated action (i.e. affecting public affairs) inspired by Islamic motives. Political Islam or Islamism is often used by popular media as an equivalent of terms such as "radical Islam", "fundamentalist Islam", and even "Islamic terrorism". However, in this study no equation is made of Islamic fundamentalism with political Islam. Within the spectrum, there are many variations of ideology and political actions, which certainly include fundamentalism and radical Islamism but do not represent it exclusively. Yet, some scholars such as Bassam Tibi describe political Islam as "an Islamic variety of religious fundamentalism.[121] In other words, in Tibi's view political Islam is one expression of religious fundamentalism rather than religious fundamentalism being one strand of political Islam.

There is another aspect of political Islam, which requires attention. This relates to the goal of political Islam: what outcome is desired from partaking in political processes? Every political action has a purpose. Political scientist Banu Eligür argues that

> Political Islamists, though differing in their means (violent and nonviolent), regard the individual and collective return to the Asr-ı Saadet – the age of happiness during the Prophet Muhammad's era – as

---

120. Graham E. Fuller, *The Future of Political Islam*, Basingstoke, 2004. p. xii [emphasis in the original text].
121. Bassam Tibi, *Islam Between Culture and Politics*, Basingstoke, 2001, p. xiii.

the solution to the political and socioeconomic problems of Muslim societies.[122]

In this sense political Islam is a utopia, an idealistic version of the past not experienced - an imagined nostalgia. Islamists desire this utopia for themselves and they also seek to impose it on others and deny personal agency to them. However, this is only one version of political Islam, expressed by some groups but not all political Islamists. Many strands of political Islam, such as expressed in Turkey by Erbakan through *Millî Görüş*, and Erdoğan, through AKP, were/are not necessarily utopian but pragmatic - although they may incorporate some elements of utopia and imagined nostalgia. This is not unusual; all ideologies, including secularism, contain an element of utopia. Their proponents idealise their perception of reality and what can be achieved if their ideology prevails. Ideologues of different persuasion hold their version of reality to be an axiomatic truth.

In the Turkish context, political Islam is an umbrella term enveloping Islamist oriented parties including the governing party of Turkey today, militant groups such as IBDA-C[123] and Hizbullah, militant tarikats and cemaats such as that of Said Nursî, but also of Fethullah Gülen. Even Nursî's movement, which primarily was interested in Quranic exegesis, can be described as political in that Nursî sought to influence Turkish society, even if not seeking political office for himself. As the term canvasses a variety of groupings with different agendas, it obscures its utility. In this study I use the term political Islam to exclude militant or violent groups.

Is "political" in political Islam a tautology, given that it is widely held that in Islam there is no difference between spiritual and temporal leadership? This synthesis was historically expressed through the office of the Caliph, following the death of Prophet Muhammad, first through the Rightly Guided Caliphs, i.e., *Rashidun* and then through the Ummayad and Abbasid Dynasties and eventually the Ottoman Dynasty, until 1924. Gareth Jenkins, a political analyst based in Turkey, notes that

> the divine revelation of the Qur'an to the Prophet Muhammad resulted in the creation of a discrete political entity defined by belief. Muhammad himself served not just as the community's spiritual and political leader, and sole source of its founding scripture and legislation, but also as its military commander in war.[124]

Jenkins's view is that there was no distinction between government af-

122. Banu Eligür, *The Mobilization of Political Islam in Turkey*, Cambridge, 2010, p. 4.
123. İslami Büyük Doğu Akıncılar *Cephesi* (Great Eastern Islamic Raiders' Front).
124. Jenkins. *op. cit.*, p. 2.

fairs and spiritual affairs, at least as far as early Islam was concerned. Nazih Ayubi held a different view, in that:

> [T]he original Islamic sources (the Quran and the Hadith) have very little to say on matters of government and the State. However, the first issue to confront the Muslim community immediately after the death of its formative leader, Prophet Muhammad, was in fact the problem of government, and Muslims had therefore to innovate and to improvise with regard to the form and nature of government.[125]

The implication is that any connection between government affairs and Islam is not of theological dictate. Ayubi's study is that the "fusion between religion and politics" in Islam was borne out by the necessities of the conditions prevalent at the time and refutes the "proposition - widely held in both Western and Muslim circles" that "Islam is by its very nature a 'political' religion":

> It is about time that this Orientalist/fundamentalist myth was dispelled once and for all. Even the common interpretation of the term umma, familiar in Western and Muslim circles alike, as a specifically Islamic community, should be subjected to serious scrutiny, for neither in the Quran itself nor in subsequent writings by Muslim authors was this term given such an unequivocally religious connotation.[126]

The investigation of whether Muhammad or the Qur'an stipulated government affairs demands a different kind of competence than one required in a study essentially within the discipline of political science. Suffices it to say that Ayubi challenges the established view and this allows for the potentiality of actual secularisation in Muslim majority countries. There are two issues emerging from this point of view warranting further attention. One issue is the reference to Orientalism, which is dealt with in the concluding paragraphs of the section.

The second is the idea that politics and religion can be separated in Islam. This is in sharp contrast to Asad's view that "'religion' was *always* involved the world of power". Asad's point is not specific to Islam but to what he considers an anachronistic term, i.e. "religion". This study is specifically on a Muslim majority country and therefore our primary concern is Islam and politics and separation of the two for the sake of secularisation/laicisation.

Political Islam is a relatively new concept; its provenance is often attributed to the Muslim Brotherhood, and in more recent times to the Ira-

---

125. Nazih N. Ayubi, *Political Islam*, London and New York, 1991, p. 1.
126. *Ibid.*, p. 14.

nian Revolution of Khomeini. However, according to Fuller

> [a] key turning point came in the [sic] 1941 when a young Indian Muslim journalist, Abu al-A'la al-Mawdudi, conceived the idea of forming a political party specifically to promote the Islamic agenda [Jama'at-i Islami (Islamic Association)]. This was a major innovation in the relationship of Islam to contemporary politics: Islam had previously been mobilized to serve the state. The Muslim Brotherhood in Egypt in the 1920s had called for political action in the name of Islam, but Islam had never functioned as a player in the form [sic] a political party in the arena of modern politics. ... 'Islamic politics' in the modern sense had been born.[127]

Though, as argued by Fuller, the first Islamic party was established in 1941, the Muslim Brotherhood as a movement was the first to emerge within the strand of political Islam. As expressed by the Salafist Muslim Brotherhood in Egypt, "Political Islam is a response to cultural modernity as much as it is a response to the realities of Western hegemony. Political Islam is a multifaceted 'Revolt against the West'".[128] Thus, in its genesis political Islam was not a utopian dream but an ideological expression and tool to counter western domination, but also modernism spreading by western domination.

Ali Mirsepassi argues of western influence on political Islam. In other words, even the anti-western ideology was influenced by ideas emanating from the West, namely, "radical anti-Enlightenment ideas of German philosophy, as well as certain French intellectuals."[129]

As noted, one view is that politics and Islam are inseparable, although in general, political Islam is seen as a new movement counteracting modernism, colonialism and western influence and domination. Bobby S. Said, interpreting Sami Zubaida's analysis, concludes that "Islamism is a phenomenon of modernity and therefore cannot be described as being anti-modern".[130] Yet, even if the genesis of political Islam is a by-product of modernism like many other ideologies, if its rhetoric is anti-modern then it can be described as such. There is no paradox; for instance, anti-democratic parties can use the benefits of a democratic system in order to bring it down. Political Islam can be anti-modern even if arising out of, and operating within, the paradigm of modernity and using modern methods and channels. As themselves thoroughly modern actors, Islamists do not

---

127. Fuller, *op. cit.*, p. 120.
128. Bassam, *op. cit.*, p. 3.
129. Ali Mirsepassi, *Political Islam, Iran, and The Enlightenment*, Cambridge, 2011, p. 2.
130. Bobby S. Said, *A Fundamental Fear*, London & New York. 1997, p. 96.

so much aim to end modernisation as to replace one form of modernity with another. It has no option but to operate in the dominant environment in order to counteract, reform or replace it. The replacement objective can take many forms, ranging from nihilistic dystopia (Taliban, ISIS) to modernity in another guise.

Whilst the origin of political Islam is associated with the Muslim Brotherhood, Bobby Said credits Khomeini with the resurgence of Islamism in more recent times: "It is Khomeini's political thought that best articulates the logic of Islamism. It is only with Khomeini that Islamism makes the transition from an opposition and marginalized political project to a counter hegemonic power".[131] Nevertheless, in the process the Khomeini revolution, which opposed certain hegemonic power, replaced it with another, a clerical hegemonic power - a theocracy. It was not a counter-hegemonic movement but "hegemony replacement", to coin a term.

The Iranian revolution has influenced Islamism in Turkey by planting the idea of revolution in the mind of the Islamists.[132] Some of the like-minded organisations in Turkey such as Hizbullah, the İBDA-C, the Hizbu't-Tahrir, and the Islamic Jihad at the extreme end of the spectrum were inspired by this theocratic revolution and even assassinated critics "who wrote and spoke openly about the dangers of an Islamist threat to secularism in Turkey".[133]

As Eligür emphasises, these militant Islamist organisations do not have mass appeal in Turkey. These violent movements remained marginal and ineffective, and they are not discussed in this study, except mentioned in passing. Furthermore, unlike Iran there has been no strong clerical movement in Turkey.

Bobby Said points specifically to the ideology of secularism in Turkey as the genesis of political Islam; essentially a by-product of Kemalism:

> Is political Islam a product of secularist ideology? By pushing Islam outside the sphere of the public and assigning it a certain role, it forced to redefine and oppose. Political Islam emerged and it sharpened its ideological tools as an opposition to secular forces. This occurred in Iran as well, as the Shah's regime which copied Kemalist principles forced Islam to become a political force.[134]

Bobby Said's argument has merit in that in the secularist narrative, there are two clear modes, which can be separated successfully. In examin-

---

131. *Ibid.*, p. 89.
132. Tanıl Bora and Murat Gültenkingil (Eds.) İslamcılık, İstanbul, 2005. p. 21.
133. Banu Eligür, *The Mobilization of Political Islam in Turkey*, Cambridge, 2010, p. 4.
134. Bobby S. Said, *op. cit.*, p. 60.

ing the term *İslamcılık*, Tanıl Bora and Murat Gültenkingil argue that the secularists have simplified a complex movement in order to define themselves as anti-Sharia. This supports Bobby Said's view. Just as the religion/secularism dichotomy emerged around the same time in Europe, the secularism/Islamism dichotomy emerged at the same time in Turkey. The state needed to define "the other" in order to define itself.

Bora and Gültenkingil contend that Islamism cannot be reduced to a single element, that of support for Sharia. They also point out that in the voluminous study (1,112 pages) they edited on Islamism, which involves many writers, including those who identify with Islam, very few of them call themselves *İslâmcı*, i.e. Islamist.[135] For instance, İbrahim Arif, known as "Islamist ", according to Bora and Gültenkingil, denies this label. Arif regards Islamism as a western, Orientalist concept and contends that it is wrong for Muslims to identify themselves as *İslâmcı*. In a conspiratorial tone Arif suggests by using this term "the missionaries of a foreign culture" (secularists?) are enabled to affect the status of Islam.[136]

Çiğdem coming from a different background also defines political Islam as an Orientalist concept. In fact, the tendency to define "Islamism" or "political Islam" as an Orientalist concept can be observed both among western and Turkish scholars, including secularists. Ali Bulaç, former writer of Gülenist newspaper *Zaman*, defines *İslamcılık* as a new mission within Islam. In his view, *İslamcılık* is a movement by cultural, political and social leaders whose quest is to establish a world in concordance with Islam's spiritual, ethical, cultural and social values.[137] Bulaç regards Islamism as an ever-changing self-producing process.[138] Bulaç also sees Islamism as by-product of modernisation and describes it as a modernisation project, which contributes to the formation of identities *sui generis* in the Islamic world, in a historical period not of its own creation.

In short, political Islam or Islamism is seen as a movement that emerged to oppose ideological currents and cultural domination emanating from the West. However, a contradiction is noticeable: political Islam cannot be recent if the view is held at the same time that politics and Islam are inseparable. As we have seen different scholars hold the view that both the inseparability of politics from Islam and political Islam itself are orientalist concepts. These attributes to Said's orientalism overextended the concept.

---

135. Tanıl Bora and Murat Gültenkingil (Eds.) İslamcılık, İstanbul, 2005. p. 14.
136. İbrahim Arif, "Fitnenin Maliyetine Giriş, in Bora and Gültenkingil, İslamcılık, p. 1097.
137. Ali Bulaç, "İslamın Üç Siyaset Tarzı veya İslamcıların Üç Nesli" in Bora and Gültenkingil (Eds.) İslamcılık, *op. cit.*, p. 50.
138. *Ibid.*, p. 51.

A critique of Orientalism is beyond the scope of the study, but as Said's Orientalism is often referred to in many studies related to the field of the study, a brief review is necessary. Said's conceptualization of Orientalism was ground-breaking as he pointed out the "colonial" attitudes in assessing societies in the East, but there were methodological flaws which were overlooked by majority of scholars ready to embrace the framework. As Bernard Lewis pointed out, the Orient is reduced to Middle East and more specifically, his study is about the Arab world. Turkish and Persian sources are ignored; German sources were also omitted even though Germany was an important centre for "Oriental" studies.[139]

Said dates Orientalism to Classical Greek times, applying such later concepts as "Europe" and to stretch the timeframe of the concept he constructed. Said arrived at this conclusion with very limited material:

> The two aspects of the Orient that set it off from the West in this pair of plays will remain essential motifs of European imaginative geography. A line is drawn between two continents. Europe is powerful and articulate; Asia is defeated and distant. Aeschylus represents Asia, makes her speak in the person of the aged Persian queen. Xerxes' mother. It is Europe that articulates the Orient.[140]

Ibn Warraq explains that

> Said's treatment of Greek intellectual themes rests only on a reading of the play The Persians. Its author, Aeschylus . . . is depicted as one of the founding fathers of modern Orientalism. The Persians is of central importance in Orientalism because Said depicts it as one of the first attempts to demarcate a sharp distinction between the West and the Orient. This play supposedly sets the tone for more than a millennium of Western perceptions of the Orient.[141]

Another criticism of Said is that its ideological framework includes and gives equal weight to the writings of ignorant travelers, amateur journalists and learned scholars.[142] Some of this criticism, however, is even expressed in much more hostile tone:

> Said has much to answer for. Orientalism, despite its systematic distortions and its limited value as intellectual history, has left Western scholars in fear of asking questions-in other words, it has inhibited their research. Said's work, with its strident anti-Westernism, it has

139. Bernard Lewis, The Question of Orientalism', *The New York Review of Books*, 24 June 1982, p. 9.
140. Edward W. Said, *Orientalism*, New York, 1979.
141. David Zarnett, "Edward Said and the West", *Democratiya,* Spring 2008, p. 51.
142. Zanett, p. 50.

made the goal of modernization of Middle Eastern societies that much more difficult. His work, wherein all the ills of Middle Eastern societies are blamed on the wicked West, has rendered much needed self-criticism by Muslims, Arab and non-Arab alike, nearly impossible. His work has encouraged Islamic fundamentalists, whose impact on world affairs needs no underlining.[143]

This seems a harsh criticism by Warraq. It is very farfetched to hold Said responsible for Islamic fundamentalism; any kind of extremist will find a way to rationalise their actions. Said's concept of Orientalism is not to be dismissed; it has utility and application. However, it has now become an orthodoxy, and orthodoxies are rarely challenged as they are the dominant form. Orientalism is the dominant discourse in Academia in the fields related to this study. Many secondary sources examined resort to Orientalism to justify their arguments and provide it as explanation to a multitude of phenomena. Said's Orientalism has been overextended to describe any opinion deviating from the norm as Orientalism.

A strand in European scholarship certainly displayed the attitude Said criticised in his seminal work. I myself used the concept of "Orientalism" above in reference to a misguided western study of tarikats, but I will have to agree that the word Orientalism has become, as Lewis pointed out, a term of "polemical abuse".[144] Scholars need to go beyond this intellectually suffocating framework to search for their answers, in this case on political Islam and Turkey. Paradigms need to be challenged until a new paradigm emerges to build on the strength of the old but remove its deficiencies. My study contributes to this by acknowledging some of the merits of the Orientalism framework in evaluating western studies of Turkey, especially of early twentieth century, but rejecting it as the only lens through which to assess primary and secondary sources on Turkey.

---

143. Ibn Warraq, *Defending the West*, New York, 2007.
144. Lewis, *op. cit.*, p. 5.

2.4 RELIGIOUS LANDSCAPE BEYOND STATE SANCTIONED ISLAM: THE CASE OF ALEVIS

Any study of Turkish politics and secularism is not complete without reference to Alevis. Alevis form a substantial proportion of Turkish society; they have been consistently supporters of Mustafa Kemal, Kemalism, laicism/secularism and privatisation of "religious" activities. By eliminating Islam from the public space, which the new state sought, the doctrinal differences between Sunnis and Alevis were bound to wither away; or so the Alevis expected. Elimination of Islam from the public space was likely to give them a reprieve from the hostile approach they experienced in the Ottoman Empire.

Alevis (also known as *Kızılbaş*) are said to be Shi'ites and due to this connection to Shi'a Islam, they are often described as "heterodox" Muslims, who occupy a position outside the state sanctioned Islam. Whatever the differences between the Shi'ites and many Alevis, *inter alia*, the belief in the twelve imams, the hidden imam and the veneration of Ali (cousin and son-in-law of Prophet Muhammad, the Fourth Rightly Guided Caliph and the First Imam)[145] remain common traits between them. The boundaries of Alevism are hard to delineate encompassing several ethnicities (Turcoman, Turkish, Kurdish/Zaza[146] and Arab), religious systems (Alevi, Bektaşi, Tahtacı), cultural subgroups (Tahtacıs, Abdals, Çepni *et al*), and languages (Turkish, Kurdish, Arabic, Zazaki).

In 1920, Wladimir Minorsky reported that an *Ahl-e Ḥaqq* dervish told him that their name, i.e., the *Ahl-e Ḥaqq*, in Turkey is Alevi.[147] Often the Nusayris (Alawis/Alawites), who are found mainly in the Hatay Province, are also referred to as Alevis, but they have a weak connection to Anatolian Alevis and their stronghold is in Syria. Neither the Nusayri nor the *Ahl-e Ḥaqq* are considered in this study, but they are cited examples of the broad Alevi umbrella.

---

145. In Turkish, Ali is referred to as Hazreti Ali (Prophet Ali), along with Muhammad and the three other *Rashidun* (Rightly Guided) Caliphs. The Twelve Imams are patrilineal descendants of Prophet Muhammed's cousin and son-in-law Caliph Ali.

146. This is an issue of contention. While there is a Zaza subgroup, which originate from Dersim and see themselves as Zaza/Zazaki, the Kurdish majority regard them as Kurdish.

147. Wladimir Minorsky, 'Notes Sur le Secte des Ahl-é Haqq', *Revue du Monde Musulman*, Vols. XL-XLI, September-December 1920, p. 53.

Heterodoxification of Alevis/Kızılbaş in the Ottoman Empire

Undoubtedly, the Alevi identity and theology has changed immensely over time. Even their appellations have gone through a transformation. Élise Massicard notes that the appearance of the Alevis cannot be reduced to a single period, though the emergence of *Kızılbaş*, a term used for Alevis, can be traced back to the sixteenth century.[148] The term Kızılbaş, literally "red heads", was due to the twelve-gore headgear they used to wear. Şeyh Haydar, the father of the founder of the Safavid Dynasty in Persia, in order to separate his supporters from others, made them were this specific headgear, which represented the twelve imams. The head gear was named "Tâc-ı Haydarî" or "Tâc". Those who wore it in time acquired the name of Kızılbaş. The term became pejorative in the Ottoman Empire, due to their connection to the Safavid Iran and Shi'ism.

Safavid leader İsmail, whose support base consisted mostly of Turcomans, became Shah and declared Shi'ism as the state religion. There were Turcomans living in Inner and Southern Anatolia at the time.[149] The term originally signified the "Saffavi supporters" or "Saffavi army"; it was therefore a political term rather than a theological one. Given the Saffavi insistence on believe on twelve imams, the terms Kızılbaş acquired a religious significance and became the name of Turcoman Shi'ism.[150]

The declaration of Twelver Shi'sm as the state religion in Persia, forced the antagonistic Ottoman palace to view Sunnism as the central ideology.[151] In short, the Sunni orthodoxy emerged as antithetical to Safavid interpretation of Islam. According to Mürüvet Harman, the term "Kızılbaş" in the Ottoman theological narrative came to acquire a variety of meanings, including "unbeliever", antithetical to Sunnism and *Râfizî* (heretic).[152] Ömer Faruk Teber's research on Ottoman documents identifies a number of terms used for mystic formations in addition to Kızılbaş and *Rafizism*: *Işık* (Light) and *Kalender*.[153] In general, the term Rafizî is connected to Shi'ite imamate. The Ottomans used the term to apply to groups who opposed state practices. The term was used even in the wider Islamic world. For instance, the fourteenth century Moroccan traveler Ibn Baṭūṭah used the term in his *Rihla* (Journey).[154]

---

148. Élise Massicard, *Alevi Hareketinin Siyasallasmasi*, Istanbul, 2007, p. 30.
149. Massicard, pp. 30-31.
150. Mürüvet Harman, 'Osmanlı Görsel Dünyasında "Kızılbaşlar Alevilik', *Alevilik - Bektaşilik Araştırmaları Dergisi*, No. 12, 2015, p. 102.
151. Élise Massicard, Istanbul, 2007, p. 32.
152. Harman, p. 103.
153. Teber, *passim*.
154. *Ibid.*, p. 24; In Arabic the term is *Râfiḍa*.

The palace started viewing the Turcomans Kızılbaş as heretics and they were persecuted. In 1720, Dürri Efendi, who served as the Ottoman Porte's ambassador in Persia for six and a half months, submitted a report to Sultan Ahmed III. In his report, he made no distinction between the Kızılbaş and the Persians, using the appellation interchangeably.[155] Moreover, as a Sunni himself, he regarded them infidels.[156]

Dressler observed that in the Ottoman documents Alevis are referred to as Shi'ites, which for many Sunni Muslims at the time meant that the Alevis were heretical. "The term Kızılbaş itself connoted in Ottoman times heresy, political disloyalty, and immorality". In the late nineteenth century Ottoman documents question the Islamic credential of Kızılbaş Alevis: "with their superstitious dogmas they have totally separated themselves from the Islamic religion".[157]

While predominantly the term Kızılbaş was used in the Ottoman records from the fifteenth century, the scant documentary evidence suggest that the appellation Alevi did not completely disappear. There is evidence of the use of Alevi in the *tahrir* tax registers. For instance, in 1455, a tahrir register related to Bayramlı, administrative centre of Ordu, recorded the expression "Nefs-i Ordu also known as Nefs-i Alevî". In the same year, a small settlement of 19 houses is recorded as "Cemaat-i Alevî" (Alevi congregation). Sadullah Gülten draws the conclusion that this particular locality was known as Alevî before the Ottoman conquest.[158]

These documents suggest that the doxa community did not abandon the emic appellation despite the imposition of the etic appellation by the Ottoman administration, and that the Ottomans occasionally acknowledged the emic term. On the whole, however, the term Kızılbaş seems to have displaced Alevi for several centuries, until its re-emergence in the nineteenth century. When the central government weakened in the nineteenth century, Alevis started using the name more openly.

While the Ottoman documents are an invaluable source reflecting the viewpoint of the palace, in the 1990s Alevi documents emerged, which seem to have been preserved in Dede families. Although it is said that Alevism is an oral culture, manuscripts in Persian, Arabic and Ottoman Turkish from the fourteenth to the twentieth century have been preserved by the Dede families. Ayfer Karakaya-Stump, who studied these manuscripts, makes a

---

155. *Relation de Dourry Efendy*, Paris, 1810, pp. 2 and 12.
156. *Ibid.*, p. 54.
157. Dressler, pp. 1-3.
158. Sadullah Gülten, 'Osmanlı Devleti'nde Alevî sözcüğünün Kullanımına Dair Bazı Değerlendirmeler', *Alevilik Araştırmaları Dergisi*, No. 11, 2016, p. 33.

number of observations. The documents show the relationship between the Wafa'i Sufi order, which seemed to have been incorporated into the Alevi *ocak* (hearth) system from the second half of the fifteenth century. The documents also show the relationship between the Alevis and Bektashis, as well as evidence of Dedes of *sayyid*[159] descent visiting the Shi'ite sacred sites in Iraq and paying homage to the convent in Karbala.[160] This highly complicated research points to the difficulties and futility in trying to trace neatly the various Alevi traditions in order to view them as a coherent unity, as it includes a number of sects and it is multi-faceted.

Slowly the term Alevi took hold, not replacing Kızılbaş entirely, but becoming the dominant appellation. According to Massicard, we can only talk about Alevis from the nineteenth century onwards.[161] Dressler concurs, noting that

> [r]eports by Western observers begin to note since the 1880s the vernacular use of the term 'Alevi' (or variations thereof), a term that in the language of Islam indicates a close relationship (by descent or chosen affiliation) with Ali Ibn Abu Talib, as a self-designation among Kızılbaş. The designation seems to become more widespread during the Young Turk period. Earlier texts of Western observers in contact with Kızılbaş groups do not mention the term Alevi. But very occasionally the term Alevi as a self-designation, apparently indicating loyalty and/ or descent from Ali, also appears in Kızılbaş and Bektashi poems that can be attributed to earlier centuries.[162]

Dressler describes Alevis as a socio-religious group, which is apt given that both religious and socio-political dimensions are articulated in their expression of identity. John Shindeldecker lists a number of statements by Alevis, he has either heard firsthand or read about. The list includes what seem to be contradictory statements about Alevi identity and "religion":

> 'An Alevi is any Muslim who loves the family of the Prophet Muhammed.'
> 'An Alevi is simply any democratic, tolerant, human rights-promoting, modern-thinking person, whatever his religious background.'
> [. . . .]
> 'Alevism is the original, true essence of Islam.'
> 'Alevism is a heterodox sect within Islam.'

---

159. A honorific title indicating descendance from Prophet Muhammad's clan.
160. Ayfer Karakaya-Stump, 'Documents and Buyruk Manuscripts in the Private Archives of Alevi Dede Families, *British Journal of Middle Eastern Studies*, December 2010, Vol. 37, No. 3, p. 276.
161. Élise Massicard, Istanbul, 2007, p. 30.
162. Dressler, *Writing Religion*, p. 1.

'Alevism is the most authentic expression of Turkish Anatolian Islam.'
'Alevism is a philosophy, a "way of life".'
'Alevism is pure Sufism.'
'Alevism is pure Shiism.'
'Alevism is simply Sunni Islam with an extra emphasis on Ali.'
'Alevism is so syncretistic that it can't be counted as Islam at all.'
'Alevism is an alternative to orthodox Islam.'
'Alevism is an example of the classic Marxist struggle by an oppressed minority.'
'Alevism is a mixture of the best elements of Islam, Christianity, Judaism, Manichaeism, Zoroastrianism, Shamanism, and 20th century humanism."[163]

The statements above express a wide variety of identities ranging from Islamic (Shi'ite or otherwise), to political (left-wing); they also include the view that Alevism is syncretic and outside Islam. In another study, by Talha Köse, additional emic views collected from field research are introduced:

> I see the Alevi creed *as a way of life*. (AA, journalist)
> At the moment, I regard the Alevi creed as a *sect* [Madhhab]. The Alevi creed is a way of believing. (H, S, anthropologist)
> Islam also included the Alevi creed, but Islam's rules are clear, its practices too, we don't have any common ground left with Islam. (AE, president of an Alevi foundation)
> The Alevi creed is an ethnic identity. Even if you were a Christian, they would call you a Christian Alevi. (DK, graduate student).[164]

From the myriad of statements of what Alevism is supposed to be, from the point of view of the individual questioned, Köse identifies two broad trends: he describes these as "ideological position" and "religious position". Köse does not believe the two positions can be separated completely as they overlap considerably, but they have different interpretation of what Alevi history is.[165] He further contends that

> [t]he Religious Position (RP) constructs an ethno-sectarian identity by defining Alevilik [Alevism] as the Turkish interpretation of Islam as opposed to 'Umayyad contaminated Sunni Islam'. RP assumes that Alevi understanding of Islam is more 'Islamic' and 'authentic' than the

---

163. John Shindeldecker, Turkish Alevis today,

   https://alevibektasi.eu/index.php?option=com_content&view=article&id=684:turk-ish-alevis-today&catid=46:aratrmalar-ingilizce&Itemid=69, [accessed on 1 January 2018].
164. Talha Köse, 'Ideological or religious? Contending visions on the future of Alevi identity', p. 582.
165. *Ibid.*, p. 582.

Sunni interpretation of Islam. There is an attribution of double authenticity and legitimacy in the RP in terms of the origins of Alevi thought and lifestyle. First, because it is perceived to have come directly from the practices of Ehl-i beyt (the Prophet's family/lineage). The Ehl-i beyt is considered to be the second important source of Islam for Alevis, after the Quran. Second, it is also presented as a tradition of belief that is blended with the pastoral Turkoman tribes' simple, genuine and 'unpoliticised' understanding of Islam. In other words, the Alevi version of Islam is considered to be both 'more Islamic' and 'more Turkish' than its Sunni alternative.[166]

This tendency to see Alevism a more Turkic version of Islam by some Alevis, is empowering and has been affected by early Republican efforts to de-pollute Islam and elevate the status of Alevis. It also shifts the hierarchical position in the horizontal dichotomy in favour of Alevis. Yet, this view is not shared by Sunnis nor by Diyanet which continue to monopolise the "religious market".

Köse also notes that "Bilici (1998), Ocak (1996) and Erman and Göker (2000) employ different taxonomies to grasp the complexity of contemporary Alevi phenomena". They classify Alevism according to institutions such as Alevi Bektaşi Federasyonu (ABF), CEM Vakfı, Pîr Sultan Abdal Kültür Derneği and Ehl-i Beyt Vakfı.[167] Though these agencies have a role to play in interpreting and shaping Alevi theology, this taxonomy is not particularly useful for the purpose of examining historical developments in Alevi history, but it may be useful in reviewing contemporary Alevi social *milieu*.

In another survey conducted in 2002 among Alevi youth by Ahmet Şık and Hatice Yaşar, some of the responses were:

I am Alevi, I am a democrat. Of course I believe in Islam. I am Kurdish but when I introduce myself I do not state it as first. Sect is at the forefront of identity."
"I am Alevi, I am Muslim."
"I am Alevi. I love Alevism. Things like tolerance and love I learned them in Alevism. I am a Muslim but I am not a bigot."
"I am Alevi, Alevism is a sect within Islam."[168]

This diversity of opinion in relation to identity is by no means unique.

---

166. *Ibid.*, p. 583.
167. *Ibid.*, p. 582. [Alevi Bektashi Federation, CEM Foundation, Pîr Sultan Abdal Cultural Association and Ehl-i Beyt Foundation respectively].
168. Cited in İsmail Beşikçi, Alevilerde Kafa Karışıklığı, 23 December 2012,
    https://www.alevihaber.com/ismail-besikciden-ezberbozan-bir-yazi-alevilerde-kafa-karisikligi-44322h.htm, [accessed on 17 November 2021].

Elsewhere I have argued that the Assyrian community in Turkey also faced not too dissimilar path. People from the same villages and seemingly same traditions followed a different path in identity construction and arrived at vastly different conclusions.[169] However, the spectrum of the variety of Alevi traditions in Anatolia is not matched by any other.

Some of the youth interviewed for the abovementioned study declared themselves to be Muslims; others declared themselves to be Muslims with a qualification: "We see ourselves within the trinity of Allah, Muhammed and Ali, and within Ehl-i Beyt". Despite the belief of many Alevis in 12 imams, the hidden imam and veneration of Ali, evidently, some do not see themselves as Shi'ite at all. These contradictions are inherent and endemic in contemporary Alevism.

These particular responses listed above motivated İsmail Beşikçi, a renowned Turkish Kurdologist, to write his article on alleged "confusion" among Alevis. Beşikçi suggested that the Alevis were confused about their religion. According to Beşikçi, some Alevi tend to say they are not Muslims, yet their allegiance to the Imams suggests otherwise. There is no doubt that there is a plurality of emic views in the Alevi doxa community, but Beşikçi in his opening paragraph seems to be critical of Alevi views which expressed non-Muslim identities, in that while they say they are not Muslims they refer to Ali and the other imams in their pantheon. Yet, it is specifically the views of those who placed themselves within Islam that attracted Beşikçi's criticism and then applied his critical views to the entire community. Beşikçi stated unequivocally that the Alevis were neither Muslims nor Shi'ites, despite some shared beliefs. In his experience, the Alevis did not conduct namaz (salah), attend mosques or make the pilgrimage to Mecca (hajj/hacı), or even use the Quran in their rituals. Furthermore, in their cems[170] the rituals are conducted with music, which in Beşikçi's view is antithetical to Islam. Beşikçi contends that the Alevi faith is Zoroastrian and therefore pre-Islamic.[171]

A prodigious writer and theoretician, Demir Küçükaydın, criticizes Beşikçi on a number of points. His primary criticism is that

> Beşikçi sees the historical authentic Alevism and Alevism of today as one and the same, and ignores the radical change in its social function. All his evidence that Alevism is a separate religion are drawn from authentic Alevism or historical Alevism. That is to say that, while he

---

169. See Racho Donef, *Assyrians post-Nineveh: conflict, identity, fragmentation and survival communities*, Mesopotamia Series 1, Sydney, 2012, *passim*.

170. Cem: Alevi ritual ceremony performed in cemevis.

171. Beşikçi, Alevilerde Kafa Karışıklığı, *op. cit.*

discusses the Alevism of today, all his evidence is from historic or authentic Alevism; he does not even regard the views of Alevis of today as Alevism. The hidden assumption here is that Alevism of today is the same as historical Alevism.[172]

Küçükaydın identifies three types of Alevism: historical and authentic Alevism, contemporary Alevism that see itself as a belief, and Alevism as social and political movement. Other criticism levelled at Beşikçi by Küçükaydın is for formulating a number of false hypotheses that Alevism is a religion, that religion is faith and that the Alevis are a faith.[173] These are themes pertinent to the present study.

In his criticism Küçükaydın refers to "authentic" Alevism presumably to differentiate it from contemporary Alevism. This raises similar range of questions as orthodox/heterodox, i.e. how does something get to be considered authentic in relation to what is the inauthentic? Who decides what is "authentic" and what is not? Is contemporary Alevism "inauthentic" by extension? Authenticity is yet another unstable term. It is claimed by many traditions but how can authenticity of a culture spanning several hundred years be objectively determined? It is a futile effort, but authenticity is claimed not because it can objectively be measured in some way, but because it bestows upon the legitimacy to the claimant. It is therefore a legitimising ideological tool, not objectively observable reality or scientifically measurable phenomenon.

Küçükaydın's criticism of Beşikçi does not end there:

> Beşikçi argues that Alevism is a separate religion in order to defend the Alevis against the injustices, in the context of a political debate. In such a context, however, to defend this proposition, the hidden assumption is that those who cannot cite scientific evidence to [demonstrate] that they are a distinct religion, do not deserve to be seen as separate religion. It is not just that, since the issue is the behaviour of the state, there is an assumption that the state can and should decide of what religion is; this is another concealed assumption, that of Kemalism, the official ideology.[174]

The core issue of contention here is what is a "separate religion": why and to whom does it matter? In this study it has been discussed that "religion" is not a stand-alone category in the first place. Furthermore, in a secular society it should not matter at all, from the state's point of view,

---

172. Demir Küçükaydın, *Tersinden Kemalizm (İsmail Beşikçi'nin Eleştirisi)*, Istanbul, 2004, p. 29.
173. Küçükaydın, p. 22.
174. Küçükaydın, p. 31.

though, granted, it may matter to the believers who argue about the content of their beliefs. In Australia, for instance, such a question will be relevant to members of a congregation, but irrelevant to the state or the rest of the population. In Turkey the issue comes to the fore because in its inception the state decided that it would be the arbiter of theological terrain in Islam. As it decided that Sunni Islam is the state religion and ignored Alevi needs, the issue constantly comes to the fore. The state still retains this monopoly through Diyanet and the Alevis keep arguing their case.

Küçükaydın wonders, what would be the point of attempting to prove that Alevism is a distinct religion? Irrespective of the merits of the lengthy and harsh criticism of Beşikçi, who has spent many years in prison defending the Kurds, Beşikçi is not the only scholar or researcher of note that believes Alevis are not Muslims. For instance, in *Ali'siz Alevilik* (*Alevism without Ali*), Faik Bulut contends that Alevism is a belief, culture and way of life outside of Islam.[175] Furthermore, Erdoğan Çınar, specifically points to the Luwians as the origin of the Alevism.[176]

Considerable scholarly effort has been dedicated to identifying the origin of Alevis, with vastly different claims and conclusions. Some Alevis are very critical of these attempts by non-Alevis to connect Alevism "to every community and every belief" under the sun, so to speak. In an Alevi journal, Hamza Aksüt argues that Çınar seem to think that Alevism is confined to Anatolia, even though Alevis can be found in Syria, Iran and Iraq. Also, Aksüt criticizes Çınar for not taken into the account the different ethnic origins of the Alevis' (Turkish, Kurdish, Arabic, Roma).[177] In the same publication, Ünsal Öztürk even accuses of Çınar of misquoting documents to support his theory.[178] It is wrong to think that only non-Alevi researchers look beyond Islam to investigate the origin of Alevism. For instance, Mehmet Bayrak, a Kurdish-Alevi, as describes himself, in his comprehensive study finds non-Islamic beliefs and influences in Alevism.[179]

To acquire an Alevi perspective from an authoritative source, an Alevi dede, journalist Hüseyin Gazi Metin, was asked in an interview, whether Alevis were Muslims. The Alevi elder Metin first mocks the premise of the question, as he finds it irrelevant, but eventually responds: "Anatolian Alevism is a different type. It has taken the beautiful aspect of Islam and Christianity, even Shamanism. It has

175. Faik Bulut, *Ali'siz Alevilik*, İstanbul, 2011.
176. Erdoğan Çınar, *Aleviliğin Kökenleri*, İstanbul, 2008, pp. 47-53.
177. Hamza Aksüt, 'Erdoğan Çınar Skandalı, *kızılbaş*, No. 9, June 2009, p. 4.
178. Ünsal Öztürk, '"mu rahipleri" (a)luvi miydi?' *kızılbaş*, No. 9, June 2009, p. 12.
179. Mehmet Bayrak, *Alevilik ve Kürtler*, ÖZ-GE Yayınları, Wuppertal, 1997, *passim*.

absorbed Anatolia like a sponge."

When the journalist pressed and sought clarification on whether Alevism is a religion at all, Metin states that Alevism does not fit into the definition of a religion:

> All religions are forms; they are cradle-to-grave investment to the other world. In Anatolian Alevism you do not live your life to receive a gift on the other side. For us the only holy being is the person. This is why we avoid harming a person, not to pass through the [bridge to the afterlife]."[180]

Metin expresses his disagreement of looking at Alevism through established precepts, which takes it for granted that any belief system is a religion. In seems, in his view "religion" is a template, which one uses in order to be rewarded in the afterlife, and that Alevism does not fit that norm. This is important because outsiders' perspectives are imposed on Alevis or are presented as the true Alevism. But the problematic is wider than that. Alevism is viewed from the perspective of Islam or Christianity, or even particular notion of what religion is. This is precisely the criticisms of Küçükaydın of Beşikçi, in that even though Beşikçi is an anti-Kemalist, in terms of religion, he thinks within the paradigm established by the Republican regime in its early years. Küçükaydın calls this "Reverse Kemalism" (*Tersinden Kemalism*). It is worth remembering that this ideological framework was borrowed from the West, by the western educated Republican elites and was adapted to the particular ideology of the early Republic.

In the Ottoman Empire, the Alevis were treated as either outright infidels or marginal Muslims at best. The Alevi theology is a complicated terrain as there is no single, cohesive form of Alevism. This is not unusual; no theology is cohesive: bifurcations, various interpretations of canon are common traits of most theological terrains. As noted, Alevis share some theology with the Bektashi tarikat. As David Shankland notes:

> Alevi religious doctrines are often based on those of Bektaşi tarikat and are very strongly influenced by a text known as the Buyruk [Command], which they attribute to Imam Cafer [the sixth Imam, Jaffar]. According to both Bektaşi doctrines and Buyruk, the first and necessary step towards personal development is mastering orthodox practice, which they know as Şeriat. In practice, however, most Alevis do not hold the Kuran to be literally true, and they go only very occasionally to mosques.[181]

---

180. Devrim Sevinay, 'Bir Dedeyle söyleşi, *Vatan*, 4 October 2004.
181. David Shankland, *The Alevis in Turkey*, London and New York, 2003, p. x.

Bektashis are mostly Alevis, but not every Alevi is a member of the Bektashi order. Erol Ayhan explains that while any person can become a member of the Bektashi order, one must be born into Alevism. Another differentiation is that Bektashis are found mostly in cities and can be referred to as "urban Alevis", while Alevis can be referred to as "rural Bektashis". Alevis also venerate Hacı Bektaş Veli, the patron saint of the Bektashis, but while "[t]he Bektashis follow an unchangeable ritual . . . the Kızılbaş-Alevi believe in myths in which legends are mingled with local folklore".[182]

In relation to Ali's position in Alevi Pantheon, Tina Hamrin-Dahl notes that:

> Ali is more or less deified and therefore Alevis are considered as being ghulat ('exaggerated', 'extremist') and heterodox. The elevated Ali personifies an aspiration to justice and righteousness. He fought on the side of the weak and oppressed against those with power in society. Theologically, Ali is assumed to be blessed by the divine light and is therefore able to see into the mysterious spirituality of Islam . . . Many Alevis today however totally dissociate themselves from Shi'ism.[183]

"Heterodoxy"

The term "heterodox" may not be accurate to describe Alevis. Marcus Dressler argues strongly against the use of the term to describe Alevis. He argues that binary pairs such as heterodoxy/orthodoxy to be problematic and he finds "it very unsatisfactory to simply put ambivalent conceptual terms such as heterodox, popular, and so forth into quotation marks, as often done."[184]

For a lack of a better term[185] and given that the majority of scholars, both Turkish, Kurdish and western alike, refer to the Alevis as heterodox, this descriptor retains its currency. Shankland, who has done extensive research on Alevis, also labels Alevis as "heterodox"; in his defence, he argues that

---

182. Erol, Ayhan. 'Re-Imagining Identity: The Transformation of the Alevi Semah', *Middle Eastern Studies*, Vol. 46, No. 3, p. 376.

183. Tina Hamrin-Dahl, 'The Alevi and Questions of Identity, Including Violence and Insider/Outsider Perspectives', Vol 19, *Scripta Instituti Donneriani Aboensis*, 2006, p. 108.

184. Marcus Dressler, *Writing Religion*, Oxford, 2013, p. 205.

185. Zarcone uses the term heterogenous (*hétérogène*), though this still does not resolve the hierarchical dimension in the dichotomy (See Thierry Zarcone, "La fabrication des saints sous la République turque" in Catherine Mayeur-Jaouen (ed.). *Saints et héros du Moyen-Orient contemporain*, Paris, 2002, p. 212.

there are groups which are more or less heterodox, or unorthodox in their belief. To ignore this, I believe, is to overlook the fact that there is a common core of ideas which these groups often define themselves in opposition to; further that they equally often do appear to have factors in common, however different their name or their doctrines appear to be from one another. 'Unorthodox' in this context is not simply a random instance of rebellion, resistance or difference, but does appear to exhibit certain patterns.[186]

In other words, the heterodoxy is not necessarily imposed by the "orthodox" group; some groups may seek to differentiate themselves from the norm. Dressler himself uses it, subsequent to his disapproval of the term, only by preceding it with a modifier ("alleged 'heterodox'")[187], which show the difficulty in extricating this label from the study of Alevis. In his ensuing study, Dressler presses the point, referring to the history of heterodoxification of the Alevis and that the Ottoman state regarded them as Muslims only towards the end of its existence, and then again still needing to be reformed.[188] Heterodoxification of Alevis/Kızılbaş was a process that started in the Ottoman Empire and the Republic inherited their marginalisation.

The history of heterodoxification can also be seen as the history of orthodoxification; these are mutually parasitic terms. Dressler notes that

[w]hile the terms orthodoxy and heterodoxy are mostly used in academic discourse, they also found their way into non-academic language, and are occasionally even used by Alevis in their self-representation.[189]

Among Alevis there are different tendencies related to the issue of orthodoxy/heterodoxy. Many accept the label heterodox (*heterodoks*) to differentiate themselves from Sunnis and other forms of Islam. That does not mean that they accept it in a hierarchical sense, orthodoxy being the norm. In fact, other Alevis may even argue that Alevism is true Islam.[190] The views among Alevis vary widely. The Alevi readiness to accept an in-

---

186. David Shankland, 'Maps and the Alevis: On the Ethnography of heterodox Islamic Groups'. *British Journal of Middle Eastern Studies*, December 2010, 37(3), p. 229.

187. *Ibid.*, p. 209.

188. Markus Dressler, 'Turkish politics of Doxa: Otherizing the Alevis as heterodox', *Philosophy and Social Criticism*, Vol. 41, Nos 4-5, May 2015; original manuscript published online, 31 January 2015, p. 3.

189. *Ibid.*, p. 4.

190. Sakir Keçeli and Aziz Yalçın, *Alevilik-Bektaşilik açısından din kültürü ve ahlâk bilgisi* [Religious culture and morality from an Alevi-Bektasi viewpoint], Ardıç Yayınları, Ankara, 1996, p. 81; cited in Stefan Martens, Being Alevi in Turkey, Unpublished Master's study, Simon Fraser University, 2005, p. 2.

ternalized God, the importance they give to Imam Ali, their permitting men and women to worship together, their distrust of mosques are unorthodox perceptions of faith within a society where orthodox interpretations of religious life are dominant.[191]

Dressler's point is that the terminology of heterodoxy versus orthodoxy suggests a hierarchy in the normative religious discourse. Though not used in this sense in the present study, it does require designating something as core, mainstream or similar. Power and historical circumstance dictates how this dichotomy is displayed in Turkey. We can see this dichotomy as vertical and therefore simply a binary without any of the poles being central, or as a horizontal and therefore stratified dichotomy.

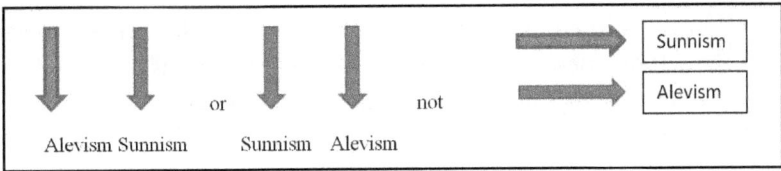

Diagram 1

It has to be acknowledged that what renders a doxa community heterodox is not necessarily their belief system but their position in the social hierarchy. In other words, power determines orthodoxy/heterodoxy.

We should be careful not to see heterodoxification of Shi'ites as exclusive Ottoman process. In fact, this process proceeded the Ottoman Empire. Eleventh century Andalusian intellectual and theologian ibn Ḥazm described the Shi'ites as some of the sects that committed depravities.[192]

It can also be argued that there is "heterodoxy" within the Sunni branch, for instance in the case of the Mevlevi, who are a Sufi order and differ widely from the officially sanctioned Sunni version of Islam. It is recognised that the boundaries between orthodoxy and heterodoxy in Islam are only constructs, but there are demarcation lines in the minds of many Sunnis and Shi'ites. The Shi'ites have the expectation of the reappearance of the hidden Imam (the Twelfth Imam). This may be regarded as a fundamental and irreconcilable difference between many Sunnis and Shi'ites.

The Ottomans used a terminology which amounted to a hierarchical dichotomy: Sunni as the right way of going about interpreting and practicing Islam and Alevism, the wrong way, the heretical was, so to speak. The

191. Erol Ayhan. *op. cit.,* p. 376.
192. Israel Friedlaender, 'The Heterodoxies of the Shiites in the Presentation of Ibn Ḥazm', *Journal of the American Oriental Society* , 1907, Vol. 28, 1907, p. 40.

terminology is obviously Christian in provenance and explains a process peculiar to them and only gained currency post-Republic.

Many Shi'ites believe the Quran edited by the third Rightly Guided Caliph Uthman was different in some respects from that brought down by Muhammad and maintained through oral tradition. They also have some different *hadiths* [sayings], as they do not trust those reported by Aisha, one of Muhammad's wives, and prefer the *hadiths* reported by Ali and Fatima (Ali's wife and Muhammad's daughter). Accordingly, it may be said that the Shi'ites are also Orthodox, albeit a different kind of Orthodox than the Sunnis. In Iran, Jafari Jurisprudence is the official Shi'ism. This is orthodox Shi'ism. As John Locke remarked once, "everyone is orthodox to himself".[193]

Undoubtedly, there is a difference between those that adhere to their respective orthodoxies, but in between there are variations of the religious dogmas. Many Alevis inhabit this theological landscape. This study is in the field of political science rather than theology and other than outlining this issue, no attempt is made to map out Alevi theological terrain. However, the heterodoxification of Alevis, the resulting tension between Sunnis and Alevis and state attitudes, are relevant themes to explore and are noted throughout the study.

This section has sketched the place of the Alevis in Turkey's religio-political landscape in order to set the context for the Sunni-Alevi conflict and the treatment of Alevis by Kemalists and Islamists. It will be argued that both ideological and political forces sidelined them. In the next section, I will examine the many facets of the ideology of the founder of the Republic and his followers.

193. John Locke, 'Letter Concerning Toleration', trans. William Popple, 1689, p. 3.

2.5 KEMALISM AS A SOCIO-CULTURAL PROJECT AND PROGRAM

The fundamental principles

Kemalism is the ideology and political practice that constituted the Turkish Republic since its inception. The ideology is represented by the six arrows found in the emblem of the CHP (republicanism, laicism, nationalism, populism, étatism and revolutionism). Laicism and its cognate secularism and nationalism are discussed throughout this study. Erik Zürcher summarises the three principles of populism, étatism and revolutionism as follows:

> 'Populism' meant the notion, first emphasized during the First World War, of national solidarity and putting the interests of the whole nation before those of any group or class. In a negative sense it entailed a denial of class interests (according to Kemalism, Turkey did not have classes in the European sense) and a prohibition of political activity based on class (and thus of all socialist or communist activity). Revolutionism - or reformism, as Atatürk's more conservative followers have preferred to interpret the Turkish term İnkilapçılık - meant a commitment to ongoing (but orderly and state-led) change and support for the Kemalist reform programme. Statism was a new concept that recognized the pre-eminence of the state in the economic field.[194]

Noticeably absent in these six defining principles of Kemalism is democracy.[195] The omission of democracy was by design. Ahmet İnsel suggested that the principle of democracy is expressed through populism, which represents a reduction of democracy and is further restricted through laicism;[196] democracy is thus curtailed. In his comprehensive book on Turkey, Frangos Frangoulis notes that one of the arrows, representing republicanism, is about a democratic form of government.[197] Thus, according to Frangoulis, democracy is represented through republicanism, which is doubtful.

Turkish novelist and nationalist Halide Edip Adıvar noted in 1930 that originally Mustafa Kemal was not in favour of the establishment of a Re-

---

194. Erik Zürcher, *Turkey*, 3rd Edition, London, 2004, p. 182.
195. Nilüfer Göle, "İslam'ın Demokratik Hak Davası" in Yerasimos, Stéphane, (ed.) *Türkler,* Ankara, 2005, p. 133.
196. Ahmet İnsel. "Önsöz" in Tanıl Bora, Gültenkingil Murat, *Kemalizm, Modern Türkiye'de Siyasî Düşünce*, Vol. 2, İstanbul, 2009, p. 26.
197. Φραγκούλης, Σ. Φράγκος. Ποια Τουρκία; Ποιοι Τούρκοι;, Athens, 2012, p. 310.

public at all. Instead, according to Adıvar, he preferred the Grand National Assembly (*Büyük Millet Meclisi*), which was established in 1920, to have continued as the framework for the governing of the country: "Yet, it was he himself who proposed to the Assembly the name of republic". Adıvar believed that it was "in spirit a personal dictatorship".[198]

A republic is not necessarily a democratic form of government *per se*; to be democratic it needs comprehensive measures to keep governments in check, a functioning opposition and independent institutions. Kemal was authoritarian and could not tolerate opposition. Both early parties *Terakkiperver Cumhuriyet Fırkası* (The Progressive Republican Party) and *Türkiye Komünist Partisi* (The Communist Party) were prohibited in 1925; the Communist Party was not even represented in the Parliament.[199] Even an opposition party established upon request by Mustafa Kemal himself, could not survive the ensuing pressure and was dissolved by its founder Fethi Okyar, on 17 December 1930, after only a few months in operation.[200] The Menemen Incident (see Chapter 4.0) and the consequent purges put *Serbest Cumhuriyet Fırkası* (Liberal Republican Party) in a precarious position and Okyar took the prudent step of dissolving the party. Multi-party democracy had to wait until 1946.

Zürcher contends that as an ideology Kemalism lacks coherence:[201] "It is best seen as a set of attitudes and opinions which were never rooted in any detail".[202] Nevertheless, Kemalism has been seen as the bedrock of the Turkish Republic. Perhaps, given its lack of coherence and detail, as suggested by Zürcher, Sena Karasipahi notes that "there exist multiple versions of Kemalism which have come into being over time, such as rightist/leftist Kemalism, conservative/liberal Kemalism, as well as reactionary Atatürkism and the like during time".[203]

As well as different forms of Kemalism as interpreted and expressed by its supporters, there are versions of Kemalism as analysed by non-Kemalist critics. Thus, the view of Kemalism by communist theoretician, Hikmet Kıvılcımlı, is different to the Kemalists' view of Kemalism. Kıvılcım-

---

198. Halidé Edib, *Turkey Faces West*, New Haven, 1930, p. 203. Halide Edib's middle name has also been spelt as Edip in some publications. Also, in one of her books in English her first name is accented in the last syllable, as Halidé. After her marriage, she received the surname Adıvar.

199. Ahmad Feroz, İttihatçılıktan Kemalizme, İstanbul, 1985. p. 161.

200. Emine Gürsoy Naskali, *Celal Bayar Arşivinden Serbest Fırka Anıları*, İstanbul, 2015, p. 117.

201. Erik Zürcher, *Turkey*, London, 3rd Edition, 2004, p. 182.

202. Zürcher cited in Parla and Davison. *op. cit.*, p. 7.

203. Sena Karasipahi, *Muslims in Modern Turkey*, London & New York, 2009, p. 4.

li's movement essentially saw Kemal's westernisation project as efforts to establish a bourgeois system.[204] Islamist intellectuals also have their own interpretation. For instance, Abdurrahman Dilipak regards Kemalism as a form of "theocracy" in Turkey, in the sense of being "religion of civilisation" - alluding to Mustafa Kemal's use of the term *medeniyet* (civilisation) as an overarching guiding principle. Dilipak also views laicism as a form of Kemalist theocracy and criticises Mustafa Kemal for "modernizing the country with oriental methods, as a result of which there occurred an identity crisis that still continues today."[205]

An aspect of Kemalism which was a characteristic of the early period but manifested itself throughout the Republic's history was the unwillingness to incorporate the non-Muslim minorities to the polity as citizens. By that I mean citizenship in the civic sense, with the ability to become a public servant, a high-ranking officer of the military, or a police officer. This avenue was closed-off. There was also restricted participation in politics, which was mainly through centre-right parties.[206] In contrast, under the Ottoman Empire, non-Muslims were well represented in the Parliament and in government services. The restriction in civic participation was the most benign form of the racist and extreme nationalist tendencies of Kemalism. In its extreme form led to movement and even extermination of minorities (e.g. Pontus in 1923, Dersim in 1938).[207]

This tendency in Kemalism was inherited and perpetuated by the presence of the Society for Union Progress (*İttihat ve Terakki Komitesi*) elements in the Republican cadres. The Republic of Turkey was arguably established on the ideological foundation of the Young Turks. Many of İttihat's upper echelon took up important positions in the Republican machinery.[208] Fikret Başkaya argues that the "regime established after 1923 was nothing but the "second Ittihadist regime".[209] Furthermore, former member of the

204. Kemalizm nedir?, Unpublished monograph, n.d., n.p., p. 2.
205. Karasipahi, *op. cit.*, pp. 81 and 98.
206. For details Rıfat N. Bali, 'Cumhuriyet döneminde azınlık milletvekilleri', *Toplumsal Tarih*, No. 186, June 2009.
207. Pontus, Sait Çetinoğlu and Dara Cibran, 'Pontus Sorunu', unpublished paper, 2007; Dersim, İsmail Beşikçi. *Tunceli Kanunu (1935) ve Dersim Jenosidi*, İstanbul, 1990.
208. For instance, Ali Cenani became Minister for Commerce in the Republic. Furthermore, İttihat's Office of Tribes and Immigration (*İskân-ı Aşayir ve Muhacirin*) Director-General Şükrü, became Minister for Internal Affairs. Mustafa Abdülhalik Renda, who before 1915 served as Bitlis and Aleppo Governor, became Finance, Education and Defence Minister and even Speaker of the Grand National Assembly (Raço Donef, 'Resmi Tarih ve Rumlar' in Fikret Başkaya and Sait Çetinoğlu (eds.) *Resmi Tarih Tartışmaları 8*, İstanbul, 2009, p. 270).
209. Başkaya, *op.cit.*, p. 14.

revolutionary left, *Dev-Genç*,[210] Melih Pekdemir, maintained that the Kemalist state did not create its own bureaucracy. On the contrary, the civil and military bureaucracy, which played a prime role in the collapse of the Ottoman Empire, established the Republic: "They became Kemalist cadres."[211] The Republic therefore did not just inherit an ideology but also a machinery ready to put this ideology into practice.

This adoption of the İttihat cadres was not *in toto*. As Zürcher noted, there were periodical purges, just as İttihat used the practice to cleanse themselves off the old guard. Nevertheless:

> In essence . . . the army of the republic was the army of the late empire. And it was this army, and certainly also the gendarmerie, which allowed the republican regime to extend its control over the population and land to a degree the empire had never achieved. In fact, one could argue that it was this establishment of effective control, more than any of the famous Kemalist reforms (clothing, alphabet or calendar), which heralded the arrival of the modern state in Anatolia. As for the bureaucracy, it was by and large the imperial bureaucracy.[212]

Kemalism and minorities

Most Kemalist reforms had some sort of provenance in the Ottoman Empire: modernisation project, laicisation, translation of the Qur'an and the adoption of the Latin alphabet.[213] Kemalism also inherited the social engineering practices of İttihat. Physical extermination, deportation, internal displacement, changing the ethnic composition of certain regions were İttihat's trademarks and Kemalism adapted and implemented their policies and practices.[214] Clause 2 of the 1934 Settlement Law (*İskân Kanunu*) divided Turkey into three regions and restricted the settlement areas of non-Muslim minorities (Greeks, Armenians and Jews).[215] Ahmet Yıldız contends that the 1934 Pogrom against Jews in Thrace were a result of the application of this law. The instigators of the attacks, a mayor, a local police chief and the president of the chamber of commerce were arrested. As a

---

210. *Devrimci Genç*, i.e. Revolutionary Youth.
211. Melih Pekdemir, *Kemalistler Ülkesinde Cumhuriyet ve Diktatörlük*, Vol. 2, İstanbul, 1997, p. 97.
212. Erik Zürcher, The Young Turk Legacy and Nation Building, London, 2010, p. 144.
213. Seyfi Öngider, *Kuruluş ve Kurucu*, İstanbul, 2003, p. 254.
214. For Ittihat's social engineering projects see Fuat Dündar, *Modern Türkiye'nin Şifresi*, İstanbul, 2008.
215. T.C. Resmî Gazete, *İskân Kanunu*, 21 June 1934.

consequence of the Pogrom, the Jewish population of Thrace migrated to Istanbul for safety.[216]

One lesser-known action taken by the regime to reduce the numbers of Greek Orthodox Christians was the establishment of the "Turkish Orthodox" Church. This was a church established in Kayseri on 21 September 1922 under the name Independent Turkish Orthodox Patriarchate" (*Müstakil Türk Ortodoks Patrikhanesi*). This Patriarchate was established to confiscate churches and poach members from the historic Greek Orthodox Patriarchate in Istanbul. Papa Eftim, who was the first Patriarch, or Pope as he preferred, of this church was a priest by the name of Eftimios Karahisaridis, a member of the Turkish-speaking Karamanlı Christians in Anatolia.[217]

The idea of establishing a separate patriarchate was first conceived in 1917, during the rule of the İttihat and after the cessation of diplomatic relations with Greece. In 1918, Cami Bey (Bayburt) wrote in *Söz Gazetesi* that the Anatolian Orthodox were Turkish. According to him, these were the Turcoman soldiers who settled in the region before the Malazgirt (Manzikert) War in 1071.[218] Mustafa Kemal found out about the project to establish a separate Orthodox church through a convert to Islam Rıza Bey in Keskin, who told him about Eftim. Kemal took up the cause and the church was discussed in the Ministerial Council (*İcra Vekilleri Heyeti*). The first step of the plan to establish a church for the Anatolian Christians was via a decree on 5 January 1921.[219]

For a brief period Papa Eftim was allowed to occupy the Greek Patriarchate in the Phanar District (Fener). Eventually he was removed though not before transferring three churches in the Galata District to his church. At its height, the flock of this project did not exceed 250 people and thus failed to assimilate the Greek Orthodox, who remained in Istanbul even after the Population Exchange. Even as early as 1926, the nationalist paper of the period *Son Saat* declared that there was no such congregation as Turkish Orthodox and advised the government to extricate itself from any involvement.[220]

216. Ahmet Yıldız, *Ne Mutlu Türküm Diyebilene*, İstanbul, 2001, pp. 253-56.
217. See Racho Donef, 'Türk Ortodoksların siyasi rolü', *Nsibin*, Stockholm, 2003; Ράτσος Ντόνεφ, 'Οι τουρκο-ορθόδοξοι', *Ανατολή*, August, 2000; Racho Donef, 'The Political Role of the Turkish Orthodox Patriarchate (so-called)', *Atour*, 2004.
218. Hasan Kocarık, *Atatürk Dönemi (1923-1938) Fener Rum Patrikhanesi*, Unpublished Graduation Study, Bozok Üniversitesi, Yozgat, 2009, n.p.
219. *Ibid.*
220. Donef, 'Türk Ortodoksların siyasi rolü', *op. cit.*

Other measures taken by Kemalists after the death of Mustafa Kemal, in line with the ideology of purification of Turkey of its foreign elements, were the actions during World War II: "Wealth Tax" (*Varlık Vergisi*), "Twenty Classes" (*20 kur'a askerleri*), the Pogroms of 1955 (Chapter 5.1) and the deportation of Greek citizens in 1964. To these 1934 Pogroms against Jews in Thrace can be added. As a result, the numbers of non-Muslims dwindled. When ethnic cleansing was not sufficient, another practice, changing place names to Turkish, aimed to remove any traces of cultures other than Turkish in Anatolia, though this culture was to be modified and put upon as well.

The cumulative effect of the policies and practices has been the reduction of the Christian population in Turkey. The population of Istanbul in 1924 was 1,065,866, of which 279,788 were Greeks, 73,407 Armenians and 56,390 Jews. The 1927 Census shows a decrease in the city's population: 809,993 of which 126,033 were Greeks.[221] Even though the population exchange with Greece exempted the Greeks of Istanbul, more than half left the city. The decrease in the Christian population in Anatolia was more drastic; by 1925 their population decreased by 84%.[222]

In general, Kemalism sought to remove, or at least marginalise, the non-Muslim groups by restricting participation in public life and by turning them into "the other". As Bozarslan notes although "[t]he question of otherness is at the heart of French laicism . . . it is posited in terms of recognition, emancipation, or domination, not extermination or total marginalization of the groups which are confessionally distinct".[223] Whereas in Turkey, the "other" was demonised and ultimately driven away to solidify the dominance of Sunni Turks.

Kemalism: rupture or continuity?

The topic of Kemalism is inexhaustible, as numerous speeches of Mustafa Kemal have been interpreted and re-interpreted by the state machinery, official historians, independent scholars, and also by party ideologues. Consequently, different facets and applications of Kemalism are discussed throughout this study. Until relatively recently, it has been difficult to separate the Republic from its founder, as the official narrative omitted the role

---

221. Christopher Houston, 'Kemalism and Beyond', *The Oxford Handbook of Contemporary Middle-Eastern and North African History*, September 2015, p. 6.
222. Cem Uzun, "Yedi Düvele Karşı Mücadele", Fikret Başkaya (ed.) *op.cit.*, p. 25.
223. Hamit Bozarslan. 'La laïcité en Turquie'. *Matériaux pour l'histoire de notre temps*, No. 78, 2005, pp. 47-48.

played by others, such as Kâzım Karabekir, in the formation of the Republic and focussed on Mustafa Kemal's real, imagined and fabricated deeds.

Current scholarship debates whether Kemalism and the Republic represented a rupture from or continuity with the Ottoman Empire. The abolition of the Caliphate and other Ottoman institutions, and the radicalism of the early years related to laicism and religion, has led many scholars to see it as a rupture. For instance, Karasipahi notes that "Kemal attempted to eliminate every symbol that had a relationship with the Ottoman–Islamic heritage. In this sense, Kemalism symbolises a radical break with the Ottoman era.[224] Mustafa Kemal wanted to accentuate this break by encouraging a historical narrative through the Turkish History Study (Türk Tarih Tezi), which glorified a pre-Ottoman, pre-Islamic Turkic past as the authentic cultural and historical heritage of the Turkish nation (this is discussed further in Chapter 4.0).

Yet, many aspects represent continuity with the Ottoman Empire. The example of the Diyanet is one case in point. One significant stage in the management of religion by the state was the establishment of Diyanet[225] on 3 March 1924. Between 1920, when the Provisional Government was formed, and 1924, the Ministry of Sharia and Pious Foundations (Şe'riyye ve Evkaf Vekâleti) looked after Islamic affairs. In the interim period, this Department formed a bridge between the *Office of Şeyhülislam and Diyanet*. Sedat Şenermen notes that Diyanet was not an institution instigated by the Republic; it was continuation of the Office of *Şeyhülislam*.[226] *It represented continuity rather than rupture.*

It is also important to point out that although Diyanet is translated as Religious Affairs, the term in Turkish for religion din "includes meanings of rulership (imaret) and government." Islam ("din-i Islam") combines temporal and spiritual affairs, whereas diyanet relates "to the worship, belief, and opinions of the jurisconsults [which were not legally binding]".[227] The Ottoman Turkish Dictionary translates diyanet as "religiosity". The Republic separated the temporal aspect from the spiritual aspect but even

---

224. Karasipahi, *op. cit.,* p. 15.
225. İştar Gözaydın notes that translations used for *Diyanet İşleri Başkanlığı* vary in literature, including terms as Department of the Affairs of Piety, Directorate-General of Religious Affairs, General Directorate of Religious Affairs, Religious Affairs Department, Directorate of Religious Affairs, Religious Affairs Directorate and the Presidency of Religious Affairs, which the Administration uses as the official title. See İştar B. Gözaydın, 'Diyanet and Politics', *The Muslim World*, Vol. 98, No. 2-3, April 2008, p. 216.
226. Sedat Şenermen, *Atatürk, İslam ve Laiklik*, İstanbul, 2015, p. 41.
227. Ismail Kara *Cumhuriyet Türkiyesi'nde Bir Mesele Olarak İslam*, 2008, p. 63 quoted in Eyup Sabri Çarmikli, Caught between Islam and the West: secularism in the Kemalist discourse, Unpublished PhD study, the University of Westminster. 2011, p. 180.

this was not an innovation. Although the Sultans were Caliphs, combining both temporal and spiritual authority, they delegated aspects of their authority to the Office of Şeyhülislam. In 1907, this office had already lost judicial and education affairs to secular departments.

Given the many aspects of the transition from the Empire to the Republic, it would be difficult to establish unequivocally either in favour of rupture or continuity and it is not the intention of the present study to do so. There were continuities with late Ottoman Empire institutions and some reforms, which Mustafa Kemal sought to implement changes in order to transform Turkish society to fit his vision. Official Kemalist narrative portrayed these changes as radical reforms, represented by the arrow of Reformism (Devrimcilik) but some scholars underline the fact that Kemalist reforms were mostly confined to the big cities and to a limited elite circle and that their effect on the vast stretches of Anatolia countryside was restricted.[228] Thus, Kemalist penetration was not deep. On the surface, Kemalism was everywhere in the public sphere, but the lower stratum did not wholeheartedly adopt the ideology and its reforms.

Kemalism as Atatürkism

That Kemalism meant different things to different people has been pointed out above. To make matters more complicated, in addition to a variety of "Kemalisms" across the political spectrum, the concept of "Atatürkçülük" (Atatürkism) also emerged soon after the death of Mustafa Kemal Atatürk. Sometimes the term is used as equivalent to Kemalism, but there are differences. Yılmaz makes a distinction by treating Atatürkçülük as a more general and milder version of Kemalism:

> Those who express their love for Mustafa Kemal Atatürk and feel respect and gratitude towards him and embraced a western lifestyle can be accepted as Kemalist. An Atatürkçü does not have to share the entire Kemalist worldview. For example, while it is very difficult to see a religious Kemalist, a religious Atatürkçü is not surprising.[229]

I see Atatürkçülük essentially as a cult of personality. An Atatürkçü has a devotion primarily to the person rather than ideology. We can see this manifestation in the social media, especially in *Facebook* with countless posts about Atatürk's supposed genius, enlightened status and treatment

228. Çarmikli, *op. cit.*, p. 109.
229. İhsan Yılmaz, *op. cit.*, p. 24.

of his every utterance as pearls of wisdom with deep meaning, in a kind of supreme hierophany. This is not to dismiss the extra-ordinary personal abilities, political acumen and charisma of Mustafa Kemal, but to point out the uncritical, unquestioning view of his personality.

This process of sacralisation of Mustafa Kemal as Atatürk intensified after his death, but it started in earnest when he was alive. As Mustafa Akyol notes:

> In just a decade, Islam was replaced by a new public faith based on Turkishness and the cult of personality created around Mustafa Kemal Atatürk. "Let the Ka'ba be for the Arabs," wrote poet Kemalettin Kamu, "for us, Çankaya is enough." That new shrine was Atatürk's residence.[230]

İnsel notes that a right-wing Kemalist group headed by Celal Bayar was responsible for the sacralisation of Atatürk's image and for the building of Anıtkabir, his mausoleum.[231] Mustafa Kemal as Atatürk was already Eternal Chief (*Ebedi Şef*) and CHP's Permanent President (*Değişmeyen Başkan*). His eternal role in the Republic history was "guaranteed". Up to the 1960s, the Turkish Dictionary of the Turkish Language Association (*Türk Dil Kurumu*) included a sentence stating that "Atatürkism is the religion of the Turks" (*Atatürkçülük Türkün dinidir*).[232] Atatürkçülük is therefore more than Kemalism, which is congruent with Dilipak's comments cited above.

Atatürkism has also been subject to gradation such as other concepts as secularist, religious and pious. For instance, Mete Tunçay notes the terms "fake Atatürkist" (*sahte Atatürkçü*) and "wardrobe Atatürkist" (*gardirop Atatürkçü*) have been used to attack people by undermining their Ataturkist credentials.[233]

In a brochure prepared for soldiers and petty officers by Colonel (Lieutenant General) Muhittin Fisunoğlu, teacher in the Military Academy, Atatürk is described as the greatest "human, commander, organiser, genius, politician, reformist and statesman".[234] This is in addition to an array of epithets such as "Liberator, Saviour, Father, Chief Teacher, great, sublime, peerless, immortal. This is a 'Superman Atatürk' narrative beyond Kemalism."[235] Even though he had a high-pitched voice, the image por-

---

230. Mustafa Akyol, "What made the Gülen Movement Possible?" in the International Conference Proceedings, *Muslim World in Transition: Contributions of the Gülen Movement*, London, 2007, p. 27.
231. İnsel, *op. cit.*, p. 26.
232. Belge, *op. cit.*, p. 37.
233. Tunçay, *op. cit.*, p. 97.
234. Doğan Akyaz, "Ordu ve Resmi Atatürkçülük" in Bora and Murat, *Kemalizm*, p. 185.
235. Hasan Ünder, "Atatürk Imgesinin Siyasal Yaşamındaki Rolü" in Bora and Murat, *Kemalizm*, p. 138.

trayed was of a person with a stentorian voice.[236] There was no aspect of his life that was not glorified or exaggerated, if not invented.

Esra Özyürek points to the omnipresence of Atatürk imagery throughout the country and to two associated phenomena: "miniaturisation" and commodification of his image. On the one hand, "gigantic" statues and posters adorn town squares and buildings, bridges and other structures are named after him, while on the other, miniature forms such as pins, and small ornaments commodified his image. Özyürek argues that the latter is a form of competition against Islamic paraphernalia that emerged in the market.[237]

Kemalism and Islamism

There are many different aspects of Kemalism in political discourse. A central preoccupation of this study is the Kemalist approach to Islam and laicisation/secularisation to which the state invested considerable energy and resources. The idea that Islam was an impediment to progress (*mani-i terakki*) emerged in the Ottoman Empire in the last quarter of the nineteenth century and it was adopted by the founding fathers of the Republic. The Kemalist cohort as positivists had two options to pursue: an anti-religious Soviet model or Luther's Protestant style of reformation. By translating the Bible into national languages, the Lutheran movement aimed at modernising Christianity.[238]

Kemalism adopted the second approach and took on the project of reforming but also Turkifying (de-Arabising) Islam. The efforts to translate the Qur'an, to conduct the *namaz* (*salah*) in Turkish, rather than Arabic, and the call to prayer (*ezan/adhan*) in Turkish, were part of this project of Reformation and Turkification of Islam. Political scientist Tunçay notes that the project was shelved as untimely as there was strong opposition. The project did not only contemplate the replacement of Arabic by Turkish as the language to conduct rituals; it also considered installing pews and conducting musical services in mosques.[239] Although this did not eventuate, these ideas of modernising the mosque services could be construed as partly imitating internal church lay outs and some form of rituals. Never-

236. *Ibid.*, p. 139.
237. Esra Özyürek, *Nostalgia for the Modern*, Durham and London, 2006, pp. 93-106
238. Tunçay, "İkna (İnandırma) Yerine Tecebbür (Zorlama)" in Bora and Murat, *Kemalizm*, p. 94.
239. *Ibid.*, p. 95.

theless, the Mevlevi used musical instruments in their rituals and therefore this cannot be described as antithetical to some forms of Islam.

It is said that much of the ideas of Mustafa Kemal were influenced by sociologist Ziya Gökalp, theoretician of Turkism. Parla regards Gökalp as the official ideologue of the Ittihadists and unofficial ideologue of Kemalists.[240] Gökalp constructed a theorem "Turkism - Islamism - *Contemporisation*" (*Türkleşmek, İslamlaşmak, Muasırlaşmak*) and summarised his social ideal as "I am from the Turkish nation, I am from the *ummah* of Islam and I am of the western civilization", combining disparate elements that for some were incompatible.[241] Mustafa Kemal adopted this theorem in part by substituting Islamism with laicism, but making Islam a constituent part of Turkism.

Ahmet Hamdi Başar, Director of Ports Operations, accompanied Mustafa Kemal on a trip to Anatolia lasting three months. The convoy included Party notables and high-level bureaucrats. Başar published his memoirs 15 years later. In these memoirs, Başar recalled one group discussion about laicism, with Mustafa Kemal present. When asked about his views, Başar expressed an opinion which was antithetical to those present. He argued that separating religion from worldly affairs is not what is required, but salvaging Islam from the clergy. Kemal interjected:

> Hamdi Bey almost wants us to create a new religion, or reform Islam [my emphasis]. The purpose of our Revolution is entirely beyond this. Islam is a thing that lived its era and worn out by revealing its benefits and harms, became old and finished its life.[242]

If we are to rely on the reporter, in this narrative, Mustafa Kemal portrayed Islam as an ideology that outlived its usefulness and any efforts in reforming it would have been in vain. Mustafa Kemal agreed with Başar on the point of neutralisation of the *ulema*, but not on the reformation project. Memoirs are very useful primary source material. However, the reliability of these sources depend on the memory, accuracy and ethical sensibilities of the writer. There are numerous published memoirs by people close to Kemal, including his butler, but there is the possibility that the writers exaggerated their role, influence and connection to Mustafa Kemal. There is also the danger of confabulation. Nevertheless, it is a matter of record that in the holy month of Ramazan of 1932 Kemal took a major step in his proj-

240. Parla, *op. cit.*, p. 40.
241. *Ibid.*, pp. 55-56.
242. Birol Caymaz, Türkiye Cumhuriyeti'nin kuruluş sürecinde laiklik tartışmaları, unpublished monograph, 2006, p. 3.

ect: on 20 January 1932, he appointed Hafız Yaşar Okur to read the *Surah Yasin* in the Mosque of Yerebatan.[243] This was the first step in the Project of Turkification of Islam.

In his memoirs, Mustafa Kemal's executive assistant, Hasan Rıza Soyak, outlined Mustafa Kemal's original program related to Islam, which included the translation of the Qur'an.[244] Şenermen notes that this program amounted to reformation of Islam.[245] Thus, even though according to Başar's memoirs, Mustafa Kemal dismissed the idea of reformation in 1930, he embarked upon precisely such a project in 1932. According to Soyak's memoirs, this was Mustafa Kemal's intention all along.

Kemal expressed a variety of opinions about Islam, many of which are contradictory. In 1923 in İzmir, journalist Kılıçzade Hakkı Bey asked Mustafa Kemal whether the new government would have a religion. Mustafa Kemal responded that Islam is the religion (of the government) and that there is no reason to reject religion as the communists did. In his *Nutuk* (Oration) delivered over five days in 1927, Mustafa Kemal mentioned the question that Kılıçzade Hakkı Bey asked him four years prior. Kemal conveyed to the CHP Congress that at the time he could not say that the state could not have a religion. "I said the opposite. There is [a religion Sir], it is Islam".[246] Kemal wanted to avoid the discussion with Hakkı Bey but upon the latter's insistence provided an answer that was acceptable at the time. In short, Kemal took cautious steps about implementing his plan about the management and Turkification of Islam.

Kemalism in stages

Kemalism is a vast canvass and had many forms, as discussed. Parla differentiates between "cultural Kemalism" and "political Kemalism", describing cultural Kemalism as an ideology and movement protecting laicism, rationalism and fundamentalist cultural reformism. In contrast, political Kemalism as a solidarist corporatism movement represents authoritarianism, statism, one-party rule and *şeflik* (chieftaincy).[247]

Given these many strands of Kemalism, Adem Çaylak and Güliz Dinç conclude that:

---

243. Dücane Cündioğlu, *Türkçe Ku'ran ve Cumhuriyet İdeolojisi*, İstanbul, 1998. p. 139.
244. Hasan Rıza Soyak, *Atatürk'ten Hatiralar*, Vol. 1, İstanbul, 1973, pp. 257-59.
245. Şenermen, *op. cit.*, pp. 213-14.
246. Cündioğlu, *op. cit.*, pp. 34-35.
247. Taha Parla, *Ziya Gökalp, Kemalizm ve Türkiye'de Korporatizm*, 2nd Edition, 1993, Istanbul, p. 10.

We cannot say that there is agreement on Kemalism's parameters. As an ideology without clear boundaries, it has had many forms: the single-party period's authoritarian Kemalism, conservative-nationalist version of the Democrat Party period, the 1960s and 1970s Kemalism with social democracy rhetoric and the 1980s militaristic-juridical Kemalism.[248]

According to Sociologist Mesut Yeğen, CHP's defeat in 1950 completed the first period of Kemalism and post-1950 Kemalism was no longer the dominant ideology but a general indicator. In essence, Kemalism retreated somewhat with the introduction of multi-party democracy.[249] There is no shortage of circumlocutions to describe the various stages of Kemalism. The post-1980 junta period is described as post-Kemalist or neo-Kemalist and the AKP period as post-post Kemalism - indeed, I am adding my own below.

Even among the Kemalists the interpretation of Kemalism has not remained uniform throughout the history of the Republic and gradually "evolved". The early period of Kemalism when Mustafa Kemal was alive, can be described as "proto-Kemalism". A distinction has to be made about the period when Mustafa Kemal was able to influence politics directly and after his death when the Republicans interpreted and applied Kemalism to suit their political agenda (post-Kemal Kemalism). Neo-Kemalism, a re-interpretation of Kemalism to allow political Islamist politicians to be in government and extend the presence of Islam in the public sphere, was largely a product of the 1980 junta (see Chapter 6.0). Finally, the later years of the AKP rule can be described as "meta-Kemalism". Although Mustafa Kemal's images as Atatürk are still ubiquitous and the ruling party AKP has not radically altered this physical reality, references to him in public discourse have been reduced.

Atatürkçülük as a cult has not disappeared but his images have miniaturised, as Özyürek pointed out, and privatised. Yael Navaro-Yashin refers to these objects carrying Ataturk's images as fetish and the personification of the state with these images as fetishisation.[250] On the other hand, Kemalism is disappearing as a dominant government discourse. A Turkish nationalism strand of Kemalism is now largely accommodated in opposition, primarily in CHP.

248. Adem Çaylak and Güliz Dinç, 'Gülenism as "Religionist" Kemalism', *Insight Turkey*, January 2017, p. 202.

249. Mesut Yeğen, "Kemalizm ve Hegemonya?" in Bora Gültenkingil, *Kemalizm*, pp. 62 and 60.

250. Yael Navaro-Yashin, *Faces of the State: Secularism and Public Life in Turkey*, Princeton, 2002, pp. 191 and 198.

To the various versions of Kemalism, we can add "pseudo-Kemalism", which manifested itself when AKP made overtures to Kemalism in 2018, by going through the motions, e.g. visiting Anıtkabir, on October 10, on the anniversary of Mustafa Kemal's death. This was a habitual practice of government leaders before AKP came to power, but it was gradually abandoned. Erdoğan thought it prudent to go through the ritual as he was seeking an expanded electoral base for the then impending elections.

Cultural Kemalism lost its influence gradually, though a proportion of the population still hangs on to the idea that Kemalism may yet become the dominant ideology again to bring about a return to their *Asr-ı Saadet* (Age of Happiness). Ironically, contemporary Turkey's strongman Recep Tayyip Erdoğan used the template established by the Kemalist to take over and concentrate all power on himself. Kemalist hegemony has been replaced by Erdoğanist hegemony. In the interregnum, the Gülen Movement (see Chapter 6.2) paved the way.

As laicism was an integral part of Kemalist thinking, scholarly attention is required on the implementation of laic/secular measures. The discussion starts from the pre-Republican period of 1920-1923, when a parliament in Ankara, independent from the withering palace in Istanbul, established itself and went about fashioning a new polity from the wreckage of the Ottoman Empire, salvaging as much as possible from this wreckage.

Conclusion

In Part A, I examined a number of key concepts central to the theoretical examination of this study and argued that, as many scholars pointed out, religion and politics are not two divergent fields. I have also argued that political Islam combines the two categories, not unlike similar strands in Christianity and Judaism. Finally, I reviewed various facets of secularism and laicism and juxtaposed different ways of approaching secularisation to evaluate its application.

This sets up the ground for Part B, which examines the period between 1920 and 1960, when a military coup temporarily ended civilian rule. Mustafa Kemal dominated the first half of this period until his untimely death in 1938. He shaped the ideology of the Republic, often pursuing contradictory objectives, trying to reconcile laicism/secularism with control of Islam, at the same time favouring a particular version of Sunni Islam over other interpretations of Islam and other religions.

PART B

CHAPTER 3:
PRELUDE TO A REPUBLIC (1920-1923)

Introduction

The official history presents the period as one dominated by Kemal. Though Kemal was the driving force, this is only partly true. From the 1980s onwards, many of the taboos related to Kemalism were challenged and later studies show that there was considerable opposition to his unrelenting ambition and tendency to dismiss opposing views. The secret parliamentary minutes and French journals of that time give us an insight to this period. What this chapter shows is that Mustafa Kemal's view on religion and Islam were in sharp contrast to what Kemalist sources have long argued.

The radicalism of the post-1923 period was absent. The major project of westernisation / modernisation and laicisation / secularisation were not part of Mustafa Kemal's discourse. In fact, in this period, Mustafa Kemal drew no distinction between "religion" and "politics", as his actions and speeches demonstrated. His provisional government even established a church ("The Turkish Orthodox") via a decree.

The First Parliament

The Sultan in Istanbul was only nominally in charge of a crumbling Empire, while the First Parliament eventually worked to replace it with a new regime. The proclamation of the Republic in 1923 only marked the end of the gradual process of the shift from the Sultanate towards a Republic. In fact, the Sultan's absolute rule ended in 1908, with the Party of the Young Turks, Committee for Union and Progress (*İttihat ve Terakki Cemiyeti*/CUP) running the Empire, virtually as a military dictatorship of a triumvirate.

Many members of the CUP, of which Mustafa Kemal was one, served in the Republic as politicians or administrators. Mustafa Kemal himself was not a high-ranking cadre of CUP, but using his undoubtedly charismatic and forceful personality, political acumen and reputation as a successful military officer, he dominated politics from 1919 onwards.

In the official narratives, Mustafa Kemal (later Atatürk, father of the

Turks)[251] had a clear vision of what sort of regime he wanted to establish. In these narratives, that vision is described as a secular, democratic state, looking to the West for its foundation principles and framework, rather than the East, the Ottoman past or Islam.[252] Yet, there are many testimonies about Mustafa Kemal's ambitions, which do not correspond to the official narratives. Enver Paşa, member of the ruling triumvirate during 1913-1918, was reputed to have said that Mustafa Kemal would want to become a Pasha (General), and once declared a Pasha, a Sultan, and then God.[253] The last Sultan Vahdeddin confided to his first *aide-de-camp*, Avni Pasha, that Mustafa Kemal wanted to become a war minister.[254]

Mustafa Kemal may well have had the ambition to rise in ranks within the Ottoman Empire, either as a Minister or Grand Vizier (*Sadrazam*), in his wildest dreams. Even so, there came a time when he decided to take a different, and it must be said, a much riskier, bold and uncertain path. Mustafa Kemal put considerable effort to establish an alternative government in Ankara and on 23 April 1920, the new Turkish Parliament was inaugurated.

Some members of the Parliament (*Meclis*) were elected, others transferred from the Ottoman Lower House (*Meclis-i Mebusân*), which was prorogued after the Allies invaded Istanbul on 16 March 1916. There is considerable confusion as to the number of the founding members of what was called the Grand National Parliament.

Mauro di Vieste notes that the chamber was composed of 190 members elected principally in Anatolia and 100 parliamentarians of the dissolved Parliament of Constantinople.[255] Pekdemir cites 104 newly elected parliamentarians and 23 parliamentarians from *Meclis-i Mebusân*.[256] Seyfi Öngider contends that on paper there were 437 members, but on its inauguration day, only 104 newly elected parliamentarians and 23 parliamentarians from *Meclis-i Mebusân* attended.[257] Ahmet Cemil Ertunç highlights these discrepancies found in primary and secondary sources and adds that

251. The surname Atatürk was only granted to Mustafa Kemal in 1934; thus, it would be historically inaccurate to use this surname before the Surname Law came in effect.
252. Tercan Yıldırım and Ahmet Şimşek. 'The Narrative of Religion in the High School Textbooks of the Early Republican Period in Turkey', *Education and Science*, Vol. 40, No. 179, 2015, p. 325.
253. Falik Rıfkı Atay, Çankaya, İstanbul, 1968; reprinted in 1999.
254. Osman Öndeş, *Vahdeddin'in Sırdaşı Avni Paşa Anlatıyor*, İstanbul, 2012, p. 270.
255. Mauro di Vieste, Promesse e tradimenti, n.p., 2008, p. 35.
256. Melih Pekdemir, Mehmet. *Kemalistler* Ülkesinde *Cumhuriyet ve Diktatörlük*, Vol. 1, İstanbul, 1999, p. 124.
257. Seyfi Öngider, *Kuruluş ve Kurucu*, İstanbul, 2003, p. 145.

Mustafa Kemal spoke at the opening of the second meeting of the Parliament on 1 March 1921, explained that the Assembly has 350 members, consisting, 12 . . . detained in Malta, 68 from Meclis-i Mebusan and 270 newly elected.[258]

Attendance may have fluctuated, given the adverse circumstances in which the Parliament operated, but there are still discrepancies that cannot easily be explained. For instance, Mustafa Kemal wrote to Karabekir, Commander of the 15th Army Corps, on 24/25 April 1920, and informed him that out of an available 120 members, he received 110 votes for the presidency of the Parliament.[259] Yet, according to Ertunç, on 24 April there were two candidates, Mustafa Kemal Pasha and Celaleddin Arif Efendi, who received 110 and 109 votes respectively. Evidently, the numbers do not add up to a fixed membership and reliable information is hard to identify.

The significance of the discrepancies in the numbers of the participating parliamentarians and the exact number of votes to elect the president may not readily be apparent. This is highlighted because the important issue emerging is the reliability of sources, primary or secondary alike. If there are such inconsistent reports on what should have been simple matters of arithmetic, discrepancies are bound to be found in other areas of contention. No single source is reliable, even the firsthand accounts of either Mustafa Kemal, or his aides and confidants, but also of those critical of him. For instance, Bertrand Bareilles, in 1923 wrote that there were "*hodjas* [*hoca*] and illiterate Anatolians in the Parliament".[260] There were certainly *hodjas* in the Parliament, but it appears that the organising committee imposed a condition of higher education as a qualification for membership.[261] Though the level of literacy skills varied, Grace Ellison, who visited the Parliament at the time, noted that the only illiterate person was a 90-year old Kurdish deputy, who spoke Turkish with difficulty.[262]

Kemal and Islam

Hidden and apparent agendas tend to cloud judgments, memories and accounts of events. As Andrew Mango noted, Mustafa Kemal was the

258. Ertunç, Ahmet Cemil, TBMM Hükümeti Birinci Meclis (1920-1923) - 1, http://ilim-cephesi.com/tbmm-hukumeti-birinci-meclis-1920-1923-1/, [Accessed on 1 February 2017].
259. Kazım Karabekir, İstiklal Harbimiz, Vol. 3, İstanbul, 1995, p. 1407.
260. Bertrand Bareilles. *Le Drame Oriental*, Paris, 1923, p. 192.
261. Karabekir, *op. cit.*, Vol. 5, p. 2225.
262. Grace Ellison, *An English Woman in Angora*, New York, 1923, pp. 155-56.

author of his own legend[263] and official historians manufactured, posthumously, a narrative Mustafa Kemal Atatürk would have liked about himself and others. Facts are likely to have been distorted; opposition to him glossed over and any person that opposed him is unlikely to have been shown in a favourable light.

One such contentious issue is the intent and extent of secularism introduced by Mustafa Kemal and his views on religion and particularly Islam. As he was the catalyst in bringing about a republic with a declared aim of secularism, it is imperative to discuss Mustafa Kemal's contradictory attitudes toward Islam; contradictory only if the pre- and post- Republic views and actions are juxtaposed. Mango asserted that "Mustafa Kemal's behaviour during his youth provide no evidence of religious conviction, while his adult life presents clear evidence to the contrary".[264]

He may well have been an atheist,[265] agnostic,[266] or non-practising Muslim as claimed by various sources, and he definitely wanted to modernise, westernise and secularise Turkey post-1923, yet he was not averse to invoking Islam when it suited. Michael M. Bisku argued:

> Although Atatürk was a non-practicing Muslim, he was not antireligious per se but rather was opposed to traditional institutions that stood in the way of modernization. Islamic traditions were inimical to the principles of Kemalism. [267]

Yet, examples of his invocation of traditional Islamic traditions are not hard to find. For instance, in this declaration "To the Muslim people of the Province of Adana", dated 5 August 1920, Mustafa Kemal praised the *mujahidin* [*mücahit*] and called them the leading fighters of the Islamic world.[268] On 13 August 1919, he wrote to Sheikh Mahmut Efendi to say: "you could not think of a Muslim who would accept the collapse of the Caliphate and the Sultanate".[269] Furthermore, he is reputed to have said: "the nation is voluntarily running to the jihad (for Allah) initiated by Mustafa Kemal. Allah forbade the Turks and the Muslims to live under the banner

---

263. Andrew Mango, *Atatürk*, New York, 2000, p. 463.
264. Mango, *op. cit.*, p. 45.
265. British Diplomat G. G. Knox, on 23 April 1928 via diplomatic cable, speculated that "The creator of the revolution is often to be reputed to be an atheist"; E 2117/128/44.
266. "Determined agnostic" as Murat Belge puts it: Murat Belge, "Mustafa Kemal ve Kemalizm" in Bora and Gültenkingil, *Kemalizm*, p. 35.
267. Michael B. Bisku, "Atatürk's Legacy versus Religious Reassertion: Secularism and Islam in Modern Turkey", *Mediterranean Quarterly*, 3(4), September 1992, p. 81.
268. Kamil Erdeha, *Milli Mücadelede Vilayetler ve Valiler*, İstanbul, 1975, p. 322.
269. İsmail Beşikçi, *Bilim-Resmi İdeoloji Devlet-Demokrasi ve Kürt Sorunu*, İstanbul, 1990, pp. 78-79.

of the infidel."[270] The language in these sources has clear Islamic overtones.

Unlike the Ottoman Lower and Upper Houses (*Meclis-i Mebûsan* and *Meclis-i Ayân* respectively), the new Parliament in Ankara was an all-Muslim chamber, as Christians were not allowed to participate. Muslim minorities, such as the Kurds, Lazes and Circassian attended often wearing their national attires in Parliament reflecting at least the ethnic diversity of Muslim communities. The Republican parliaments later included Christians and Jews, but while Mustafa Kemal was fighting Greeks and Armenians, it was deemed inappropriate to include representatives of those communities.

The primary reason therefore appears to be nationalism and politics rather than "religion". Identifiable religious minorities were able to be incorporated as long as they were not suspected of acting in state-like ways. The *millet* system in the Ottoman Empire accorded considerable jurisdiction in family and civil law to the Greek and the Armenian Patriarchates and the Jewish Rabbinate.[271]

In line with Goldenberg's theory, one can argue that they acted in state-like ways in exercising their authority. The new regime was not willing to cede any of its authority to them. Nationalism and the desire for a homogenous Sunni Muslim Turkish nation were the driving forces, not concern about any threat posed by these minorities whose numbers were severely depleted. They allowed Muslim minority groups to be incorporated into the system since they did not have their own "religious" structures.

In general, Mustafa Kemal's stated views on religion, pre- and post-Republic, were contradictory. This is not so in the period leading up to the Republic. From 1919 to 1923, Mustafa Kemal consistently employed Islamic terminology and symbolism to register support for his endeavour. The opening of the Parliament is but one example.

The day of opening of the Parliament was scheduled to be on a Friday, the Muslim *Sabbath*. This was not coincidental. Öngider argues that Friday was selected to wrap the opening around a *Jihad* (Holy War) theme.[272] On 11 April 1920 a meeting in Ankara involving the prospective parliamentarians took place and it was decided to inaugurate the Parliament on Thursday, 22 April 1920. This was changed by Mustafa Kemal in his capacity as the Chair of Representatives' Committee (*Heyet-i Temsiliye Reisi*). He sent

---

270. Nuri Aydın Konuralp, *Hatay'ın Kurtuluş ve Kurtarış Mücadelesi Tarihi*, İskenderun, 1970, p. 52.
271. Racho Donef, *Identities in the Multicultural State*, Unpublished Doctoral Study, Macquarie University, 1998, pp. 13-18.
272. Öngider, *op. cit.*, p. 146.

a lengthy telegram on 21 April 1920, marked urgent and circulated widely to all key military and administrative posts. In *this telegram Mustafa Kemal outlined his plan for the opening of the Parliament:*[273]

1. With God's grace, the Grand National Assembly will open Friday, 23 April, after the Friday prayers [namaz].

2. By causing the opening day of the Grand National Assembly, which is to carry out the most vital tasks such as the independence of the homeland, the liberation of the exalted Caliphate and the reign of the Sultan, to be Friday, we are to take advantage of the sanctity of the day. The *namaz* will be performed with all the parliamentarians in the Supreme Mosque of Hacı Bayram Veli and be enlightened by the radiance of the Quran and the prayer [*namaz*]. After the prayer, *Sakal-ı Sharif* and *Sancak-i Sharif* will be taken where the assembly is to be convened. Before entering the Parliament, a prayer shall be read and animals shall be sacrificed. In this ceremony starting from the Supreme Mosque to the building of the Parliament, the Army Corps Command with the military units shall take special ceremonial formation.

3. In order to express the sanctity of the opening day, starting this day, in the provincial centre, to be organised by His Excellency the Governor, the Quran will be read in full, Buhari-i Şerif will be read and, in order to bring good luck, the last section of Hatm-i Şerîf will be read, the Friday after prayers, in front of the meeting place of the Parliament.

4. From this day forward, in every corner of our sacred and wounded country, we will start reading Hatm-i Şerîf and Buhari-i Şerif and on Fridays before the call to prayer, in the minarets the sâlâ will be recited, khutba [hutbe] will be delivered, while prayers will be read for the blessed existence of our Sultan Efendi, his glorious country and his subjects to be liberated as soon as possible and reach happiness, and after the performance of the Friday prayers khatm [hatim] will be completed and speeches will be delivered emphasising the importance and sanctity of the National Struggle which was undertaken for the exalted maqam [the office] of the Caliphate and the Sultanate and the liberation of all the soil of the homeland and explaining the obligation of each individual of the nation and the Grand National Assembly consisting of its delegates to carry out their patriotic duties. Later, prayers will be read for our Caliph and Sultan, the liberation, salvation and independence of our religion, our state, our homeland. After this religious and national ceremony are held and after departure from

---

273. Ahmet Cemil Ertunç, *op. cit.; Sakal-ı Sharif:* hair from Prophet Muhammad's beard, *Sancak-i* Sharif: curtain from Aisha's tent; *Buhari-i* Şerif : the most trusted book of hadiths; *Hatm-i* Şerîf: a surah from Quran.

the mosques, official congratulations will be delivered to government houses for the opening of the Parliament. Everywhere Mevlid-i Sharif will be appropriately read before Friday prayers.

5. In order for this notification to be able to reach everywhere immediately, every means will be used and will be delivered to the most remote villages, to the smallest military units and to all the organisations and institutions of the country. In addition, it shall be hanged everywhere, and where possible shall be reproduced and distributed free of charge.

6. We beg the Almighty God to enable a complete success for us.

On behalf of the Representatives' Committee
Mustafa Kemal

These religious ceremonies were conducted on 23 April 1920, as prescribed above.[274] Kâzım Karabekir, a hero just as significant as Mustafa Kemal, of the "Liberation War" (*Kurtuluş Savaşı*), who often disagreed with him on many matters, was very critical of this choice. Karabekir wrote that he was not privy to this decision beforehand,[275] though he should have been a recipient of the abovementioned telegram. He went on to criticise severely the decision to select Friday as inauguration day as well as the religious ceremonies, going so far as to call it *dervişâne* (in the manner of a dervish, dervish-like):

> In our history no parliament opened with such zealotry. Perhaps it was thought that . . . these grandiose ceremonies [would constitute] an insurance against rebellions that started in some places. No matter what it would have been prudent to separate faith and zealotry, from the inauguration day of the National Parliament. That is, there was no need to select Friday or for so much fuss. A nice prayer would have had a better effect. As it would not be possible to continue with the zealotry displayed, its counter effect may be more dangerous.[276]

No parliamentary business was conducted on the 23rd of April. On the 24th of April, one of the aims of the Parliament was declared to be the protection of the Caliphate and Sultanate.[277] This may appear odd, given Mustafa Kemal's supposed hostility to the Sultanate and the Caliphate, but in light of the sources cited, it appears to be a logical progression towards

---

274. Mango, *op. cit.*, p. 276.
275. Karabekir, *op. cit.*, Vol. 3, p. 1399.
276. *Ibid.*, p. 1401.
277. Pekdemir, *op. cit.*, p. 125.

that aim. Mustafa Kemal gave a speech on the 24th of April emphasising the role of Islam:

> It was our own wish not to want to pursue the politics of Turanism. Because we wished all our power, material, spiritual, and strength to be manifested within our stated homeland. We refrained from being dispersed outside these borders . . . We even felt obliged to steer away as far as possible from the overt expression of Islamic politics, which is what the foreigners fear the most, what they dread. But in the face of material and spiritual forces of all the world and against the Christian politics' most avid battles of the crusaders, the obligation to think of forces outside the borders to be formed for us to rely on, was self-evident. You see, even though we did not express this externally, in fact, we did not refrain from seeking this point of support. Naturally, for salvation and safety, the only fountain has been the strength of the Islamic world. From many perspectives, the Islamic world has been intimately and extraordinarily concerned about the independence of our nation and state and [showed] religious allegiance and, by the way, we accept that the entire Muslim world is assisting and supporting us morally. Consequently, it was necessary to approach our co-religionist in the areas that come into contact with our borders.[278]

It is noteworthy that although later in his speech Mustafa Kemal defined the enemies as the British, the French, the Greeks, the Italians *etc.*, initially they are identified as Christians only, and the Muslims as an opposing force. The struggle against foreign forces is presented in religious rather than in nationalist terms. As nationalism was unlikely to excite the masses, Mustafa Kemal often used religious symbolism to motivate soldiers. In August 1920, in an appeal to his troops, he claimed that the Crescent was lying on the ground defeating the Cross.[279] Goldenberg's theory about religion as vestigial states is also applicable in this circumstance, as religions' state-like aspects were utilised by a leader of an actual state, so as to attach greater affect to a struggle between states.

As well as giving speeches extolling the virtue of Islam as a unifying force, Mustafa Kemal also talked about the importance of the Sultanate and the Caliphate. Mazhar Müfit Kansu, who kept notes of his meetings with Mustafa Kemal, noted that in the opening speech of the Erzurum Congress in 1919, the latter used a number of stereotypic palace expressions to praise the office of the Caliphate and stated the objective to be the guarding of the offices of the Sultan and the Caliph. Mazhar Müfit asked Mustafa Kemal

---

278. *T.B.M.M. Gizli Zabıtları*, Vol. 1, İstanbul, 1999, p. 2.
279. Bareilles, *op. cit.*, Paris, 1923, p. 63.

the reasons for such a speech, also likening it to a mufti's prayer. Mustafa Kemal just laughed off these comments and responded thus: "I understand your point, I do, but now our responsibility is to make the people believe that our aim is to save the country and our captive Sultan."[280] Thus, if this information is accurate, there was a great deal of cynicism on his part, just before the Parliament was to be inaugurated: on the one hand employing Islamic discourse, while on the other contemplating ambitious plans to bring about radical change.

Despite the government of Ankara pledging support for the Sultanate and the Caliphate, the Palace issued a *fetva* (*fatwa*) against Mustafa Kemal and the nationalists in Ankara. The *fetva* was issued by the Şeyhülislâm Durrizadé El-Seid Abdullah, holder of the second highest religious office in the land after the Caliph. The *fetva* of 10 April 1920 proclaimed a holy war against the nationalists (*millis*). The unionist, i.e. CUP, newspapers did not publish it.[281] In his inaugural speech to the Parliament, Mustafa Kemal mentioned this *fetva*: "You all know the *fetva* we just read yesterday, consisting of a ruse. Could a Caliph such as this in possession of his freedom and liberty have [issued a *fetva*]?"[282]

It is hard not to draw the conclusion that the *fetva* was issued by the Palace, as Mango notes, in an attempt to "to mobilise Islamic feelings against the nationalists, by presenting them as Bolsheviks or at least 'Godless Unionists' – the residue of the 'masonic' CPU".[283] Mustafa Kemal's countermove was to issue his own *fetva*. The *fetva* was issued by the Ankara *müftü* (*mufti*) Mehmet Rıfat (later Börekçi). Mustafa Kemal asked *kaza* (district) muftis to sign the fetva[284] and eventually was signed off by 250 muftis across Anatolia.[285] He used traditional Islamic means at his disposal to counteract traditional Islamic means.

The *fetva* proclaimed that the Istanbul Caliph, as a prisoner of the allies was not in the position to issue such a ruling and his fetva lacked validity.[286] This was an accurate description; the Caliph/Sultan was indeed captive and powerless. The Nationalist *Yeni Gün* (New Day), which mainly expressed Mustafa Kemal's point of view, argued that a *fetva* against Muslims was

280. Mazhar Müfit Kansu, *Erzurum'dan* Ölümüne *Kadar Atatürk ile Beraber*, Vol. 1, Ankara, 1986, p. 85.
281. *Bulletin périodique de la presse Turque*, No. 4, Du 20 Mars au 25 Avril 1920, p. 4.
282. *T.B.M.M. Gizli Zabıtları*, Vol. 1, p. 9.
283. Mango, *op. cit.*, p. 276.
284. Karabekir, *op. cit.*, Vol. 3, p. 1357.
285. Mango, *op. cit.*, p. 275
286. See full text in Karabekir, Vol. 3, pp. 1358-9.

contrary to the spirit of Sharia law.[287] The use of theological argument is notable.

Karabekir, once again, was in disagreement about issuing a counter *fetva*, calling fetvas a chain of disasters in the Ottoman history. He argued that the *fetva* may affect the relationship with the Bolsheviks in the ongoing negotiations and thought that "to request the fetva to be signed by many people is a sign of weakness". He also wondered that "[P]articularly, what are we going to be able do to those who are not going to sign it?" He was sceptical both of the medium and the method. Despite his criticism of the *fetva* as being wrong both in terms of its religious symbolism as well tactical move, he felt duty bound to convince the Erzurum *ulema* and persuaded the *müftü* to sign it.[288]

In the next two years, Mustafa Kemal continued to draw on Islam to further his aims. On 4 March 1921, in another speech to the Parliament, he stated that "Islam is a force not to be defeated by force". The members of the Parliament applauded.[289] Around the same time he initiated a project which was unanimously accepted by the Parliament. The project emphasised the importance of co-operation of Islamic countries against Christian Europe and envisaged a Confederation or the United States of Islam directed by the Ottoman Empire.[290] Kemal, in this period was not "Kemalist" at all. We may call him pre-Kemalist in this period.

In March 1921, a Pan-Islamic Conference took place in Ankara with delegates from Egypt, Algeria, Tunisia, Morocco, Tripoli, Syria. Mesopotamia, Afghanistan and Azerbaijan. This was hardly Pan-Islamic, but given the resources available at the time, understandably more Islamic nations could not send delegates. Later that year, the leader of the Sufi Sanusi order, Sheikh Ahmaed Sharif As-Senussi arrived in Anatolia to deliver Pan-Islamic propaganda. His sermon of Sivas was reproduced in summary by the Nationalist *Yeni Gün* on 10 May 1921. The sermon in Arabic was directed at the Muslims in Anatolia and asked them to join the *Jihad* and extolled the virtues of being a *mujahidin*. Both *Yeni Gün* and *Hakimiyeti Milliye* (*National Sovereignty*) enthusiastically reported on the speech and published a summary.[291]

Unlike the radical reforms Mustafa Kemal initiated once the Republic was established, in this period he acted cautiously, and perhaps cynically,

287. *Bulletin périodique de la presse Turque*, No. 4, Du 20 Mars au 25 Avril 1920, p. 4.
288. Karabekir, *op. cit.*, Vol. 3, p. 1366.
289. *Bulletin périodique de la presse Turque*, No. 13, Du 9 Mars au 11 Avril 1921, p. 2.
290. *Loc. cit.*
291. *Bulletin périodique de la presse Turque*, No. 14, Du 12 April au 24 Mai 192, pp. 8-9.

about Islam. As Mardin explained:

> During the years when he was leaving [sic] the resistance movement between 1919 and 1922, he was dependent on sympathies of Muslims outside Turkey, and often used the theme of unity Islam. He also made use of it to mobilise the feelings of Anatolia religious notables against the Ottoman administration which continued to function in the capital as a virtuous prison of the Allies. He took advantage of the prestige of the Caliphate at the time when, paradoxically – he was about to suppress it. In both cases he had made up his mind very early concerning the Turkey he visualised in the future.[292]

Mardin may have been right in that Mustafa Kemal may have made up his mind about visualising Turkey's future, though whether or not the system he envisaged and the framework he put in place were one and the same is debatable. Praxis often strays from theory and a perfect idea in mind may not translate well on the ground. It is also important to remember Karabekir's assertion that "Gazi wants the Caliphate and the Sultanate for himself".[293]

One of the ways to mobilise the Islamic feelings of Anatolian notables was the expression of support for the office of the Caliphate and the appointment of two leaders of religious orders (tarikat) as ministers (Konya Mevlevi Çelebi Abdülhamit Efendi and Kırşehir Bektaşi Çelebi Cemalettin Efendi).[294] He also emulated the Istanbul government's Cabinet structure by appointing a Şeyhülislam and placing him as second only to the president in the Cabinet protocol. Mustafa Kemal therefore imitated and reproduced traditional Ottoman practices when it was necessary and expedient to do so.

It is important to point out that certain elements in the CUP were much more radical in their approach to Islamic institutions than Mustafa Kemal between 1920-1923, though leading members such as Enver Pasha were also Pan-Islamists. In 1916, the CUP excluded the Şeyhülislam from the Cabinet, confining his role to religious matters. At the same time, the courts were separated from the Şeyhülislamate and were attached to the Ministry of Justice. The medreses were separated from the ulema and the administration of the pious organisations (vakıf/wakf) were placed under

---

292. Şerif Mardin, "Religion and Secularism in Turkey" in Ali Kazancigil and Ergun Özbudun (eds.) Atatürk, founder of a Modern State, London, 1981, p. 208.
293. Karabekir, Vol. 5, p. 2226.
294. Öngider, op. cit., p. 146. Çelebi, is a title given to the leaders of these tarikats. Both of these religious orders have been traditionally very liberal in their interpretation of Islam. When Mustafa Kemal met Çelebi Cemalettin Efendi, they both drunk rakı (Mango, op. cit., p. 261).

the authority of the Cabinet. At the end of the War, the role of Şeyhülislam in the Cabinet was reinstated.[295]

Mardin's information related to the short-lived abolition of the office of the Şeyhülislam is contradicted by Halide Edib Adıvar's account, co-editor of nationalist *Yeni Gün*, a novelist and advocate of women's rights. Adıvar confirmed that the reforms were carried out in that Şeyhülislam's portfolio was reorganised but the office of Şeyhülislam was not abolished:

> Although [Ziya Gökalp] was not able to get the Sheikh-ul-Islam out of the Cabinet, he managed to end the Sheikh-ul-Islam's jurisdiction by placing the Sheriat courts under the authority of the Ministry of Justice.[296]

These reforms were based on Gökalp's ideas and were instituted when the Sultan was still on the throne, even if nominally. Mustafa Kemal, an admirer of Gökalp and himself a radical reformist in the post-Republic years, chose to re-establish traditional Ottoman theocratic institutions under his authority in this period.

Karabekir was also concerned about the titles Mustafa Kemal was amassing (*Gazi*, Marshal) and his utilisation of Islam to further the aims of his movement. In his memoirs, he recounts that he received Princess Kadriye Hanım's French book, *Letter from Sacred Ankara* (*Mukaddes Ankara'dan Mektuplar*) on 25 January 1920. He was concerned particularly with page 139, which contained a picture of Mustafa Kemal. Among those turbaned people, Mustafa Kemal was sporting a turban and gown, traditional Islamic attire.

295. Mardin, p. 208.
296. Halidé Edib, *Turkey Faces West*, New Haven, 1930, p. 212.

Image 1: Mustafa Kemal wearing traditional Islamic attire[297]

Karabekir was disturbed that Mustafa Kemal labelled this photo as "ideal memory" (*mefkûre hatırası*).[298] Karabekir emerges as a person, who in the early years, was much more radical in his approach to Islam and disagreed with Mustafa Kemal's cautious and perhaps cynical approach.

This cynicism is evident during the prohibition of alcohol, which the Parliament brought about when it opened. The prohibition of alcohol is a Quranic precept and no doubt it was imposed to demonstrate the new entity's Islamic credentials and appease the Anatolian masses whose support was essential for the success of the new regime. Yet, the alcohol prohibition did not stop parliamentarians consuming contraband alcohol smuggled by Ankara's police chief.[299] Mustafa Kemal himself was also known for his *penchant* for *rakı*, which he consumed late into the night and early mornings, at tables where he conducted government and political business.

In these three years, Mustafa Kemal and his cohorts tried to keep a balance between their desire to introduce changes and a war-weary con-

297. https://twitter.com/mustafarmagan/status/505850622516936706, [Accessed on 30 May 2019].
298. Karabekir, Vol. 5, p. 2226; Kadriye Hanım or Pesend Hanım was born Princess Fatma Kadriye Achba; She was the Empress consort of the Ottoman Empire as the eleventh wife of Sultan Abdul Hamid II.
299. Öngider, *op. cit.*, p. 146.

servative population which saw their world already changing dramatically. Feroz Ahmad points out that the Ankara government "had to cope with a secret opposition and suspicious, malcontent and sullen masses who could not conceive the new order that was about to rise."[300] To a certain extent the strategy, to keep a balance and utilise Islam to ensure support for the new regime is justified, given the social and political context.

The Ottoman ruling class sovereignty existed for a very long period of time, creating a wide range of institutions and attachments, and also religious affiliations, in the social groups. Even a revolution, noted Ahmad, could not have destroyed this network in a night.[301] Accordingly, Mustafa Kemal and Ankara took cautious steps before abolishing the Sultanate. The Ankara government's Foreign Affairs Minister even went to Istanbul to meet with Vahdettin, to convey Ankara's loyalty and repeatedly requested recognition from the Parliament.[302]

This recognition never came, which paved the way for Mustafa Kemal to purge Vahdettin. He tried to recruit the Crown Prince Abdülmecit Efendi to his cause. According to French intelligence agencies, which intercepted a letter, Mustafa Kemal wrote to offer the crown to Prince Abdülmecit in February 1921, which the latter did not accept, despite his initial enthusiasm.[303] Regardless, Abdülmecit was still briefly arrested on suspicion that he was escaping to Ankara.[304] By November 1922, the Sultanate was abolished. Bisku argued that the delays can be interpreted as some uncertainty about the regime "Mustafa Kemal and his cohort wanted to establish".[305]

While the Sultanate was abolished, which ended the Ottoman Empire, Mustafa Kemal thought it prudent to retain the office of the Caliphate (Halifelik). Vahdeddin, the last Sultan, left the country, never to return, Abdülmecit became the Caliph, the last Caliph as it turned out.[306]

---

300. Feroz Ahmad, İttihatçilıktan *Kemalizme*, Istanbul, 1985, p. 161.
301. Ahmad, *op. cit.*, p. 161.
302. Öngider, *op. cit.*, p. 205.
303. Perkdemir, *op. cit.*, p. 157.
304. Öndeş, *op. cit.*, p. 258.
305. Bisku, *op. cit.*, p. 82.
306. In exile, Vahdettin objected to Abdülmecit referring to himself as the Caliph (Öndeş, *op. cit.*, p. 338).

Conclusion

In this period, as demonstrated, Islam and politics were clearly inseparable. Irrespective of what Mustafa Kemal was contemplating about the path he wanted to follow, at this early stage, secularism/laicism, or modernisation and westernisation for that matter, were not openly discussed. It was clear, however, that notables such as Karabekir were secularist inclined and wanted to reduce the visibility and extent of Islam in public affairs. Mustafa Kemal, a staunch secularist after the Republic was declared, appeared to be an Islamist before the Republic. This was no doubt due to the circumstances in that period, as he needed to form coalitions across the spectrum to further his agenda. Nonetheless, this "anomaly" contradicts the official narrative at least until the 1980s, and still persists among Atatürkists. After 1923, with increased authority, Mustafa Kemal ushered in the Kemalist period proper, an era with significant differences from the pre-Kemalist period.

While pre-Kemalism was an Islamic-oriented ideology, the forthcoming Kemalism proper appeared to be anti-Islamic. The next chapter will argue that after 1923, Kemal's rhetoric and attitude changed towards Islam, displaying hostility towards it. Yet, I will argue that this hostility was exaggerated in the narrative constructed by Kemalist historians. While it is not denied that, on the surface, the public discourse by politicians, the state machinery, pro-government media (*Milliyet, Cumhuriyet*) displayed an intolerant attitude towards the public expression of Islam, it is posited that Kemalism still favoured it, specifically Sunni Islam. I will also argue, concurring with many scholars, that laicism, the cognate concept of secularism, failed.

CHAPTER 4:
THE REPUBLIC AND EARLY KEMALISM:
The Cultural Revolution, restriction of religious activities and the construction of the secular public sphere (1923-1938)

Introduction

One of the arguments postulated in this study is that laicisation failed in Turkey. This chapter sets outs the reasons. The project Mustafa Kemal initiated in much hurry, once the major opposition (Caliphate, Islamic institutions, the ulema, the tarikats) were either taken under control or eliminated, was implemented through a variety of measures, including through the brutality of the Independence Courts. The reforms were impressive. Much of the official historiography praises Kemal for his resolve, especially in relation to what they consistently called "backward" forces. Much of this orthodox view is that the enlightened Mustafa Kemal reformed a "backward" Turkish society, though the propensity for brutality he displayed in the process is omitted.

The religious terrain was complicated. It included tarikats, cemaats, folk Islam practices, mosques, Alevi/Kızılbaş practices and myriad others. Kemal wanted to homogenise this terrain and weed out the undesirable elements. In this quest, conflicting paths were pursued. "Islamist" İsmail Kara argued that the Republic wanted to eliminate all religious organisations "that were autonomous of the state control".[307]

Sources related to tarikats vary from those romanticising them to those that demonise them. Contemporary western scholarly sources in English cited tend to idealise and romanticise Sufism and are reluctant to criticise any aspects of their operation (except for think tanks with anti-Islamic agendas). Certain Turkish sources are not so hesitant. Kemalist ideologues label these tarikats as "backward" and analyse them through this prism. *The Menemen Incident* of 1930, involving the Nakshibendis, is used in this chapter as a case study to demonstrate the vast differences of views amongst different cohorts, with competing narratives employed to analyse the event. Most studies related to his period tend to be partisan.

---

307. Ismail Kara cited in Murat Es. "Alevis in *Cemevis*: Religion and Secularism in Turkey" in *Topographies of Faith*, Irene Becci *et al*, 2013, p. 27.

A major primary source used in this chapter is the parliamentary proceedings covering the discussions that took place about the parliamentary bill to close the tarikats. These discussions give us a comprehension of the Republican thinking about different aspects of Islam. These "secret proceedings", which were not published until 1985, contribute to our understanding of the ideological framework of the elite of the period. The chapter relies heavily on these proceedings to trace the Republican mindset. These proceedings are generally underutilised, particularly in contemporary western scholarship, probably due to linguistic impediments.

End of the Caliphate

The Republic was officially declared on 29 October 1923. Mustafa Kemal's Party CHP, as stated, had six principles, which were regarded as the foundation principles and objectives of the new State. Until his untimely death in 1938, at the age of 57, Mustafa Kemal managed, to a certain extent, to separate Islam from the state and the public sphere. "Religion was pushed to the margins of private life", as Hakan Köni noted.[308]

In reality, Mustafa Kemal made Islam subservient to the state in order to restrain the clergy and control religious activities. By establishing an agency for religious affairs, he failed to implement fully a laic state, a state that does not partake in religious matters. Yet, the Republicans had some notable success in the construction of the public sphere as the domain of the profane. The sacred was to be privatised.

If the stated objective of the First Parliament were truthful, then it partially failed as the Sultanate collapsed but the Caliphate remained, still hanging by a thread. The language employed during the period of the First Parliament was distinctly Islamic and there were no clear signs of what was to come; that is a radical transformation during which the state was to introduce draconian measures to replace Islamic and traditional values with a combination of secular concepts and contrived notions of nationalism.

During this period a de-Ottomanisation and secularisation process was undertaken using both the force of the law but also propaganda, especially through the school system, where an official history was taught to new generations born within the Republican period. The Ottoman - Islamic past was demolished and pre-Islamic Turkic past reconstructed and glorified.

Referring to the Kemalists, Lütfi Levonian, of Armenian background, wrote, in 1928:

---

308. Hakan Köni, 'Religion and Politics in Turkey', *JLSS*, Vol 1, No. 2, July 2012, p. 79.

[T]hey are in revolt against Islam, because Islam is Arabian . . . They are in revolt against all religions because they think religion and science, faith and knowledge cannot agree; they are essentially opposed to one another . . . religious creeds, teachings, and books are unreliable. Religion is for primitive-minded people.[309]

After 1923, Mustafa Kemal expressed opinions on Islam, and, "religion" in general, which were diametrically opposed to those he expressed between 1919 and 1923. For instance, Grace Ellison wrote in 1928 that Mustafa Kemal told her in an interview: "I have no religion, and at times I wish all religions at the bottom of the sea".[310] This was consistent with his views expressed openly after 1923. In 1925, in a visit to Kastamonu, he articulated his dissatisfaction with what he described as superstition by criticising those who attended shrines of Muslim saints: "[i]t is a disgrace for a civilized society to appeal for help to the dead".[311] The association of Islam as practised in Turkey with superstition was a theme that the Republicans employed as argument for its control by the state.

Köni notes that as "admirers of western enlightenment", Kemalists viewed Islam as a "source of fanaticism and ignorance".[312] Thus, as positivists well versed in French intellectual traditions, Mustafa Kemal and his cohort put a strategic plan in place to eliminate Islam from public life, to the extent that is possible in a Muslim majority country where the Caliph resided. Firstly, the Caliphate was to be abolished. Given Mustafa Kemal's personality, it was unlikely that he would have tolerated such an office for long. Before the establishment of the Republic, he thought that it may still be useful for Turkey to be in control of this office. After the proclamation of the Republic, Mustafa Kemal was voted as the President (*Reisicumhur*). A prayer recited by Hoca Kâmil Efendi completed the proceedings of the day.[313] Mustafa Kemal was biding his time before putting an end to such religious ceremonies in the Parliament, ceremonies which he himself initiated in the First Parliament.

In the First Parliament of 1920-1923 an opposition group emerged known as *İkinci Grup* (The Second Group), while Mustafa Kemal's faction was known as *Birinci Grup* (The First Group). Mustafa Kemal dissolved the

---

309. Lutfi Levonian, *Moslem mentality*, 1928, p. 141, cited in Kemal H. Karpat, *Turkey's Politics*, Princeton, New Jersey, 1959, p. 58.

310. Mango, *op. cit.*, p. 463 [Mango notes that the interview took place either in 1926 or 1927].

311. *Ibid.*, p. 435.

312. Köni, op. cit., p. 79.

313. *Bulletin périodique de la presse Turquie*, No. 32, Du 16 Octobre au 20 November 1924, p. 5.

First Parliament and managed to exclude any of the Second Group members being elected to the Second Parliament.[314] Kemal's hegemony was being constructed and opposition could not be tolerated, as it did not fit into the grander plan. The Republic was launched with no official parliamentary opposition.

Mustafa Kemal, who was uncomfortable with any opposition, labelled efforts of formation of such opposition as signs of efforts "to return to the past", "reaction" (*irtica*) and "backward".[315] Ahmet Demirel notes that the official historians neglected this period and at best, argued of the existence of *dinci* and *gerici* opposition.[316] This presentation of the differences between the two groups as laicist/progressive (*laik/ilerici*) and religious/conservative (*dinci/muhafazakâr*), has prepared the ground in time for the Islamists to stake a claim to the Second Group.[317]

After his election as the President of the Republic, the Caliph congratulated Mustafa Kemal by sending him a telegram which he did not undersign as Caliph but simply as Abdülmecit İbn [son of] Abdülaziz Han. *Bulletin Périodique de la Presse Turquie* notes that the Caliph did not use the words "Republic of Turkey" in his salutation.[318]

The question of the Caliphate emerged again with the declaration of the Republic. It was an anomaly to have the office of the Caliphate occupied by a former prince, whose lineage dated back to the beginning of the Ottoman Empire. Originally, the concern was that there would be a backlash in the Muslim world if the office were to be abolished. Yet, apart from Indian Muslims, there was no great interest in the Caliphate any longer. The Arabs, who were liberated from the Ottoman Empire, were indifferent. As can be surmised from a cable from the British Embassy in Constantinople on 28 April 1924, some Muslim nations were not pleased, but they did not make formal protestations to Ankara:

> Persian Ambassador to Turkey called on me yesterday in order to say good-bye . . . Though himself an oriental, he could not understand the mentality of the Angora Government. . . . this gentleman spoke most bitterly of the neglect and lack of courtesy now shown by Mustafa Kemal towards the mission. The Ambassador criticised severely the action of the Turkish Government in abolishing the Caliphate and in expelling Abdul Mejid Khan and the members of his family. This action has thoroughly estranged opinion against Turkey in Egypt and

314. İsmail Göldaş, *Takrir-i Sükûn Görüşmeleri*, İstanbul, 1997, pp. 10-80.
315. *Ibid.*, p. 31.
316. Ahmet Demirel. *Birinci Meclis'te Muhalefet*, İstanbul, 2015, p. 17.
317. *Ibid.*, p. 30.
318. *Ibid.*, p. 9.

in Afghanistan, and even in Persia, which was unaffected by the substance of the action, the discourtesy and indignity of the forms adopted were most unfavourably regarded.[319]

This cable also gives the impression that having played the card of Islamic unity during the First Period of the Parliament, Mustafa Kemal was no longer interested in that theme, soon replacing it with nationalism. The Caliph himself made it easier for Mustafa Kemal by not restricting himself to the role to which he was confined. Certain meetings he held with politicians critical of Mustafa Kemal were not conducive to his retaining the office. Barely four months since the proclamation of the Republic, the last Caliph was gone, without any protestations, as the British envoy, Sir Ronald Charles Lindsay, reported to the Prime Minister of Great Britain via a cable dated 17 March 1924. Lindsay also noted that the government had already taken measures to eliminate the Caliph from the Friday prayers starting on 7 March: "[p]rayers for the nation and the republic were substituted".[320] Not only the *hanedan* (the Ottoman dynasty) was being erased, but the state was also using Friday prayers as a tool to legitimise the regime. Why would a laic Republic need the blessing of the "pulpit"? Evidently, the regime still did not feel secure enough yet and sought this blessing.

The abolition of the Caliphate was not sudden; it was a work in progress. Işıl Çakan points out that the regime signaled its intention to abolish the office during the budget discussions in 1923 and 1924. Çakan contends that this aspect is generally overlooked by researchers. On 26 September 1923, before the proclamation of the Republic, when the bill was discussed, the Caliph was still a candidate for the presidency of the Parliament and the state. Yusuf Akçura, Member for Istanbul, criticised Caliph's and his entourage's expenditure as payment for no service at all.[321]

> I do not know how many men and women will get money in the name of the dynasty. These men, together with the grooms and misfortunes [sadme], form a very large cluster. These are parasites. And to feed them without them performing any such work is to harm them. These are robust men, well-fed and men of wealthy families. It is never a good thing to reduce them to [receiving] a kind of alms. Rather than eating and sitting around like the hocas and hacis of old times, let them render a service to the nation, earn [a living] like everyone else.[322]

319. Australian Archives, A981, TUR 13 Part 1, [E 3680/3680/44], 28 April 1924.
320. Australian Archives, A981, TUR 13 Part 1, 182400, Cable from Sir R. C. Lindsay to Mr MacDonald, E 2358/1752/44, 17 March 1924.
321. Işıl Çakan, *Türk Parlamento Tarihinde II. Meclis*, İstanbul, 1999, p. 165.
322. TBMMZC, İ: 26, C:1, 26.9.1339, p. 292.

Akçura equated the *hanedan* with the clergy as representatives of the old world and as an unproductive class. The sort of rhetoric attacking the old establishment was the order of the day. The approach to the matter of the Caliphate as removal of a financial burden, barely masked the ideology of the Republicans.

On 25 February 1924, during budget discussions again, Şükrü Saraçoğlu from İzmir argued that religion should be separated from politics, so as not to be exploited by politicians. The hodjas in the Parliament reacted strongly, perhaps sensing what the future held.[323] Unperturbed, and eloquently, Saraçoğlu, warmed to his theme:

> Let us liberate our judicature erewhile from those who do not speak a word other than Arabic and Persian, and from laws that are far from the spirit of being national, and let them erewhile shape the national soul and deliver the justice the country expects.[324]

The conservative elements of the Parliament responded by using a language that was slowly becoming obsolete in the Parliament. Hafız İbrahim Efendi[325] from Isparta responded angrily:

> There is no monasticism in Islam Şükrü Bey. The religion of Islam is constant. That Power is with government; manifestly, only the Islamic religion is unchangeable. Islam is everlasting until the Judgement day. The religion of the government is Islam. It cannot be demolished by the conviction of three to five people.

Hüseyin Hüsnü Efendi, also from İsparta, echoed the same sentiments: "[t]hree to five people cannot demolish it [Islam]; those who attack it will wither away".[326] Here the Islamist section was pointing to the inseparability of Islam from government, which was contrary to the idea of laicism. Although Mustafa Kemal dispensed with the Second Group, there were still members of the Parliament from his party who would not approve of the forthcoming changes. These individual members opposing the changes were concerned about the reduction of the content of Islam in public life.

If there was any doubt as to the views of Mustafa Kemal's party, Vasıf Bey from Sarihan clarified. He contended that the Sultanate was being in danger of being revived and that the Caliph was living opulently, while the poor nation was footing the bill and that there could be no place for the Caliph's expenditure in the budget:[327]

---

323. Çakan, *op. cit.*, p. 167.
324. TBMMZC, İ: 111, 25.2.1340, p. 329.
325. *Hafız* is a person who memorised the Quran.
326. TBMMZC, İ: 111, 25.2.1340, p. 334.
327. Çakan, *op. cit.*, p. 167.

[A] number of legal matters are intended in civil courts. A number of legal matters are also enshrined in the Sharia Courts. The jurisdiction of the Court of Justice is entirely the same as that of the Sharia Court. Why is this so, friends?

Vasıf Bey went on to respond to his rhetorical question by positing an argument that it was untenable to have two legal systems in the land.[328] But, perhaps to moderate his stance and not be accused of being anti-Islamic by the *ulema* class still present in the Parliament, he concluded his speech saying:

> [e]steemed friends, you all know that religion is an order of conscience. Particularly, Islamic religion, our beloved religion; it is deferential and respectful to everyone's freedom and conscience. In the history of religions, in the history of humankind, there is no other religion, which respects conscience as much the Islamic religion does.[329]

The regime newspapers also played their role by reflecting the views of those who wanted to remove the Caliph from office. *İleri* newspaper went so far as to circulate a story that the rumours of the Caliph abdicating were not true. The British envoy, Henderson, reported to Marques Curzon that the article curiously uses the term Sublime Port (*Babıâli*); a term that fell into disuse with the departure of the last Sultan. Henderson wondered whether the article constituted a *ballon d'essai*,[330] a fabrication to test the waters.

On 9 February 1924, Yakup Kadri, the deputy from Mardin, expressed his view that the Budgetary Commission was too complacent for the *princes du sang*. Furthermore, both *İleri* of 21 February and *Akşam* (*Evening*) of 26 February argued that the times have changed.[331] The media was playing its role.

The position of the Caliph was becoming untenable, as the Parliament moved closer to abolition. On 26 February Mustafa Kemal had a secret meeting with high importance, with the Minister of Religious Affairs, Mustafa Fevzi. It has been reported that the meeting extended to the late hours of the night.[332] Only one day later, on 27 February, Vasıf Bey, outlined the three important reforms to be discussed on 1 March 1924: elimination of the Caliphate and expulsion of the remaining members of the dynasty, unification and laicisation of jurisprudence and education and elimination

---

328. TBMMZC, İ: 113, 27.2.1340, p. 416.
329. TBMMZC, İ: 113, 27.2.1340, p. 416.
330. Australian Archives, op. cit., E 10923/199/44, 12 November 1923.
331. *Bulletin périodique de la presse Turque*, No. 34, Du 19 Janvier au 26 Mars 1924, p. 4.
332. *Loc. cit.*

of the Ministry for Sheriat, Religious and Pious Foundations.[333] The Presidency of Religious Affairs was now to be attached to the office of the Prime Minister.

This office, Religious Directorate (*Diyanet Başkanlığı*) continues to exist as established in 1924, an enduring legacy of Kemalism in the name of laicism, continuously marking the failure to implement said laicism. Adıvar prophetically declared, in a disapproving tone, in 1930:

> Unless the Presidency of Religious Affairs is made free, unless it ceases to be controlled by the office of the Prime Minister, it will always be a governmental instrument. . . . The Islamic community is chained to the policy of the Government. This situation is a serious impediment to the spiritual growth of Islam in Turkey, and there is always a danger in it of the use of religion for political ends.[334]

Two weeks after the budget discussion when the idea of elimination of the office was flagged, the Caliph's position was formally abolished by the Parliament on 3 March 1924. In terms of the convoluted arguments used to justify this act, Halide Edib Adıvar argued that

> [h]ad the Caliphate been instituted in the person of an individual who did not belong to the old dynasty of the Ottomans, it would have taken root as a new spiritual institution, a departure from the old sense of Caliphate, but nevertheless an institution which would have persisted. But the Caliphs were to be chosen from the members of the House of Osman. The House had ruled for seven centuries. The Turkish Republic naturally feared that it might lay plans to restore the sultanate and blot out the Republic. Therefore the Caliphate had to be abolished.[335]

Thus, the new regime freed itself of a significant symbol of the imperial past, using theological, as well as financial arguments. Neither theology nor government expenditure were the real reasons for their action, they were just the pretext. Mustafa Kemal and his allies seem to have already decided to take the next step in their program and in any case a republic and religious office of this high standing was incompatible, especially since the office holder was part of the *hanedan*, presenting a constant reminder of the past Mustafa Kemal wanted to erase. They were building something new and the old had to go.

The office of the Caliphate relates to the concept of a vestigial state, or, as Goldenberg puts it, a "once-and-future-state". The presence of the

---

333. *Bulletin périodique de la presse Turque*, No. 34, Du 19 Janvier au 26 Mars 1924, p. 5.
334. Adıvar, *op. cit.*, p. 230.
335. *Ibid.*, 207.

Caliph was a physical manifestation of a once-and-future state explaining why Kemal was sometimes ready to invoke Islam, as mystifying helped his cause but came down hard on state-like institutional forms, which could potentially emerge again as actual states.

Next target: tarikats and the ulema

Mustafa Kemal had his radical hegemonic agenda to pursue now that the Caliph was out of the way. His program was to be implemented in several stages. First organised religion, which could mount resistance, needed to be brought under the control of the state or, if need be, dismantled. Then he planned to introduce legislation which was going to affect the general population's way of life. To this end, he targeted the *tarikats* and the *ulema* first.

Adıvar notes that the "class of clericals, the supreme support of conservatism, disappeared when the office of Sheikh-ul-Islam (or the Commissariat of Sheriat) was abolished in 1924 and their jurisdiction and political power in the state came to an end".[336] The ulema easily disbanded measures against the tarikats followed.

The question arises though, why Mustafa Kemal decided to close down *all* tarikats. After all, the Mevlevi had sent battalions to the First World War.[337] In fact, both the Mevlevi and the Bektashi orders sent battalions to form part of death squads of *Teşkilat-ı Mahsusa* (Special Organisation) to massacre Christians.[338] Their nationalist credentials were impeccable and their leaders (*Büyük Çelebis*) joined the first Cabinet in 1920 and unlike other religious orders, they were moderate in their interpretation of Islam, their participation in massacres notwithstanding.

Zürcher believes the key to explain Mustafa Kemal's stand to close down all tarikats lies in understanding the "tarikat culture": the relationship between the *şeyh* (sheikh) and the *mürit* (disciple) is one that required obedience.[339] This was incompatible with modern central governments. In other words, the state requires obedience only to itself and it was jealous of any other relationship outside its control. Furthermore, Kemal was to

---

336. Adıvar, *op. cit.*, p. 217.
337. *Loc. cit.*
338. Racho Donef, "The Role of Teşkilat-ı Mahsusa (Special Organization) in the Genocide of 1915" in Tessa Hofmann, Matthias Bjørnlund and Vasileios Meichanetsidis (Eds) *Studies on the State Sponsored Campaign of Extermination of the Christians of Asia Minor (1912-1922) and Its Aftermath*, New York & Athens, 2011, p. 187.
339. Pekdemir II, *op. cit.*, p. 60.

establish a hegemonic state and independent institutions were an impediment to the formation of such a state, whether or not some tarikats were not antagonistic towards to his cause.

Definitional issues: tarikats and cemaats

The term Sufi, associated with tarikats mysticism, encompasses all tarikats, irrespective of their classification as Sunni and non-Sunni. Such classification may even be irrelevant from the point of view of the Sufi sects, such as the Mevlevi and the Bektashi. This second order classification is employed only for the requirements of the structure of the present study, and only partly, as it is not possible to isolate the Alevi Bektashis from a discussion on the closure of tarikats. On the other hand, the categorisation of tarikat and *cemaat* as distinct religious formation is significant. The tarikats were not allowed to function after 1925, while cemaats such as the Nurcu were - notwithstanding the restrictions and persecutions they faced. The Nurcu cemaat did not spread until the 1940s and it was not necessary to curtail cemaats in the early years. When the Nurcu movement became a problem, the regime tried to use whatever means necessary to contain its activities.

Halil Peçe in his study of religious group classification of tarikat and cemaats, noted the difficulties in separating these two formations. Though "the terms and concepts traditionally used by the tarikats are different than the cemaat jargon, this is not sufficient to be evidence of distinction".[340] Peçe further points out the different origins of the tarikat and cemaats:

> The concept of tarikat has traditionally pointed to the institution of Sufism, while the concept of cemaat cannot be said to have a long history. The cemaat concept was introduced to our literature to describe the non-Muslim elements [in the Ottoman Empire].[341]

Mehmet Yanmış points out that tarikats have a sheikh, a system of caliph-deputy and a specific zikr/*zikir* ritual.[342] Tarikats are hierarchical and organised structures with strict rules and rituals. The cemaats do not necessarily rely on a sheikh tradition and tend to be discussion circles, though

---

340. Halil Peçe, "Dinî Çeşitliliğin Artması: Dinî Grupları Sınıflandırma Sorunu Bağlamında Tarikat-Cemaat Ayrımı", *V. Türkiye Lisansüstü Çalışmalar Kongresi*, İstanbul, 2016, p. 198.
341. Peçe, p. 197.
342. In Islamic mysticism repeating, silently or aloud, the word Allah, the ninety-nine names of God, or formulae that praise God.

a charismatic preacher still stands at the apex. Also, participation in cemaats are freer;[343] meaning requirements for joining are less stringent.

Frangos Frangulis points to the connection between the two even though Islamic cemaats in Turkey are post-Republic formations:

The tarikats are traditional Islamic organisations, which reflect various cultural, social and political needs. In the past, they have undertaken significant political and social initiatives. The Cemaats appeared after the establishment of the Republic in Turkey and they have organisational ties with the tarikats, whence they drew their fundamental elements.[344]

As well as closing the tarikats, the Republic put measures in place to combat the activities of "religious movements", but around 1945 there was a revival of such movements, as Şerif Mardin pointed out. Mardin also argued that

[i]n this interim period, continuation of religion concentrated on three focal points. We can call one of these cultural 'conservatism' [muhafazakârlık]. (The Ottoman word emphasizes this development in this area better than 'tutuculuk' [conservatism]). The second focal point is the tarikats; and the third is the movements that try to reconcile religion with modern societies and try to revive it at the same time.[345]

The Said Nursî movement was such as that described by Mardin as the third focal point. The significance of tarikats and cemaats led the regime first to outlaw the tarikats and monitor the cemaats. With the benefit of hindsight, it can be observed that this approach failed.

The question about the differences between tarikats and cemaats is not merely an academic one; at least it was not at the time when Said Nursî was alive and had many followers. By describing the Nurcu cemaat as tarikat, it would have enabled the regime to outlaw it. Said Nursî himself during his trial in Eskişehir, in 1935, addressed the issue: "Hey messieurs. I am not a sheikh [. . .] I am a hodja [. . .] to whoever approached me I might have said 'faith is necessary, Islam is necessary, it is not time for tarikat'". Akgündüz points out that if Nursî's movement were a tarikat, he would not have been afraid to declare it. This is a credible conjecture. Nursî had already stated in court that he dedicated himself to *Şeriat* (Sharia), which was an anathema

343. Mehmet Yanmış, 'Post-modern Kabileler veya Cemaat-Tarikatlar', *Milliyet*, 27 October 2016.
344. Φραγκούλης, *op. cit.*, p. 420.
345. Şerif Mardin, *Türkiye'de Din ve Siyaset*, İletişim Yayınları, İstanbul, 1991, pp. 30-31.

to the regime in the first place.[346] While Nursî was pursued throughout his life as his cemaat grew, the action against the tarikats was swifter.

The process of closure of tarikats

Mustafa Kemal did not act immediately against the tarikats after the proclamation of the Republic. Initially, the dervish lodges transferred to the jurisdiction of Diyanet. On 3 March 1924, a new law abolished the old Department of Sharia and Waqfs (*Şe'riye ve Evkaf Vekaleti) and replaced it with Diyanet İşleri Başkanlığı.* Clause 5 of the Law 429, states that the *tekke* and *zaviyes* were henceforth to be managed by Diyanet. Cem Apaydın notes that this law amounted to the recognition of the dervish lodges initially, but that the Şeyh Said uprising in February 1925 caused a debate about the lodges.[347] Thus, the first tranche of measures was taken to *control* the tarikats, as well as the mosques, but new circumstances forced the Republicans to re-assess their policy and moved to *eliminate* them. Having the "vestigial states" organised was a considerable risk.

To prepare the ground for the closure of the tarikats, it was necessary to describe them in most negative terms, even as "enemies of Islam":

A small book, published in 1925 the same year, entitled Tekkeler Yıkıl-malıdır [Tekkes must be destroyed], criticizes these institutions and associates them with the revolt of Şeyh Said: 'We must destroy these tekkes which are the source of stupidity, fanaticism and debauchery and the impious enemies of Islam, of humanity and civilization' (Ö. A. Zülfi-zade, 1925, 3).[348]

The Republicans saw the dervish lodges as a nest of reactionaries and they portrayed them as such. In their quest to tackle the tarikats, they would use whatever arguments and means necessary. Mustafa Kemal himself expressed his thoughts on this matter and issued a warning in Kastamonu on 30 August 1925:

Under no circumstances do I accept the existence of such primitive people in the civilised community of Turkey, who under the [influ-

---

346. Yet, he was acquitted in three trials, in Eskişehir, Denizli and Afyon, managing to defend himself successfully: *Ibid.,* p. 123.

347. Cem Apaydın, 'Belgeler Işığında Tekke Zaviye ve Türbelerin Kapatılması Üzerine Bir Değerlendirme, *Yakın Dönem Türkiye Araştırmaları*, Vol. 16, No. 2, 2017, p. 152.

348. Thierry Zarcone, "Confrérisme, maraboutisme et culte des saints face au réformisme", Paris, 2009, p. 325; Zülfizâde Ömer Adil, Tekyeler Yıkılmalıdır, İstanbul, 1925 [Written in the Ottoman script], İstanbul, 1925.

ence] of such and such sheikh search for material happiness and spiritual enlightenment in the face of today's science and the full scope of
enlightening civilisation. Sirs and O nation! Know well that the Turkish Republic cannot be a country related to sheiks, dervishes and disciples. The most right, the truest [hakikî] tarikat is civilisation. Doing
what civilization demands is sufficient to be human.[349]

This unequivocal statement indicated his views and intention about
the tarikats. The Şeyh Said Rebellion in 1925 simply precipitated the
process.[350] Şeyh Said was Kurdish and of the Nakshibendi order. His
uprising had both Islamic and nationalist overtones: "The explicit aim
of the revolt was to establish an independent Kurdish state in which Islamic law would be respected".[351] Both aspects were unacceptable to the
new regime, as they were intent on building a nation-state built on
Turkish ethnicity only, and different measures were undertaken to
counteract actual and potential opposition.[352]

Dervish lodges (*tekkes* and *zaviyes*)[353] were formally closed down on
30 December 1925. The operation of tarikats and the use of an assortment
of honorific titles became illegal. We cannot be certain as to when Mustafa
Kemal made up his mind, but it is highly likely Mustafa Kemal had always
the intention of ending practices related to tarikats and dervish lodges,
once their support was not needed. His views on modernisation, seculari-
sation/laicism and religion, discussed above, were a clear indication of his
agenda, once he felt powerful enough to proceed. Mustafa Kemal waited
only to decide on the best form of action. Tarikats, as they operated, were
not compatible with his vision. They were seen as an impediment to the
progress of Turkish society towards the three pillars of modernisation, secularisation and westernisation. They had no place in this science-oriented,
rational society Mustafa Kemal and his cohort desired to build, albeit with
many inconsistent tendencies and practices.

Parliamentary debate on tarikats

The discussion that took place in the Parliament on the future of tarikats traces the prevailing mood in the Republican elite circles. The parlia-

349. Cited in Apaydın, p. 152.
350. Zelyut, Rıza. 'Tekke ve Zaviyeler Niçin Kapatıldı?', *Güneş Gazetesi*. 25 May 2011.
351. Itzchak Weismann, *The Naqshbandiyya*, New York, 2007, p. 104.
352. Şeyh Said was eventually captured and executed after a military operation.
353. A *zaviye* is a smaller *tekke*.

mentary minutes also give us a window to the paradoxical view of this elite *vis-à-vis* Islam; on the one hand always quick to demonstrate reverence to it, but on the other, claiming that tarikats, tekkes and zaviyes represented "backwardness or the most negative aspect of Islam. These were significant Islamic institutions with a tradition stretching back to the thirteenth century in Anatolia. The Republic addressed this paradox by placing tarikats outside, or at least to the margins, of Islam. In other words, they were purging the polluting elements to purify Islam. While the Republican discourse was laicist, in practice the Republicans worked to shape Sunni Islam into a form, which Murat Es noted, was to be a "secular, rational version of Sunni Islam as the state religion".[354]

On 16 November 1925, Konya deputy, Refik Bey (Koraltan) submitted a motion related to dervish lodges and tombs (and mausoleums).[355] This was discussed on 30 November of the same year and passed into law. Refik Bey, who introduced the bill, described these places as sinister, though he conceded that there were innocent people among tarikat members.[356] Further, Refik Bey labelled tarikats as depraved places, and even accusing them of treachery, despite tarikat involvement in the Liberation War:

> Honourable friends .... I need to add to the sentence that fundamentally for centuries among the household members of such places as türbes [tombs], tekkes and zaviyes there were innocent citizens who were swayed and seduced in these houses. They become a source of depravity inside the country and at times constituted the groundwork to cause tremendous treacherous malice on the country and the nation.[357]

Rize deputy Ekrem Bey continued on the theme:

> No doubt today another significant law is added to the history of the Republic. There will no longer be sheiks or tekkes. I am happy to see that. The tekkes which hitherto were a nest for hideous social scenes, in the country's most distressed periods carried out inauspicious (meşulm) and destructive political activities.[358]

Having described the tarikats as exploiters of common folk and also

---

354. Es, *op. cit.*, p. 27.
355. *T.B.M.M. Zabıt Ceridesi*, İçtima: 9, Cilt 1, 16 Teşrinisani 1341 [16 November 1925], p. 125.
356. Ayşe Yanardağ, 'Tarikat ve Zaviye ve Türbelerin Kaldırılmasına Dair Devrim Kanunu ve Uygulamaları', *I. Uluslar Arası Tarih ve Kültür Kongresi*, Gaziantep, 19-22 August 2017.
357. *T.B.M.M. Zabıt Ceridesi*, İçtima: 17, Cilt 1, 30 Teşrinisani 1341 [30 November 1925], p. 282.
358. *Loc.cit.*

groups with involvement in politics outside the sphere of their control, the deputies passed Law 677 "Regarding the Closure of Dervish Lodges, Tombs and the prohibition or abolition of the profession of tomb-keeping and a number of honorific titles," stated:

> Generally tarikats and the use of honorific titles as sheikdom, dervish-ism, discipleship, *dedelik*, sayyidism, çelebism, babalık, emir, *nakip* [dervish leader], caliphship [position of deputy sheikh], fortune telling, sorcery, üfürükçülük [breathing on sick people in order to cure them], foretelling, *nüshacılık* [making of amulets] to fulfil hopes and to perform services and wear related vestments is prohibited.

> Within the Republic of Turkey tarikats or all . . . related tombs will close down and the profession of tomb-keeping [türbedarlık] is prohibited. Those who re-open or establish dervish lodges that were closed down, or those who provide space even temporarily for tarikat rituals, and those who bear the above titles or offers services or wear vestments related to them shall be punished for imprisonment of no less than three months, and a fine of no less than fifty liras.[359]

The views of the deputies cited above demonstrate very clearly that the new regime distrusted tarikats. Furthermore, the "sacred" places of tarikat members were viewed as "profane" by the regime, as well as clusters of "superstitious" activities. The spiritual scope of the tarikats, their mystical and esoteric approach (*tasavvuf*/Sufism) to Islam was not of interest to them. They abhorred their clothes which they viewed as anachronistic, their archaic titles and "backward" practices. Seemingly, there was no point of compromise.

Law 677 did not define the tarikats as such but used their physical structures, i.e. the dervish lodges *etc.*, as the basis to single them out. In other words, it was implied that a tarikat is a religious formation, which functions primarily through dervish lodges. This aspect may have been an oversight, which Kütahya deputy Nuri Bey alluded to:

> As you know magicians, fortune-tellers, soothsayers with a tray on their hands they sell things like 30-40 bottles of hacıyağı [a heavy perfume used by hajjis], kalemis yağı and other oils [and ointments] and even ıkannica [karinca? (ant)] prayer, Uğru Abbas prayer; these [people] are mobile türbes. These mobile dervishes walk around the streets

---

359. Emir and Seyit are titles used by descendants of the Prophet Muhammad; *Tekke ve Zaviyelerle Türbelerin Seddine ve Türbedarlıklar ile bir Rakım Ünvanların Men ve İlgasına Daır Kanunu*, Law Number: 677, Date of Acceptance: 30 November 1925, published in *Resmi Gazete* on 13 December 1925.

and both intimidate the people and propel them to the wrong path; many murders were committed because of this.[360]

Other than making a statement about needing to keep an eye on these sorts of activities performed by *seyyar derviş* (mobile dervishes), no additional measures were constituted. It was the organisational aspect of tarikats that was of concern, rather than the so-called mobile dervishes who scraped a living utilising aspects of cultural practices and folk Islam. There was no Church of mobile dervishes, or in Goldenberg's terms, they did not act like a future state. Certainly, as pointed out above, the Republicans had an ideological aversion to the practices of the mobile dervishes, but the immediate goal was to shut down the organisations which, in the future could have formed the nucleus for an uprising with more participation than that of Sheikh Said's. There were thus both ideological and practical reasons to remove the tarikats from public life.

Baki Öz notes that some deputies showed hostility, especially against Bektashi tarikats, in fact, the only one mentioned by name during the debate. This was peculiar considering it was the Nakshibendi resistance that precipitated the process. The underlying Sunni-Alevi dichotomy, which persisted throughout the Republic's history, came to the surface during the parliamentary debate. Bozok deputy Süleyman Sırrı Bey described Hacı Bektaş Lodge as *mezellegâh* (abject place) and its resident dervishes as Albanian murderers.[361]

There were also deputies who were openly hostile to Alevism.[362] They combined their aversion to tarikats and Alevism. The original bill in its list of honorific titles did not include 'dede', a title used by Alevi elders or the institution of Alevi "dedelik". Malatya deputy Reşit Bey requested *dedelik* to be prohibited as well, and Zonguldak deputy Tunalı Hilmi, supporting the motion, proposed *dedelik* to be included in the list of titles following *şeyhlik, dervişlik*, and müritlik.[363] The motion was accepted and Alevism was also affected beyond just the Bektashis.

---

360. *T.B.M.M. Zabıt Ceridesi*, İçtima: 17, Cilt 1, 30 Teşrinisani 1341 [30 November 1925], p. 284.

361. Baki Öz states that Süleyman Sırrı Bey used the term *mezbelehane* (midden) to describe the *Dergâh* (Lodge), which included Hacı Bektaş' tomb but the transliterated minutes clearly state *mezellegâh* (see *T.B.M.M. Zabıt Ceridesi*, İçtima: 17, Cilt 1, 30 Teşrinisani 1341 [30 November 1925], p. 285). The original Ottoman transcript states *mezeltegâh* (see page 316). The harshness of language is to be noted. Baki Öz. *Tarikatlar ve Tekkelerin Kapatılma Olayı*, İstanbul, 2004, p. 157.

362. Baki Öz, *op. cit.*, p. 168.

363. *T.B.M.M. Zabıt Ceridesi*, İçtima: 17, Cilt 1, 30 Teşrinisani 1341 [30 November 1925], p. 285.

Tunalı Hilmi Bey also warned that despite the prohibition of sheikhs and dedes, they could still carry on with secret organisations. Hilmi Bey wanted to increase the penalty for those involved in secret organisations but received no support. Yet, the concerns that Hilmi Bey articulated, that the closure would simply push the tarikats underground, proved correct. Physical structures were eliminated but elimination of entrenched customs and behaviour was going to be much harder to achieve. This was to be tackled partly through the school curriculum to prevent the next generations from participating in practices the regime did not approve, but also through the monopoly of radio and state-controlled print media spreading appropriate messages.

In light of the evident hostility to tarikats and what they represented in the eyes of the regime, it may be superfluous to investigate the reasons for their closure. Mardin pointed out that Mustafa Kemal's approach towards the tarikats related to his attack against the suffocating *gemeinschaft*. He wanted to break the influence of charismatic leaders such as Nursî and tarikats' leaders who, in his view, were ignorant and immoral and exploited the lower classes. "In the future, Turks were to be governed not by dissolute sheiks but according to the *modus* governed by science".[364] The view of supremacy of science over other modes of thought affected Mustafa Kemal's approach to Islam post-1923.

Still, İlber Ortaylı argued that the closure of the tekkes and zaviyes should not be viewed as a consequence of

a radicalism invented by the Republic; their roots were based on an official control and suspicions extending to Tanzimat. The modernised administration could not tolerate those who have gathered around the tekkes and zaviyes and have been institutionalized.[365]

Certain tekkes were closed down by Sultan Mahmut II during the nineteenth century.[366] As pointed out in Chapter 2.2, the modernisation process did not start with the Republic but was a product of the *Tanzimat* period (1839-1876). However, the extent and scope of the Republican modernisation process was more radical, and it must be said, more aggressive in its implementation. The dervish lodges were steeped in tradition and they were seen as custodians of the old way. Modernisation is a process of trans-

364. Mardin, *Türkiye'de Din ve Siyaset*, p. 77.
365. İlber Ortaylı. 'Tarikatlar ve Tanzimat Dönemi Osmanlı Yönetimi'. *Ankara Üniversitesi Osmanlı Tarihi Araştırma ve Uygulama Merkezi Dergisi*, No. 6, 1995, p. x.
366. Mustafa. Özsaray, Arşiv Belgeleri Işığında Osmanlı'da Devlet Tekke ilişkileri (XIX. Yüzyıl), Unpublished Ph.D. Study, Fatih Sultan Mehmet Vakıf Üniversitesi, 2018, p. 569.

forming to modern anything that is not; tarikats could not have been part of this process, or at least, Mustafa Kemal and his cohort did not think so. Apaydın points to the inevitability of the process leading to the closure of tarikats, given

that they were outside the new regime's concept of civilization. It seems normal to believe that a mentality that claims to create a secular and civilized society, would close down the dervish lodges, which, as they were structured, represented the old regime and what they produced was seen as a source of superstition and as an obstruction to modernisation.[367]

Yet, the Bektashi, for example, were in favour of the Republic and secularism. Accommodation could have been reached with some tarikats, such as the Bektashis. Thierry Zarcone notes that "(Ziya Gökalp, for example) developed a more nuanced critique [of tarikats], aware of the positive role that these institutions have played in Ottoman society and their recent efforts to reform themselves".[368]

Modernity is not an ideology that precludes "religion" but confines it to the private space via a gradual process. Rather than attempting to transform the tarikats to adapt to the new reality, the Republicans chose the option of ending them, which in the long run was not achievable. Ultimately, Mustafa Kemal decided to keep only Sunni Islam in the fold and marginalise other forms of Islam (Sufism, Alevism, folk Islam).

Some of the discussions that took place prior to the passing of the tarikat law were not recorded in the parliamentary minutes. In his memoirs, Hamdullah Suphi Tanrıöver[369] noted that Mustafa Kemal presided over the session. He told Mustafa Kemal about a *türbe* in his neighbourhood and other türbes, pointing out that some of these türbes may belong to people "who made our history and left us the liberated nation" and asked Mustafa Kemal "can you please correct this?" Mustafa Kemal became very angry, gave Tanrıöver a stern look and said, "all of them", "all the türbes", but added "wait for ten years, I will give you all the türbes".[370] This suggested that it was a temporary measure, at least that is how Tanrıöver presented it. Yet, as long as Mustafa Kemal lived only two Mevlevi lodges reopened as museums.[371] He did not shift on this.

---

367. Apaydın, *op. cit.*, p. 162.
368. Zarcone, *op. cit.*, p. 325.
369. Tanrıöver literally translates as "one who praises God". Like most Turks in 1934, when the Surname Law passed, he would have chosen his own surname.
370. Baki Öz. *op. cit.*, pp. 170-71.
371. *Ibid.*, pp. 192 and 197,

The Bektashi narrative is that Mustafa Kemal only reluctantly included Bektashi tarikats and institutions to the tekke and zaviye prohibition. The provenance of the information subject to the narrative is the *postnişin*[372] of Eryek Baba Lodge, Halifebaba Turgut Koca. According to Turgut Koca, it was not Atatürk's intention to close down the Bektashi tekkes. During preparation for the bill, İsmet Pasha, Kâzım Karabekir, Kâzım Özalp, Abdul Halik Renda and others had a meeting with Mustafa Kemal. Mustafa Kemal asked, "should we close the Bektashi tekkes as well?". Kâzım Karabekir and Abdul Halik Renda said, "not possible" (*olmaz*). But İsmet Paşa insisted "all or nothing". Atatürk listened to İsmet Paşa".[373] The source of this apocryphal story, Turgut Koca, shifted the blame to İsmet. This rationalisation is in accordance with Alevi idealisation of Mustafa Kemal as Atatürk.

The British legate in Constantinople, Sir Ronald Charles Lindsay, captured the context of the tarikats' closure insightfully, as described in the cable he sent to Austen Chamberlain, Secretary of State for Foreign Affairs, on 14 September 1925:

In January of this year when Mustafa Kemal spent a few days at Konia, it was reported that the Turkish Government was thinking of laying hands ·on the valuable properties of the Mevlevi order of Dervishes; and when I was in the same town in May I heard that the Buyuk Chelebi, the head of the order, though he liked seeing visitors, preferred that they should stay away because their visits could only have the result of exciting the suspicions of the civil authorities. The blow that has now fallen, though sudden, is hardly surprising. As to the causes of the action taken, the decree itself mentions the observations of the Independence Tribunals made after the Kurdish insurrection, and doubtless the Dervish orders, the tekkes and zaviehs, constituting as they do rallying points for the religiously minded, have contributed somewhat to the movement of last spring; but they are not political organizations properly so-called; and if in the East religion and politics could be divorced, I have no doubt that the Buyuk Chelebi himself would have welcomed a decree of divorce. The Government in its passion for secularisation has had good reason for the action it has taken if it can afford to despise the possible by-products of that action, and mere police considerations have doubtless reinforced its determination; for apart from the regular and unrolled [sic] members of the orders there are vast numbers of unorganised adepts all over the country, inscribed on no·

---

372. A title used by Bektashi Dervish Lodge head.
373. Baki Öz. *op. cit.*, p. 171.

lists and bound by no fixed formula or obligation, yet held together by a vague kind of esprit de corps and mutual sympathy.[374]

In total, 773 tekkes and 905 türbes were closed. The tarikats that abided by this prohibition were the Bektashis and the Mevlevis, while, as we shall see, the Nakshibendi resisted.[375]

Further reforms towards westernisation, secularisation and modernisation

In addition to the closure of the tarikats, two more laws passed in 1934 as part of the modernisation project. On 26 November 1934, a new law abolished the use of such titles as *müşür* (Marshall), *paşa* (General), *ağa*, *hacı*, *hoca*, *efendi bey* and *hanım* (Lady). According to *Milliyet* newspaper, these titles denoted class differences. The terms *bay* and *bayan* (Mister and Miss/Mrs) were introduced at the same time with the instruction that they were to be used before the name of the person.[376] The project required change in terminology to break with the past and in the process, new terms were invented and imposed.

On the same day, a bill was submitted to prohibit the wearing of religious vestments outside places of worship. This law was to apply to Muslims and non-Muslims alike.[377] On 3 December 1934, "The Law Regarding Some Vestments That Can Not Be Worn" (*Bazı Kisvelerin Giyilemeyeceğine Dair Kanun*) was enacted.[378] Cumulatively, these reforms were restricting and eliminating "religious activities" and presence in the public space and confined them to the private space (i.e. mosque and domestic sphere). In the opening of the First Assembly in 1920, Kemal employed the services of the Supreme Mosque of Hacı Bayram Veli to conduct prayers to endorse the new Assembly. In that instance, the mosque was exercising a public function. This was entirely consistent with the proto-Kemalist period (1920-1923), as I described in Chapter 3. After 1923, the mosques were regarded as private places for prayers and rituals. The regime's objective

---

374. Australian Archives, *op. cit.*, E 5527/4706/44.
375. İsmail Saymaz, *Şehvetiye Tarıkatı*,İstanbul, 2019, p. 13.
376. 'Mecliste Büyük Bir Gün', [A great day in the Parliament], *Milliyet*, 27 November 1934, p. 1.
377. 'Ruhanî kisve ile sokaklarda dolaşılmıyacak', [One will not be able to walk in the streets wearing religious vestments], *Cumhuriyet* 27 November 1934, p. 1.
378. 'Kıyafet Kanunu Dün Meclisten Geçti', [The Law on Attire Passed Yesterday], *Millliyet*, 4 December 1934; 'Dinî kıyafetlere dair kanun Meclisten çıktı', [The law regarding religious vestments passed in the Parliament], *Cumhuriyet*, 4 December 1934, p. 1.

was for Islam to retreat to this private space. In other words, the mosques' conceptual status shifted and this law reinforced this new status.

Kılıçzade Hakkı, Muş deputy, during the discussion suggested that this reform was delayed for too long and that the office of mufti (*müftülük*) should also be abolished, which was a radical approach even by the early Republican standards. In essence, however, the abolition of these offices would have made it harder to control local mosques, which was an integral part of the network of control. This tendency to control was stronger than the desire for true laicism, which requires the state not partaking or interfering in religious affairs. Although mosques were treated as private space on the one hand, the regime still wanted to control this space from potentially becoming a springboard for an uprising. The Interior Minister did not accept the amendment and said that this was an unrelated issue.[379] Kılıçzade Hakkı addressing the Parliament stressed the importance of the new law:

> Gentlemen. Today the law that was brought before you is about superstition and those representing superstition. . . . This law will act as a stone of pressure; it will stop them from spreading their superstition. Our children and we will no longer see this superstition. (Sounds of 'hear, hear'). Gentlemen, this law is the most blessed of the laws created by our great revolution.

> The heart desires that this law should have accompanied the Hat Law. But as our friend the Interior Minister said it was not its time. It passed late, finally; it passed. It made all free thoughts happy. Freedom of opinion has already spread throughout the country. In the spirit of Islam there is no governance. There is a namaz issue, there is an imam. There is no special türban and gown, no [special attire]. A person of virtue and a scholar takes the mihrab380 and leads people's namaz. Today whoever wants to satisfy their conscience with a divine service can go to whichever temple they want.[381]

Not an eloquent speech by any means, Kılıçzade Hakkı made three key points: certain clothing reflected "superstition"; Islam did not need institutions; and simplicity in worship was desirable. This ignored the historical reality of the existence of the Caliphate for centuries as an Islamic institution. Also, Diyanet was the organisation that was set up to control mosques and *mesjids* and activities of the clerics.

379. 'Dinî kıyafetlere dair kanun Meclisten çıktı', *Cumhuriyet*, 4 December 1934, p. 1.
380. A niche in a mosque, that indicates the qibla (direction of Mecca), and into which the imam prays.
381. *T.B.M.M Zabit Ceridesi*, İçtima 11, Cilt 1, 3-12-1934, p. 75.

Although these two reforms, regarding titles and vestments, were not directly related to the tarikats, they enabled the authorities to extend the restrictions and use the additional legislation to arrest tarikat members. The law can also be seen partly as an attack on aspects of Anatolian traditions and what Mardin called "cultural conservatism". The Kemalist project was comprehensive in its scope with little respect for local sensitivities, which facilitated the building of resentment among those outside the designated core.

Hegemony, modernisation, brutality

To facilitate the implementation of these measures, *Takrir-i Sükûn*, Maintenance of Order Law, was passed in 1924 which turned the country into a dictatorship. Even if the foreign sources of the time can be dismissed as biased, Adıvar, once a co-editor of *Yeni Gün* and a person representing Kemal's view, cannot easily be dismissed. She called the regime "in spirit a personal dictatorship"[382] and refers to a "dictatorial regime from 1925 to 1929" when the Law of Maintenance Order was in operation.[383]

> Mustafa Kemal Pasha played a superb political game. He proposed the Law of Maintenance of Order, which would reestablish Revolutionary Tribunals, with absolute power to arrest and execute anyone suspected of endangering public order.[384]

The Revolutionary Tribunals referred to by Adıvar, were the *İstiklâl Mahkemeleri* (Independence Tribunals) which carried out summary executions. These courts aggressively eliminated any opposition to the Kemalist reforms.

It was then time to introduce reforms which potentially were going to alter the life of the majority of the citizens. The dismantling of the old edifice was well under way. The Sharia Law was gone and the Swiss Civil Code, the Italian Criminal Code and the German Commercial Law were introduced to replace it. It is also clear that the Republic embraced a secular ideology as its wider ideological framework. These significant laws were supplemented with other measures, some of which had profoundly affected daily life. This was a comprehensive and radical program to bring about change, a cultural revolution, the likes of which very few countries have seen. The changes were ambitious, bold, untested, the pace was unrelenting

---

382. Adıvar, *op. cit.*, p. 203.
383. *Ibid.*, p. 223.
384. *Ibid.*, p. 220.

and the implementation unforgiving.

On 26 December 1925, the Gregorian calendar was adopted instead of the lunar *hijri* calendar and the Rumi calendar previously used by the Ottoman administration. In the same year, the "Hat Law" declared the wearing of the *fez* and the male turban (*sarık*) a criminal offence. Religious attire was forbidden outside mosques (or churches for that matter).

Only a few years prior, citizens of the new Republic were subjects of an Empire, with a public life different than what was being laid out at that point. In this process, even their clothes were being questioned and altered. The Hat Law was significant because as well as forcing ordinary male citizens to change their attire to look more like westerners, it was criminalising aspects of their culture and traditions. The state was rapidly purging what was perceived as Islamic from public life. The Hat Law warrants some attention because unlike the abolition of the Caliphate, it attracted significant resistance from the population. The Office of the Caliphate had lost its significance in day-to-day life, but the Hat Law was to disrupt customs and habits.

Pekdemir refers to the mobile (*seyyar*) Ankara Independence Court which travelled around meting out justice, as it saw fit, against what the new establishment summarily labelled as "backward". Pekdemir also talks about "Muslims that were executed for not wearing a hat", though he later specifies that they were executed for protesting against the new law.[385] This is a fine distinction, but the Hat Law represented a significant cultural shift and the determination of the Kemalist cadres to do what it takes to implement it.

On 27 November 1925, in Maraş, a small so-called "reactionary" group, took the green flag from the mosque of the district and protested in front of the government building crying "Islam is being lost, we do not want hats". Forty of them were arrested. For most ordinary Muslims the western-style hat became a symbol of a foreign, non-Islamic world, even though it was being imposed by Turks.

Not all of the proceedings of the Independence Courts are available given the huge volume of records. Those that are available demonstrate that the Courts were obsessed with the Hat Law and questioned many of the accused to detect any level of involvement in religious orders and, at the very least, their views on wearing western hats.[386] The panel of judges even accused some defenders, e.g. Erzurumlu Zühdü Efendi, for not wearing

385. Pekdemir, Vol. 1, *op. cit.*, pp. 205-06.
386. Ahmed Nedim, *Ankara İstiklâl Mahkemesi Zabıtları – 1926*, İstanbul 1993, passim.

a hat, even though under the new law this was not a crime.[387] The Tribunal treated the reluctance to wear a hat as suspicious activity. The same defendant, Erzurumlu Zühdü Efendi, pointed out that there were no hats available in Erzurum:

> Some hats arrived with the mail. Some of them were handed out to postal workers before being distributed. Public servants were without hats. Officials of the Republic had to wear hats. There was not even a hat in the province.388

For Kemalists, the hat was a symbol for modernisation and westernisation, and opposition to it was considered to be an opposition to their entire project. Much like the headscarf issue in the 1980s, when wearing it was deemed to be "reactionary" and opposition to secularism, opposition to wearing the hat was deemed to be seditious and "reactionary". The Independence Courts also relentlessly pursued members of religious orders and other organisations opposing the changes. For instance, on 15 August 1925 the Ankara Independence Tribunal sentenced eleven members of *Tarikat-ı Salâhiyye*[389] to death, which was not a tarikat but an organisation formed to oppose the Ankara government in 1920. The brutality of these courts meting out summary justice is well documented.

The torrent of reforms stopped momentarily in 1926 so that the new regime could take stock and consolidate its grip on the popular opposition. In 1928, the phrase "Islam as the religion of the State" was removed from the constitution. Subsequently, the Ottoman script, consisting primarily of Arabic but also some Persian letters, was replaced with the Latin alphabet.[390] As Geoffrey Lewis notes "[t]he aim of the Turkish language reform was to eliminate the Arabic and Persian grammatical features and the many thousands of Arabic and Persian borrowings that had long been part of the language."[391] Ostensibly, Arabic and Persian words were replaced with "authentic" Central Asian Turkic words. Kemalist reformers called this new language *Öztürkçe* (Pure Turkish), but in reality these were manufactured words.

This radical change deprived the ulema and other Islamist elite of their cultural capital. After political power, cultural power was also shifting to

---

387. *Ibid.*, p. 152.
388. *Ibid.*, p. 151.
389. Pekdemir, Vol. 2, *op. cit.*, p. 198.
390. On the background to the adoption of the Latin script, see Ayşe Hür, 'Arap elif-basından Türk alfabesine', [From the Arabic alphabet to the Turkish alphabet], *Radikal*, 6 October 2013.
391. Geoffrey Lewis, *The Turkish Language Reform*, Oxford, 1999, p. 2.

the western educated and oriented elites who were well-versed in the Latin script. Nationalism cannot be separated from the other dimensions of the language reforms (*Dil devrimi*). Kurdish words and even certain letters key to the Kurdish language were banned (q, w and x). Indeed, the existence of the Kurdish language and Kurdish people was denied. As well as erasing the existence of a large minority, the language reform aimed to reduce the influence of Ottoman thought and knowledge.

Replacing historical memory

As the state actively worked to erase the memory of the Ottoman Empire, it created a vacuum. This vacuum was filled with two pseudo-historical theses in the 1930s. It was asserted that all peoples in the world were in fact Turks and all languages derived from Turkish, even Ancient Greek, Chinese or Syriac for that matter. These were the so-called Sun-Language Theory (*Güneş-Dil Teorisi*) and the Turkish History Study (*Türk Tarih Tezi*). The Council for Research into Turkish History, consisting of four academics and six parliamentarians, produced a book entitled *Türk Tarihinin Ana Hatları* (The Main Points of the Turkish History). This ideological project headed by Mustafa Kemal himself placed Turks at the centre of all major civilisations in Mesopotamia, the Mediterranean region and beyond.[392]

Büşra Ersanlı, who conducted a comprehensive analysis of the background to the construction of the Turkish Historical Study, noted that Mustafa Kemal asked the Council members to produce the book within a short period of time. The resulting product was poor and Kemal did not approve the last draft. The book was to be used in teaching middle school students but only 100 copies were printed. The authors relied mostly on foreign secondary sources, while Ottoman sources were systematically ignored. Thirty thousand copies of an expanded second edition, in which the Ottoman political existence was entirely omitted, were printed.[393]

In June 1932, in the First Congress of Turkish History, the Minister for Education opened the congress by maintaining that when the rest of the world was in caves, the Turks of Central Asia were already using wooden and metal tools and cultivating the soil. According to his study, by 7,000 B.C.E. Turks had already developed farming and pastoralism, discovered gold, copper, tin and iron and migrated from their homeland to form, no

---

392. Originally published as Türk Tarih Heyeti, *Türk Tarihinin Ana Hatları*, Ankara, 1930; reprint *Türk Tarihinin Ana Hatları*, 3rd Edition, İstanbul, p. 18.
393. Ersanlı, Büşra. İktidar ve Tarih, İstanbul, 2003, pp. 120, 121 and 125.

less, the Chinese, Anatolian, Mesopotamian, Egyptian, Mediterranean, Roman and Etruscan civilisations.[394]

It should be pointed out some European historians and geographers of the time had described the "Turkish race" as second class. To some extent the Turkish History Study, was a reaction to these racial and racist theories. By emphasising the pre-Ottoman Turkic past the Republicans wanted to change this view.[395] Nonetheless, Ersanlı notes that no genuine debate took place during the congress as no participant wanted to appear opposing nationalism and science. Even the slightest criticism of the official study was not tolerated.[396] In short, European racial theories were counteracted with Turkish racial theories.

A linguistic conference was held later in the year on 26 September. This congress put in place a process whereby any foreign words in the Turkish language, mostly Arabic and Persian, were being replaced with "authentic" Turkic words. The congress was called *Kurultay* a central Asian Turkic word for assembly. This was a neologism; others were introduced. The title of the president (of the Republic) changed from *Cumhurreisi* to *Cumhurbaşkanı*, which still contained the Arabic loan word "Cumhur" (people). De-Arabising Turkish remained a constant challenge to pursue at least until the 1970s.

This linguistic congress also reiterated the assertion that

> [t]he language of the Hittites, Sumerians, Medes, Hindus, Hellenes and Egyptians were derived from a single idiom, that originally spoken in Central Asia, i.e., primitive Turkish. Thousands of years before the Christian era the Turks dominated all civilised countries. The honour of having invented all systems of writing, particularly the Phoenician, Hittite, Sumerian, Cyprian and Cretan, belongs to the glorious Turkish race.[397]

The British envoy who reported these proceedings also noted that the Minister of Education visited "Stanbul University", the local headquarters of Halk Evi and other educational institutions to impress upon them the importance of linguistic reform. What ensued was gradual replacement of Arabic and Persian words with new ones (Öztürkçe) in an attempt to de-Islamise the Turkish language in parallel of the de-Arabisation of Sunni Islam in Turkey. A second Turkish History Congress was held in 1937. Almost no discussion was held during the congress and the "conclusive vic-

---

394. İsmail Beşikçi, *Türk Tarih Tezi ve Kürt Sorunu*, Stockholm, 1986, p. 6.
395. Ersanlı, *op. cit.*, p. 14.
396. *Ibid.*, p. 143.
397. Australian Archives, *op. cit.*, E 5494/3822/44.

tory" of the Turkish Historical Study was officially declared.[398] The regime felt that the pre-Islamic Turks were connected to contemporary Turks and the Ottoman represented a rupture in the process.

Intensification of the secularisation process

There were other measures, which also contributed to the secularisation process. The re-organisation of the built environments is an important cluster in itself in this process. For instance, Hagia Sophia (Ayasofya, the Byzantine Church Αγία Σοφία) became a museum. It had become a mosque in 1453 after the Conquest of Constantinople to symbolise the dominance of Islam, but was converted into a museum by 1935 to symbolise the dominance of secularist ideology. The sacred space of the mosque became profane, but to many Islamists it remained sacred (and efforts to convert it back to a mosque increased in intensity once AKP came to power). Thus, the same space is regarded sacred by the opposing camps.[399] Eventually was converted to mosque again in 2020, as part of Erdoğan's de-secularisation process and the dismantling of the symbols of the Kemalist hegemony.

As Taves demonstrated with the example of the shrine at Lourdes, there is no limit to what can become sacred. It can be argued that the museum itself is a certain kind of "sacred space". Gretchen Buggein, who visited several museums in New York, noticed the respect and contemplation visitors demonstrated, and, in the case of the National Museum of the Native American, "the entire museum presenting itself as a sacred place". Buggein argues that visitors can experience, in certain museums at least, "revelation, transcendence, transformation", which are no longer the exclusive domain of religion.[400] In the case of the Şişli Atatürk Museum cited above, the museum was deliberately built to be a sacred place, while the Museum of Ayasofya was designed to convert a sacred place to a profane one.

Conceptually, this re-organisation of the built environment in Turkey was not just about secularisation but also de-Ottomanisation of space. Houston notes that "the Kemalists' de-Ottomanization of the city [was] via policies of Turkification/ethnic cleansing after 1923."[401] We may call this

---

398. Ersanlı, *op. cit.*, pp. 15 and 28.
399. Eventually, Erdoğan succeeded in re-opening of the Museum of Hagia Sophia as a mosque, on 24 July 2020.
400. Gretchen Buggein, 'Museum space and the experience of the sacred', *Material Religion*, Vol. 8, No. 1, pp. 33 and 37.
401. Chris Houston, Shaping the City: Three Urban Events in Istanbul, *Idealkent*, Vol. 9, No. 24, 2018, p. 345.

de-Christianisation or de-Judaization of such cities as İzmir and İstanbul. The Great Fire of Smyrna (İzmir), for instance, as Kolluğlu argues, gave the opportunity to the Republicans to rebuild the city, eradicating its Ottoman, Christian and Jewish heritage.[402] The city was to be rebuilt without a reference to its non-Muslim, non-Turkish and perhaps Islamic heritage.

Köni lists a number of other reforms which eroded further the influence of the Islamic/Ottoman past: introduction to the Surname Law (Soyadı Kanunu) in 1934, adoption of the western European metric system of measurement, change of the weekly official holiday from Friday to Saturday in 1935, prohibition of going on pilgrimage to Mecca in 1934 and the change of the language of prayer calls from Arabic into Turkish in 1932. As Köni notes, this holistic secularism was implemented by state elites: the Office of the President, Prime Minister, the government, the Parliament and the CHP.[403]

The process was completed with the term laiklik being enshrined in the constitution as of 5 February 1937. The Turkish state was declared to be laic, though implementation and penetration of secularisation into the wider Turkish society was another matter.

Through state efforts, Mustafa Kemal tried to instill a sense of nationhood to rely on pre-Islamic Turkic culture, as reconstructed. Before the Islamisation of the Turkic tribes, they were under the influence of different religions, though in general shamanism dominated. For instance, the playing of the drum during Ramazan (Ramadan) is a likely shamanistic trait brought to Anatolia from Central Asia.

Ahmet Yıldız notes that the Kemalist nationalism, in order to create a secular "present", secularised the "past"; it tried to reconstruct a Turkish past freed from Islamic influence.[404] To do so, it had to draw its references from the distant - and not well documented at the time - past. The reconstructed identity has not been sufficient as a marker, without reference to Islam. Accordingly, some Turkish intellectuals are not convinced that secularism of this period eroded the Islamic feeling of the nation or that Mustafa Kemal completely eradicated Islam from the new identity he fashioned for the Muslim Turkish population. Soner Çağaptay argued that Islam

> remained central to Turkish society as its culture and identity. Notwithstanding its secularism Kemalism was compelled to sanction such nominal Islam as a marker of Turkishness. An analysis of the relations between the state and minorities in the 1920s demonstrates that despite

---

402. Kolluoglu, *op. cit.*, pp.25-44.
403. Köni, *op. cit.*, p. 80.
404. Ahmet Yıldız, *op. cit.*, pp. 119-120.

its commitment to secularism as well as territorial-voluntaristic-linguistic forms of citizenship, to a large extent, Kemalist nationalism was still molded by Islam.[405]

While pre-Islamic Turkic culture was emphasised by the early Republicans, Islamist intellectual Kara argued that:

> Turks in Turkey have no histories outside of Islam and Muslims in Anatolia. For them it is Islam which is the constituent and sustaining element of their experience in Anatolia. The establishment elite that founded the Republican ideology was cognizant of this even when they sought to isolate Islam. . . . in Arab nationalist movements, Muslim Arabs and Christian Arabs were able to come together; it was also like this in Albanian nationalism. In Turkish nationalism, there was not a strong strand like this, and Muslim-ness defined Turkish-ness.[406]

Starting at different angles, both secularists and Islamists came to the same position in support of the supremacy of Islam in the construction of Turkish nationalism.

Paradox: The Book of Religion for the Soldier

While the Republican regime embarked upon a laicisation / secularisation project and started a process of instituting measures to eradicate religious formations outside state control, paradoxically it also set a course for heavy involvement in religious matters. The establishment of Diyanet is often cited by scholars as an example of this contradictory strategy. Diyanet was to be a control mechanism. Even more inconsistent is the commissioning in 1925 of a religious handbook for soldiers by Marshal Fevzi Çakmak, Chief of General Staff. Çakmak, under orders by Mustafa Kemal, requested Diyanet to prepare such a handbook. Diyanet complied and produced *Askere Din Dersleri* (Religion Lessons for the Soldier) by Ahmed Hamdi Akseki, who was to become the President of Diyanet in 1947. In its second edition, the book was renamed as *Askere Din Kitabı* (Book of Religion for the Soldier). Another book published in 1928 entitled *Askerî Din Dersleri* (Military Religion Lessons). This was as a result of a competition initiated by the General Staff and the winning entry by Muallim [Teacher] Cevdet [later İnanç Alp] was officially recognised by the military.[407] However, as

405. Çağaptay, *op. cit.*, p. 15.
406. 'Islam and Islamism in Turkey: A Conversation with İsmail Kara', *Maydan*, 24 October 2017, https://www.themaydan.com/2017/10/islam-islamism-turkey-conversation-ismail-kara/ [Accessed on 28 January 2019].
407. Muallim Cevdet, *Askerî Din Dersleri*, Yeni Matbaa, İstanbul, 1928.

the book was written in the Ottoman Script and the government adopted the Latin alphabet in 1928, it was not distributed to soldiers.[408]

This book, prepared under the watchful eye of Mustafa Kemal,[409] is an example of cognitive dissonance in play. While the state was purportedly removing "religion" from state affairs and public life, it also required and encouraged the army to practice religion. The book, hastily put together, claimed that "the only right and true religion is Islam".[410] This was a clear example of religion in the service of the nation-state; it served for nationalistic purposes. To be an ideal citizen, you had to be a particular type of Muslim and this book promoted that idea. In short, the book did not reflect any Republican radicalism but followed traditional norms.

While the various practices of the tarikats were described as superstitious in the Parliament, *Askere Din Desleri* discussed at great length the existence of angels and their attributes, the hereafter and Doomsday as certainties.[411] The book instructed soldiers on what to do to avoid going to Hell. At the same time, *Askere Din Desleri* warned soldiers not to fall prey to superstition, which Akseki did not define. Taves regards such terms as "religion" and "religious", "unstable and contested" and warns that

> [t]heir meanings. . . overlap in some cases and compete in others with a variety of other terms derived from both Greek and Latin, including 'magical,' 'religious,' 'sacred,' 'superstitious,' 'worshipful,' 'possessed,' 'insane,' 'inspired,' and 'secular.'[412]

Though Akseki tried to make a distinction between Islam and "superstitious practices", in the minds of the Republican elite, there was no clear distinction between religion and superstition. Islam, whether practised in the mosque or tekke or in other forms, was anti-modern, and the Republicans wanted to reform it and weed out the undesirable aspects. While they did not believe in differences between the categories of "religion" and "superstition", they did believe they could reform Islam so as to be practised by the population, but not themselves. As Christopher Dole notes:

> The attempted suppression of religious formations alternative to state

---

408. Hasan Işık, Muallim Cevdet'in Türk Eğitim Tarihindeki Yeri ve Derslerinde Yerel Tarih Uygulamaları, TUHED, Spring 2020, Vol. 9, No. 1, p. 15.
409. Ohannes Kılıçdağı, 'Genelkurmay "Askere Din Kitabı Hazırlatmış"', *Agos*, 29 April 2016, http://www.agos.com.tr/tr/yazi/15171/genelkurmay-askere-din-kitabi-hazirlatmis, [Accessed on 6 March 2018].
410. Ahmed Hamdi Akseki, *Askere Din Kitabı*, Diyanet İşleri Başkanlığı, Ankara, 1976, pp. 24 and 26.
411. Akseki, pp. 37, 84 and 88.
412. Taves, *op. cit.*, p. 25.

sponsored orthodoxy would thus serve two agendas: to subvert bases of political opposition found among the country's network of religious orders and to eliminate the sorts of 'superstition' deemed contrary to the national and technological promises of reason, freedom, and science that were to chart the nation's future. Here, numerous religious figures regarded for their ability to bring relief to the sick and dying, such as the cinci hoca or üfürükçü" [Quranic healers], would become entangled within the state's redoubled efforts to exert its control over and re-imagine the nation's religious life.[413]

Just as Akseki's book was full of contradictions, so was the Republican approach to "religion". On the one hand, the Republicans displayed a very radical approach against Islam and shamanism was singled out as the only "authentic" religion of the Turks; and on the other, a Sunni version of Islam was imposed on soldiers, including Alevis. Akseki's book gave instructions on how to perform the daily rituals (*namaz*). *Askere Din Desleri* also suggested that drinking was the devil's dirty trick; but in Ankara, alcohol was consumed by the Republican elite, including Mustafa Kemal.

It is evident that the Republicans attacked religious practices with which they disagreed by labelling them superstitious and outside of Islam, and impediments to modernisation and secularisation projects. Yet, they also showed willingness to exploit Islam whenever it proved to be useful. Controlling soldiers by instilling a sense of moral duty based on familiar themes and sentiments was much easier than instilling a sense of moral duty based on new republican and nationalist principles. Instilling nationalism and a sense of nationhood on a country, which only recently rose from the ashes of a fallen empire, was a much longer project. While nationalism was embraced by the ethnic groups, both Muslim and Christians alike, in the Ottoman Empire in the nineteenth century, nationalism arrived relatively late to the Turkish element. Until the Young Turks embraced nationalism, by rejecting both Ottomanism and Islamism as the bases of identity, there was no cohesive Turkish nationalist movement in the Empire.[414] The new Republic could not alter this reality in a short time.

Akseki's book also touched on matters not related to worship or spiritual aspects, such as the relationship between husband and wife. Akseki's views, which were approved by higher authorities, were no different from those expressed by Said Nursî in his *Risale-i Nur* (see Chapter 5.2.2). Though the *Askere Din Desleri* conferred responsibilities on both men and women, it did so from a patriarchal framework. The heavier burden was

---

413. Christopher Dole, *Healing Secular Life*, Philadelphia, 2012, pp. 37-38.
414. Racho Donef, Identities in the Multicultural State, *op. cit.*, 1998, pp. 17-21.

placed on women who were not even supposed to fast (during Ramazan) without their husband's permission, and informed soldiers that "it should not be forgotten that women are angry by nature and touchy".[415]

These issues did not necessarily reflect Islamic precepts but traditional norms of expected behaviours. Paradoxically, in the quest for modernisation/westernisation, it was these sorts of attitudes that the Kemalist "Revolution" sought to stamp out, but the book was providing advice contrary to state goals. In Kemalist historiography, aberrations such as Akseki's book, which do not fit into the radical laicist narrative, have been ignored.

The core issue here is whether the Republicans were inconsistent or expedient, or even both? The instrumentalisation of religion by the young state points towards expediency. It can be argued that the state is not really against religion as such, but it seeks to establish and maintain its power. Religion is useful when it supports that project but dangerous when it asserts state-like characteristics of its own.

Between 1920 and 1923, Mustafa Kemal, by his own admission, pretended to go along with a group who would not have approved his future plans. He needed to placate them at that point to ensure their support. At the same time, it has to be recognised that the Republicans did not have a handbook on how to go about imposing secularisation in a Muslim majority country. They were guided by the French Revolution, positivism and modernism in Europe, but these were movements of the Christian West, products of specific historical circumstances. Adaptation of this ideology to local conditions required ingenuity, creativity, but more importantly, an iron fist - a hegemonic system. It is therefore not surprising that contradictory practices can be observed in the way they went about implementing the project.

Also, this was an attempt to teach a standardised version of prayers, consistent with the policy of control. Stamping out "religion" all-together was not a viable option. Very few societies eliminated "religion" totally from the public; but they replaced it with a different form of worship, that of the party and leaders. Even secular extremists have a pantheon of their own. The profane took on the characteristic of the sacred in these places. However, as we have seen, the profane and the sacred are not that separable, at least not in the scholar's mind.

Mustafa Kemal wanted the army to be obedient and at the time he could only do this by using an ideology and traditional practices familiar to soldiers. Nationalism was to replace tradition to transform the army into

---

415. Akseki, *op. cit.*, p. 202.

custodians of laicism/secularism.[416] In the meantime, Mustafa Kemal unleashed a torrent of measures to realise his three pillars.

Nakshibendi backlash and the Menemen Incident: a case of contested narratives

The main opposition to the Kemalist reforms came from the Nakshibendi order including its off-shoots. The *Menemen Incident* is an early example. In the official secularist narrative, a group of "reactionaries" carrying an Islamic flag ran rampant in Menemen in western Turkey on 23 December 1930, asking for the restoration of the Sharia Law and the Caliphate. The flag carried the following statement: "إِنَّا فَتَحْنَا لَكَ فَتْحًا مُبِينًا", a *Sura* from the Quran translated as "Indeed, We have given you, [O Muhammad], a clear conquest".[417] It means we will conquer the enemy; the enemy being the Kemalist regime. This was a clear message of defiance against the regime, emanating from the extreme end of the tarikat spectrum; an act of political Islam.

A teacher and reserve officer, Mustafa Fethi Kubilay, tried to stop them but he was seriously wounded when a member of the pack, Şamdan Mehmet (Mehmet of Damascus), discharged his gun, upon the order issued by their leader Derviş Mehmet. Subsequently, Derviş Mehmet followed the wounded officer Kubilay, dragged him onto a mounting block, severed his head using his dagger and placed the poor officer's head on the flagpole. The mob, which by then had grown in size, applauded. Two guards (*bekçis*) were also killed by the crowd.[418] It is even claimed that Derviş Mehmet drunk Kubilay's blood as a symbolic act (i.e. "saving Islam").[419]

Giritli Derviş Mehmet [Dervish Mehmet of Crete] (Bedâvaki), "who claimed to be a *Mahdi*"[420], was the leader of the group but "[i]t was claimed that this incident occurred as a result of the incitement by Mohammed Es'ad Erbili, the famous Naqshi sheikh".[421] Notably, Erbili had not gone out of his home after the closure of the tekkes

---

416. It has to be noted that this book was reproduced with amendments in 1945 and 1976 and extended its original scope.

417. https://quran.com/48 [Accessed on 5 March 2018].

418. İsmet Üzen, 'Çankırıda Yayınlanan Gazetelere Göre Menemen Olayı', No. 83, July 2012, p. 46.

419. Çetin Özdek, *Türkiye'de Gerici Akımlar*, İstanbul, 1968, p. 158.

420. Necdet Aysal, 'Yönetsel Alanda Değişimler ve Devrim Hareketlerine Karşı Gerici Tepkiler "Serbest Cumhuriyet Fırkası - Menemen Olayı', *Güz*, No. 44, 2009, pp. 601.

421. Hülya Küçük, "Sufi Reactions Against the Reforms After Turkey's National Struggle: How a Nightingale Turned into a Crow" in Touraj Atabaki (Ed.). *The State and the Subaltern*, London, 2007.

[he] withdrew to his mansion in Erenköy, Istanbul, after the shutting of the tekkes and zaviyes, but he continued his activities through deputies and disciples. He was referred to as 'Kutbilaktab' [Kutb-ul Aktab], which meant the pole of poles, a title given to a person known by the order as the material and spiritual president of the religious community at all times. With the appointment of Laz Ibrahim, one of the most important and most trusted men of Esat, as the chief caliph [deputy] of the Manisa region, a great mobilization has started as part of the activities of the sect.[422]

There is no doubt about the veracity of the general sequence of events, though the newspaper *Cumhuriyet's* pictorial representation of an alleged event during the incident is contrived. The symbolic depiction of the "reactionaries" shooting at the crowd using a minaret goes against the depiction of the official narrative itself, which reported that the crowd applauded and supported Derviş Mehmet.[423] Yet, *Cumhuriyet* was not interested in solely reporting the event, which by all accounts was gruesome. *Cumhuriyet*, as a mouthpiece of the regime, went a step ahead by representing the mosque as a base for "reactionaries", even though the mosques were under the tutelage of the government, at least administratively.

Image 2: Representation of the local mosque during the Menemen Incident[424]

422. Aysal, *op. cit.*, 600.
423. 'Dirilen ve boğulan irtica', [Reaction resurrected and strangled], *Cumhuriyet*, 28 December 1930, p. 1.
424. 'Maktul Derviş Mehmet bir nakşibendi şeyhidir!', [Slained Dervish Mehmet was a

There were many eye-witnesses to the incident and many were questioned by the authorities. The difference between the official narrative and that of the alternative sources lies on the explanation of the causes of the events and the strength of the connection of the incident to the Nakshibendi order. One thing is for certain, the appropriately named Kubilay[425], who was brave and unfortunate to be in the wrong place, was elevated to martyr status: "Kubilay, the heroic victim of the incident, has been an icon of Kemalist secularism."[426] Even secular iconography requires its own martyrs to counteract the Islamists.

Azak notes that

[t]he Menemen Incident has been studied mostly by amateur historians and journalists, and referred to by several, mostly Kemalist, sources, with little sociological or political analysis. These sources narrate the event from the state's perspective and bring into focus the 'martyrdom' of Kubilay. They all point at a Sufi order, the Naqshbandiyya, as the organization behind the uprising, and emphasize the fact that the latter was effectively suppressed.[427]

This was probably the case in 2007 when Azak's article was published, but since then the Menemen Incident attracted the attention of more scholars. For instance, Eyüp Öz who conducted extensive research by reviewing archival material in 2015, examined the incident from a different angle. He even attempted to interview Halil Yılmaz, aged 96 at the time, who knew Giritli Mehmet. The request was initially refused and only when Yılmaz's son remarked to his father "[a]t this stage of your life, what are you afraid of?", Yılmaz accepted a restricted interview.[428] Even after 75 years, the incident was still regarded as a sensitive topic, given that it signified a clash between the secularist-minded and Islamists. Kubilay's martyrdom proved to be an enduring symbol for many Kemalists.

Eyüp Öz makes a number of observations which are contrary to the official interpretation of the events. In the official narrative, Giritli Mehmet is presented as a peon, yet Öz argues that Giritli Mehmet was the instigator. Originally, of the Bektashi order, he was only permitted to join the Nakshibendi when he promised to give up drug use (*esrar*). According to Öz, in December 1930, Giritli Mehmet organised an "army" of seven

Nakshibendi Sheihk!], *Cumhuriyet*, 28 December 1930.
425. Name of a Mongol Khan.
426. Umut Azak, "A Reaction to Authoritarian Modernization in Turkey: The Menemen Incident and the Creation and Contestation of a Myth, 1930-31" in Atabaki, p. 144.
427. *Loc. cit.*
428. Eyüp Öz, 'Yasak Bir Hafızayla Yüzleşmek: Menemen Olayı İrtica mı, Komplo mu?', *İnsan ve Toplum Bilimleri Dergisi*, No 5, 2015, p. 411.

and decided to conduct *hijra* (migration). He named four of his soldiers Mehmet, two Hasan and the last Ramazan, following the Seven Sleepers tradition found in both Christianity and Islam.[429] *The Times* depicts him as the leader: "Dervish Mehmed, the leader of the religious reactionaries . . . had prepared the movement a long time ago in conjunction with other members of the Nakshibendi order of Dervishes".[430]

In Menemen, Giritli Mehmet gave a speech in the central square, asking the town residents to join him in his quest and declared himself to be the *Mehdi* and expressed his claim that he was "impervious to bullets":

> O you folk throw away your hats on your heads and unite with us under this banner. Otherwise, our army, which will conquer Ankara as of midnight and begin to besiege everywhere, will punish mercilessly the unfaithful who did not believe us. . . . The Mahdi will not die, bullets do not work on him, to fire a weapon on him is pointless. You can not kill us, there are seventy thousand people behind us. Throw me in the fire; just like Prophet Abraham, you will see that I will not be set alight and I will not burn in the fire. Whatever happens tonight, the apocalypse will break. Kıtmîr [Ashâb-ı Kehf's, Seven Sleepers dog] will save us.[431]

Öz notes that this claimed extraordinariness is not commensurate with Sunni belief related to mahdi description and points out that it is rather a tradition that can be found among Bektashis and the belief in The Twelfth Imam. Öz concludes that there is no reliable evidence connecting any of the perpetrators of this incident and the ageing sheikh in Istanbul.[432] Even *Cumhuriyet* originally claimed that Derviş Mehmet was inspired and received strength from Keçeci Süleyman of Manisa. Derviş Mehmet is also described as an old sheikh with disciples of his own; no mention of the ageing Sheikh Esad in Istanbul.[433] It was beneficial for the regime to connect Derviş Mehmet to the Nakshibendi sheikh, even if the link was tenuous.

The one inescapable conclusion is that Derviş Mehmet was not a stable person, with obvious adjustment issues. Derviş Mehmet, like many of the residents of Menemen, was originally from Greece and were exchanged in 1924 with Greeks residing in Anatolia. As Eyüp Öz points out these émigrés who gathered and applauded Dervish Mehmet had problems with expressing themselves in Turkish, as their first language was Greek. Coupled with economic difficulties they faced, they felt that the regime was against

429. *Ibid.*, pp.412 and 414.
430. 'The Menemen Affairs in Turkey', *The Times*, 30 December 1930, p. 9.
431. Eyüp Öz, *op. cit.*, pp. 416 and 419.
432. *Ibid.*, pp. 419-21.
433. 'Dirilen ve boğulan irtica', *op. cit.*, p. 1.

them. Many became members of the Nakshibendi order as they felt the order represented their interests.

Islamist historians constructed a different narrative, blaming the state for orchestrating these events and to use it as a pretext to murder the most prominent Nakshibendi sheikh, Esad.[434] Kısakürek, himself an influential Nakshibendi - important to remember - was amongst them. In an article, entitled *Tertip* (The Scheme) (1969), he expressed his thoughts thus: "The Menemen Incident was organised by the government to annihilate all honourable Muslims, especially the elders of the Nakshibendi order. It constitutes the most unscrupulous *tertip*."[435] This theme was taken up by other Islamists historians:

> Later descriptions of the incident by Müftüoğlu, Ceylan, Bursalı and İslamoğlu were duplications of his narrative. These writers questioned the glorification of Kubilay as a heroic martyr, but they appropriated the same theme of victimhood, though with a different content. Instead of Kubilay, they portrayed the Naqshbandiyya Order in general, and specifically Sheikh Es'ad . . . as the 'real victim' of the event.[436]

In effect, the accusation is that this was a "false flag" operation. While there are such documented operations in the history of the Republic,[437] it is doubtful that this is the case on this occasion. What is not in contention, however, is the severity of which the regime responded and using the incident *ex post facto* to liquidate the order which still operated in some fashion despite the prohibition. Sheikh Esad and his son were arrested in Istanbul and were transferred to Izmir. The Sheikh was still in his traditional attire:[438]

Mustafa Kemal's initial reaction was to declare Menemen *ville modite*, a motif borrowed from the French Revolution: "This is severing the Republic and our heads. The entire Menemen is responsible". In January 1931, the Ministerial Council established a Court Martial. Its president, General Mustafa Muğlalı, echoed this mentality of mass punishment: "Logic dictates that we should not burn an entire mattress because of one flea. Nevertheless, for this anti-Republican incident, I do not hesitate to demolish

434. M. Hakan Yavuz, *Islamic Political Identity in Turkey*, Oxford, 2003, p. 140.
435. Eyüp Öz, *op. cit.*, p. 434.
436. Azak, *op. cit.*, p. 144.
437. For instance, the bombing of Mustafa Kemal's house in Salonica to instigate the 1955 Pogrom; see Donef, '6-7 Eylül olayları 50 yıl sonra', [The 6-7 September incidents 50 years on], *Nsibin*, Stockholm, 2006.
438. 'Mevkûflar dün sabah İzmir'e sevkedildiler', [The arrested were transferred to Izmir yesterday morning], *Cumhuriyet*, 3 January 1931.

Image 3: Nakshibendi Sheikh Esad[439]

the entire Menemen, the value of which is less than a flea." Cooler heads such as that of the Prime Minister, İsmet İnönü, prevailed and Menemen was not destroyed.[440] İnönü insisted that measures were to be taken only against the principal instigators of the "reactionary movement" and not all tarikats.[441] We can infer from this statement that the government was aware that the tarikats were still operating.

Martial Law was declared in Menemen and in the ensuing investigation cast a very wide net. Even a Jewish resident of Menemen, Josef Hayim, was arrested, accused of applauding the Mahdi. Twenty-eight people held responsible for the incident were executed.[442] It was not about justice; it was about show of force. This gruesome episode in 1930 came to dominate the Kemalist narrative against the *gerici* for a long time to come. It served as a focal point in the ideological battle against the forces that opposed Kemalist projects.

Whither tarikats? Tarikats post prohibition

Many tarikats went underground and continued their activities clandestinely until the political environment allowed them to operate openly

439. 'Mevkûflar dün sabah İzmir'e sevkedildiler', *Cumhuriyet*, 3 January 1931.
440. All citations in the paragraph by Eyüp Öz, pp. 419-20.
441. 'Le movement reáctionnaire en Turquie', *Le Populaire*, 31 December 1930, p. 3.
442. Küçük, *op. cit.*, pp. 153-54.

again. There is a gap of information as to the immediate aftermath of the closure of the tarikats. Hülya Küçük contends that any studies of that period

> are generally fragmentary and lack detail. Additionally it can be sometimes dangerous for scholars to write about the era, and Sufis themselves were uncomfortable discussing or recording their memories of that time. Consequently, how Sufis reacted to the events of the era is not easy to depict.[443]

In general, Küçük finds there were both "progressive" and "reactionary" Sufis, in contrast to the regime's rhetoric in 1925 that all tarikats were "snakes" (*yılan*). Küçük classified well-known Sufi sheiks as to their attitude for or against the new regime. Their reaction varied; some opposed it silently, others openly. Many just accepted the new reality:

> Because Sufism is based on an intimate and personal contact with God, and because the secularism presented in that period stressed the necessity of practising Islam privately, there seemed to be no conflict. Thus Sufis, who were not interested or involved in political activities, had no problems with the abolition of the caliphate and the Ministry of the Shar'iyya wa Awkaf, or banning the Sufi orders etc. Many were even ready to be used as a medium of legitimizing these reforms. However, their costumes, culture, tradition and cosmology would not be helpful to the modernization process. Therefore they were not selected as a legitimizing medium.[444]

In Küçük's classification, which still reflects the Kemalist nomenclature, Said Nursî is listed among those that opposed the changes. The list also includes some Nakshibendi and Süleymancı sheikhs, as well as the Ticani order, which smashed Atatürk statues and staged a protest in the Parliament in 1949. Mevlevi and Bektashi sheiks predominantly accepted the new status quo and some notable Bektashis moved to Albania.[445] Subsequently, neither the Bektashi nor the Mevlevi caused any significant problems to the regime. Although they were capable of militancy as demonstrated during the First World War and Liberation War, they were not motivated to oppose the regime.

---

443. Hülya Küçük, "Sufi Reactions Against the Reforms After Turkey's National Struggle" in Atabaki, Touraj. (Ed.). *The State and the Subaltern*: Modernization, Society and the State in Turkey and Iran, London, 2007, p. 124.
444. Küçük, p. 126.
445. *Ibid.*, 127.

The Republic and the Nakshibendi

The Nakshibendi proved to be troublesome and recalcitrant. In 1936, the daily *Cumhuriyet*, which supported the official Republican regime's point of view, described a group of former Nakshibendi members as bigots (*yobaz*), arrested for secretly carrying out such activities as "Dervishism, soothsaying, charm writing, witchery". *Cumhuriyet* continued to equate tarikats with "superstition", magic and folk-exploiting activities. [446] Another daily *Milliyet* followed suit. [447] These newspapers continually reinforced the idea that tarikats were not compatible with modern Turkey.

According to Hakan Yavuz,

[T]he Kemalist establishment always has been particularly fearful of the Nakşibendi movement, because the Nakşibendis were able to demonstrate their continuing ability to arouse mass resistance across ethnic and tribal lines in their protests against the radical antireligious programs of the Republican elite from 1925 through 1930. [448]

Yavuz contends that 18 rebellions took place between 1924 and 1938, most of which "were led by the Nakşibendi orders". [449] Yavuz who, in general, is sceptical of Kemalist claims, surprisingly relies on Reşat Hallı as the sole source of this information. This research, published by the General Staff (*Genel Kurmay*) in 1972, exaggerated the number and nature of these "rebellions". The original publication of 1972 by Colonel Hallı, entitled *Türkiye Cumhuriyeti'nde Ayaklanmalar* [450] (*Rebellions in the Republic of Turkey*), was reprinted as *Genelkurmay Belgelerinde Kürt İsyanları* (*Kurdish Rebellions in the Documents of the General Staff*) [451] in 1992, presumably to suit a different purpose than the original publication.

The first "rebellion" listed in this publication is the so-called "Nestorian uprising" in Hakkâri. The incidents and the army operation resulting in massacres and expulsion of remaining Nestorian Assyrians in Hakkâri have no connection to Nakshibendi whatsoever, and only a tenuous connection to a Kurdish uprising:

446. 'Yakalanan Yobazlar', [Captured bigots], *Cumhuriyet*, 27 January 1936, p. 1.

447. '63 Nakşibendi âyin yaparlarken yakalandı', [The Nakshibendi caught performing religious ceremony], *Milliyet*, 3 July 1951, pp. 1 and 3; 'Ayin yapan tarikatçılar cezalandı', [The tarikat members who performed religious ceremony punished], *Milliyet*, 11 July 1951, p. 2.

448. M. Hakan Yavuz, *Islamic Political Identity in Turkey*, Oxford, 2003. p. 139.

449. *Loc. cit.*

450. Hallı, Reşat. *Türkiye Cumhuriyeti'nde Ayaklanmalar (1924–1938)*, Genel Kurmay Yayınları, Ankara, 1972.

451. *Genelkurmay Belgelerinde Kürt İsyanları 1*, İstanbul, 1992.

It has to be mentioned in passing, that part of the force, which came to attack the Assyrians, including officers, were of Kurdish background. Of those officers, İhsan Nurî with four other Kurdish officers Rasim, Tewfik, Qorsit (Hursit) and Ali Rıza Bey, abandoned their posts and escaped to Iraq. These officers, members of the illegal Kurdish organisation, Āzādī, absconded for the purposes of a Kurdish uprising.[452]

Though it is doubtful that the Nakshibendi staged 18 uprisings (which required military intervention), they were involved in sporadic incidents post-Menemen. On 1 February 1933, in Bursa, a group of people under the leadership of Nakşibendi Kozanlı İbrahim staged a protest against reading the call to prayer in Turkish. In 1935, in Siirt, a person by the name of Halit declared himself a Nakshibendi Sheikh and Mehdi and caused unrest, which was suppressed by government forces. The third incident occurred in 1936 in İskilip. Nakshibendi Kayserili Ahmet Kalaycı invented a new fasting period ranging from 40 to 90 days and asked to be worshipped. All these incidents may be described as Nakshibendi related, as Çetin Özdek argues,[453] acts of political Islam to be sure, but they were hardly of great threat to the regime.

The Republic and Alevis

While the Republicans had a clear and unmistakable animosity towards the tarikats, their attitude towards the Alevis was ambivalent, but still treated them as occupying an outer Islamic space. With the advent of the Republic the view of the state changed in favour of Alevis - however briefly. The new state was reconstructing the past to alter the future; history, religion and identity were to be re-interpreted and re-imagined, including Alevism. Élise Massicard notes that "[w]hen the nationalists focused on the pre-Islamic past and on Anatolian people's culture, they encountered the Alevis and henceforth they equated it [i.e. Alevism] to Turkishness".[454] The historian Fuat Koprülü, the first director of the Türkiyat Enstitüsü within *Darülfünûn*,[455] initiated many studies on Bektashis and Alevis regarding them the same.[456]

Reportedly, in the nineteenth century the missionaries saw the Alevis as either influenced by Christianity or even as Crypto-Christians. Yet, the

---

452. Racho Donef, *The Hakkâri Massacres*, Sydney, 2014, *passim* and p. 29.
453. Çetin Özdek, *Türkiye'de Gerici Akımlar*, İstanbul, 1968, p. 160.
454. Élise Massicard, *Alevi Hareketinin Siyasallasması*, İstanbul, 2007, p. 43.
455. Literally the House of Sciences; i.e. university.
456. Massicard, *op. cit.*, p. 43.

new regime saw them as custodians of pre-Islamic Turkic traditions in that they interpreted their ritual practices as shamanistic. The regime wanted to connect Turkish culture and religion to a "pure" imaginary Turkic past, bypassing Islam and the "polluting" Arabic influences. Shamanism was one useful theoretical springboard. Dressler notes that the study that the ancient Turks of Central Asia were Shamans was originally developed by Russian Turkologists such as Friedrich Wilhelm Radloff (in *Das Schamanenthum und sein Kultus*)[457], in the late nineteenth century and enthusiastically promoted by the Young Turks and later the Republicans.[458]

Alevi manuscripts from the fourteenth to the twentieth centuries preserved by Dede families contain no information to support the study that Shamanism formed the basis of proto-Alevism.[459] Just like in the case of the Turkish History Study the scientific basis of the contention was less relevant than the desire to make a connection, however tenuous. Whether or not there is any truth in the theory,

> the introduction of the term 'shamanism' into the discourse of Turkish nationalism fulfilled two purposes. First, shamanism became a token for the asserted unbroken continuity of elements of Turkish culture from Central Asia to contemporary Anatolian life and played thus a vital role in providing evidence for the narrative of the Turkish nation. . . . the Bektashi and the Kızılbaş groups, which in this time period began to be labelled 'Alevi,' were depicted as Anatolian carriers of remnants of this shamanistic past. This move, second, helped to integrate the Kızılbaş - Alevi into the national domain against claims of their political subversiveness, as well as their alleged relation to non-Turkish elements. However, from an Islamic point of view the connection with shamanism also pointed to the Alevis' alleged 'syncretistic' and 'heterodox' character, further cementing their religious otherness relative to Sunni Islam.[460]

Ayşe Hür notes that there were two streams of official researchers in the early twentieth century, who focused on Alevis. She identifies these two streams as "Ittihadist, Kemalist" and "Turanist, racist Turkist". The first stream, which she calls Ittihadist and Kemalist, dated back to 1915, encompasses efforts to enlist the Bektashis to form a Jihadist Battalion. One such battalion was formed in Dersim, with the participation of Bektashi

---

457. Turkish translation: Wilhelm Radloff, *Türklük ve Şamanlık*, Istanbul, 2008.
458. Dressler, *Writing Religion*, p. 206.
459. See Ayfer Karakaya-Stump, 'Documents and Buyruk Manuscripts in the Private Archives of Alevi Dede Families, *British Journal of Middle Eastern Studies*, Vol. 37, No. 3., December 2010.
460. *Ibid.*, p. 209.

Turcomans, but Kızılbaş Kurds showed no interest. The İttihadist asked the help of the Çelebi of the Hacı Bektaş Dergâh (i.e. Dervish Lodge), Ahmed Celaleddin Efendi, to form the battalion. Hür notes that Ahmed Celaleddin Efendi lost some prestige because the battalion was formed on the basis of Sunni Jihadist ideology,[461] which was presumably antithetical to Kızılbaş Kurdish beliefs.

At the same time, under the leadership of Gökalp researchers were sent to study the "Kızılbaş, Mevlevi, Bektaşi, Alevi and Nusayrî" and Gökalp himself was carrying out sociological research on Arab, Turcoman and Kurdish tribes. Another researcher, Baha Sait Bey, produced many texts from his work between 1914 and 1915, but it was not possible to publish them uncensored at that time, because the Palace (Sultan Mehmed Reşat V. and the Şeyhülislam) regarded this project of Ittihat's as "Kızılbaş propaganda". Baha Said Bey's writing suggested that Alevism, Kızılbaşism and Bektashism were original Turkish beliefs and that they were a mixture of shamanism and Islam.[462]

This ethno-political project continued when Mustafa Kemal seized power. Hasan Reşit (Tankut) was sent to the Dersim region by Mustafa Kemal as the Coordinator of the Eastern Provinces Public Order and the Turkish Hearths. In one of his reports, he divided the Kurdish area into the Zaza-Kızılbaş in the North, Alevi-Kızılbaş Kurmancı in the West and Shafi Kırmancı in the East, and proposed to establish a Turkish buffer zone between them to separate them from each other,[463] thereby breaking any social cohesion between those groups.

The second stream of researchers of Turanian ideology concentrated on proving that Turks were Shamanists originally and that the Alevists were Shamanist. The conclusion was to be drawn that the Alevis were pure Turks.[464] This was an attempt to incorporate the Alevis to the polity as orthodox, by defining shamanism as authentic (i.e. orthodox). The term orthodox was not used but it was an attempt of orthodoxification of Alevis as authentic Turks. Goldenberg's theory of religion as vestigial state is helpful here: shamanistic practice as pre-Islamic seem un-state-like and therefore not threatening to a state trying to assert its own unassailable status. Of course, wandering dervishes can also be described as unthreatening to the

461. Ayşe Hür, İttihatçı ve Kemalistlerin Alevi-Bektaşi politikaları, [İttihadist' and Kemalists' Alevi-Bektaşi policies], *Radikal*, 30 June 2013.
462. *Loc.cit.*
463. *Loc.cit.*
464. Ayşe Hür, '72 milletle barışık' Alevi – Kızılbaşlar, [Alevi – Kızılbashs in peace with 72 nations], *Radikal*, 25 May 2014.

state, but as we saw the Kemalist/Republican regime had an ideological aversion to it.

However, while this approach was adopted in one strand, in the other the Sunni version was adopted as the right form of worship. This apparent contradiction eventually gave way to the same approach the Ottomans adopted of treating the Alevis as the other. Despite this historical reality of marginalisation even by the new regime, the Alevis have been supporters of the Republican Party and Mustafa Kemal.

The process of remaking an Alevi consciousness did not extend to the point of being recognised by Diyanet, which did not employ Alevi religious leaders, dedes, or fund *cemevis*. Nevertheless, the Alevis were left alone to practise their rituals in their private space. This was acceptable by both the secularist regime and the Alevis, at that point. In a way, to have incorporated Alevism would have meant to expunge Alevism under the suffocation of state control.

The Republic and the Kurds

Via a separate process, there was an attempt to shape Kurdish identity; the Kurds were called "mountain Turks".[465] The state wanted to create a country with citizens adhering to one type of identity: Sunni Turkish. The Christian minorities were largely disposed of during the First World War, the Independence War and Population Exchange with Greece. There remained too few Christians to be of any threat but there were substantial number of Kurds (Sunni and Alevi) and Turkish Alevis, who did not fit into the ideal identity. The Alevis were already declared to be Shamanist and therefore pure Turks but this construct was more appropriate for the Turkish Alevis. The state was ambivalent about Kurdish Alevis. On the one hand they were Turks on two accounts (mountain Turks and Shamanist), on the other they were not Turks at all.

Tanıl Bora summarises this ambivalence: "[e]ven though they are all Kurds, they are Turks" [*Hepsi Kürt olmakla beraber Türktür*].[466] The phrase referring to Dersim Kurds belongs to Tahsin Uzer, the Third Inspector of the General Inspection established to keep an eye on Kurds. Erzurum Deputy Tahsin Uzer occupied this post from 1935 onwards.[467] Hasan Reşit Tankut described the Kurds as "Turks who forgot their language". Bora de-

465. Racho Donef, Identities in the Multicultural State, op. cit., p.95.
466. Tanıl Bora, Türk Milliyetçiliği Söyleminde Dersim, *Tiroj*, Vol. 7, No. 47, December 2010, p. 15.
467. Erdal Aydoğan, 'Üçüncü Umumi Müfettişliğinin Kurulması ve III. Umumî Müfettiş Tahsin Uzer'in Bazı Önemli Faaliyetleri, *Atatürk Yolu Dergisi*, May-November 2004, p. 1.

scribes this logic as "Okay. They are Turks, but they are Kurds, they are Kurds, but they are Turks". [468] These ideologues tried to reconcile competing and conflicting ideas to fit different and divergent purposes the primary focus being the homogenisation of the Muslim population of Turkey to Sunni Turkish form.

Conclusion

Kemalists did not tolerate what was deemed to be outside of what they designated as the core. Furthermore, modernisation required removal of reminders of the immediate past and the tarikats with their rituals and practices and dress code seemed very distant to the Republican vision. The closure of tarikats represented a radical step and demonstrated the willingness of the regime to break-away from traditional norms and eliminate the old guard of Islamic institutions. Removal of the tarikats also served the purpose of de-Ottomanisation, which the Turkish History Study facilitated.

The Menemen Incident, with its many layers and antagonistic narratives, showed the incompatibility and interpretation of different visions post-Republic. Muslims, Kemalists and non-Kemalist secular scholars interpreted the events from different vantage points, which still inform the intellectual environment in the continuing debate about Islam and the state. The Menemen Incident, as the narrative of fanatics versus the enlightened, rational state, endured in the minds of staunch Kemalists/secularists.

What the chapter has shown is that despite the radical ideas to transform the Turkish society, the ideal was not to build a pluralistic, democratic society, free of prejudices against minorities (Muslim or non-Muslim); a society in which expressions of different cultural identities are welcomed. Instead, a brutal regime without respect for local cultural traditions, tried to impose an ideological form of identity removing any "polluting" elements. In the process, even as avid positivists, hostile to "religion", they embarked upon building a predominantly Sunni Turkish society, in which those who wanted to practice a different version of Islam were either prohibited from doing so or discouraged – except briefly for the Alevis in the early years of the Republic.

Kemalists sought to homogenise the country into a Sunni Muslim Turkish identity, devoid of Arabic, Persian, Ottoman, Sufi and Alevi influences. Sunni Islam was to be de-Arabised, Turkified, to serve the pur-

---

468. Bora, *op. cit.*, p. 15.

pose of constituting one of the core elements of Turkish identity. The clean sweep served another purpose; it was another step in the formation of Kemalist hegemony. Nationalism played a significant role in this process.

Their approach to "religion" was to view it as a potential threat to the actual state and to take measures to reduce this potential threat. What they could not homogenise, marginalise or eradicate, they pushed it outside the state sanctioned space. The secularisation process they undertook as part of their three-pronged approach was in the form of reducing the visibility of Islam in the public sphere and emancipation from Islamic institutions and norms.

Mustafa Kemal Atatürk died on 10 November 1938, leaving behind a remarkable edifice he constructed. Kemalists were to maintain this legacy and extend his project. The system he left as his legacy can only be described as hegemonic. Though his presence was kept up through a myriad of statues, pictures and his name on boulevards, institutions *etc*, his departure left a void. Cracks already appeared on the edifice he had built; it was likely that these cracks would widen and his vision dilute.

CHAPTER 5:
THE REPUBLIC POST-KEMAL: POLITICS AND RESISTANCE

The two preceding chapters focused on Kemal and Kemalism. In these chapters I argued that the interrelatedness of religion and politics was evident in the first period of the rule of the Republicans, before the Republic was formally declared. After Kemal and Kemalism prevailed the public discourse adopted was in favour of separating the two fields, though as it has been shown this was not consistently observed, with many contradictions noted.

These contradictions were analysed in terms of the incompatibility of many divergent aims, arguing that even though separation of religion and politics was sought through laicism, in fact the state interfered in religious affairs, nullifying the effect of laicism. The persecution of tarikats constituted interference in religious institutions. The Republicans sought to remove Islam from the public sphere, while at the same time sought to elevate Sunni Islam as a constituent element of Turkish national identity. In their endeavour to cement this identity, they employed Diyanet and the mosque network. These contradictions can be explained in terms of Goldenberg's study of vestigial states. Some vestigial states were useful to control (mosque network), used for purposes of identity building and to keep them in check to prevent them from becoming a future state. Other vestigial states, with grass roots organisation that is difficult to control or an esoteric philosophy that cannot be converted to an ideology the state may exploit, were dangerous to the actual state. While one vestigial state was kept in close proximity, other vestigial states were singled out for elimination.

In this chapter I argue that while Kemalism remained an overarching ideology of the state, the emergence of political Islam disturbed the order. The mutual relation between religion and politics will be discussed in light of the emergence of political Islam as an opposition to Republicans. While in the preceding period, the state ostensibly eliminated one form of vestigial state (*tarikats*), this form in fact morphed into a *cemaat* and still behaved as a future state. Kemalists could not eradicate Islamic opposition; *they simply stalled its advent.*

Two key areas are examined in this chapter: the test of secularist ideology and Kemalism in a multi-party environment and Islamic opposition by two key intellectuals: Kısakürek and Nursi. In the Kemalist version of history both Kısakürek and Nursî are presented in a negative light, as expected. Western scholars, on the other hand, have been less critical of Nursî, and often an admiring tone can be detected in many such studies, overlooking any infirmities. Kısakürek has not drawn the same attention in the West as Nursî, as the latter's influence as a cemaat leader overshadowed the former. Sources on Kısakürek are mainly studies by Turkish scholars.

The approach taken in this chapter is to be critical of both the Kemalists and the Islamists, with the main focus being their approach to secularisation and modernisation, areas that pre-occupied both poles. While it has been pointed out that laicism was a doomed project, laicism/secularism was fiercely defended in government and the CHP discourse. Proceedings of the 1947 CHP Congress during which members of the party discussed laicism/secularism at length, along with the DP party program, Nursî's writings and Kısakürek's journal (*Büyük Doğu*) were used as primary sources for this chapter. The congress proceedings show the extent of ideological variation within the party, hard-core secularists and those who wanted to relax the regime's control of Islam.

While the political context of the CHP-DP squabble dominated the post-war years, the initial position of these two Kemalist parties on the issue of laicism/secularism did not much differ, but the DP varied its policy as a ruling party. In government it sought support from Islamists such as Nursî and Kısakürek. The connection between "politics" and "religion" is demonstrated by the review of the parliamentary political context as well as Islamist writing and action.

5.1 Politics post-Kemal

By the time of Mustafa Kemal Atatürk's death, the system of chieftaincy and his hegemonic rule were well established. He was named the "Eternal Leader" (*Ebedî Şef*). When the Eternal Leader died, İsmet İnönü succeeded him. On 26 December 1938, a CHP Congress convened and elected İnönü Permanent Leader (*Değişmez Başkan*) of the Party, and National Chief (*Milli Şef*). Cemil Koçak notes that this title was influenced by the European "chief system", prevalent in some European states at the time (Hitler – Führer, Mussolini – Il Duce, Franco – Caudillo). Koçak adds that the main reason for the designation was to boost İnönü's authority. There was an enormous power vacuum created by the death of Atatürk, and it needed to be filled quickly. The title of *Milli Şef* for İnönü was already used by the newspapers earlier; officially it was bestowed upon him by the congress.[469] The hegemonic system required a leader with exaggerated titles.

İnönü was entirely of a different character from Mustafa Kemal, and did not approve the latter's predilection for discussing and running state affairs at tables, drinking *rakı*. İnönü and Mustafa Kemal co-operated for a long time, both in the National Struggle (*Milli Mücadele*) and Republican politics; yet, disagreements in 1937 led İnönü to resign and retire.[470] Even though continuing to be deputy for Malatya, he was rarely seen in public post-resignation.[471] It appears that Mustafa Kemal favoured him as successor, despite the altercation.

Certainly, İnönü did not have Mustafa Kemal's charisma or boldness; he was a cautious person and had overcome the "handicap" of being a Kurd among Turkish nationalists. When Mustafa Kemal appointed him as the head of the delegation to the Lausanne Conference in 1923, Dr Rıza Nur complained: "İsmet is Kurdish; moreover a pure Kurdish! We threw out Rauf [Orbay] as head of delegation because he is Abkhaz. We brought a pure Kurd, what a pity!"[472] At the Lausanne Conference, İnönü's prefacing his speeches as "we the Turks and Kurds" enraged the Second Delegate Rıza Nur, who was, according to Ayşe Hür, "from the racist-Turkist wing of the Parliament".[473] In his memoirs, Dr Nur complained about Orbay and İnönü: "Isn't there a Turk to look after Turkish affairs?"[474]

The death of Mustafa Kemal Atatürk marked the end of an era, but not the end of Kemalism. Kemalist ideology was already the official ideology of his party, CHP. In the 1935 CHP Party Program, it is stated that the Party's principles are the principle of Kemalism.[475] The ideology took shape in the following years and became the guiding principle of the state and civil society to a larger extent.

As noted in Chapter 2.4, Kemalism was not a cohesive ideology and different versions of it co-existed. Kemalism therefore is an ideology which is sufficiently elastic to be adapted to divergent ideological precepts and

469. Cemil Koçak, "Siyasal Tarih (1923 – 1950)" in Mete Tuncay et al. Çağdaş Türkiye 1908-1980, İstanbul, 1989, p. 124.
470. 'İsmet İnönü dün istifasını verdi', [İsmet İnönü submitted his resignation yesterday], *Kurun*, 26 October 1937, p. 1.
471. Koçak, *op. cit.*, p. 118.
472. Ayşe Hür, 'Musul'u neden ve kaça sattık?' [Why and for how much did we sell Mosul?], *Radikal*, 15 June 2014.
473. *Loc. cit.*
474. *Dr Rıza Nur'un Lozan Hatıraları*, İstanbul, 1992, p. 23.
475. *C.H.P. Programı*, Ankara, 1935.

Mustafa Kemal's potent symbol. It was the obligation of the CHP to safeguard Kemalism and Kemal's ideals, a role that the party still professes to cherish. In its 7th Congress, the CHP reiterated their commitment to Kemalism in the introduction to the party program: "The main principles of the Party in this program are the expression of the 'Kemalist' path to which we always remained loyal".[476]

One of the early projects of the CHP was the building of an appropriate mausoleum for Mustafa Kemal Atatürk. His final resting place, *Anıtkabir*, took 15 years to complete and was built in a way that it cannot be regarded as Islamic. The symbolism of *Anıtkabir* cannot be overstated:

> Even though Anıtkabir is a burial site, which is a sacred location that would customarily be under the jurisdiction and authority of Islam, there are no religious inscriptions or any sign of Islam on any part of the monument. The only place that makes a reference to Islam is the burial chamber where Atatürk's body rests, which is oriented toward the qibla, the holy direction toward which prayers are oriented in Islam. However, this chamber is underground, below the symbolic sarcophagus, a pre-Islamic, ancient Greek-Anatolian form of burial, before which visitors pay homage to Atatürk and the nation, and official ceremonies are held. . . . In other words, the only reference made to Islam in the mausoleum is buried underground, is hidden from and inaccessible to regular visitors and the public at large. Therefore, the mausoleum stands as an articulation of the triumph of the secularist ideology of the state over its Ottoman-Islamic contender. . . .[477]

Racism as government policy

Soon after Mustafa Kemal's death, the Second World War was in progress. It is said that Turkey remained neutral and İnönü is often credited with avoiding embroilment in the war. Researcher Sait Çetinoğlu argued, it would be more accurate to say that Turkey did not participate in the war but was not neutral; her sympathies lay with Nazi Germany.[478] On 18 June 1941, a friendship treaty was signed between Turkey and Germany, for a period of 10 years. The two countries were to avoid any direct or indirect confrontation against each other.[479] The Parliament approved the treaty on

---

476. C.H.P., *Yedinci Büyük Kurultayı*, 18 November 1947, p. 49.
477. Çınar, *op. cit.*, p. 109.
478. Ali Sait Çetinoğlu, *Varlık Vergisi 1942-1944*, İstanbul, 2009, p. 45.
479. 'Türk Alman Dostluk Paktı İmzalandı' [Turkish German Friendship Treaty Signed-off], *Cumhuriyet*, 19 June 1941, p. 1.

25 June 1941. The newspaper *Vakit* announced the news and praised the Prime Minister Refik Saydam for his achievement, and, inexplicably, also announced: "we are loyal to the English Ally." At the same time, the foreign affairs minister Hasan Safyettin Menemencioğlu praised Hitler: "with the talk in the Reichstag, Hitler sparked the hearts of the Turkish nation and Turkish children".[480] This cheerfully announced connection between Hitler and Turkish children is very obscure, to say the least.

The interwar governments were certainly influenced by ideas emanating from Germany. Two incidents occurred during the war which were contrary to one of the principles of laicism that the state should keep equal distance from all "religions". In these two incidents, Christian minorities (Greeks and Armenians primarily) and the Jews were targeted. The first such incident was in 1941, the conscription of all non-Muslim males born between 1889 and 1913 (*Yirmi Kur'a Nafıa Askerleri*/Twenty Classes Public Works Soldiers). Though the conscription was meant to apply to those aged between 24 and 39, in reality the age gap ranged from 20 to 60.[481]

It was a secret decision made by the ministerial council and was immediately put into practice from 1 May 1941, by checking identity cards to identify non-Muslims: mainly Greeks, Armenians and Jews. Even though this was a military conscription, in practice, the interned non-Muslims were not provided arms or even military uniforms. They were given uniforms, which Greece sent to Turkey in 1939, as assistance after the earthquake in that year. These uniforms were designed for refuse collectors.[482] The conscripted lived-in internment camps and mainly worked in infrastructure projects breaking rocks and building roads. Though many internees believed they were to be executed, eventually they were allowed to return to their homes in July 1942.[483]

Once the dust settled on the conscription of non-Muslims, the government instituted the Wealth Tax (*Varlık Vergisi*) in December 1942. Ayhan Aktar argues that the Wealth Tax was as a result of the Turkification process established by Kemalists from the beginning of the one-party rule. Their view of "us and them" depicted ethnic Turks as "us" and non-Muslim minorities as the "other". The Muslim groups that lived in Anatolia (Kurds, Lazes, Circassians and others) were deemed to be ethnically Turkish, while

---

480. *Vakit*, 26 June 1941.
481. Rıfat N. Bali, *Yirmi Kur'a Nafıa Askerleri*, İstanbul, 2008, p. 45.
482. Çetinoğlu, *Varlık Vergisi 1942-1944*, p. 57.
483. The Assyrians living in Mardin have also been affected by these two government campaigns against non-Muslim minorities; see Jan Beth-Şawoce and Abdulmesih Bar Abraham, "Cumhuriyet Tarihi Boyunca Doğu ve Batı Asurlara Karşı Baskı, Zulüm, Asimile, Kovulma" in Başkaya and Çetinoğlu, *op. cit.*, pp. 229-235.

the non-Muslim groups who, for a variety of reasons could not be Turkified, designated as minorities and even "foreigners". Greeks, Armenians
and Jews dominated commerce. The Tax aimed to break the dominance of
those who could never be regarded as Turks.[484]

Although it was promoted as a tax imposed on the wealthy, it was an
"arbitrary tax", as described by one of its architects, Faik Ökte.[485] The tax
was imposed on the bases of religion and ethnicity with the following per-
centages:[486]

Ethnicity / Religion	Tax to capital ratio
Armenian merchants	232%
Jewish merchants	179%
Greek merchants	156%
Muslim-Turkish merchants	4.94%

Table 1

In the tabulated lists, those who were burdened to pay the tax were
designated as:

G for Gayri-Muslim	Non-Muslim
M for Müslüman	Muslim
E for *Ecnebi*	Foreigner
D for *Dönme*[487]	Crypto-Jew

Table 2

The tone for the treatment of non-Christian minorities in the Republic
was set on 16 March 1923, when Mustafa Kemal, in a speech in Adana,
said that Armenians and others did not have a place in Turkey.[487] What
was striking in this instance was the treatment of *Dönmes*, converts from
Judaism to Islam in the seventeenth century:

> Let us look at the issue of 'Dönme'. They were designated as 'D' in the
> tabulated lists. Why were the Sabbetaists, who converted to Islam three
> hundred years prior, registered as 'D', rather than 'G', in the records?
> There are two issues here: the first, how did the state know who was
> a 'Dönme'? It was easy to identify Greeks, Armenians and Jews, since

484. Ayhan Aktar, *Varlık Vergisi ve 'Türkleştirme' Politikaları*, İstanbul, 2000, p. 136.
485. Faik Ökte, *Varlık Vergisi Faciası*, İstanbul, 1951, *passim*.
486. Çetinoğlu, Varlık Vergisi 1942-1944, 129.
487. Ayşe Hür, 'Cumhuriyetin "azınlık raporu"', *Kızılbaş*, March 2012, p. 52.

their religion was recorded in identity registries. The Dönme bore Turkish names and they were supposed to be recorded as Muslims. . . . How they identified the Dönme was one issue, but why they differentiated them was more important. The state did not recognise as Turkish a community which bore Turkish names, appearing to be Muslim for three hundred years ([though] it is certain that they practised a different religion at home). . . . I believe the government of the day saw Turkishness as a matter of origin. You were either Turkish by birth or not at all; changing names, becoming Muslim was not sufficient.[488]

This was an example of weak laicism. The state which professed to eliminate religion from the public place and treat its citizens equally, did the opposite, and meted out differential treatment to its citizens, based on designated religion. Elimination of "religion" from the public space, did not mean elimination of religious prejudices. It has to be also pointed out that the *Dönme* were secularists and practised their rituals in private, i.e. in domestic settings, not in a readily identified public temple, such as a mosque. The mosque was deemed private in the ideology of the state, but the state provided for the mosques financially, it oversaw appointments, supervised staff and provided guidelines and sermons.

Ostensibly, a laic state would have wanted its citizens not to practise religion in the public space, i.e. outside a temple. Yet, nationalist ideas overtook laic principles and the *Dönme* were punished along with other minorities simply because their ancestors were Jewish. Those who could not pay the heavy tax were interred in labour camps and formed labour battalions (*amele taburları*), to carry out the same sort of work the non-Muslim internees carried out just a few short months prior.

Multi-party democracy and reversal of certain reforms

After the war, the CHP ended the one–party system, though it rushed to launch the elections in 1946, when opposition was only just forming. The 1946 elections are widely known as the fraudulent elections. This guaranteed four more years in government before finally the multi-party system produced a change of government in 1950.

In power until 1950, the CHP continued the stated policy of laicity but also made some concessions. Between 1935 and 1950, 800 mosques and *mescits* [*masjids*] were closed down; some because of lack of congregations,

---

488. Raço Donef, "Sunuş" [Presentation] in Çetinoğlu, pp. 7-8.

others due to their use during the war as either barracks or depots.[489] At the same time, the regime was unwilling to train clerics, which resulted in some villages lacking clerics to conduct funerals. This situation led to the training of clerics underground.[490] While the Republican elites pushed for the westernisation, modernisation, and secularisation projects, there was significant reluctance by the subaltern to adapt to the requirements of these projects. Sensing that the hard laic policies would eventually lead to their electoral demise, the CHP showed some flexibility eventually. In the meantime, in 1940, it allowed the appointments of Imam Chaplains in the Army.[491]

In 1946, the CHP allowed private classes (in *dersanes*) on religion, but under the watchful eye of the Ministry of Education. It was also specified that the classes were to run in Turkish only (i.e. not in Arabic).[492] The issue of training of clerics was still outstanding and the CHP was dragging its feet in respect of this, as well as the teaching of religion classes in public schools. The struggle between professed ideology and practical problems on the ground dictated the necessity of a compromise. A 17-member *ad hoc* Commission discussed the issue in 1948, but there were disagreements.[493] The CHP Party Group decided to allow for classes but in a way that would not contradict the principles of laicism and *çağdaşlık* (contemporariness, modernity).[494]

Eventually, on 30 August 1948, CHP decided to introduce religion classes as an optional subject for Muslim children only, in the fourth and fifth grades of primary schools.[495] This was subject to textbooks being prepared and the school year was to start in September; it was at least one more year before these classes were introduced. On 3 January 1949, a CHP deputy representing the province of Van, İbrahim Arvas, criticised the government in the Parliament for delaying tactics.[496] There was thus some

489. Ömer Akdağ, Çok Partili Dönemin Başlarında CHP'nin Laiklik Politikası, Konya, 2012, p. 67.
490. Akdağ, op. cit., p. 68.
491. Ibid., p. 93.
492. 'Din öğretimi serbes' [Religious education free], Akşam, 3 July 1947, p. 1; 'Yurdda din öğretiminin serbes olması kararlaştı', [It was decided to free religious education in the country], Cumhuriyet, 3 July 1947.
493. 'Dinî tedrisat meselesi hakkında tartışmalar', [Discussions regarding the issue of religious teaching], Cumhuriyet, 18 February 1948.
494. 'B. Hilmi Uran İstanbulda', [B. Hilmi in Istanbul], Ulus, 13 February 1948, p. 1.
495. 'Din tedrisatı yeni ders yılında başlayacak', [Religious instruction to start in the new school season], Akşam, 31 August 1948; Turkish primary school at the time consisted of five-year compulsory education.
496. 'Din öğretimi yüzünden Mecliste çıkan tartışmalar', [Disputes in the Parliament because of religious instruction], Cumhuriyet, 4 January 1949.

reluctance to expand religious education. The generation that established the Republic was still in power and some of the more radical elements were still present in its ranks.

This contradictory attitude can also be observed in the approach regarding religious publications. Between 1939 and 1945, 104 such publications were allowed.[497] Publications of a religious nature were carefully studied before permission. When the books were not commensurate with either the Religious Directorate's or the government's views, they were prohibited. For instance, in 1943, *İslam Muhtırası* (Islamic Memorandum), was deemed to be a work of propaganda, rather than a study of religion and it was prohibited. Moreover, in 1944, *Namaz Surelerinin ve Fatiha Şerifin Manası* (The Salah Suras and the Meaning of al-Fatihah Sura), was deemed to be influenced by Shia propaganda and also erroneous in the interpretation of the Quran.[498]

The self-designated laic state was therefore involved in interpreting Islam and blocking other interpretations such as those of so-called heterodox sects. Nevertheless, Ömer Akdağ notes that the CHP and Diyanet did not necessarily see eye to eye on all matters Islamic. For instance, in 1950, before the general elections, CHP headquarters sent a circular to party branches instructing them to be close to Alevis.[499]

After 1946 a multitude of parties was formed, many using religious expressions in party programs. The eventual winner of the first multi-party election in 1950, the Democrat Party (*Demokrat Partisi*/DP), was not one of them. Clause 14 of the general principles of DP's party program referred to laicism as follows:

> Our party understands laicism as the state not having a connection with religion and no religious thought influencing the regulation and enforcements of laws. It recognises religious freedom as other freedoms, one of humanity's holy rights.[500]

Clause 14 also set the principle that religion is not to be used in politics. When in power, Adnan Menderes, one of the DP party founders, violated this principle, but back in 1946, as former CHP deputy, he pledged to support the *status quo* on the cleavage of religion and politics. The principle espoused in Clause 14 seemed to contradict laicism as envisaged and practised by the CHP and the state. CHP's laicism was about control over religion, while the DP suggested disengagement. In the 1947 CHP Congress it

497. Akdağ, *op. cit.*, p. 94.
498. *Ibid.*, pp. 76-77.
499. *Ibid.*, p. 78.
500. *Demokrat Parti Programı*, 1946.

was stated that "our party separates state and political matters. As religion is a matter of conscience, it has been protected from all kinds of attacks".[501]

By 1947, the CHP could no longer ignore pressures for religious reforms, both from within the party and without. Akdağ notes that there were demands from the community related to religious matters, such as the teaching of religion in schools and training of imams and hatips. CHP had taken some steps to address some of these concerns, but overall it treated such demands as reflections of "medieval mentality" and was reluctant to allow for a debate.[502] On 24 December 1946, Tanrıöver and Muhittin Baha Pars insisted on religious education as an enforcer of morality and a shield against communism. Menderes, who by then had established the DP, supported the proposal. However, the government of the day, under Prime Minister Recep Peker's leadership "did not agree to open the gates to religious propaganda".[503]

The CHP Congress of 1947 was the forum at which these matters were debated by the members of the parliamentary group. During the Congress, Sinan Tekelioğlu, deputy for Seyhan, was one of the first to be very critical of the situation regarding the lack of clerics. Tekelioğlu argued that the Christians and Jews were in a better position than the Muslims, as they were able to train their priests and rabbis and asked that Diyanet be allowed to open schools to train clerics: let them train for us "modern" and "civilised" clerics (asrî and medenî). His choice of words suggests that he was very careful in using a language that most CHP deputies would approve ("politically correct", so to speak). But it was his claim that clerics were "hungry and miserable" that attracted ridicule by his colleagues. Some deputies interjected with cries of "Allah, Allah", expressing their anger. Tekelioğlu tersely responded "no point in saying Allah, Allah".

Tekelioğlu also alluded to moral decay in Turkish society due to lack of religious education and alleged absence of religion in public life: "rather than holding iftar[504] tables, we accept as novelty drinking sessions at the tables, men and women playing bridge and poker till the early hours of the morning".[505] Perceived moral decay was a favoured concern of Islamists and evidently of some Republicans.

Tanrıöver, deputy for Istanbul, in his long speech argued that laicism among Turks was not new, in that, in their long history they implemented

---

501. *C.H.P. Kurultayı*, 1947, p. 448.
502. Akdağ, *op. cit.*, p. 93.
503. Dankwwart A. Rustow, "Türkiye'de İslâm ve politika 1920 – 1955" in *Türkiye'de İslâm ve Laiklik*, İstanbul, 1995, p. 78.
504. The breaking of the fast, in the evening during the holy month of Ramadan.
505. *C.H.P. Kurultayı*, 1947, pp. 448-52.

laws not derived from Sharia. Tanrıöver cited the examples of *Fatih* the Conqueror (Fatih Sultan Mehmet) and Süleyman the Lawmaker (Kânunî Sultan Süleyman), as well as Timurlenk (Tamerlane). He then argued that laic countries such as Switzerland, Belgium and the United States, did not overlook the needs of congregations. In other words, laicism, as practised in those countries, did not disregard religious needs. Tanrıöver estimated over 50,000 mosques, including small mosques (*mescits*) extant in Turkey and he pointed out the need for the training of the clergy to staff these places. Tanrıöver also criticised the closure of the tombs being a bad policy,[506] though over 20 years had already passed since their closure. Tanrıöver consistently maintained a line which contradicted the CHP's laicism policy.

Cemil Sait Barlas, deputy for Gaziantep, who opposed Tanrıöver's assessment, informed the congress that he provided private tuition on religion for his nine-year-old daughter. Having established his credentials as a good Muslim, he then expressed his understanding of laicism to be antithetical to that of Tanrıöver. In his view, the "Turkish nation's survival [does not depend on] religion or faith. That is between the conscience of the Turk and God. The Turk's ultimate strength is his/her noble blood in his veins". [507] Islam in private was the message, but divorced from rituals, and the primacy of nationalism as the key factor in determining identity - though expressed in racial terms, in defining Turks by descent rather than citizenship.

Cemil Sait Barlas also responded to Tanrıöver's ideas about reforming the system, slightly making light of the latter's comments:

> we cannot carry out religious reforms. It is impossible for a person who is trained as a soldier to carry out religious reform. Luther was a priest. The religious reforms they call Reformation originated from Catholic priests. Hamdullah Suphi Tanrıöver, are you a priest that can carry out religious reforms; or are you a hoca? (Applause).[508]

Finally, Tahsin Banguoğlu, deputy from Bingöl, summed up the demands for reform by Tanrıöver and others as: conduct religious education, look after religious institutions and take care of the clergy. Banguoğlu commented that he surmised that all his colleagues were in agreement with these demands, but added that Tanrıöver seemed to be promoting a new religious ideology. Expressing his disagreement with this ideology, Banguoğlu asserted that their ideology was based on the nation not religion.[509]

---

506. *Ibid.,* pp. 454-58.
507. *Ibid.,* 459.
508. *Loc.cit.*
509. *Ibid.,* p. 466.

It was clear that there was no place for Tanrıöver in the CHP any longer; eventually he resigned to join the DP, just as other former members of the party who did not agree wholeheartedly with all of Mustafa Kemal's reforms did.

After the congress, the CHP, concerned about the population's dissatisfaction with its policy on laicism and Islam, took "a series of measures aimed at establishing a more tolerant climate with regard to religion . . . without affecting the principle of secularism."[510] As part of these measures 15 İmam Hatip Kursları (courses for Muslim clerics) were authorised in 1948 and, in 1949, religious classes were introduced as an optional subject for Muslim children only, in primary schools. The CHP also lifted the prohibition against going to Mecca for the pilgrimage (hac) during the election campaign in 1946, and formally in 1947. It reintroduced the prohibition in 1948, due to the financial circumstances of the country.[511] It also established a theology faculty in Ankara University and transferred the administrative control from the Pious Foundations (Evkaf) to the Religious Directorate.[512] The CHP even allowed the opening of certain tombs of significant Ottoman heroes and some dervish lodges in 1950.[513] The CHP was displaying an ambivalent attitude but was weary of the subaltern Islamic opposition. The CHP tried to preserve the Kemalist edifice by introducing measured counter-reforms, which Kemal would not have approved.

It is to be noted that since the establishment of the Republic and up to 1948, the training of clerics was neglected. This approach demonstrated that the majority of the Republicans were not interested in practising rituals. They were nominally Muslims, in the sense that they derived part of their identity from local cultural norms, but the practice of Islam as required by Islamic and cultural traditions were not of interest. Furthermore, they did not appreciate the need of the majority to continue to express themselves within those local, traditional, cultural and Islamic norms.

In opposition (1946-1950), Menderes did not express any antithetical view to the regime's views on laicism/secularism. On 9 March 1947, in a speech he gave in Karagümrük, he expressed the view that laicism should be seen within the context of freedom of conscience.[514] The gap be-

---

510. Pongiluppi, Francesco. "La Turchia di Adnan Menderes: Il Demokrat Parti dalla Fondazione al Declino", in E. Locci (ed.), Volti della Politica, Rome, 2015, p. 118.

511. Cemil Koçak, 'CHP, İnkılap ve hac yasağı', [Revolution and prohibition of pilgrimage], Stargazete, 17 January 2015; http://www.star.com.tr/yazar/chp-inkilap--ve-hac-yasagi-yazi-991929/ [Accessed on 15 June 2017].

512. Rustow, op. cit., p. 79.

513. Şükrü Şur, 'Demokrat Parti ve Atatürk'ün üç ilkesi, Ankara Üniversitesi Türk İnkılâp Tarihi Enstitüsü Atatürk Yolu Dergisi, No. 176, Spring, 2015, p. 152.

514. Süleyman İnan, Muhalefette Adnan Menderes, (1945-1950), unpublished Ph.D.

tween the parties was not so wide. By the late 1940s, the CHP was not the monolithic party of laicism which it once may have been. The divergence of views on laicism and religion came to the fore in the Party's 1947 Congress, as discussed above.

The *Demokrats* were in general liberal laicists who had embraced the fundamentals of Mustafa Kemal Atatürk's westernisation, modernisation and laicism projects, but Menderes believed that the CHP used laicism against Islam and that religion should be protected by the state.[515] Yet Sunni Islam was not in any danger, protected and controlled as it was by Diyanet. On the other hand, in its 1950 program the DP promoted "religious tolerance" over "Turkish secularism". Francesco Pongiluppi notes that for the first time in the history of the Republic, a debate on secularism and, in particular, on rehabilitation of religion in the public space was being held.[516] Changes to the laic/secular system were inevitable and in the next 10 years, until it was stopped by a *coup d'état*, the DP did its best to amend the socio-political and cultural environment that Mustafa Kemal conceived and built. Menderes believed that Sunnism could be and should be compatible with laic society:

> On the one hand, the DP reforms were lifeblood to religious institutions, on the other the government strengthened the laws against each religious fanaticism and those who, through belief, have attacked free thought and manipulated religion for economic or political reasons.[517]

According to Metin Toker, journalist and İnönü's son-in-law, in the 1957 elections the Demokrats were disseminating propaganda, that "if İsmet Pasha[518] came to government, he would shut down the mosques and prohibit the call to prayer [*ezan*] and the reading of the Kuran [Quran]".[519] In the 1957 elections, in a speech in Adana, Menderes became "brazen" enough to promise to "make Istanbul a second Mecca and Eyüp Sultan [mosque] a second *Kâbe* [*Kaaba*]".[520] The religious discourse was becoming more and more public after more than three decades of circumspection.

Menderes was inspired by the writings and thought of theologian

---

study, Süleyman Demirel Üniversitesi, Isparta, 2012, 342.
515. Muhammed R. Feroze, "Laiklikte aşırılık ve ılımlılık" [Excesses and Moderation in Laicism] in *Türkiye'de İslâm ve Laiklik*, İstanbul, 1995, p. 36.
516. Pongiluppi, *op. cit.*, p. 118.
517. *Ibid.*, p. 121.
518. The Ottoman titles such as Pasha were prohibited in 1934 but were widely used, regardless. Officers who attained the rank of general were referred to as Pasha, until recently.
519. Metin Toker, *DP Yokuş Aşağı (1954-1957)*, İstanbul, 1991, p. 193.
520. Şur, *op. cit.*, p. 170.

Bediüzzaman Said Nursî.[521] Nursî's movement, *Nurcular* (the Lightists), was influential during the DP reign, as well as in the post-DP period. Said Nursî, himself, participated in the 1957 election by criss-crossing the country advocating for a DP government.[522] Another figure from the Islamist movement, Necip Fazıl Kısakürek, had also been sufficiently influential to attract DP's interest. As both Kısakürek and Nursî were thinkers who influenced Muslim intellectuals of subsequent generations, they are discussed in Chapters 5.2.1 and 5.2.2 respectively.

Reforming the reforms

Though Menderes started as a laicist/secularist no different from most Republicans, he slowly shifted his views. One of the early "reforms" by Menderes was the abolition of the law prohibiting Arabic as the language of the *ezan*. The DP parliamentary group decided to lift the prohibition on 13 June 1950[523] and expressed its desire to do so before *Ramazan* (*Ramadan*), which was to start on 17 June 1950. The *ezan* was not a trivial matter; hitherto it was a red flag issue for the laicist nationalists who insisted it should be in Turkish.

Their views were reflected in the like-minded press. For instance, on 13 April 1950, during the funerary procession of a national hero Mareşal Fevzi Çakmak, a group of people shouted the *tekbir* "Allahu ekber" (Allah is greater) in Arabic ("Allahu akbar").[524] This was regarded as disrespectful to Atatürk's reform but was also unlawful and a number of transgressors were arrested.[525] The CHP softened its stand somewhat in 1948, and allowed the *tekbir* to be recited in very restricted circumstances, which were listed in a Diyanet. Any person who recited the *tekbir* outside the specified circumstances, whether or not inside a mosque, was subject to penal sanction.[526]

Thus, until the lifting of the prohibition, the public call to prayer in Arabic was an arrestable offence; the law of the land was overriding traditional Islamic practices. In another instance, in 1949, two people were arrested for reading the *ezan* in Arabic in a hall within the parliamentary building. Interestingly, the two law-breakers were described as mentally unbalanced

---

521. Pongiluppi, *op. cit.*, p. 121.
522. Şur, *op. cit.*, p. 170.
523. 'Ezanın istenen dilde okunması kararlaştı', [It was decided the call to prayer to be in the language wanted], *Milliyet*, 14 June 1950, p. 1.
524. *Takbir* in Arabic.
525. 'Gençlik Takbih Ediyor', [The Youth condemns], *Vakit*, 14 April 1950, p. 1.
526. Azak, *op. cit.*, p. 70.

(*mezcub*).[527] The matter was also recorded in parliamentary minutes, given that the incident disrupted the parliamentary proceedings.[528] What the newspapers were not aware of, or chose not to report, was that the two individuals reading the *ezan* in Arabic were members of a religious order which originated in North Africa: *Ticaniler* (*Tijanis*). "Ticanis, travelled throughout the 1940s to several towns just to recite the Arabic call to prayer, as a way of conducting a holy war (*cihad*) against the regime."[529] The same group also broke some Atatürk statues in Ankara, considering it idol worship. This time, 400 members were arrested and about 40 of them, including the leader Kemal Pilavoğlu, received long sentences.[530] This was not wide-spread resistance to the reforms; nevertheless, the regime could not tolerate it.

Given the huge majority the DP enjoyed, the prohibition was to be easily lifted on 16 June 1950.[531] The law allowing the *ezan* to be read out in Arabic passed unanimously, with members of the CHP who were present, acquiescing. Some CHP members chose not to attend the session: Head of the CHP İsmet İnönü, Cemal Reşit Eyüboğlu, Cevdet Kerim İncedayı, Yusuf Ziya Ortaç and Hasan Reşit Tankut. Perhaps, they could not bring themselves to vote in favour of lifting the ban. Though the amendment to the Turkish Penal Code did not prohibit the use of Turkish in the call to prayer, to date the *ezan* is read out in Arabic only.[532] This was a complete reversal of a reform which aimed to de-Arabise Islam in Turkey.

Menderes introduced a number of other changes, slowly undermining the laic/secular edifice, such as it was. Religious classes expanded to the secondary schools in 1956; though still as an elective subject.[533] In addition, the DP made religious classes compulsory in primary schools, though it allowed parents to exclude their children from these classes. Other than the ezan and the religious classes, Rustow argued in 1957 that the DP did not do much else. Rustow concluded that it was doubtful that these changes could be called religious renaissance.[534] This is debatable; for instance, Muhammed R. Feroze, who wrote around the same time, believed there

---

527. 'İki mezcub dün Mecliste arabca ezan okudular', [Two unstable people read the ezan in Arabic in the Parliament] *Cumhuriyet*, 5 February 1949, p. 1.
528. *TBMM Tutanak Dergisi*, Kirk Birinci Birleşim, Cild 16, Dönem 8, Toplantı x, 4 February 1949, p. 20.
529. Umut Azak, *Islam and Secularism in Turkey*, London, 2010. p. 69.
530. Rustow, *op. cit.*, p. 82
531. 'Meclis, ezanın Arapça olarak okunmasını dün kabul etti', [The Parliament accepted the Arabic call to prayer], *Milliyet*, 17 June 1950, p. 1.
532. Şur, p. 167.
533. Pongiluppi, *op. cit.*, p. 121.
534. Rustow, *op. cit.*, p. 80.

was a religious revival in Turkey, which terrified the laicists. The *status quo* favoured them; any changes would have endangered their privileged position.[535]

According to Toker, the CHP at the time attributed their loss in the 1950 elections to their adherence to two principles: laicism and etatism. Toker confides that many CHP deputies approached him and told him that "the country does not approve this [hard attitude]".[536] İnönü did not agree with their assessment:

> Can you compete with the DP in the field of concessions? So? If we make the most minor concession in etatism and especially in laicism, we can never catch up. Your analysis is not correct. In Turkey, the CHP is held in [high] esteem because it is the custodian of Atatürk's reforms.[537]

The DP circles frequently alleged İnönü and the CHP were irreligious (*dinsiz*)[538]. They were not averse to using Islam for political gain. DP leaders Bayar, Menderes, Bölükbaşı, all former CHP deputies, started and ended their speeches by references to "Allah". As Toker notes, all that İnönü had to do to counteract the allegation was to invoke the name of Allah at least once. Yet, İnönü did not budge:

> Why do you want me to say this? In order to attract votes, is not it? Does not that mean using religion for politics? If I use these methods am I likely to be more of a Muslim, and meritorious? Is that what you think? No. Your aim is politicking. Come on!539

Clearly İnönü and Menderes approached politics differently and the DP members resorted to religious discourse, but despite Toker's assertions, it would be wrong to see the DP as entirely anti-laic. Just as the CHP was not unified on how laicism should be applied, The DP members also held divergent views. A DP deputy, Ahmet Tahtakılıç (Kütahya representative), considered the CHP's congress of 1947, "a political get-together of reactionaries".[540] This was the kind of language the CHP used against Islamists, but evidently it did not have a monopoly over the term and its application. This also presents a difficulty in the narrative of clearly demarcated lines between the secularists in the CHP and Islamists of the DP.

---

535. Feroze, *op. cit.*, p. 37.
536. Toker, *op. cit.*, p. 48.
537. *Loc. cit.*
538. The term *dinsiz* can also be translated as atheist, but it literally means without religion.
539. Toker, *op. cit.*, p. 193.
540. Akdağ, *op. cit.*, p. 127.

Moreover, Celal Bayar, a founding member of the DP and former Prime Minister, who had even replaced İsmet İnönü in 1937 in that position, was a secularist and tried to keep in check anti-laicist forces within DP. There is no doubt that the CHP has been more of a stalwart of laicism than the DP, as it represented urban dwellers and those with vested interests in the system: public functionaries and the military. It is also evident that the DP's commitment to laicism/secularism wavered considerably in the course of its 10 years in government.

In 1959, Fahri Ağaoğlu submitted a motion requesting a constitutional amendment to render Islam as the religion of the state. This motion did not receive sufficient support for parliamentary debate, but similar motions were submitted intermittently until the military intervention in 1960.[541] Such motions would have been unthinkable before the 1950s; no MP would have dared. In short, the political environment in the 1950s was markedly different to that of the preceding 20 years, and not only because of the shift to the multi-party system. The hardcore Kemalists still retained power in all significant state institutions, but allowances had to be made to placate the emerging opposition to Republican reforms. Most of the opposition was propelled by the Islamic sector which was led by such intellectuals as Nursî and Kısakürek. The subaltern was opposing the hegemony of the laicists, though Kısakürek can be categorized as representative of the elite Islamists, in contrast to Nursî's movement which was clearly more grass-roots grounded.

Menderes survived a plane crash at Heathrow airport in 1959, in which 14 people, including a minister, died. This accident made him feel invincible and may have bought him some time. The military was becoming anxious, not necessarily only because of his approach to religious matters, but also due to allegations of financial mismanagement. Eventually he was toppled by the military, through a coup led by young officers on 27 May 1960. He was charged and tried for, *inter alia*, violating the constitution, organising the Pogroms against the Greeks in Istanbul on 6-7 September 1955,[542] and corruption. Menderes was eventually executed.

Prophetically, in 1960, Walter F. Weiker thought that

[t]here will be arguments in Turkey for many years about whether the Democratic party period was one of the betrayal of secularism, the exploitation of religion, the restoration of freedom of worship, or the beginning of a new period of 'modernized Islam'.[543]

541. Feroze, *op. cit.*, p. 38.
542. Donef, '6-7 Eylül olayları 50 yıl sonra', *op. cit.*
543. Walter F. Weiker, *The Turkish Revolution*, The Brookings Institution, Washington,

Conclusion

The reformist zeal of the Republic ran out of steam by the 1950s. This was not simply as a result of an anti-laic, anti-modern party coming to power. It was more complicated than that as the 1947 CHP Congress minutes showed. Secularisation of the mind required secular education but pressures from the subaltern required some compromises in religious education. CHP members were not all of the same mind, as the minutes demonstrated. The Islamists slowly found more ways of undermining the reforms by using their voting base and pressuring politicians.

The 1950s were certainly a period in which the cracks expanded in the dominance of the laicist/secularist practice and narrative. Two key intellectuals contributed to this shift; two intellectuals with different characters and strengths. One austere and willing to make sacrifices, even of personal liberty, the other with a more western lifestyle, Nursî and Kısakürek respectively. They were selected for this chapter because their legacy lived on after their passing and their ideas continue to influence Islamic thought. Up to the 1950s, the Islamists lacked political power and the sporadic acts of resistance did not alter the *status quo*.

The significance of these intellectuals for the broader theoretical concerns of this study is that both Nursî and Kısakürek were involved in politics through different mechanisms they controlled. The next two sections will be show that these Islamists saw very little difference between the two categories. It should be added though that Kısakürek had more direct involvement in politics than Nursî, who preferred a more spiritual role, though not exclusively.

1960, p. 9; cited in John Obert Voll, 'Renewal and Reformation in the Mid-Twentieth Century, *The Muslim World*, Vol. LXXXIX, No. 3-4, July-October. 1999, p. 257.

5.2.0 THE SHIFTING OF THE IDEOLOGICAL GROUND AND PERSPECTIVES OF ISLAMIC INTELLECTUALS

5.2.1 Necip Fazıl Kısakürek

While the politicians disagreed about how to go about protecting laicism (or dismantling it), conservative Islamists and poet Necip Fazıl Kısakürek, a Nakshibendi, published a journal, *Büyük Doğu* (The Great East), in which they approached Islam as a "social, cultural and political system".[544] Kısakürek would have certainly denied the label political Islamist, or Islamist, as meaningless. His journal was widely read, considering the low literacy level of the period.[545] According to Ayşe Nevin Yıldız, who analysed *Büyük Doğu* editions between 1943 and 1951, 10,000 issues were printed in 1943, and sales were estimated at 20,000 by 1946.

In this first period of the journal, *Büyük Doğu* promoted an Islamic and nationalist structure under the concept of Anatolian Islam.[546] Indeed, in its first issue, its manifesto was careful to state that, despite its name, *Büyük Doğu* did not have any ambitions beyond Turkish boundaries. This point is emphasised several times in the manifesto published in the first issue.[547] Kısakürek was therefore not advocating Pan-Islamism or Pan-Turkism. Yet, Edel Edelma noted that

> Kısakürek's writing clearly pointed to the need for an Islamic state, and furthermore, to Turkish leadership of the "Great East", a pan-Islamic union with a Great Islamic Shura at Medina.[548]

This assessment is not based on *Büyük Doğu* texts or other writings of Kısakürek's but entirely on a secondary source, Burhanettin Duran's doctoral study. Duran indeed contended that *Büyük Doğu* had the goal of the unification of the Islamic world, including the establishment of the great Islamic shura (*Büyük İslam Şurası*) among Islamic nations in Medina. However, Duran makes a significant qualification in the footnote:

544. Akdağ, *op. cit.*, 49.
545. In 1935, 80.8 percent of the population was illiterate; Eligür, *op. cit.*., p. 148.
546. Ayşe Nevin Yıldız. 'Türkiye modernleşmesine bir muhalif basın olarak Büyük Doğu', İletişim Fakültesi Dergisi, Vol. 0, No. 13, 2012, p. 582.
547. 'Büyük Doğuya Doğru', [Towards the Great East], *Büyük Doğu*, No. 1, 17 September 1943, p. 2.
548. Edel Edelma *et al. Turkey Transformed*, Bipartisan Policy Center, Washington D.C., October 2015, p. 22; [Bipartisan Policy Centre is a U.S. based think tank which has a number of projects including U.S.-Turkey partnership].

It should be stated that Kısakürek wrote less on the possible unification of [the] Islamic world; he rather focused on the Islamic revolution that would start from Turkey. His nationalist inclination and the realities of a nation state was clear enogh [sic] in this situation.549

Büyük Doğu started its circulation on 17 September 1943, but was shut down in May 1944, by a Ministerial Council decision, for publishing the phrase: "you cannot obey those who do not obey Allah."550 This was an obvious reference to the CHP government. The journal was allowed to circulate again in November 1945.551 This was one of its many closures by the state in its publication life, which ended in 1978. *Büyük Doğu* represented a segment of society which did not embrace all the reforms.

As well as acting as opposition to the CHP, at a time when there was no parliamentary opposition, *Büyük Doğu* expressed Islamic viewpoints on a range of topics. Kısakürek was critical of fashion and luxury, which he saw as products of modernisation; consumption of alcohol; gambling; and even co-education.552 Yıldız adds that Kısakürek did not necessarily see modernisation as cultural degradation but he preferred the transfer of technology and information from the West, rather than its values.553

Some articles in *Büyük Doğu* were designed to scandalise a conservative audience with far-fetched stories, such as allegations of sexual intercourse in co-educational schools, or an unnamed man using a room next to the tombs of Sultan Bayezit and Reşit Paşa for womanising.554 Though this type of stories appeared, perhaps in an effort to expand circulation, it was a serious publication, which occasionally could not help falling to tabloid standards of embellishing news to manufacture outrage.

Yıldız argues that, in general, *Büyük Doğu* employed a moralising tone. This is a fair assessment, which can be observed by reading any of the extant *Büyük Doğu* issues. The journal started with a simple language

549. Burhanettin Duran, Transformation of Islamist Political Thought in Turkey from the Empire to the Early Republic (1908-1960), Unpublished Doctoral Study, Bilkent University. Ankara, 2001, p. 243.
550. Hasret Yıldırım, '1952 senesinden bir manşetin hatırlattıkları', [What a headline from 1942 evokes], *Yenisöz*, 3 October 2015, http://www.yenisoz.com.tr/1952-sene-sinden-bir-mansetin-hatirlattiklari-makale-6013 [Accessed on 4 July 2017].
551. *Loc. cit.*
552. Yıldız, *op. cit.*, p. 584.
553. *Ibid.*, p. 585.
554. Abdürrahim Zapsu, 'Hani, bize sahip çıkacak biri?, [Where is someone to advocate for us?], *Büyük Doğu*, Vol. 6, No. 23, 8 September 1090, p. 6.

but with the passing of time became a professional tool of an "Islamic party propaganda".[555] By 1951, Kısakürek established *Büyük Doğu Cemiyeti* (The Association of the Great East), as the power of his journal increased, and he became influential in swaying public opinion and politicians. Thus, the journal instigated a movement to be formed, opposing laicism/secularism.

Right from its first issue *Büyük Doğu* opposed Mustafa Kemal's reforms and the CHP. When the DP was formed, and was formally in the Parliament as opposition party, Kısakürek believed there was no difference between them. In 1949, reportedly, he alleged that Celal Bayar, Chair of the DP, did not believe in Allah and the Prophet. The newspaper *Sabah Postası* attacked Kısakürek by calling him a "sorrowful" (*bedbaht*) and mentally deranged (*mezcub*) individual.[556] The day before, the same newspaper used strong language against Kısakürek, calling him, *inter alia*, a charlatan, for publishing an unflattering drawing of Atatürk, in which the latter is depicted holding a beer glass.[557] Thus, there was a concerted attack against Kısakürek by the secular minded press.

Eventually, Kısakürek treated Menderes on a more positive note and became more supportive of the DP.[558] As was revealed in the Yassıada trials, held after the military intervention, *Büyük Doğu* had received substantial financial support from the concealed state funds (TL 147,000) between 1951-59.[559]

At the same time as criticising the state, Kısakürek entered into polemic with the newspaper *Vatan*, whose owner, Ahmet Emin Yalman was of Sabbetaist background. Yalman's strong stand against Islamism was interpreted as a result of his Sabbetaist roots; anti-Semitism was one of the themes the journal employed.[560]

Duran and Cemil Aydın argued that Kısakürek's opinions about Jews contained racist aspects as "he regarded them as the corrupting element within Western civilization".[561] Kısakürek also blamed Jews for the decline

555. Yıldız, *op. cit.*, p. 595.
556. 'C. Bayar, Allahı ve Peygamberi tanımıyor mu?', [Does not C. Bayar believe in Allah and the Prophet?], *Sabah Postası*, 7 November 1949.
557. 'Hükûmeti, Savcıyı, Gençliyi, vazifeye çağırıyoruz' [We call upon the Government, the Public Prosecutor, the Youth to carry out their duty], *Sabah Postası*, 6 November 1949.
558. Yıldız, p. 590.
559. Ayşe Hür, 'Necip Fazıl Kısakürek'in öteki portresi' [The other portrait of Necip Fazıl Kısakürek], *Radikal*, 6 January 2013.
560. For his collection of articles on Jews, Masons and Dönmes, see Necip Fazıl Kısakürek, *Yahudilik – Masonluk Dönmelik*, İstanbul, 2008.
561. Burhanettin Duran and Cemil Aydın, 'Competing Occidentalisms of Modern Islamist Thought', *The Muslim World*, Vol. 13, 2013, pp. 491.

of the Ottoman Empire. Given that the "Ottoman Jews remained loyal to the Ottoman Empire", note Duran and Aydın, his assertions lacked historical validity.[562] Manufacturing history was not a monopoly exercised by government and academia only.

While anti-Semitism was a constituent element in the antagonistic approach to *Vatan*, it was also the newspaper's strong laic/secular views that intensified the enmity. Ahmet Emin Yalman, who kept warning the DP about the danger of *irtica* (reaction), thus echoing the Kemalist establishment, became an adversary of *Yeni Sabah* and *Büyük Doğu*.[563] On 22 November 1952, an assassination attempt took place against Yalman, in Malatya. The assassination attempt was carried out by a supporter of an extremist Cevat Rıfat Atilhan, a Nazi sympathizer and anti-Semite.[564] Atilhan had contributed articles to *Büyük Doğu*[565] as well as another Islamic ideological publication, *Sebılürreşad*. The would-be assassin, Hüseyin Üzmez, was a high school student, aged seventeen. Over 50 years later, Üzmez admitted having been influenced by *Büyük Doğu* writings in carrying out the assassination attempt.[566]

Whether or not Kısakürek had any personal involvement, he was charged as accessory, along with a number of people belonging to the Islamist circle. Undoubtedly, *Büyük Doğu* was the instigator as they published strongly worded articles against Ahmet Emin Yalman, which seemed to encourage his assassination:

> Spiritually the murderer of Islam and the Turk, you need to be silenced. Sower of discord; that's you! Be afraid of us and die of fear! Due to your words and cognovits actionem, we will be the executioner who will fasten the noose on your neck.[567]

There is no doubt that Islamists were attacking Yalman both for his support of secularism and his Sabbetaists background. According to *Vatan* newspaper, 11 people were arrested for the assassination attempt; collectively they were members of Büyük Doğu Association, Islamic Democratic Party (*İslam Demokrat Partisi*) and the Association of Nationalists (*Milli-*

---

562. *Loc. cit.*

563. Sanem Gök, Türk Siyasal Yaşamında Vatan Gazetesi (1950-1960), unpublished post-graduate study, Ankara University, 2003, pp. 510-52.

564. Rustow, *op. cit.*, p. 83.

565. For instance, Cevat Rıfat Atilhan, 'Nasıl Yahudi ve Mason düşmanı oldum' [How I became an enemy of Judaism and Masons], *Büyük Doğu*, 25 August 1960, Vol. 6, No. 23, p. 12.

566. Hasan Pulur, 'Bilse bilse "o" bilir', [If anyone knows, it is "him"], *Milliyet*, 27 April 2007.

567. Gök, *op. cit.*, p. 52f.

yetçiler Derneği).[568]

Evidently, in the 1950s, the Islamist section emerged as a threat to the political system and Kısakürek was pivotal as the intellectual driving force. This movement may not have been strong enough to topple the regime, but it was an expression of discontent vis-a-vis laicism/secularism. In this period, *Büyük Doğu* added the communists, the Jews and laicists/secularists to its list of enemies, using inflammatory language. For instance, the 4 July 1952 edition stated: "Satan worshippers clash with God worshippers: Jewish investors and communists".[569]

The 1960 military coup led to the arrest of many people who were perceived as a threat to the regime. Kısakürek was among them. In Yassıada trials, when the issue of funds received by the DP came to the fore, he defended himself by trying to take the moral high ground:

> All I received, I spent it on my path of struggle. . . . Adnan Menderes did not use me through the concealed funds, in reality I tried to use him for the sake of my ideal; but due to his non compos mentis and fickle character, I did not succeed.[570]

In 1952, Kısakürek was arrested in a gambling house. In his defence, he said that he was there to observe gamblers' behaviour. He may well have fallen victim to a conspiracy by the establishment, as suggested by Altan Öymen, a one-time CHP leader.[571] Yet his personal failings (including gambling) have been sufficiently documented. Kısakürek is not the first- or last-person advocating purity, but fell short of adhering to the stated standards. Kısakürek has been a polarising figure and, today, while secularists loathe him, Islamists revere him.[572]

Duran and Aydın noted that Kısakürek and another influential Islamist, Nurettin Topçu, were products of the thirties and early forties. They were both modern, western-educated Islamist intellectuals. They represented "new sensibilities, arguments and credentials corresponding to the changing cultural and political climate of the Turkish Republic". The old

---

568. *Ibid.*, p. 52.

569. Hasret Yıldırım, *op. cit.*

570. Mustafa Yürekli, 'Necip Fazıl'ın Yassıada'daki savunması', [Necip Fazıl's defence in Yassıada], http://www.haber7.com/yazarlar/mustafa-yurekli/973425-necip-fazilin-yassiadadaki-savunmasi.

571. Hasan Pulur, 'Necip Fazıl'ın kumarhanesi . . .', [Necip Fazil's gambling house . . .], *Milliyet*, 7 November 2009.

572. For diametrically opposing views see: 'Din sahtekarlar için en kullanışlı bir maskedir', [Religion is most useful mask for imposters], in which, just as the title suggests, Kısakürek is treated as a fraud; and **Mustafa Yürekli**, *op. cit.*, in which he is represented as a proud man, even as he explained to the court how he came to receive funds from the DP government.

guard of Islamic intellectual tradition of the late Ottoman period had almost disappeared, "they were forced into silence or exile".[573] The new guard emerged to take their place and act as the opposition, albeit outside the Parliament.

Kısakürek expressed his views on Islam through a framework he called *Ideolocya Örgüsü* (The Web of Ideology). He had an eclectic view of Islam and East-West relations. He believed that

> Western civilization as a Greek-Latin construction . . . had been shaped by the three constitutive elements, producing the Renaissance: Greek reason, Roman order and Christian morality. Western domination over nature thanks to modern science had culminated in technical developments in the nineteenth century. In the twentieth century, the Western failure to balance reason and spirit had burst out as a crisis in the spiritual, political, social and economic fields.[574]

Duran and Aydın argued that Kısakürek believed that a new Asianism of the Great East was able to synthesis the West's achievements in material and positive sciences with the East's achievements in spirit and belief.[575] This notion suggests that he did not entirely reject the West. While Duran and Aydın interpret his writings as a desire for synthesis, it may well be argued that he was in favour of weakening the West vis-a-vis a strengthened East, albeit using western technology. In one of his manifestos, in 1954, he castigated the country for not being productive:

> This nation, which has not even manufactured a needle for a hundred years, will manufacture its radio, its car, its tractor, its motor, its whatever, with its own hands. It will be compelled to do so. If need be, it will do it using tin, but it will do it.[576]

In the same manifesto, Kısakürek suggested that western products will be prohibited from entering the country. Duran and Aydın note that by embracing an eclectic method, Kısakürek was able to argue that any good cultural values that have already transferred to the East "were already inherent in Islam".[577] In essence, in his Occidentalism, Kısakürek reduced the West to one worthy dimension, technological superiority; Kısakürek argued that natural and physical sciences as abstract matters were products of Islam. As a source for this assertion, Kısakürek quoted selective *hadiths*.

573. Both quotes by Duran and Aydın, *op. cit.*, pp. 480-81.
574. *Ibid.*, p. 486.
575. *Ibid.*, p. 489.
576. 'Ideolocya Örgüsü: Program, [The Web of Ideology: the Program], *Büyük Doğu*, No. 7, 18 July 1954, p. 2.
577. Duran and Aydın, p. 485.

Furthermore, Kısakürek asserted that the West used these sciences to trap Islam for four centuries (since the Renaissance).[578] As we can see, at different times, he argued that both positive cultural values and sciences were borrowed from Islam.

In his 1954 manifesto, he decreed that gambling houses, which by many accounts he frequented, as well as coffee houses would be shut down. Reading "the third item" of his 1954 manifesto, it can be deduced that the closing down of these places is not necessarily an attempt to address perceived moral decay, but rather to address perceived loss of productivity. Consequently, Kısakürek seemed to have been expounding an "Islamic Calvinist" work ethic for the East, emulating western processes of rationalisation. Kısakürek did not use the term "Islamic Calvinist" but by 2005 the notion was debated and was accepted by influential members of the AKP, for instance Abdullah Gül, Deputy Prime Minister and Foreign Affairs Minister at the time.[579]

Kısakürek's ideas influenced several generations of Islamists who eventually came to power to alter Turkish society once again and purify it from the polluting elements brought by the Republic; in the process he incorporated principles espoused by Republicans (westernisation, modernity, positivism) albeit from a different vantage point. While Republicans wanted to purify Islam to mould it into a model they wished, Kısakürek saw the Republic as polluting Islam.

---

578. 'İslâm İnkilabı: Müsbet Bilgiler', [The Islamic Revolution: Natural and physical sciences], *Büyük Doğu*, Vol. 6, No. 23, p. 2.
579. European Stability Initiative, *Islamic Calvinists*, Berlin, Brussels, Istanbul, 2005, p. 2.

5.2.2 Beddiüzaman Said Nursî

While Kısakürek has been influential in Islamist circles, Beddiüzaman Said Nursî through his *Dersanes* (study circles) and spiritual authority, reached more people. Nursî was of Kurdish background, but his ethnicity did not seem to have played any role on the expansion of his ideas to a wider Sunni audience, Turkish or Kurdish. Emrah Cilasun argues that Nursî was influenced both by Kadiri and Nakshibendi thinking.[580]

Nursî's whole life was marked by imprisonments and exiles because his ideas brought him into a collision course with the secularist regime. Not surprisingly, there are two dominant and competing narratives regarding Nursî, as far as Turkish sources are concerned. The secularists present him as a dangerous Islamist, while his followers present him as a person with extraordinary intellect and a person who believed secularity and Islam could co-habit.

This influential Islamic intellectual was born in 1877 and represented the old guard of Islamist thinkers. He served in the Ottoman Army and after the war he wrote nationalist brochures, which

> put him in the good graces of the nationalist government in Ankara. But this prestige dissolved when he reminded the representatives to the assembly of the nationalist government that their success was not due simply to their own work but was the result of divine intervention.[581]

Nursî also "wrote a treatise that called politicians to pray daily and perform other acts of worship for the sake of God. He even published it as a booklet on the importance of the five daily prayers".[582] This was unlikely to go down well with the new elite, who believed that Islam as practised was the problem that needed to be overcome. Though he was offered the position of "Kürdistan Umumi Vaizliği" (General Preacher of Kurdistan) in the new regime when he visited Ankara,[583] he did not get along with Mustafa Kemal and eventually departed to be an adversary. Said Nursi in his *Emirdağ Lahikası* (*Emirdağ Appendix*) noted that Mustafa Kemal offered him such position with 300 lira salary but relationship deteriorated

---

580. Emrah Cilasun, Yeni Paradigmanın Eşiğinde Beddiüzzaman Efsanesi ve Said Nursî, İstanbul, 2018, pp. 153-54.

581. Şerif Mardin, "The Nakshibendi Order of Turkey" in Martin E. Marty & R. Scott Appleby (eds.) *Fundamentalisms and the State*, 1993, p. 218.

582. Mustafa Gökhan Şahin, 'Said Nursi and the Nur Movement in Turkey', *Domes*, Vol. 20, No. 2, Fall 2011, p. 232.

583. Cilasun, op. cit., p. 256.

when Said Nursî stated that the person not conducting *namaz* is a traitor.[584] Mustafa Kemal reprimanded him stating that "We invited you so that you can provide high level thought. You came and wrote things about namaz and caused disagreements amongst us".[585]

Later, his position as a popular religious teacher made the new reformist government of Mustafa Kemal even more suspicious and Nursî spent much of his subsequent life in prison, exiled to remote places in Turkey. The Republican Party demonised him, while the Demokrat Party was more sympathetic. Although the state mechanism still pursued him, through the courts, the DP allowed him to publish his work and gave him room to manoeuvre. In turn, Nursî was involved in the political campaign in 1957 in favour of the Demokrats. İnönü, the leader of the Republican Party and former President, is even reported to have declared that it was the *Nurcus* who defeated him.[586]

Nursî himself divided his life into three parts, reflecting his philosophical leanings for each period: Old, the New and the Third (*Eski Said, Yeni Said, Üçüncü Said*). The Old Said partly accepted human philosophy and positive sciences. However, as Babacan and Karaman note his views on positivism were modified, as he believed that the intellectuals using western positivists writing as a model tried to impose these ideas without filtering them or taking into account the cultural structure of the community. He also believed that religion had stopped becoming a reference point for the Westernist Ottoman intellectuals.[587]

The New Said, returning from Russia, where he was a prisoner of war, withdrew from public life to start writing his *opus magnum, Risale-i Nur* (The Message of Light), to address the challenge of taking "the Qu'ran as his sole master". The Third Said was the period in which his book *Risale-i Nur* was allowed to be published in Latin letters. The original text in Arabic script was illegally distributed all over Turkey as his followers bought mimeograph machines.[588] In 1956, the book was allowed to be printed in Latin script.[589] In this period, Voll notes, the students of *Risale-i Nur* became a cohesive movement.[590] However, they were never organised along the *tari-*

584. Bediüzzaman Said Nursî, *Emirdağ Lâhikası*, Sahdamar Yayınları, İstanbul, 2014, pp. 7 and 182.
585. Cilasun, op. cit., p. 190.
586. *Şükran* Vahide. *Islam in Modern Turkey*, Albany, 2005, p. 330.
587. Hasan Babacan and Mehmet Ali Karaman, *Said Nursi:* Siyaset ve Devlet, Ankara, 2013, p. 125.
588. Cilasun, *op. cit.*, p. 355
589. Azak, *op. cit.*, p. 117.
590. Voll, *op. cit.*, p. 247.

kat lines, which in any case would have been illegal and Said Nursî himself stated repeatedly that they were not a tarikat.[591]

A question set in the introduction of this study was to explore Turkey's conceptualisation of laicism/secularism and the role of Islam. As reported by Nursî followers, Nursî seemed to believe that Islam was compatible with secularism. He also thought that Islam was compatible with modernity. The secularists denied that is the case and painted him as a religious fanatic. Indeed,

> [h]e was portrayed as a mysterious (esrarengiz), oddly dressed (acip kılıklı) old man, his unusual outfit of traditional Kurdish clothing (şal û şapik and koloz) being a major attraction. Falih Rıfkı Atay, the editor of Dünya, found Said Nursî's clothes to be 'more backward than those of the sheikhs of Yemen'. These clothes were seen as a statement against the secular dress code. Although, with the exception of Said Nursî himself, none of the Nurcus wore traditional outfit or clothes which were against the law (Kıyafet Kanunu), they were depicted in cartoons as stereotypical reactionaries with baggy trousers and long black beards with spider webs around them.[592]

From the early years the new regime treated him with derision and regarded him as a danger to secularism and a representative of *irtica* (reactionary Islam). While the secularists continue to depict him in a negative manner,[593] sympathetic accounts, such as that of Şükran Vahide, interpret his ideas as compatible with secularism:

> While, for his part, Nursî denied that he had opposed [secularisation], arguing that 'the secular republic means the separation of religion from [the matters of] this world' and that 'since, according to the principle [of secularism] the secular republic remains impartial and does not interfere with those without religion, so too of course it should not interfere with those with religion on whatever pretext.' That is to say, secularism should ensure freedom of conscience, and of expression, and other liberties. This conflict of interpretations over the meaning of secularism and how it should be applied remains unresolved to this day.[594]

Recent hagiographies present Nursî as a moderate, interested in inter-faith dialogue. Perhaps these contradictory approaches can be ex-

---

591. Cilasun, *op. cit.*, p. 154.
592. Azak, *op. cit.*, p. 125; Falih Rıfkı Atay's view can be regarded as "orientalist", the kind which Edward Said lamented.
593. For instance, see Alpaslan Işıklı, *Said Nursi Fethullah Gülen ve "Laik" Sempatizanları*, Ankara, 1998.
594. Vahide. *op. cit.*, p. 224.

plained away by separating the "political Said" from the "philosophical Said". The political Said supported a conservative party such as the DP, while the philosophical Said was more open in his approach to Christianity. Foreign admirers, seduced by the inter-faith dialogue narrative, present him in a much more positive light than the Turkish secularists. Partly, his reputed embrace of technology and advancement has played a role.

In this narrative, inter-faith dialogue is presented as something positive, and it might be - as long as the dialogue is about understanding and respecting each other. But what about inter-faith dialogue with one party trying to convince the other of the superiority of their own beliefs? Hamid Algar contends that 'interreligious dialogue'

> was not a primary concern of Nursî. True, he came to believe in the necessity of Muslim-Christian collaboration against godless Communism - supposedly exemplified by Turkish membership in NATO.[595]

The inter-faith dialogue, in this context, was more of a temporary political alliance between the West and the East, as well as future and actual states, to defeat communism, a common enemy. Communism threatened both vestigial states with anti-religious rhetoric and practice, but also actual states. The alliance therefore was a political strategy. In 1946, in a letter he sent to Hilmi Uran in, Interior Minister at the time, warned that if the country does not "spread . . . the truths of belief and the Qur'an", the Turkish nation would be "overwhelmed by the fearsome monster that has appeared in the north".[596] Said Nursî also tried to establish relationship with Vatican before Turkey established diplomatic relations with it and visited the Ecumenical Greek Patriarchate in Phanar (Fener). Yet, in other instances spoke in a derogatory manner of Christians by referring to "semi-nude Christian girls".[597]

M. Zakyi Ibrahim notes that "quite unique to Said Nursî, even if naïve, is the metaphorical jihad that he urges Muslims to wage against the 'civilized world'".[598] Nursî did not define "civilisation" "other than the prevailing perception in his time that, due to its scientific and technological advancements, Europe is the 'civilized group of nations." Turner and Horkuç expand this notion:

> As far as religion is concerned, Nursî says, the civilized can be conquered not through force but through peaceful persuasion: to this end,

595. Hamid Algar, 'An introduction to Said Nursi', *Journal of Shi'a Islamic Studies*, Vol. 6, No. 3, Summer 2013, p. 341.
596. Vahide, *op. cit.*, p. 279.
597. Cilasun, *op. cit.*, pp. 383, 404 and 413 respectively.
598. M. Zakyi Ibrahim, 'Said Nursi', *Contemporary Islam*, 2011, p. 86.

all that Muslims have to do is demonstrate the elevated nature of Islam with the 'tongue of mute eloquence' namely by adhering to the precepts of Islam in their own lives and thus acting as ambassadors of Islam in the presence of others.[599]

It appears that the embrace of technology and inter-faith dialogue were for the purpose of advancing the cause of Islam. Said Nursî's followers used the technology of the time (mainly radio) and this has been put forward as an embrace of modernity. However, using modern means (i.e. up to date technology) to disseminate a message is not necessarily a sign of accepting modernity. After all, the so-called Islamic Caliphate used up-to-date technological means and a multitude of social media to disseminate their message of hate, but in areas they controlled, the arts, dance, sports, television, study of sciences, or any kind of activity outside an austere and archaic life style, were prohibited. On the other hand, to give a broader perspective, fundamentalists of various persuasions (Christian, Muslim or Jewish) using modern means to disseminate an "anti-modern" message is not unusual. It does point to the fact though that such anti-modernism is, in itself, a product of modernity.

In the "Rays" collection of *Risale-i Nur*, Nursî responded to allegations by the state, *inter alia*, of being against modern progress:

[B]ecause I criticised the evils and faults of civilization, unimaginable things are ascribed to me in the police reports: as though I do not accept the use of the radio, aeroplane and railway, they accuse me of being opposed to modern progress.[600]

. . .

[A]lthough mankind should have responded with endless thanks to Almighty God's supreme bounties of the aeroplane, railway, and radio, they did not respond in that way, so He rained down bombs on their heads from the planes. The radio is also a supreme bounty, and thanks for it may be shown by making it a universal reciter of the Qur'an with millions of tongues, allowing all the people on the face of the earth to listen to it. Also, I said when explaining in the Twentieth Word that the Qur'an makes predictions about the future wonders of civilization, that one of its verses indicates that the infidels will defeat the Islamic world with the railway. Although I had urged Islam to lay hold of these wonders, some of the prosecutors in previous courts, accused us of being

599. Colin Turner and Hasan Horkuç cited in M. Zakyi Ibrahim, 'Said Nursi', *Cont Islam*, 2011, p. 87.
600. *The Rays*, p. 389.

against modern progress, and made the aeroplane, railway, and radio the basis of charges against us.[601]

Given Nursî's highly allegorical language, it is hard to interpret his text. The passage above encompasses several ideas. One idea is that technology such as radio is useful because it transmits the Quran to many people. The radio as a means for providing entertainment and information outside the Islamic context is not treated. Another idea is that technology can also have negative consequences. For instance, nuclear bombs represent technological advancement but not necessarily human progress: the ultimate aim of such technology is to destroy humanity. In relation to the destructive ability of technology, Nursî's position seems to describe it as an instrument of divine judgment for insufficient gratitude. The third idea is that Islam, presumably Islamic peoples and nations, should be weary of technology because technology can be used to conquer them. Evidently, his writing is contradictory at times but given the scale of the *Risale-i Nur* collection in Turkish which far exceeds 5,000 pages, this is to be expected.

Tuğrul Keskin contends that the Old Nursî believed in the idea of Pan-Islamism:

> in order to prevent the collapse of the Ottoman Empire, Muslims would need to adopt the technological changes and industrialization of Europe. Said Nursî understood the power of the newly emerging technological advances, and had the foresight to understand the way in which these advances would eventually alter the social and political structure of Muslim societies. Therefore, he was able to bring together elements of science and religion, and in so doing, was able to use science to advance the objectives of Islam.[602]

Voll notes that Nursî tried to synthesise science and religion, looking for a middle way.[603] As Nursî's life progressed and the political climate changed, his views evolved to accommodate the new context. That being said, Nursî employed an ambivalent language regarding modernity and laicism. However, there are different definitions of these concepts. He notes in *Risale-i Nur*:

> Mr. Prosecutor and Members of the Court! You are accusing me of holding an idea the opposite of which I have held for fifty years. If you are asking about the secular republic, what I understand by it is that secularism means being unbiased; that is, in accordance with the principle of freedom of conscience, it refers to a government that does not

---

601. *The Rays*, p. 390.
602. Tuğrul Keskin, *op. cit.*, p. 124.
603. Voll, *op. cit.*, p. 252.

interfere with religiously-minded and pious people, the same as it does not interfere with the irreligious and dissolute. I have withdrawn from political and social life for ten, and now it is twenty years.[604]

It is not surprising that Nursî supported the DP, as Menderes had similar ideas about secularism, in that he also believed that religion was a matter of individual practice and the state should not interfere. This approach can be described as "upholding religion" in Laborde's schema. The Republicans were of the view that Islam should be controlled, even shaped, and if it was not, the religious sphere would take over and not allow for the expression of other views.

Ian S. Markham and Suendam Birinci Pirim, an admiring Christian theologian and a Lightist (*Nurcu*) disciple, teamed up to study Nursî, note that he

> illustrates that Islam, properly understood, is compatible with the best that modernity brings. One can be a Muslim and an advocate for technology and science; one can be a Muslim and operate effectively in a secular state; and one can be a Muslim and commit to peaceful co-existence with those who disagree with Islam. Furthermore the arguments for these positions are all found in the Qur'an. The embrace of science, pluralism, and dialogue are not, for Nursî, a betrayal of the teaching of the Qur'an and the Prophet Muhammad. Instead this constructive attitude to modernity is directly derived from these Muslim sources.[605]

Setting aside the very subjective nature of the study, the question of compatibility of Islam and secularism is answered in the affirmative. Although Nursî, according to Markham and Pirim, is not saying that arguments for modernity or secularism can be found in the Quran, the Quran is providing a context for an attitude addressing these notions.

Azak notes that "[t]hroughout the 1950s, Said Nursî supported the DP as opposed to the RPP [CHP], as he considered Menderes's "respect for Islam" a bulwark against atheism and moral decay."[606] This perceived moral decay was also a preoccupation of Kısakürek, as we have seen in the preceding pages. Nursî had similar parochial views on morality. The following passage from the *Risale-i Nur* may reflect these views:

> [T]he woman is charged with protecting and preserving her husband's property and possessions, and his children. Carelessness in dress and

---

604. *The Rays*, p. 305.
605. Ian S. Markham and Suendam Birinci Pirim, *An Introduction to Said Nursi*, Surrey, 2011, p. 2.
606. Azak, *op. cit.*, p. 119.

morality destroys that loyalty, and her husband loses confidence in her and makes her suffer pangs of conscience. In fact, if the two qualities of courage and generosity, which are desirable in men, are found in women, it damages this loyalty and confidence and so are undesirable for women and are considered to be bad qualities. But since the husband's duty is not loyalty and stewardship, but protection, kindness, and respect, he cannot be restricted and refined, and may marry other women as well.[607]

[I]ncreased freedom for women led to a sudden unfolding of bad morality in mankind. The represented forms of little smiling corpses have played a large role in making the evil-polluted perverse spirit of modern man what it is.[608]

In these passages Nursî seemed to embrace a negative view of modernity, though it is not entirely clear what he meant by "modern man", or the "little smiling corpses" for that matter. In the same collection, "The Words", Nursî appealed to this hypothetical modern and educated man:

Oh, modern-educated Sir whose brain has shrunk through studying the soulless matters of astronomy, whose mind can see no further than the tip of his nose, and who cannot squeeze the mighty mystery of the above verse into his constricted brain! The heaven of the verse may be reached by a stairway of Seven Steps. Come, let us climb them together![609]

It appears that Nursî was offering a helping hand to "modern man" to see reality the way Nursî understood it, and ultimately to attain a higher level of existence. The "modern man" may have been a westerner or a secularist; there is a lot of room for different interpretations. It is these sorts of passages though, that formed the nucleus of the idea of "inter-faith dialogue" as promoted by Nursî sympathisers.

While Nursî believed that the way secularism was practised in Turkey was wrong because in his view it did not allow for freedom to practice religion, his struggle against the state was not violent; he preferred to use the power of persuasion. According to Hakan Yavuz,

[h]e was a dedicated advocate of positive action and strongly challenged the use of violence. By encouraging constructive behavior, Bediuzzaman Said Nursî interpreted jihad as spiritual struggle or struggle with words.[610]

607. *The Flashes*, p. 257.
608. *The Words*, p. 259.
609. *Ibid.*, p. 191.
610. M. Hakan Yavuz, *Islamic Political Identity in Turkey*, Oxford, 2003, 11.

Quranic exegesis, Nursî's lifelong project, is not central, or even peripheral, to the theme of this study. His texts, however, were studied by thousands of disciples and affected the way they think. At times, his text reads like Islamic apologia:

> The Messenger (UWBP) was such that from the age of fifteen to forty when the blood is fiery and exuberant and the passions of the soul enflamed, with complete chastity and purity he sufficed and was content with a single older woman, Khadija the Great (May God be pleased with her) – as is agreed by friend and foe alike. His having numerous wives after the age of forty, that is, when bodily heat subsides and the passions are quietened, is decisive, self-evident proof for those who are even a little fair-minded that such marriages were not to satisfy the carnal appetites, but were for other important reasons and instances of wisdom.

> Companions transmitted the outward, public things, and his wives were the transmitters and narrators of the private matters of religion and injunctions of the Shari'a that became clear from his private conduct in the personal sphere; they performed that function. Perhaps half of the personal matters of religion and the injunctions concerning them come from them. That is to say, numerous wives of differing temperament were required to perform this necessary duty.[611]

This passage justified polygamy. The text in Latin script was not widely available until the mid-1950s, but the Ottoman text circulated widely and almost certainly the public prosecutors would have had a copy of it. As long as he was not advocating polygamy for contemporary Turkey, explaining away polygamy at the time of the Prophet Muhammad was acceptable. However, it is these kinds of ideas which made the Republican secularists wary of him.

Nursî never married, led an austere life and died in 1960, at the age of 87. The regime was so concerned about Said Nursî's final resting place becoming a focal point for an Islamic resistance that they destroyed his *türbe* (tomb) built by his followers and removed his remains from Urfa to an unknown location in Isparta. His followers reconciled with the absence of a cenotaph to Said Nursî reported preference for his gravesite not to be known. Necmeddin Şahiner interviewed gendarme and army soldiers who were tasked with the interment of Said Nursî's remains in 1960 after the military coup of 27 May.[612]

---

611. *The Letters*, p. 44.
612. Necmeddin Şahiner, *Bediüzzaman Said Nursî'nin Kayıp Mezarının Sırrı*, Ankara, 2012, pp. 66-93.

After his death, a number of groups emerged as followers, transmitters and interpreters of his ideas. Despite the periodic protestation by Gülen, there is an undeniable connection between the Gülenists and the Nurcu. The ideas of inter-faith dialogue and education, attributed to Nursî's writing, are especially significant aspects of the Gülenist *modus operandum*, especially after his exile in Pennsylvania. The Gülenist network and their involvement in politics, education and social life in Turkey are analysed in Chapter 6.2.

Even this brief review of Nursî should demonstrate that to present him as "backward", i.e. anti-modern and against progress, does no justice to reality and the depth of his writing. No doubt many of his ideas, especially conservative views on gender relations were not congruent with modern society, but his philosophy was wider than these ideas.

Conclusion

There were intellectual differences as well as life-style differences between Kısakürek and Nursî. More importantly, while Kısakürek tended to represent elite Islamists, Nursî mostly represented the subaltern, both segments of which saw their culture and traditions being undermined by the Republican regime. They were not against modernism and were open to borrowing technology from the West. At the same time, they opposed western lifestyle.

Secularity does not have to be equated with western style secularity. A Muslim-majority country can find its own path. Both Kısakürek and Nursî advocated different paths to undergo, rather than emulate the western track.

Nursî was neither in favour of *secularism*, as Vahide portrays him to be, nor in favour of harsh Sharia law, the way the Kemalist traditionally portrayed him. He made statements in favour of *laicism*, as quoted above, describing it in a way that allowed him to form an alliance with the DP. In other words, he couched his language in terms that were acceptable in governing circles. The DP was still dominated by Kemalists, albeit not to the same extent as the CHP. Much before Taylor expressed his theory of the Immanent Frame, Nursî was aware that he operated in the kind of environment Taylor described. Nursî described "secularisation as fulfilment in worldly experiences" and was concerned that "secularisation would come after secularisation of the mind."[613] By the time of the Third Said, gener-

---

613. Necati Aydin, *Said Nursi and Science in Islam*, Oxon, 2019, pp. 29-30.

ations of students had been through the secular education system. Their minds were secularised.

Nursî was against Kemalist positivism, believing that "secular science brings many calamities for humanity", such as atheism, individualism, secularism, nihilism, hedonism, *etc.*[614] However, as Necati Aydın notes "[r]ather than completely rejecting science, Nursî decided to first filter out secular ideology from scientific knowledge and then use the de-secularized scientific knowledge as a means to get to know God (*ma'rifatullah*)".[615] De-secularisation of the mind and deconstruction of the Immanent Frame were required in the process.

Markham and Pirim suggest that Nursî argued for an alternative, which they call "Grounded pluralism", that is "grounded in the truths found in the Qur'an". In their interpretation, this vision encompassed diversity and commitment to the public nature of religious traditions".[616] Whether this argument for pluralism is genuine, for instance, in light of his ambivalent attitude to Alevis, for instance, is to be questioned.[617] However, it is important to note that Nursî explored an alternative to the binary of theocracy/secularism.

Chapter 5 discussed how the emergence of political Islam changed the political and cultural landscape hitherto dominated by Kemalists and forced laicists/secularists to make concessions. This concludes the argument of Part B, namely that Kemal established a hegemonic system in which he made efforts to curtail Islam (except between 1920 and 1923) and confine it to the private realm and separate religion from politics through the principle of laicism. This attempt has been shown to be problematic. The difficulties faced by the state in attempting to continue confining "religion", specifically Islam, inform us about the understanding of the fields of "religion" and "politics" in Turkey in this period. The illusion of separation of the two fields could not be maintained as well as in the period leading up to multi-party democracy. The non-official vestigial states, through the emergence of political Islam, and the efforts of intellectuals such as Nursî and Kısakürek, showed the fragility of the Kemalist project.

Laicism was also implemented through many contradictory practices, as I often pointed out. These contradictions did not mean that the state did not know what it was doing. Laicism was a useful banner under which to

---

614. *Loc cit.*
615. *Ibid.*, p. 2.
616. Markham and Pirim, *op. cit.*, p. 52.
617. Both Markham and Pirim and Vahide stay clear of Nursi's view on Alevism. As it does not fit the portrayal of him to a Western audience.

disseminate state propaganda. In practice, the policy of laicism concealed a number of objectives. The state wanted to harness Islam; at the same time, it wanted to employ Sunni Muslim identity as a constituent part of the Turkish national identity, excluding non-Muslims, as Aktar argued. In its endeavour the state decided to bring the Sunni mosque organisation into the fold. This "vestigial state" was thus neutralised by the close proximity to the state. It pursued an eradication and suppression policy in relation to tarikats and cemaats, which had the potential to become "future states", or at least to take on increasingly state-like attributes. The actual state actively pursued measures to eliminate this antagonistic element.

Alevis, other than the Bektashi lodges, which were banned, did not have any other institution that could be controlled. *Dedelik* would have been a difficult grass-roots institution to be brought under state control and did operate in the private sphere. In any case, the Alevis were supportive of the Kemalist project and they did not act as a "future state".

The Christian churches in Turkey did not directly operate under state management but the state had a say in the election of the Greek and Armenian Patriarchates, which were institutions established in the Ottoman Empire and which still exist in Turkey. Given the limited influence of these churches in Turkey - though the Greek Patriarchate controls churches across the world - the state does not interfere in the day-to-day affairs of the churches.

The state adopted different strategies to deal with different communities: it designated some phenomena as "religion" but not others; it suppressed some of the phenomena it had identified as "religion" portraying it in a negative light, but not others; and mobilised and used some of the phenomena it had identified as "religion", but not others.

As it was shown in the second part of Part B, the principles of laicism were diluted in the post-war era, even with the acquiescence of the CHP in part, to accommodate growing opposition to state policies and practices involving Islam. This opened the door for the emergence of political Islam, an ideology that clearly linked "religion" and "politics". To develop this argument further, Part C investigates the re-transformation of Turkish society, which gradually merged the fields of "religion" and "politics", increasing the visibility of Islam in the public square, starting the process of de-secularisation and replacing Kemalist hegemony with Islamist hegemony.

PART C

RE-TRANSFORMATION OF TURKISH SOCIETY: THE SECOND, THIRD AND FOURTH REPUBLICS (1960-2018)

Turkish society went through a radical and traumatic transformation in the early years of the Republic, but the reforms affected urban areas more than the periphery. The regional areas resisted the reforms to the extent they could. On the whole, with some exceptions, this was a passive, not militant resistance. When they were able to oppose reforms through the ballot box, they supported the DP and Menderes, who in turn responded by reversing some reforms, as discussed.

This part examines the slow re-transformation of Turkish society from a relatively secular, or an aspiring secular country, to a "post-secular" one. Kemalism failed to hold the opposing forces in the shadows forever; they re-emerged to claim their place in the political spectrum. Furthermore, it was the Kemalists who facilitated this transition. This period is marked by the emergence of Islam as a political force and more overt participation of Sunni tarikats in politics.

This part argues that political Islam finally managed to control the government and the state machinery, with facilitation by the Kemalists in the early years of the period examined. It advances the overall argument by demonstrating that the two fields of religion and politics as they had been conceptualised in the First Republic clearly merged by 2018 in the official government discourse, as well as in the self-understanding of political Islam. The state went to great effort to separate the two fields but in essence it created them as two separate things and then merged them. In other words, the state deconstructed the framework of separation it had created. Consequently, laicism failed *on its own terms*.

Chapter 6 examines a period which I call pre- post-secular. This is a period in which the Kemalist military took over government, ostensibly to safeguard Kemalist principles, including laicism/secularism. In effect, however, concessions were made to political Islam, as discussed in that chapter. Chapters 7 and 8 review two Islamist entities, which first co-operated but eventually fell out: the Gülen Movement and the AKP respectively. Gülen's intricate and ubiquitous network, which facilitated the AKP's ascendancy to power, is discussed in some detail in Chapter 7, while Chapter 8 discusses the re-transformation of Turkish society into a new form. Chapter 9 provides concluding remarks, forming a conduit to the last chapter of the study.

CHAPTER 6

THE SECOND AND THIRD REPUBLIC: PRE – POST SECULAR

Between 1960 and 1980, the military intervened three times to right perceived wrongs. This period is characterised by revolving governments between the CHP and the AP (*Adalet Partisi*), mostly through coalitions between likeminded, and even not-so-likeminded parties on occasion (e.g. the "Islamists" - "Secularists" alliance in 1974). With the notable exceptions of Jenny White, Phillip Dorroll and Nilüfer Göle, most scholars perceive Turkish history as a continuous struggle between the Islamists and the Kemalist secularists. Though, no doubt, there is an element of antagonistic attitude between the two camps, they both have a vested interest in exaggerating the gap.

There is a plethora of secondary studies related to this period, a selection of which are utilised in this chapter. The most important primary sources are party programs in the 1960s and 1970s, State Security Council (*Milli Güvenlik Kurulu*/MGK) minutes and *Wikileaks*, containing secret US diplomatic cables, generally overlooked, which are also used to trace and analyse the events of the period.

The military as the sentinel of secularism

The military, which traditionally saw itself as the guardian of laicism and the principles of Kemalism, did not hesitate to intervene to save democracy from itself. In the sixties:

> . . . if an unexpected visit to the house of an officer found [the officer] to be married a woman wearing a headscarf or refuse an offer to have any alcoholic drink or caught in flagrante delicto while praying, would cause disciplinary referral and certain discharge from the army without a trial before any court and with no appeal rights against the decision.[618]

The relationship between Diyanet and the Kemalist establishment was tested. The 1960 junta removed the President of Diyanet immediately. While there have only been 18 Presidents since 1924 to 2019, in the 1960s

---

618. İhsan Yılmaz, *op. cit.*, p. 33.

alone there were six appointed and removed. Until 1965, no President of Diyanet had undertaken an official visit abroad; the first to do so was İbrahim Bedreddin Elmalılı. Elmalılı went to Tunisia first and reportedly was greeted and treated as *Şeyhüilislam*. He was then invited to Libya, which he also visited. These visits alarmed somewhat the Kemalist establishment and he was removed from his post in less than a year. This was a brief period when Diyanet was not trusted by the Republican elite.

There was a degree of Kemalist radicalism among the military elite, which forced the government to take action against Diyanet presidents not deemed suitable, reflecting the peculiar Kemalism of the period. The tension with Diyanet was evident in the way appointments were handled. While several presidents of Diyanet were removed, its role was also strengthened by adding morality (*Ahlâk*) to its charter. Clause 1 of the Diyanet mission expanded in 1965 to include "moral principles" as part of its duty. This way it enveloped a central preoccupation of Islamists, such as Kısakürek:

> To carry out works related to the beliefs, worship and moral principles of Islamic Religion, to enlighten society about religion and to manage places of worship; the Presidency of Religious Affairs is established under the Office of the Prime Minister.[619]

Thus, any radicalism on the part of the army and government was about personalities and not about the role of Diyanet in the management of Islam and even civic life. While the army continued to pontificate about laicism, it extended the scope of Diyanet in a way that contradicted said laicism.

One important ingredient of proto-Kemalism and early Republican ideology was the belief that "scientific ideas must replace theological ones".[620] This positivist idea and positivism, an important element of Kemalism, was no longer pursued. It was inevitable that the content of Kemalism would change over time but the military reduced Kemalism to an ideology with much of its content removed. Positivism in the Kemalist thought was eroded. This became clearer when the National Culture Report (*Milli Kültür Raporu*) was released in 1982 (see below).

Alevis and politics

Paradoxically, the junta introduced measures which expressly facilitat-

619. Diyanet İşleri Başkanlığı Kuruluş ve Görevleri Hakkında Kanun, No 633, *Resmi Gazete*, 2 July 1965.
620. Parla and Davison, *op. cit.*, p. 102.

ed the right to unionise and the right to assembly. The presence of the left became more noticeable, with the *Türkiye İşçi Partisi* (TİP) gaining seats in the Parliament. Alevis have also benefited from this brief democratisation. Alevi participation in politics has been on the side of the left and secularism, while the Sunni tarikats such as the Nakshibendi entered into politics on the side of Islamic and conservative parties. The Alevis even experimented with running their own political party: *Birlik Partisi* (Unity Party/BP).

Image 4: Emblem of Türkiye Birlik Partisi[621]

The party chose to represent and express itself through the Alevi/ Shi'ite pantheon, the lion representing Ali and the 12 stars representing the imams, thereby reinforcing the "otherness" of Alevis and entrenched Sunni attitudes. In 1969, during its second congress, the BP was renamed "The Unity Party of Turkey" or *Türkiye Birlik Partisi* (TBP), in order to put an end to the rumours which accused it of working for a division of Turkey, or on behalf of Iranian interests.[622] The TBP was not very successful and it had to compete with the CHP as well as the TİP for the Alevi vote. Eventually the TBP folded and the Alevis returned to the CHP.

It was not only the coup that affected the Alevi path. In the 1960s, Turkey experienced the beginning of migration to urban centres. Modernisation in Turkey penetrated slowly to the regional areas, but, with internal migration, the people of the periphery were finally exposed fully to it. This assessment applies to both Alevis and Sunnis, whether Turks or Kurds. Urbanisation facilitated the modernisation process:

> Official authorities then considered urbanisation as a necessary step in the modernisation process, and strove to foster it. In 1950, about 25% of Turkey's population lived in urban areas, and this percentage

621. https://tr.wikipedia.org/wiki/T%C3%BCrkiye_Birlik_Partisi [Accessed on 2 May 2020].
622. Elise Massicard, 'Alevism in the 1960s: Social Change and Mobilisation', *Isis*, 2005, p. 20.

increased to 42% in 1975.[623]

Massicard noted that "many Alevi rituals were abandoned" in this process. This urbanization affected the traditional institutions such as *dedelik*, which needed to re-adapt to an urban environment:

> Village communities and the relations between dede and talip, which were the framework for religious practice, were dismantled by migration: "Before, we were conducting cem every winter in the village. But with migration, it was not possible any more, and we could only do it every third or fifth year. (Interview with a dede from Sivas, November 27th 2000)".[624]

Mustafa Kemal's vision was to break such relationships between traditional leaders and followers, as Mardin noted,[625] but during his life-time he could only break the tarikat structures, including Alevi Bektashis; Alevis living outside urban environments continued to rely on traditional structures of leadership. The *dedelik* institution was outlawed in 1925 along with other tarikat-related titles, but that had little affect outside the area of greater control and continued to operate along traditional lines.

With urbanisation, *dedelik* was tested again; it eventually became bound on Alevi organisations. In a sense, Kemal's vision was fulfilled by the weakening relations between *dede* and *talip* with *dedelik* becoming under the tutelage of cultural institutions. The proliferation of Alevi organisations in itself, as Subaşı observed, was a result of siege mentality among the Alevis. It represented a movement that was formed to defend themselves against Islamism, which they perceived to have emerged against them.[626]

Erbakan and Islamism as a political force

In the context described above, in light of a more tolerant constitution, Erbakan, an engineer by profession, tested the waters to establish an Islamic party. There were short-lived Islamic parties before the resilient Erbakan established *Millî Nizâm Partisi* (National Order Party/MNP). A party by the name *İslam Koruma Partisi* (Party of Protection of Islam) survived seven months before it was closed down by the Martial Law Command in 1946. The Islamic Democratic Party (*İslam Demokrat Partisi*),

623. *Ibid.*, p. 2.
624. *Ibid.*, p. 4.
625. Mardin, *Türkiye'de Din ve Siyaset*, p. 77.
626. Subaşı, *op. cit.*, p. 113.

mainly preoccupied with anti-Semitism, was also shut down soon after its foundation in 1951.

These two are parties rarely mentioned in the historiography of Islamic parties, as they had no lasting effect on Islamic politics, though Resul Türk notes "[w]e can see the discursive and intellectual influence of this party in the National Order Party, which was to be established many years later".[627] The early Islamic Parties tested the system's resolve and found that the establishment was not ready to accept a party with Islam in its title.

Erbakan, originally elected as an independent in 1969, formed *Millî Nizâm Partisi* and when it was closed down by the second junta without facing any elections, established *Millî Selâmet Partisi* (National Salvation Party/MSP) in 1972. Erbakan's parties were all closed for being involved in "religious politics", "religious exploitation" and acting against the principles of laicism. When the 1980 junta also prohibited his new party, along with all the other parties, Erbakan established his third party, *Refah Partisi* (The Welfare Party/RP), which eventually led him to the post of Prime Minister, in coalition with "secularist" Tansu Çiller, Turkey's first female Prime Minister. This coalition of seemingly opposing ideologies was brought down by a "soft-coup" in 1997.[628] On that occasion, the military forced Erbakan to resign.

Erbakan was connected to the İskender Paşa Cemaat of the Nakshibendî-Hâlidî order.[629] He therefore did not emerge in a vacuum; he was a member of a vestigial state which had ambition to become a future state. After his election to the Parliament as an independent from the Konya Province, he approached Nakshibendi notables such as Kısakürek, Sheikh Mehmet Zahit Kotku Efendi and Bayburtlu Paşa Dede Efendi to canvass the idea of establishing a new party. Eventually a party was formally founded on 24 January 1970, poaching two deputies from the Justice Party (Adalet Partisi/AP). Rather than using other parties, the Nakshibendi decided to form their own as a vehicle to push their agenda, thus testing the tolerance of the military.

The MNP's program expressly opposed laicity, which it saw it as curtailment of "religion":

We oppose laicism, which is described as a guarantee of freedom of

627. Resul Türk, 'Türkiye'de Siyasal İslam'ın Örgütlenme Faaliyetleri', *Journal of the Academic Elegance*, Vol. 2, No. 3, 2015, p. 114.

628. Also known as "the 28 February process", M. Hakan Yavuz, *Secularism and Muslim Democracy in Turkey*, Cambridge, 2009, p. 67.

629. Tosun, *op. cit.*, p. 676.

religion and conscience, to be a tool in the aim to repress religion and show irreverence to religious [dindar] people.[630]

The MNP also declared itself to be against Marxism, cosmopolitanism and all kinds of foreign ideologies. Much like Islamists before them, the party was also preoccupied with morality. However, providing guidance on morality was already added to Diyanet's role in 1965 and there was therefore no difference between the laicists and the Islamists, as far as the scope of Diyanet's role was concerned in certain aspects of civic life.

Despite his xenophobic discourse, Erbakan, a mechanical engineer, who received his doctorate in Germany, much like Kısakürek, was not against western technology and technological development. He was one of the first politicians who talked about manufacturing cars in Turkey, a sensible policy objective. Erbakan wanted technological advancement to avoid foreign dependency in this field. His frequent anti-western discourse was to appease his emerging constituency: the subaltern who never embraced Kemalist reforms. Irrespective of Erbakan's personal views, the MNP and later the MSP

> largely represented Anatolian cities controlled by religiously conservative Sunnis, and the small traders and artisans (esnaf) of the hinterland. These groups had long waited to benefit from the state's modernization policies but had rarely done so, partly due to their own resistance to modernization in the name of religion and tradition (e.g., female children were not often sent to school). In addition to the frustrated periphery, the NOP [MNP] also represented religiously conservative people who were informal members of outlawed religious orders. These people formed silent but powerful pressure groups with a large network.[631]

The MNP saw itself as balancing "spiritual" with "material" development and in this quest, positive science was to play an important role:

> Our Party is in favour of our nation's spiritual development, liberated from imitation in the positive sciences and technology, and aims to develop a science true to creativity, discovery and invention.[632]

In this part, the party program was not contradicting Kemalism, at least not proto-Kemalism and the early Republican views, in which science was to play a primary role in Turkish society. The party program echoed

---

630. *Millî Nizam Partisi: program ve tüzük*, Ankara, n.d., p. 7.
631. Nilüfer Narli, 'The Rise of the Islamist Movement in Turkey', *Middle East*, Vol. 3, No. 3, 1999, pp. 38-9.
632. *Millî Nizam Partisi: program ve tüzük, op. cit.*, p. 5.

Kısakürek's views on science, morality and the West, in itself an "occidental" narrative (see Chapter 5.2.2). None of their stated views were particularly radical to cause the closure of the party, but as a new party with a new discourse with strong emphasis on Islam, the party caused some alarm in the Kemalist establishment. The party was closed partly because of its opposition to laicism.

The indictment against the National Order Party suggests that all speeches given by Erbakan and his deputy, Abbas, were monitored and reported to the Office of the Public Prosecutor (*Savcılık*), which initiated the process to close the party.[633] Some of the allegations were laboured, for instance that Erbakan greeted the public with the expressions of "Esselamünaleyküm" and "Esselamünaleyküm my Muslim brothers". Both *Esselamünaleyküm* and the most common term for greeting *Merhaba* are of Arabic origin, but the term *Esselamünaleyküm* has an Islamic tone to it. Even so, it could hardly be a rational reason to form the basis of allegations against a party.

In his speeches, Erbakan played up Occidentalism and claimed Europeans did not know how to wash themselves and that they were "superstitious", as well as "hippies". However, anti-European discourse was not a sufficient reason to close the party either. Careful though Erbakan may have been, he attacked aspects of the Kemalist project. For instance, on 6 October 1970, in Kırklareli, he criticised the Civil Code for allowing a woman to work without her husband's approval. This was opposite to one of the westernisation/modernisation reforms of Mustafa Kemal to improve the status of women, and reflected Erbakan's voter base biases, and perhaps also Nakshibendi views.

In addition to the frequent references to Islam and Allah, the party also expressed a nationalism based on the Ottoman past. On the day of the launch of the party, Erbakan stated that the MNP was the party of the Sultans. His continuous reference to a history of 1,000 years went beyond the establishment of the Ottoman Empire and stretched it to the Seljuk tribes' arrival in Anatolia, but fell short of the Kemalist version of Turkish history, expressed through the Turkish History Study. The Kemalist establishment of the day still preferred to trace the provenance of the Turkish nation to an earlier, pre-Islamic time, and derive its mythology and inspiration from that of the distant past. There was thus still a gap between the Islamists and

---

633. 'Millî Nizam Partisi'nin kapatılmasına ilişkin savcılık iddianamesi', [The indictment of the office of the public prosecutor for the closure of National Order Party], Decision No. 1971/1, Decision date: 20 May 1971.

the Kemalists in respect of a number of issues, *inter alia*, Turkish history, secularism and gender roles.

Erbakan had an interest in showing the ideological gap to be wider than it was and attacked other sacred cows of the establishment of the time, alleging that the Lausanne Treaty of 1924 was a ploy to annihilate Islam. As well as making some incoherent, ahistorical claims, Erbakan's party expressed the same anti-Semitic views of Kısakürek's and alleged that the Justice Party was a party of freemasons; though he himself was initially a candidate for that party in Konya.[634] In launching the party, Erbakan re-iterated that his party would not accept Zionists or Masons, as though many were trying to become members.[635] He was simply trying to differentiate himself from other right-wing parties. This was expedient populism, pure and simple.

Much of the language of his speeches aimed at procuring votes from a conservative and pious audience. The AP was competing for the same votes, along with several other smaller parties. Following the junta of 1970 and the closure of his party, Erbakan left for Switzerland, purportedly for health reasons.[636] When he returned and was able to do so, he formed his second party, the MSP. The language of the new party was more circumspect for fear of prosecution. The anti-laicist language shifted to "[l]aicism is the assurance of freedom of thought and conscience", as prescribed in the party's program.[637] Thus, laicism was interpreted as protection of "religion". A crucial difference between the Kemalists and the Islamists was eliminated. Furthermore, the party program also addressed other concerns of the regime in relation to the indivisibility of the country by stating that "[i]n order to ensure spiritual development to gather around our nation's national consciousness and objectives and form an indivisible whole".[638]

Party programs did not necessarily reflect the true views of their leaders, but Erbakan and his cohort, the second time around, went to some length to moderate their discourse and express themselves in the language that would be acceptable by the establishment. In an interview by a renowned journalist, Abdi İpekçi in 1973, when Erbakan was asked about

---

634. Süleyman Demirel leader of the Justice Party personally vetoed Erbakan, 'AP, Erbakan ve 13 adayı veto etti', [AP, vetoed Erbakan and 13 candidates], *Millîyet*, 19 August 1969.

635. 'Millî Nizam Partisi Kuruldu', [National Order Party founded], *Cumhuriyet*, 27 January 1970.

636. A great irony is that his anti-western language did not preclude him from seeking to benefit from western medicine, in a western country.

637. Millî Selâmet Partisi, *Program ve Tüzük*, Ankara, p. 8.

638. *Ibid.*, p. 5.

the National Order, he gave a convoluted response, arguing that MSP was a different party.[639] Understandably, Erbakan did not want to provide an excuse to a Kemalist public prosecutor to start proceedings for the closure of the party.

Erbakan's own views can be found in his manifesto published in 1969, under the title *Millî Görüş*. These ideas were influenced by the Nakshibendi around him. Millî Görüş developed to become a "religio-political" movement (*Millî Görüş Hareketi*) in Turkey as well as in the Diaspora, under the leadership of Erbakan, promoting Islam and nationalism.

Islam and Nationalism

According to Tanil Bora and Nergis Canefe:

> The Millî Görüş movement expressed itself as the core perspective of the people. Furthermore, employing the daily life rituals and symbols of the religious people as references for identity, [it promoted] an ethno-populism, which stresses being Muslim as an obligatory prerequisite of being from the people/nation - or envisaged the people/nation as a Muslim nation, [thus] representing a fascist tendency in Islamism.[640]

This harsh reflection represents a "left-wing" view of the movement. Bora and Canefe also contended that Millî Görüş did not clearly identify the differences between Islamism and nationalism, thereby creating a tension.[641] Alpaslan Türkeş, the main instigator of the 1960 coup and later the leader of the ultra-nationalist *Millîyetçi Hareket Partisi* (Nationalist Movement Party/MHP), at times criticised Millî Görüş for being non-nationalist and contended that the movement did not represent "sincere Muslims" (*samimi müslümanlar*), whoever they might be.[642] In effect Türkeş was saying that Millî Görüş was neither sufficiently nationalist nor Islamist. Türkeş was in favour of violent nationalism and Pan-Turkism under an Islamic banner:

> The pride and consciousness of Turkishness is the full and harmonious unification of the spiritual elements that constitutes our nation with Islamic morality and virtue. If only our material development is raised on such an exalted basis, it becomes meaningful, becomes valuable; it

639. Abdi İpekçi, 'Her hafta bir sohbet', [A conversation every week], *Milliyet*, 8 August 1973.
640. Tanıl Bora and Nergis Canefe, "Türkiye'de Popülist Millîyetçilik" in Tanıl Bora and Murat Gültenkingil (eds.), *Millîyetçilik*, İstanbul, 2002, p. 659.
641. *Loc. cit.*
642. Kemal Can, "Ülkücü Hareket Ideolojisi", in Bora and Gültenkingil, op. cit., p. 679.

is not possible to ascend without a nation and development without morality. . . . we can see that some people are trying to cause a clash between nationalism and Islam. Such an attitude is misplaced, nugatory and ignorant; if it is done consciously then it is betrayal and discordant [nifak]. A struggle occurs between ideals, which are enemies. Yet, Islam and Turkishness have been merged in the same sacred pot for a thousand years, and it has become impossible to separate them, just like a finger and finger nail. The Turkish Nation by being a Muslim has gained the highest values of religious life, and Islam has found a Mujahideen with the love of the faith that is unique with the Turkish Nation. . . . An understanding of 'religiosity' rejecting nationalism and an understanding of nationalism hostile to Islam is alien to us.[643]

Türkeş expressed these sentiments in 1975, 15 years after he formed part of the Kemalist junta. Millî Görüş itself eventually arrived at a synthesis of Islam and nationalism, but this was hardly an innovation. As just argued, Türkeş had already launched this synthesis, the nucleus of his ideas having developed in the 1960s. The difference between Millî Görüş, Erbakan's parties and Türkeş's parties was that that one emphasised Islam the other nationalism, though their doctrines were similar. (It is not surprising that in the 2018 elections Erdoğan's Justice and Development Party (AKP) and Devlet Bahçeli's MHP formed an alliance; the two parties were already close allies. Fundamentally, they both agreed to exclude non-Kurds and non-Sunnis from their imagined ideal citizenry).

Furthermore, the synthesis itself is a proto-Kemalist construct. Yılmaz explains this construct, which he calls *Homo LASTus*, as an acronym of four parameters required to be "the best and 'the most acceptable citizen'": Laicist, Atatürkist, Sunni Muslim and Turkish.[644] All four parameters were required. For instance, a fervent Kemalist and Turkist (*Türkçü*) author of Jewish extraction, Munis Tekinalp (a.k.a. Moiz Kohen), was still subjected to the Wealth Tax in 1947 and was closely watched by the state until his death in 1961.[645] He did not fully satisfy the criteria, along with many others (Kurds, Alevis, Christians, anti-laicists).

The secondary project supported by Diyanet was to create "the good or acceptable citizen" as an ideal type for the masses. Yılmaz calls this *Lozan Müslümanları* (Lausanne Muslim), as the Lausanne agreement between Greece and Turkey used religion as a surrogate for a nation by exchanging Turkish speaking Greek Orthodox and Greek speaking Muslims.

Yılmaz's analysis regarding the constructed ideal citizen is very in-

---

643. Alpaslan Türkeş, *Temel Görüşler*, 190-91, 1975.
644. Yılmaz, *Kemalizm'den Erdoğanizm'e*, pp. 9-10.
645. *Ibid.*, p. 24.

sightful. Yet, his work contains many contradictions. For instance, while he argued that the Sunni Muslim component was a requirement for the most ideal citizen, as a Gülenist, he also contends that the Kemalists hated religion, as opposed to the Atatürkists, who tolerated it so long as there are no political demands from them. As we have seen, there have been periods where some Republicans showed an antagonistic attitude towards Islam; or at least aspects of Islam encompassing local traditions. This antagonism was not about hatred of Islam, but about control of Turkish society.

In the early years, the Republican elite looked down on the masses, but it was not Islam *per se* but cultural practices, which they regarded as "backward", that formed the basis of their antagonistic and elitist view. Irrespective of his personal views on Islam, Mustafa Kemal chose to include Sunni Islam as a requirement for his acceptable and ideal citizen. "The emblematic citizen was a Turkish Muslim with a secular lifestyle, dedicated to a state-led program of modernization believed to be Ataturk's design."[646]

Mustafa Kemal could have embraced Alevism to form a new Turkish identity rather than Sunni Islam, or simply not included Islam at all in the construct of an ideal citizen, Sunni or otherwise. Ultimately, the Republican elite chose their own background as the ideal and tried to impose it on the masses through hegemonic methods.

Yılmaz explains that the dislike of the Republican elites against Islam as practised, led them to reform it through Diyanet to create a "laic, nationalist, religious doxa".[647] The term "Lausanne Muslim" may not be a suitable description, but Yılmaz's analysis of a two-tiered ideal citizenry is apt, one for the elites, one for the masses. The evident failure of this social engineering is not surprising, as they attempted to agglutinate disparate and contradictory elements into one synthesis.

Erbakan and politics in the 1970s: Convergence of seemingly opposing ideas

Erbakan claimed that until the period when he defined Millî Görüş,

[t]his period has multiple parties, but it is single-minded. It has a single mindset. You can have as many parties as you want, but provided you express ideas within a rigid [framework of] ideas. This is the action and the practice.

646. White, *op. cit.*, p. 9.
647. İhsan Yılmaz, *op. cit.*, p. 39.

According to Erbakan, these parties, which have been established since the transition to the multi-party system, were far from being parties of ideas, they had become mass parties. In effect, Erbakan was accusing the other parties of operating within the framework of Kemalism and espousing laicism. The two major parties, the AP, partly, and the CHP were certainly in this camp, but there was a number of small parties competing for votes. One of those small parties, the New Turkey Party (*Yeni Türkiye Partisi*), referred to nationalism, laicism and adoption of western democratic lifestyle and modernisation in its program, which looked somewhat antithetical to Erbakan's views. Yet, their program devoted attention to religious education as a state responsibility:

> We conceive laicism as separation of religious affairs from the state affairs. However, we believe in the necessity of conducting the religious affairs and particularly the religious education within a program to be prepared by qualified committees. We believe that if the religious discipline and inculcation were in the hands of the ignorant, it would be detrimental to the purity and sublimity (ulviyet) of religion.[648]

Another small party, The Nation Party (*Millet Partisi*) did not use the term *laik* in its party program, but referred to the separation of religion, party and state matters: [Our Party] accepts politics as an activity based on the moral principles to ensure the welfare and happiness of the nation".[649] In turn, *Güven Partisi* (Reliance Party), in its program declared its support of laicism, with a peculiar definition of it:

> Our party refuses the apprehension of laicism as disrespect of religion and worship. Laicism requires religious beliefs and sentiments to be held at such height that cannot be exploited.[650]

The party program also referred to the aim of ensuring material and spiritual development as the aim of the Turkish state.[651] These spiritual values, never defined, can be found throughout the party program and were no different from those of Erbakan.

Cumhuriyet Köylü Millet Partisi (Republican Peasants' Party), which morphed into MHP once Türkeş took over the party, also emphasised the importance of spiritual and material foundations as a necessity and announced their policy of an extensive reform of religious education: "We will develop the Faculty of Theology, the Higher Institute of Islam. We re-

---

648. *Yeni Türkiye Partisi Tüzüğü ve Programı*, 1967, pp. 54-55.
649. *M.P. Millet Partisi Programı*, Ankara, 1967, p. 8.
650. *Güven Partisi Programı*, 1967, pp. 8 and 73.
651. *Ibid.*, p. 8.

gard Imam Hatpin schools as vocational high schools; our aim is to expand them".[652]

Erbakan, therefore, with his Millî Görüş principles, was not as radical as he is credited to be; much of the ideas espoused can be found embedded in other parties' programs. Many of the parties in the 1960s and 1970s referred to spiritual values, morality, religious beliefs and the perceived importance of religious education. The difference between the other conservative parties and Millî Görüş Parties was that the latter were much more overt in their language, interspersed with Islamic references.[653] They also omitted references to Kemalism or Atatürk. In a rally in Izmir on 4 October 1973, marked by violent protest, Erbakan spoke to a mostly middle-aged audience, which was its vote base at that point. His speech, reportedly, "was most notable for its failure to mention Atatürk among the heroes of Turkish history".[654] That they disliked Mustafa Kemal is not in dispute.

Erasing Mustafa Kemal from the party's public discourse was not an impediment to form an alliance with Kemalist secularists eventually. Erbakan operated in the same framework of political expediency he criticised and used the opportunity presented, in 1973, to be in government with its supposed arch nemesis, the party of laicism *par excellence* CHP. A United States diplomatic cable reported that the military was strongly objecting to this coalition and preferred a CHP-AP coalition instead, to represent a broad spectrum of the "secularists". Press of the day also reported that the Armed Forces Commanders presented a memorandum to the President Korutürk to that effect: "The President immediately issued a denial that . . . any memo exchanged hands, but this denial in effect acknowledged that there have been several talks on political affairs between the President and the top military leadership."[655]

Though this coalition of Islamists and Republicans did not survive the full term in the turmoil of the politics in the seventies, Erbakan used the opportunity to staff the public service with his supporters. Here there was a departure from the previous policy of recruiting only the most ideal citizens to the public service. People not fitting the archetypal public servant

---

652. *Cumhuriyetçi Köylü Partisi Seçim Bildirisi*, 1965. p. 10.
653. Indeed, originally when Erbakan was contemplating names for his first party, considered risky names such as *Cihat Partisi* (the Jihad Party) and İmanlı Türkiye Partisi (Faithful Turkey Party); 'Erbakan'ın Yeni Partisi Pazartesi Kuruluyor', *Milliyet*, 24 January 1970. p. 11.
654. *WikiLeaks*, Public Library of US Diplomacy, Canonical ID: 1973IZMIR00443_b, Subject: Violence Mars NSP rally, 5 October 1073.
655. *WikiLeaks*, Public Library of US Diplomacy, Canonical ID: 1974ANKARA00269_b, Subject: RPP and NSP Ready to Form Coalition, 14 January 1974.

profile were now recruited to administrative positions, diluting the constitution of the public service, though still Sunni Muslim. Homo LASTus was slowly being replaced by "Homo Islamicus" and Islamo-nationalists:

> During the legislature, Erbakan placed its members in the different bureaucratic institutions and even approved a bill that equated the imam-hatip to the secondary schools, thus facilitating the students of these schools to reach universities. Between 1974 and 1978 the number of these schools tripled.[656]

Millî Görüş

As noted, Millî Görüş was an ideology in which the Nakshibendi tarikats had an influence. The parties they established and re-established as the state kept shutting them down, were not simply vehicles through which to transmit ideas, but also to gain power. Millî Görüş was not an ideology of a party; it was the ideology of a group around Erbakan who established a number of parties to implement their thinking.[657] Part of this group included Zahit Kotku who had a much more direct influence upon Turkish Islamist discourse. Kotku had a seminal role in the formation of the Millî Görüş movement, which can clearly be described as a Nakshibendi project.[658]

In a way, Millî Görüş parties embodying the Nakshibendi tarikat can be said to have been competing primarily in the religious market. Yet, by operating within a framework of Islamo-nationalism, Millî Görüş was not competing in the religious market, but in the market of nationalism, so to speak. In the Turkish political *milieu,* this was a crowded arena. The religious element gave Millî Görüş an edge to exploit. The MSP newspaper *Millî Gazete* announced on 4 October 1973 that it was not the parties fighting in the elections but faiths[659]; this was hardly the case, as can be attested by other party programs cited above.

Resul Türk notes all the parties established by Erbakan reflecting Millî Görüş principles were functioning as *cemaat* and Erbakan was called a "Commander of mujahideen", party demonstrations were called *gaza* ("sa-

656. Laura Fernandez, 'El desarollo del Islamismo politico en Turquía', Unisci Discussion Papers, No. 9, October 2005, p. 139.
657. Yılmaz, Selma. 'Millî Görüş Hareketi: Toplumsal Hareketlerde Çerçeve Değişimi Etkisi', İnsan ve Toplum Bilimleri Araştırmaları Dergisi, Vol. 5, No. 4, p. 1165.
658. Anne Rose Solberg, *The Mahdi Wears Armani,* University of Gothenburg, Goteborg, 2013, p. 56.
659. Ihsan Yilmaz, *Kemalizm'den Erdoğanizm'e,* p. 66.

cred battle"/war against non-Muslims) and "heterodox" people, mainly Alevis, were called *fitneci* (seditious).[660] Thus, they acted like a future state. Their construct of Islamism and nationalism, just like the original ideal of an acceptable or ideal citizen, excluded non-Sunnis.

Millî Görüş ideology was a synthesis of Islam and nationalism, but broadly speaking so was Kemalism. Despite all the rhetoric of laicism, the Kemalist state defined the nation using Sunni Islam as a surrogate and excluded non-Muslims from participating in certain aspects of public life, for instance, from public service employment. There are definitely some differences in the discourse, but it is to be wondered why the state kept closing down Erbakan's and Millî Görüş parties, when the divergence was not wide. The army and the Republicans locked in their peculiar view of laicism, continued to view any kind of Islamism as a threat; all the while Diyanet under their watch produced Islamic literature and kept excluding Alevis.

Erbakan used opportunities that were presented when his party was a coalition partner to promote supporters to the public service during 1996-97. Though he was eventually forced to resign, he paved the way for the current governing party, AKP. The public service now had functionaries that were not expressly laicists or even Atatürkist.

The chasm between Erbakan and the "neo-Kemalists" was not as wide as both sides portrayed. Even in terms of preferred clothing some of the differences were minimised in later years, when Erbakan sought to transform his image and extend his vote base by wearing fashionable suits and Versace ties:

> Similar to Atatürk, who had made a public appearance wearing a suit and a top hat, thereby inscribing on his own body the norms of 'civilized' modern governance, Erbakan also used his own body to create an image of modern and competent Islamist statesmanship. Erbakan's suits and trademark ties served a twofold function. First, they served to vest the Islamist elite with agency and ascribe to it the qualities of a competent leader who was capable of ruling and transforming society toward a new Islamist nationalist ideal. . . . Second, this intervention with regard to the male body of the Islamist leadership served a crucial function toward unsettling the dominant view of Islamism as backward, 'uncivilized', fundamentalist, incompetent, and lacking taste and culture. [661]

660. Resul Türk, 'Türkiye'de Siyasal İslam'ın Örgütlenme Faaliyetleri', *Journal of The Academic Elegance*, Vol. 2, No. 3, 2015, p. 123.
661. Çınar, *op. cit.*, p. 88.

Neo-Kemalism

As frequently pointed out in this study, the Kemalist elite made an artificial distinction between themselves and the rest of the population by defining themselves as the enlightened (*aydın*) elite and the large masses as those that needed to be reformed. Mustafa Kemal himself noted that they needed to set the Anatolian Turks right (*adam etme*).[662] By this rationalisation, they aimed to perpetuate their hold on power. They did not allow for other parties to function until 1946 and when the parties did not play to script, the military intervened to continue guiding and governing. It was not just about religion or laicisation, it was about power.

The establishment redefined Kemalism in the 1970s and 1980s through a conservative nationalist advocacy group called *Aydınlar Ocağı* (Hearth of Intellectuals) by merging it with Islam. This was not an innovation by any means, but the element of Islam and the Ottoman past was strengthened in the synthesis:

> [B]y constructing a new ideology based on the fusing of Turkish nationalism with Ottoman-Islamic myths and symbols. This new ideology was incorporated into the 1982 constitution, thus attaining the status as a semi-official ideology of the state. According to the Turkish-Islamic synthesis, there is an innate compatibility between the Turkish national character and Islam, so that the supposed character traits of pre-Islamic Turkish culture such as a strong sense of justice, monotheism and emphasis on family and morality were enhanced through the Turks' conversion to Islam, and that Turks were therefore ;the soldiers of Islam'.[663]

In essence, any differences between the "laicist" elite and the "Islamists" were reduced even further. Positivism was ignored in this emerging neo-Kemalism. Post-1980, the dismantling of the laicist structure eroded further some laicist measures still in place, such as the equivalence of Imam Hatip Schools, religious education in schools becoming compulsory and other measures that sought to appease a segment of society Kemalists traditionally did not favour. In order to suppress the growing leftist movement, including the violent left, the military sought to strengthen the Islamist segment. Between the secularists and the Islamists, the supposedly laic military chose the latter.

---

662. Yılmaz, *op. cit.*, p. 10.
663. Solberg, *op. cit.*, p. 56.

The 1980 junta sought to transform Kemalism once again, even trying to portray Mustafa Kemal as "religious", in a three-volume biography of Atatürk, reinventing him "as a pious Muslim whose reforms were designed not to reduce the influence of Islam in public life but to free it of obscurantist accretions and restore it to its original state as an enlightened, rational religion".[664]

Yüksel Taken calls this period a "Kemalist Restoration Attempt", which at times vulgarised Atatürkist.[665] If this simulacrum was not sufficient to transform Kemalism, the principal leader of the junta Kennan Even would express his eclectic views under the rubric *hakiki İslam* ("true Islam"). Just like Türkeş's *samimi* (sincere) Muslim, Evren used his construct to differentiate from other imagined categories of Muslims. These sorts of terms alluded to the existence of a mass of insincere or untrue Muslims as a category, which somehow needed to be moulded to the "true" form.

Kenan Evren took it upon himself to preach at rallies about "true Islam" giving speeches using religious motifs and reciting verses from the Quran.[666] Jenkins notes that

[e]ven though he was - unusually for a member of the Turkish military - the son of an imam, there is no evidence to suggest that Evren had an Islamist agenda. He appears rather to have been attempting to instrumentalize Islam as an ideological bulwark against communism and, in eastern and southeast Anatolia, separatist Kurdish nationalism.[667]

Evren may not have had an "Islamic agenda", meaning he did not want the state to be governed by Islamic law, but the evidence shows that he promoted Islam as a defining element of Turkish society. In short, post 1980 the military transformed the Kemalist notion of acceptable citizen. In the original synthesis, the Islamic element was moderated by laicism. This construct of disparate elements held together by state control lost its strength and meaning. A new era, sometimes described as post-Kemalism or neo-Kemalism, was ushered in. The Kemalist restoration required the maintenance of Kemalism as a framework but with transformed content.

This neo-Kemalism distanced itself from proto-Kemalism:

664. Jenkins, *op. cit.,* p. 143. It is also important to remember that Diyanet's *Askere Din Kitabı* (Book of Religion for the Soldier) was reproduced in 1982; Kürşat Bumin, 'Askere Din Kitabı (2)', *Yeni Şafak,* 16 April 2006.

665. Yüksel Taşkın, "12 Eylül Atatürkçülüğü ya da Bir Kemalist Restorasyon Teşebbüsü olarak 12 Eylül" in Tanıl Bora, Gültenkingil Murat, *Kemalizm,* Vol. 2, İstanbul, 2009.

666. Savaş Çoban, 'Türkiye'de Siyasal İslamın Kısa Tarihi', *biamag Cumartesi,* 10 May 2014, https://bianet.org/biamag/siyaset/155563-turkiye-de-siyasal-islamin-kisa-tarihi, [Accessed on 21 April 2018].

667. Jenkins, *op. cit.,* p. 142.

In 1983 the junta published a Milli Kültür Raporu, or 'National Culture Report.' It was prepared in collaboration with the ultranationalist Intellectuals' Hearth organization and argued that Turks were united by a shared national culture based on the three institutions of the family, mosque, and military.[668]

The junta, in co-operation with *Aydınlar Ocağı* redefined Turkish identity, strengthening the Islamic component. This component had always been inconspicuously present but now it was expressed unambiguously. This report also criticised positivism and by doing so, it "represented an implicit critique of Atatürk and of the origins of Turkish nationalism".[669] The report also stated that "[s]cience without Religion . . . causes a disaster",[670] whereas Mustafa Kemal and the early Republicans believed the positivist notion that scientific ideas must replace theological ones.[671] The neo-Kemalists were now reflecting Nursî's views and challenging the Immanent Frame.

While Atatürkism was retained, Kemalism was being reconstructed and even Erbakan once said that "if Atatürk were alive, he would have definitely been a Millî Görüş supporter".[672] This was politically expedient to say. The term *Millî* needs to be dicussed to assess Erbakan's contention. Although it is translated as such:

> Milli does not mean simply 'national' but also connotes religious ethnos, and it continues to be articulated as an ethical signifier of justice, loyalty, and community. Milli easily could be used interchangeably with 'religiously defined community'.673

The concept of *Misak-i Millî* (National Pact), which was the doctrine of the new boundaries of Turkey, was announced in 1920 by a group of deputies in the Ottoman Parliament. These deputies participated in the Independence War instigated by Mustafa Kemal. Kemal's Misak-ı Millî was clearly defined and restricted; whereas, in the usage of the deputies, within the framework of *Darul Harb* and *Darul Islam*, *millî* referred to the places where Muslims lived. The deputies participated in the National Pact because they thought it was about liberation of all Muslim lands.[674] This is an important distinction: while Kemal's vision of the new country's borders

---

668. *Ibid.*, p. 142.
669. Eligür, *op. cit.*, p. 106.
670. *Loc. cit.*
671. Parla and Davison, *op, cit*, p. 102.
672. Ahmet Akgül. *Erbakan'ın Farkı*, İstanbul, 2013, p. 349.
673. Yavuz, *Islamic Political Identity in Turkey*, p. 208.
674. Aytunç Altındal, *Laiklik*, 2nd Edition, İstanbul 1994, p. 63.

were more realistic and, with some exceptions, took into account the lands where the majority of Turks lived, the deputies, who joined Mustafa Kemal's efforts, had a much broader Islamist-oriented territorial vision. It is this vision Millî Görüş supported.

Re-emergence of religious formations as a political force

Some tarikats disappeared completely proving to be ephemeral. One group, the Ticanis mentioned in Chapter 4.0, was active for several years leading up to the arrest of their leader, Kemal Pilavoğlu, in 1950. The Ticanis were formed post-Republic and did not have the long history and the embedded tradition and popular support base of the other tarikats. They dissolved without causing much damage to the regime, although they contributed to the reversal of the prohibition of the reading of the Quran to be in Arabic.

A few years later, in 1954, their confiscated belongings such as cones (*kulâh* and *takke*) and any instruments facilitating the performance of religious ceremony were destroyed.[675] This marked the end of Ticanis. The ceremonious burning of the vestments and assorted paraphernalia showed the importance assigned to any physical reminders of tarikats. The buildings of the formal tarikat could not be demolished as they had historic significance, but hostility to non-western clothing and fear of physical reminders of the existence of the tarikat led authorities to destroy the relics.

A few incidents involving the Bektashis have been reported in the press between 1930 and 1960, receiving the same negative treatment as the Nakshibendi.[676] After the prohibition the Bektashi changed their normal practices and conducted their ceremonies in houses in presence of women and children.[677] The following picture from *Milliyet* in 1952, attest to this change.

---

675. 'Ticanîlerin eşyaları merasimle yakıldı', [Ticani belongings were burned ceremonially], *Milliyet*, 12 November 1954, p. 1.
676. 'Bektaşiler!', [Bektashis!], *Cumhuriyet*, 9 June 1930, p. 4; Bektaşiler tahliye edildi', [Bektashis released], *Cumhuriyet*, 9 June 1930, p. 5; 'Ayin yapan Bektaşiler dün tevkif edildiler', [The Bektashi who performed a religious ceremony were arrested yesterday], *Milliyet*, 6 October 1952, p. 1; 'Bektaşi Ayini' [Bektashi religious ceremony], *Milliyet*, 23 October, p. 2; '13 Bektaşi yakalandı', [13 Bektashis captured], *Cumhuriyet*, 13 June 1932, p. 2.
677. Cemil Hakyemez, 'Tekkeler ve Zaviyeler Kanunu Çerçevesinde Alevîlik-Bektaşîlik', *Hitit* Üniversitesi İlahiyat *Fakültesi Dergisi*, Vol. 13, No. 25, 2014, p. 166.

06.10.1952, Milliyet, Sayfa 1

Ayin yapan bektaşiler dün tevkif edildiler

Sanıklar evvelâ nişan yaptıklarını söyledilersede delliler karşısında suçlarını itiraf ettiler

Image 5: Arrested Bektashis

At first glance, it is hard, to comprehend the reason for arresting these Bektashis, or any other Bektashis. They were performing their rituals in private, just as the ideal secularism demanded and did not antagonise the regime. Also, men and women were together in a social function, which fit the purported Kemalist worldview about the position of women. All tarikats were seen as anachronistic, irrespective of their practices.

It can be surmised that the clandestine activities of Bektashis and Nakshibendis, for that matter, continued throughout the prohibition. The dervish lodges were simply replaced with houses and apartments and the ceremonies became discrete so as not to attract attention of neighbours. The *Milliyet* newspaper called these houses 'tekkes' and 'dergâhs'.[678] By defining any place in which tarikat functions were undertaken as lodges, the prohibition law extended its application.

Both the Bektashis and the Nakshibendis survived the difficult years, but it is the latter that went from strength to strength. Angel Rabasa and Larrabee F Stephen contend that:

The Nakşibendi are known for their tolerance and flexibility. Members

---

678. 'Bektaşi tekkesi dün basıldı', *Milliyet*, 5 October 1952, p. 1.

divide life into two spheres: the private and the religious. This leaves room for enjoying life. Some members have been known to indulge in moderate drinking in private.[679]

Rabasa and Stephen do not provide a source for this information; perhaps it is a general observation. Nevertheless, İsmet Zeki Eyüboğlu, who joined the tarikat at the age of 14 and stayed several years, paints a different picture. To be sure, Eyüboğlu's negative experiences may have clouded his judgment but with his insider knowledge, he was able to outline the Nakshibendi practices and their conservative attitude toward women.[680] One possible explanation of the contradictory information is that Eyüboğlu's joined in 1939 at the age of 14, when the order was illegal, and the order evolved since then to some extent to keep up with the times. Hakan Yavuz noted that:

> In recent decades, the Nakşibendi order has become mobilized on an internal level because of increasingly worldly concerns. To a certain extent, the order has become secularized, and its religious views, in turn, have been modified by more profane interests.[681]

This claim will be examined in the following chapters but it has to be pointed out that at least one of the branches of the Nakshibendi, the Cemaat of İsmail Ağa, insisted its male members to wear beard, shalwar (baggy trousers), turban and *cübbe* (gown). The female members were required to wear *çarşaf* (black headscarf).[682] Probably not the branch Rabasa and Stephen had in mind, when described them as flexible. This was precisely what Mustafa Kemal wanted to stamp out in his quest for modernisation of the Turkish society. In contemporary Kemalist sources these sorts of practices by these formations justify retrospectively Mustafa Kemal's hostility towards the tarikats and reinforce the view of their "backwardness".

While the Nursî followers supported the conservative AP in the 1960s, they largely stayed away from party politics. İhsan Yılmaz attributes this to the difference of philosophies between Nursî (who also was Nakshibendi) and the Nakshibendi notables of the 1970s:

> One of the reasons for this is their divergent view of the state. Said Nursî is the person who most clearly states that is not possible to Is-

679. Angel Rabasa, and Stephen F. Larrabee, *The Rise of Political Islam in Turkey*, Santa Monica, 2008. p. 14.

680. İsmet Zeki Eyüboğlu, İslam *Dininden Ayrılan Cereyanlar*, Cumhuriyet Gazetesi, n.p., 1998, *passim*; especially pp. 6, 14 and 104.

681. M. Hakan Yavuz, *Islamic Political Identity in Turkey*, Oxford, 2003, p. 35.

682. Necdet Tosun, 'Nakşibendiyye'in Ceyhan, Semih (ed.), *Türkiye'de Tarikatlar*, İstanbul, 2015, p. 679.

lamise society from top to bottom by taking over the state. According to him, the state is not a structure to be sanctified or conquered, it is a service tool.[683]

This was a fundamental difference between Nursî and other Islamists who intended to capture and control the state mechanism, the latter behaving like a future state, as Goldenberg would suggest. Service, *Hizmet*, has also been a preoccupation of the Gülen Cemaat, a branch of Nurcular. However, they departed from Nursî's view relating to the state, and, as we shall see, they sought political power and infiltration into state mechanisms.

For a period of 20 years (1960-80), politics was dominated by military coups or the threat of one. The Islamists became an element of politics, but their concern about potential closure of their parties forced them to be circumspect in their articulation of their message and to wait for the right time. However, they threw caution to the wind, when they felt the time was right, at a rally held in Konya on 6 September 1980:

> MSP supporters openly called for the destruction of the secular Turkish state. . . . During the rally, the demonstrators, while marching in long robes and fez and carrying green flags, called for the restoration of a Sharia order in Turkey by shouting such slogans as 'Sharia will come, brutality will end,' 'Sovereignty belongs to Allah,' 'The Constitution is the Quran,' 'Secularism is atheism,' 'Government with Allah's rules,' 'We are ready for jihad,' 'We want [an] unlimited, classless Islamic state,' and 'Sharia or death.' The Islamists refused to sing the national anthem . . . 'We want the call of prayer (ezan); we do not sing this anthem.'[684]

Only a few days later the army took over again. While it appeared that the Islamists may have alarmed the Kemalist establishment in the immediate term, the main reason for the intervention this time around was the pacification of an overtly politicised population and also to achieve economic stability.[685] Both the far left and the far right had militant wings and they fought each other in many arenas, such as schools, universities and neighbourhoods.[686] I myself witnessed this first hand in 1978, when my high school was briefly overtaken by left-wing students before the police arrived and struck students indiscriminately. The military managed to

683. İhsan Yılmaz, *op. cit.,* p. 61.
684. Eligür, *op. cit.,* pp. 87-88.
685. Hacı Hasan Saf, 'Türkiye'de Yükselen Siyasal İslam'ın Postmodern Nedenleri', *Karadeniz Teknik Üniversitesi İletişim Araştırmaları Dergisi*, Vol. 3, No. 12, p. 113.
686. For instance, *Devrimci Sol* or *Dev Sol* (The Revolutionary Left) and *Bozkurtlar* (The Grey Wolves).

eradicate the leftist threat to a great extent by both judicial and extra-judicial executions, but in the process, it precipitated the politicisation of Islam, increased the Islamist penetration in state mechanisms, and the eventual dominance of political Islam.

By political Islam, I mean the action of individuals and/or groups who seek to transform the nature of society to revitalise an Islamic vision through political engagement. There is obviously a distinction between the terms Islamists and Muslims. As White puts it:

> Islamists are Muslims who, rather than accepting an inherited Muslim tradition, have developed their own self-conscious vision of Islam and the ideal Islamic life, which they bring to bear on social and political events.[687]

Many communities talk as if they are simply accepting an inherited tradition, but every community in fact develops its own - more or less - self-conscious ideal of how that inherited tradition relates to the modern world, including social and political events. White goes on to say that in many parts of the world, this vision is the implementation of Sharia Law, or at the very least some form of systemic social and political change. The content and meaning of Islamism therefore may vary across a continuum.[688] This vision could be a utopia or a pragmatic goal, which takes into account the social and political realities. Turkey is a country in which increasingly Islamic groups and precepts appear in public life, but no Sharia law, such as polygamy or gender segregation, is enshrined in law. The penal and civil codes remain secular, but it has to be pointed out that some Islamic practices such as polygamy are not prosecuted, the state thereby ceding certain territory in family law.

The most important factor that accounts for the Islamist mass infiltration into the state apparatus was the shift of the political will of the neo-Kemalist regime and its need to recruit allies in its war against the Kurdish separatist guerrillas. Hitherto, the state's policy in relation to the Kurdish question was to approach it as a military operation. The junta pursued the same policy. In its attempt to resolve the Kurdish question by force, it chose to recruit allies from the Islamic sector. As noted by Eligür,

> [t]he military regime also established a new Department of Propagation (İrşad Dairesi) within . . . Diyanet in 1981 as a countermeasure to the Kurdish separatist movement, the PKK, in the southeastern part of Turkey. The department had regularly organized conferences and

687. White. *op. cit.*, pp. 38-9.
688. *Ibid.*, p. 39.

217

lectures regarding the dangers of the PKK and of Marxism.[689]

By doing so the military instrumentalised Diyanet in its effort to fight the PKK, and Islam was used as an ideology to keep the Kurdish community under control and stop its national emancipation. Political Islam has always had and continues to have, a great impact on the Kurds, as opposed to the parties that represent Kemalist orthodoxy.

The change of attitude of the military, which till then presented itself as the guardian of Kemalist principles, especially laicism/secularism, required a change in its charter. Thus, a new project was undertaken to re-interpret and shape Kemalism, to produce neo-Kemalism. Different names have been used by scholars to label this shift, including "Kemalist Restoration", or the Third Republic. The Islamists had to be integrated into the system in order to pursue the goals of economic development and eliminate the relative threat posed by the Left and the Kurdish insurgency.

In the aftermath of the coup, the National Security Council (*Milli Güvenlik Kurulu*/MGK), consisting at the time of the top brass of the Chief of Staff, shut down leftist associations and unions. It even purged left-leaning scholars from universities.[690] The vacuum was to be filled by the newly emancipated Islamist sector. The new project of Kemalism enticed the Islamists to government but they expected the extremist elements to be isolated, which they regarded as *irtica*. This term can be translated as either "reaction" or "reactionary" Islam[691] and was used by Kemalists to indicate an Islamic movement of which they did not approve. Thus, the new policy shifted to regard some political Islam as acceptable. As Hakan Yavuz noted, it was decided that this integration could be done only by accepting a "soft Islam", that is an Islam that the state carefully domesticated and monitored. Consequently, Islamist groups entered the system through the expansion of educational opportunities, economic activity and party politics.[692]

The early Kemalist project to control and shape Islam failed. On the ground, many Muslims were influenced by tarikats and cemaats, which the regime could not eradicate. This failure was evident in the rapid emergence of these religious formations in the public sphere. The newer project was to accept the reality of Islam not fully controlled by the state, and still try to chisel out the extreme elements (*irtica*) and share power with those that

---

689. Eligür, *op. cit.*, p. 105.
690. Saf, *op. cit.*, p. 114. Post 1983, the NSC included the Prime Minister and the President.
691. Parla and Davison translate it as 'regressive" or "obsurantist", *Corporatist ideology on Kemalist Turkey*, p. 103.
692. Hakan M. Yavuz. *Islamic Political Identity in Turkey*, Oxford, 2003, p. 214.

were willing to enter into a mutually beneficial arrangement.

One of the early measures taken by the MGK was the introduction of religious classes as a compulsory subject into the school curriculum. Though the Kemalists tried to control and manage Islam under the guise of laicism, at times governments of different persuasions maintained an ambivalent attitude towards religious education and this was reflected in changes in policies about the status of the *İmam-Hatip* schools and religious education in schools. Religious education, which was restricted in the early years of the Republic, was gradually accepted in Kemalist circles and was introduced at different school levels. However, compulsory religious education in secular schools remained a figurative red line. The military under the leadership of Evren wanted to take a new direction and cross this red line as well.

Discussion on the introduction of compulsory religious education as draft Clause 24 of the Constitution took place in the MGK meeting of 18 October 1982. The clause in question stated: "Religion and moral education is carried out under the watch and supervision of the State. Religious culture and moral education are among the compulsory subjects in the primary and secondary education institutions".[693] General Tahsin Şahinkaya proposed removing the word "compulsory" to soften the clause and make it judicious but Kenan Evren, presiding over the meeting, did not think it was necessary to change and insisted on the word "compulsory" (*zorunlu*).[694]

One rationale for introducing the subject was about control, as Evren clearly expressed it. Evren thought that the number of *İmam Hatip* Schools was too high (357) and in addition he pointed to the proliferation of Qur'anic courses running across the country, given that parents wanted their children to receive religious education.[695] In Evren's thinking, rather than letting different Islamic groups teach the Qur'an and provide their own exegesis, the state was to fulfil this role. This was already done through the *İmam Hatip* schools but now it was to be extended to secular schools so as to "corner the market" in religious education. The State first sought to monopolise the field of "religion" and "religious life", then monopolise

---

693. The Turkish term *ahlâk* can be rendered both as "morality" and "ethics". Different scholars have translated the subject as Religious Culture and Morality or Religious and Ethics. Given the content of the curriculum it is more apt to call these lessons Religion and Morality. The subject is taught within the context of Sunni Islam rather than as a philosophy course of ethics. See, Nurullah Altaş, 'Türkiye'de Örgün Öğretimde Dinin Yeri', *Marifet*, Vol. 2, no. 1, Spring 2002, p. 229.
694. *Milli Güvenlik Konseyi Tutanak Dergisi*, Vol. 7, 18 October 1982, p. 340.
695. *Ibid.*, p. 342.

clerical training and finally religious education.

Evren also thought that religious culture and morality education went hand in hand, which is compatible with the view of the early Islamist thinker Halil Pasha, but also the Millî Görüş Movement, which the Kemalists detested. The implementation of the rapprochement policy with the Islamic sector required a compliant government and state machinery, given that secular-minded public functionaries were still prevalent. It was necessary to remove the old guard from the equation. The military delayed elections, relying on appointed technocrats, and unlike the previous juntas, banned parliamentarians who were holding seats at the time of the coup, from participating in the first elections of 1983. The ban, which was lifted in 1987, excluded the main stalwarts such as Demirel, Erbakan, the former CHP leader Bülent Ecevit and Türkeş. These circumstances provided opportunities for politicians who either failed or did not attempt to run for a parliamentary seat in the then current session.

Post-Junta period and facilitation of Islamism in public life and the economy

One such politician Turgut Özal, who failed in his quest to be elected with the MSP, emerged and used the opportunity to become Prime Minister, with his *Anavatan Partisi* (The Motherland Party, ANAP). In the interim he worked in the Public Service (undersecretary to the Prime Minister Demirel) and before the coup he was instrumental in Demirel's economic reform package. After the coup he was appointed by the military as Deputy Prime Minister. Özal had also worked for the World Bank and was "a supporter of the İskenderpaşa Nakşibendi Sufi order".[696]

As a technocrat before the military intervention, Özal was instrumental in the construction of the financial reforms known as *24 Ocak kararları* ("24 January Decisions") - due to the day of their announcement in 1980. As undersecretary and as Deputy Prime Minister Özal embarked upon the implementation of changes to the economic terrain and as Prime Minister affected the political landscape with the participation of the Islamists increasingly successful in both spheres.

Although Özal was not the military's preferred person for the prime-ministership, it is hard not to conclude that he turned out to be the ideal person to implement the military project, both in terms of his economic credentials and his connections to the Nakshibendi tarikat. Turgut

---

696. Rabasa and Larrabee, *op. cit.*, p. 13.

Sunalp, the military's favoured candidate, was simply a retired officer lacking Özal's experience, ability and connections to the tarikats and the world of finance. Özal was uniquely placed to embark upon this project even if his elevation was circumstantial.

As Prime Minister, Özal removed barriers to Islamic activities and essentially sought to form a regime in Turkey that would combine moderate Islamic principles, economic neo-liberalism and geopolitical ties with the West. The full scope of his agenda included the resolution of the Kurdish question through reform rather than force, but he was not able to progress it. His enduring legacy, the massive penetration of the Islamists into the state apparatus, has remained. The proliferation of *İmam-Hatip* schools got under way in an intense manner during the Özal period.[697]

Until the 1980s, the Turkish economy was controlled by firms headquartered in Istanbul which were well connected to the state and the Kemalist ideology. Özal reduced the power of the State over the economy and opened up a wider space for companies without ties to the circle that surrounded the state apparatus.[698] As a result of these changes, a new class of capitalists emerged of "businessmen known with their religious and conservative identities", as Alper Mumyakmaz noted. They emerged without the support of the state, which traditionally did not favour them; but at least the state stayed out of their way.

This new breed emerging from Anatolia was variably called "Anatolian Tigers", "Green Capital", "Islamic Capital" or "Islamic Bourgeoisie". They mostly preferred to be known as Anatolian Tigers (*Anadolu Kaplanları*), rather than with Islamic labels. Mumyakmaz interviewed several such businessmen and they told him that they would not be concerned about conducting business with Christians or Jews, though they would prefer "devout" (*dindar*) Muslims as partners.[699] This view suggests that despite their Islamic leaning principles, this new breed of businessmen was pragmatic when it came to business.

Mumyakmaz also notes that this previously marginalized Islamic sector, established by 1990s as a counter elite, with financial strength launched their own publications to voice their point of view and attained the ability to mobilize masses and promote an "Islamic way of life".[700] Thus, the Islamists' penetration into the media extended their ability to influence

697. *Ibid.*, p. 19.
698. Joost Lagendijk. 'Turquía en la Encrucijada', *Colección Mediterráneo Económico*, No. 12, December 2007, pp. 245 and 248.
699. Alper Mumyakmaz, 'Elitlerin Yeni Yüzü, Islami Burjuvazi', *Mustafa Kemal* Üniversitesi *Sosyal Bilimler Enstitüsü Dergisi*, Vol 11, No. 27, 2014, pp. 372-74.
700. Mumyakmaz, *op. cit.*, p. 378.

politics. They even established their own peak industry body MÜSIAD (*Müstakil Sanayici ve İşadamları Derneği*/Independent Industrialists and Businessmen Association) to counteract TÜSIAD (*Türk Sanayicileri ve İş İnsanları Derneği*/Turkish Industry and Business Association, TÜSIAD), which was seen as a secularist agent, and were able to finance political parties of their choosing.

In this period, Turkish society underwent a transformation reducing the distance between the Kemalists and sections of the Islamist sector. Nilüfer Göle calls the deep change in the interaction between the state and civil society, a "catharsis", which eliminated adversarial dichotomies:

> This catharsis and the entry of those who internalised the Muslim culture into the political field, dispensed with such antagonistic categories as the values of higher classes and the newly urbanised, the elite and the people, the progressives and the backward people, the modernists and the Islamists.[701]

The political and intellectual landscape was thus reconfigured as a result of Özal's neo-liberalism. Was this new *millieu* evidence of the Kemalists' failure to counteract political Islam? Yavuz argued that the reinvigoration of Turkish Islam cannot be attributed to the "failure of Kemalism", though, he added that "the Kemalist project played an important albeit inadvertent role" in this transformation. Yavuz contended that the new opportunities allowed Turkish Islam to disseminate different ideas:

> The history of . . . the Republic shows that the Turkish authorities seldom have been consistent in counterpoising nationalism and Islam, secularism and religion. If any concept could capture this tendentious relationship it is that of contradiction.[702]

Another way of approaching this is to differentiate between Kemalism of the early period (proto-Kemalism) and the Kemalism of the 1980s (neo-Kemalism). Even if the new environment could be regarded as a failure of early Kemalism, it was a "triumph" of this neo-Kemalism. The Kemalists entered into a sort of power-sharing arrangement of their choosing. They still retained key positions, army command, the MGK, Devlet Güvenlik Mahkemesi (State Security Court, DGM), Constitutional Court (*Anayasa Mahkemesi*) and other judicial positions, but in return they tolerated the presence of tarikat members and other Islamists in government. They thought they could continue to control a process perhaps they did not

---

701. Nilüfer Göle, "İslam'ın Demokratik Hak Davası" in Yerasimos, Stéphane, (ed.) *Türkler*, Ankara, 2005, pp. 127 and 134.
702. Hakan Yavuz, *Islamic political identity in Turkey*, p. ix.

fully understand. Their narrow frame of reference based on the Kemalist precepts prevented them from appreciating the full force and pent-up frustration of a segment of society they viewed as the subaltern.

The neo-Kemalists approached the Islamists as divided into two forms, acceptable and unacceptable, on the grounds that the most extreme end of the spectrum, advocating Sharia Law (*irtica*), was not acceptable. For instance, the *Menzil Cemaat* of the Nakshibendi was regarded as unacceptable. This cemaat was under surveillance by the junta on account of the excessive number of visitors of its sheikh Muhammet Raşit Efendi, from both within and without the country. Raşit Efendi was even exiled to Gökçeada in the Aegean Sea for a short period, quite away from his base in Menzil, Adıyaman Province.[703] By softening their position and allowing what they regarded as acceptable Islamists into the political and economic arena, they kept themselves in power for two more decades or so, until their edifice crumbled with the AKP coming to power and transforming the political landscape once again.

Erbakan as the first Islamist Prime Minister

Eventually Özal's ANAP collapsed and gave an opportunity for Demirel to become Prime Minister again, in 1991, succeeded by Çiller. In the ensuing two years, Çiller simply spent whatever good will she had in the electorate, tired of financial scandals and corruption at higher levels. After the reduction of her party's electoral power, Çiller began to appear as a faithful Muslim. To contain the leaks to other parties, she met with Fethullah Gülen, who was a "red flag" for many Kemalists, still hanging on to the idea that Turkey should be laic/secular and that the two fields of "religion" and "politics" should not interact.

While previously references to Kemalism and loyalty to Atatürk were standard discourse in Turkish politics, from the mid-1980s, gradually even parties describing themselves as secularists, such as *Doğru Yol Partisi* (True Path Party/DYP) under Çiller's leadership, found it significant to court the conservative Muslim vote by making overtures to it. Power brokers invoked Islamic symbols to carry out their campaigns, and the centre-right parties competed with the religious right in representing Islamic interests in parliament.[704]

703. Necdet Tosun, "Nakşibendiyye" in Ceyhan, Semih. (ed.) *Türkiye'de Tarikatlar*, İstanbul, 2015, p. 678.
704. Hakan Yavuz, *Islamic Political Identity in Turkey*, p. 216.

As discussed in the previous chapter, the differences between laic/ secular and Islamic parties were exaggerated. While in the 1970s Erbakan sought to receive votes by competing in the nationalist market, by the 1990s the laicist parties sought to compete in the religious market to increase their shrinking vote base. This further politicized Islam and moved it into the centre of political debate. For example, a week before the 1995 election, the DYP controlled Ministry of Education gave full status to 70 new religious high schools and opened 6,000 new positions for religious functionaries.[705]

Çiller formed a coalition with Erbakan in 1996, as she could not form government on her own. By private agreement they were to take turns to occupy the post of prime-ministership. Erbakan was to go first, who with the RP this time mostly represented the urban poor, rather than the country conservative people, owing to internal migration to urban areas.[706] He was trying to cater for different political needs and reach voters that previously would not vote for a party that was seen as "Islamist".

Two-fifths of those who voted who for the RP in 1995 identified themselves as secularists.[707] Even an Alevi dede Izzetin Doğan stated that they "[did] not frown on Refah", which attracted criticism by other Alevis.[708] At that point the Millî Görüş Movement accommodated members of various sects, but also others who did not consider the tarikat systems as essential.[709] Consequently, the RP was not a monolithic Islamist party, though the Islamic Millî Görüş element prevailed in its ranks. This flexibility allowed the party to grow and come to power.

Despite the pluralism of its voter base, when Erbakan was in government he accelerated the pace of appointments of sympathisers from his core; thus facilitating the on-going transformation of the public service. The military once again remembered Kemalism and laicism, but they were primarily concerned about their privileged positions. The top military brass, who kept an eye on politicians through the MGK, presented Erbakan and Çiller with a memorandum on the meeting of 28 February 1997. It appeared that the military still imagined some red lines, as far as Islam was concerned, and believed that Erbakan crossed those lines. The military looked for allies among the Kemalists to facilitate their coup:

---

705. *Ibid.*, p. 216.
706. Tayfun Atay, *op. cit.*, p. 31.
707. White, *op. cit.*, p. 41.
708. Altındal, *op. cit.*, pp. 200-1.
709. Talip Tuğrul, 'Milli Görüş Hareketi'nin Temel Karakterleri', *Mezhep Araştırmaları Dergisi*, Vol. 10, No. 2, Fall, 2017, p. 628.

A major characteristic of the 1997 coup was that judges and journalists, rather than bullets and tanks, supported and implemented it. The military authority used the mass media, as well as briefings, conferences, and regular public announcements to inform the judges and the public about the existential threat to the state stemming from political Islam and Kurdish ethnonationalism.[710]

Erbakan had no viable option but resignation. This was not the end of the Islamist presence in government. The soft coup only managed to erase Erbakan, not the Islamic movement.[711] Erbakan did all he could to further an Islamic, Milli Görüş, Nakshibendi agenda, while he walked a tight rope to appear also a sort of modernist. The environment following the soft coup was not conducive to the continuation of the RP which was shut down just like the previous two iterations of the Millî Görüş Parties.

The Nakshibendi in politics

Islamism has undergone many changes throughout the Republic. It originally represented a vehicle through which to express opposition to changes, but it was not sufficiently organised (for instance, the Menemen Incident). There was an expression of frustration to the changes to the traditional way of life, as well privatisation of "religious" activities. In the next stage, Islamic opposition was expressed through Nursî's teachings through circles called *Dershane* and Kısakürek's writings through *Büyük Doğu*, which operated as an opposition force to Kemalism. Both forces used their voter base to seek influence but did not directly participate in party politics, with the exception of Nursî in the 1957 election campaign. This approach changed with Erbakan's foray into party politics in the late 1960s. The Islamists now made the metamorphosis.

The tarikats, especially the Nakshibendi, exercised enormous influence on political parties in the 1980s. While they supported conservative parties before, they were becoming more overt in their involvement, as the Kemalist regime was becoming more tolerant and ignoring the law about the prohibition of tarikats. In the 1983 election, the junta's handpicked candidate Sunalp and his party MDP was supported by the tarikat known as Süleymancılar, also a branch of Nakshibendi, while in general the other branches and tarikats supported Özal. By 1986, more parties were allowed to run and in the by-elections held in that year, the Nakshibendi supported

710. Yavuz, *Islamic Political Identity in Turkey*, p. 244.
711. Tayfun Atay, *Parti, Cemaat, Tarikat*, Istanbul, 2017, p. 29.

both Özal's ANAP and the RP. The Nursî cemaat and the Süleymancılar supported the centre-right DYP, which was re-incarnation of the AP.[712] The Nakshibendi voter base spread its vote across conservative parties and its influence grew exponentially.

The political aspirations of the Nakshibendi stood them apart from other tarikats. In general, the Sunni tarikats such as the Mevlevis, and the Alevi Bektashis stayed out of politics after the prohibition and retreated into the private space, away from the prying eyes of the regime. In contrast, the Nakshibendi put up some resistance against the Kemalists in the 1930s; though they eventually also retreated to the private sphere to conduct their rituals. They re-entered the public sphere by supporting the Democrat Party in the 1950s, the Justice Party in the 1960s, and eventually through the Millî Görüş Project to affect policy and politics. Consequently, the Nakshibendis demonstrated the propensity for involvement in the civic life.

Svante Cornell, Director of the Stockholm based Institute for Security and Development Policy, makes a distinction between the Nakshibendi and other tarikats in the way they interpret Islamic tradition and practice their rituals:

> Sufi orders are known for their esoteric nature, in contrast to orthodox Islam. This has often implied an emphasis on mysticism over literalism and strict interpretation of Sharia law. It would be a mistake, however, to view the Naqshbandi order through this lens. It stands out among Sufi orders for its compatibility with orthodox, official Islam. Indeed, the Naqshbandi differs from most Sufi orders, almost all of whom trace their 'silsila' - their chain of spiritual transmission - back to Muhammad via his son-in-law Ali, who is the first İmam in the Shia branch of Islam. By contrast, the Naqshbandi is the only order to trace its chain of transmission through the first Sunni Caliph, Abu Bakr. This explains the order's firm allegiance to the orthodox Sunni tradition, and its strict adherence to Sharia, with mysticism only a second story subservient to the fulfilment of formal Islamic duties.[713]

These theological differences between the Nakshibendi and other Sufi tarikats may explain the tendency of the Nakshibendi to enter into political action more than other major tarikats, such as the Mevlevi and Bektashi, which focus on their mystical inner journeys rather than participate in political action. However, this view has been challenged by Brian Silverstein,

---

712. 'Tarikatlar da Özalı bırakıyor', [Tarikats too are abandoning Özal], *Milliyet*, 17 October 1986.
713. Svante E. Cornell, 'The Naqshbandi-Khalidi Order and Political Islam in Turkey', Hudson Institute, 3 September 2015, n.p.

who conducted research with the Gümüşhanevi branch of the Khalidi cemaats. To be sure, Silverstein also notes that the cemaats did not discuss "the classic themes of Sufism . . . [namely] intimate experience of God's and 'self-effacement (in the Reality of God)'". However, they were concerned with such concepts as "the good (*iyilik*) and morality (*ahlak*), and how one can become predisposed to ethical practice and avoidance of sin". In essence, the cemaat saw "Sufism is essentially an ethical discipline" rather than focusing "on something called 'mystical experience'". Silverstein's conclusion is that

> an interpretation of the nature of Sufi practice in contemporary Turkey (and likely in other contexts as well) requires an analytic shift away from the infinite calculus of 'real Sufi' experience (or its absence) and toward the relationship between traditions of discourse and practice and the kinds of ethical selves associated with them.[714]

Thus, some outsiders did not understand or appreciate the subtleties and the nuances of Nakshibendi Sufism, as Silverstein perceived. Irrespective of interpretation of Sufi theology and its practices, indisputably, the Nakshibendi have a long and well documented tradition of activism. Their practice of infiltrating Turkish institutions of which they do not approve, in order to benefit in some way, has been pointed out even as early as 1953 by Abdülbaki Gölpınarlı.[715] Birol Yeşilada also noted that

> [t]he Nakşibendis always emphasized the need to conquer the state from within by aligning themselves with powerful sources of capital and political actors (ultimately including the armed forces). As coalition partners of main center-rightist parties Refah was able to place many activists in key positions within the state apparatus.[716]

The Nakshibendi political project managed to have a prime minister for the first time with Özal. This is not to say that Özal simply followed orders from the tarikat's leaders. In fact, Professor Esad Coşan, who succeeded Kotku, his father-in-law, as the leader of the tarikat, had some reservations about him. In Coşan's view Özal "had 'excessively' politicised religion".[717] Coşan reportedly also distanced the order from Erbakan, and

714. Brian Silverstein, "Sufism and Modernity in Turkey" in Martin Van Bruinessen and Julia Day Howell (eds), Sufism and the 'Modern' in Islam, London and New York, 2007, pp. 42-43.
715. Abdülbaki Gölpınarlı, *Mevlâna'dan Sonra Mevlevilik*, 1953, p. 319 cited in Ismet Zeki Eyüboğlu, İslam *Dininden Ayrılan Cereyanlar*, n.p., 1998, p. 33.
716. Birol A. Yeşilada, "The Refah Party Phenomenon in Turkey" in Birol A. Yeşilada (ed.) *Comparative Political Parties and Party Elites*, Michigan, 1999, p. 139.
717. Rabasa and Larrabee, *op. cit.*, p. 14.

for all practical purposes severed the link between his lodge and Erbakan's politics.[718] Coşan was critical of Erbakan's focus on politics.[719]

This criticism was inconsistent with Nakshibendi's own approach, turning its members into voters of particular parties. In any case, Erbakan's third attempt as the leader of the RP was still supported by the Nakshibendi order as part of the Milli Görüş movement.[720] The Nakshibendi tarikats, with their different lodges, were not always acting as a coherent unit; nonetheless they encased themselves into the political landscape and affected civic life.

De-secularisation of everyday life

The junta's re-shaping of Kemalism was characterised by the growing influence of what Erik Zürcher called "unofficial Islam", or "acceptable Islam" as I prefer to call it; acceptable to the Kemalists that is. Zürcher outlines the ensuing changes which started to alter the predominantly secular nature of society and created tension between those who practised and those who did not. This is in contrast to Göle's view, as cited above, who saw the changes as reducing or even alleviating antagonistic dichotomies. Zürcher suggested that

> [f]rom 1984 onwards the press, both Kemalist and socialist-oriented, constantly drew attention to the growth of Islamic currents as manifested in the building of new mosques; the enormous growth in the number of İmam-hatip (preacher) schools, whose graduates were now allowed to enter university; the growing religious content of school books and of the state-controlled radio and television; the growing number of Islamic publications and bookshops and incidents during the month of fasting, Ramazan, during which people who were smoking or drinking were attacked. The fiercest criticism was reserved for the explicit way in which members of the cabinet took part in religious ceremonies. All these developments were seen as so many attempts to undermine the secular character of the state.[721]

---

718. Cornell, Svante E., 'The Naqshbandi-Khalidi Order and Political Islam in Turkey', Hudson Institute, 3 September 2015.

719. Itzchak, op. cit., p. 154.

720. Ruşen Çakır, 'Esad Coşan-Erbakan çekişmesi tekerrür mü ediyor?', [Is the Esad Coşan-Erbakan conflict being repeated?], Vatan, 28 November 2013. Reportedly, the disillusionment lead Coşan to a self-exile in Australia, where he was killed in a traffic accident.

721. Zürcher, Turkey, op. cit., pp. 288-89.

Individual attacks during *Ramazan* can be described as markers of the de-secularisation process; nonetheless, we need to bear in mind that the periods of *Ramazan* and *Bayrams*[722] always had a special treatment in the Turkish culture. These periods, especially the *Ramazan* month, represented the temporary sacralisation of the profane space. Even if not every Muslim fasted during the month, they were likely to participate at least in the evening meal of *iftar*. The dawn meal *sahur*[723] was announced by a wandering *davul* player until the 1970s, even in large cities such as Istanbul. For this month at least, the profane used to retreat to a more restricted space.

Respect of the sacred space during *Ramazan* is one thing, physical and verbal abuse of those who did not want to partake is another. The demarcation line was not respected by more extreme elements in the Islamic camp. These attacks began in the fast changing of the socio-political landscape of the 1980s, when some Muslims felt that their sacred place expanded and that not fasting was a sacrilegious act and that it was now acceptable to take matters into their own hands. As the Islamists were becoming more visible in the public space and openly participating in politics, they felt more confident in interfering to insult, harass and even physically attack those not practising.

Another example of de-secularisation and the influence of the Islamic sector is attacks on women for not being veiled and attempts to separate men and women in public transport,[724] which would have been unthinkable until then. Gender segregation was practised in the Mosque and religious ceremonies. There were now attempts to expand this segregation from the private to the public sphere, thereby de-privatising certain traditional practices.

Göle notes that "[t]he penetration of secularism in daily life is best illustrated by women's physical and social visibility. Secularism pushed for the emancipation of women from religious practices such as veiling and the segregation of sexes."[725] Conversely, the increasing segregation of sexes and veiling of women and this sort of harassment can be regarded as the penetration of the secular space.

As we have seen, the term "secular" refers to the nature of civil society and laicism refers to the state. The laic nature of the state was already undermined both by the founders and by subsequent governments, including

---

722. Religious festival.
723. *Sahur* is the early morning meal before the day break, which marks the fasting period of the day.
724. White, *op. cit.*, p. 40.
725. Göle, 'Secularism and Islamism in Turkey', p. 51

the military. It was the secular character of civil society that was transforming further. The question is to what extent the Islamists influenced public
life to reduce the secular, if it can be measured at all. Clearly, when we compare the 1980s with the preceding decades the influence of political Islam
increased. There is a plethora of studies, some of which are cited here, that
attest to this. There is a clear pattern of de-secularisation and merger of the
categories of religion and politics. As pointed out in Chapter 2.2 in Berkes's
assessment:

> To understand the process of secularization in a non-Christian society,
> one must examine the extent of domination of religious rules over all
> areas of life and discover whether or not this domination is either im-
> plemented or supported by the state.[726]

While in the period leading up to the 1980s, the state managed to a
certain extent to confine religious practices into the private sphere, the
cracks in the edifice that appeared in the 1950s, gradually became more
pronounced. The influence of tarikats and cemaats in the public sphere
were becoming more evident. Some tarikats were no longer formations
simply focused on their particular rituals and spirituality. Their involvement in politics was increasing. and so was their influence in daily life. In
one such example of provision of advice contrary to the laic view, in one
of his sermons to 3,500 "head scarfed" women in 1985, Mahmut Hoca of
the İskender Paşa lodge advised the audience not to watch television, not to
read newspapers and not to handshake with men. In other words, he asked
women to reduce their participation in the public space and even detach
from it completely.[727]

This over-the-top sermon attracted the attention of the State Security
Court's public prosecutor as being contrary to laicism.[728] Mahmut Hoca
was acquitted but the Presiding Judge Süheyl Deliorman noted that the
court received many letters of support for the *Hodja*, which he interpreted
as the existence of *gericilik* in Turkey.[729] As member of the elite, the judge
expressed his dissatisfaction with the changing nature of public life, but
still went along with the neo-Kemalist project parameters and acquitted
Mahmut Hoca.

As noted in Chapter 2.2, secularity is a spectrum, not an absolute. Total domination of religious rules over all areas of life has never been im-

---

726. Berkes, *op. cit.*, p. 6.
727. 'Mahmut Hoca'nın kadınlara vaazı', [Mahmut Hodja's sermon to women], *Milliyet*,
    7 October 1985, pp. 1 and 9.
728. *Ibid.*, p. 13
729. 'Mahmut Hoca beraat etti', [Mahmut Hoja was acquitted], *Milliyet*, 4 December
    1985.

plemented or supported by the Turkish state, even under the increasingly Islam-oriented AKP's rule. The point is that there are some grey areas and no country is completely secular. As Arnal and McCutcheon put it, the secular and religious are a co-dependant pair, with the boundary between them rather arbitrary.[730]

In secular Australia, governments provide funding to schools run by religious organisations and recognise marriages conducted in churches. In contrast, in Turkey, marriages officiated by either imams or priests were not recognised until recently. Furthermore, in Australia, in limited form, the sacred manifests itself in the prayers in the opening session of parliaments. This practice in the public space can only be described as non-secular.

In most "secular" European countries there is some sort of interaction between the Church and the State. For instance, in Denmark, priests are paid by the state, just as in Turkey imams are paid by *Diyanet*. Furthermore, in Sweden until 2000, the Lutheran Church was a state institution, in the same way the mosques are run by *Diyanet* in Turkey. In Greece, the clergy were removed from the public payroll and stopped being civil servants only in 2018. A country can be secular on one aspect (e.g. demographics) or not in another (state endorsement of religion).

What other criteria can be used to identify the process of de-secularisation, if such a process is occurring at all? As discussed in Chapter 2.1, Pratt suggested that the dwindling numbers of churchgoers is not a sufficient marker of secularisation.[731]

Conversely, may increase attendance in mosques be regarded as a marker for de-secularisation? In 1990, compared to 20 years prior, there was a noticeable increase in mosque attendance in Turkey. It is suggested in this study that the rate of attendance of mosques is not a sufficient marker of de-secularisation. Furthermore, while in 1945 there was one mosque for 1,000 Turks, in 1990, the corresponding ratio was one mosque for 700.[732] In the same period, the Turkish population increased from 18.7 million to 51.4 million. The number of mosques outpaced the rate of growth of the population. Even so, these numbers in themselves cannot be used as markers, because in the rush to build many mosques in the 1980s, many were built in Alevi villages, despite the lack of interest among the Alevi population and were poorly attended. The increase in the numbers of mosques points to the intention of the state to promote Sunni Islam.

---

730. Arnal and Mccutcheon, *op. cit.*, pp. 22 and 132.

731. Pratt, *op. cit.*, p. 1.

732. *Amerikan Gizli Belgelerinde Türkiye'de* İslamcı *Akımlar*, trans. Yılmaz Polat, İstanbul, 1990, p. 40.

Another marker, which is more pertinent in its application to the review of the de-secularisation process, is the proliferation of *İmam-Hatip* schools facilitated by governments of seemingly different persuasions. These were originally established in 1952 at the level of Middle School (*Orta Okul*) to train clerical staff for the mosques. They were later extended to High School (*Lise*) level. In 1970, there were 40 *İmam Hatip* high schools. The number increased to 249 in 1980 and to 383 by 1988.[733] Under the watch of Evren's junta 140 such schools were added. While the original scope of these schools was training of imams and hatips, by this period they had become schools of general education. For example, there were 50,000 girls attending these schools, even though they could not become clerics.[734] Other than de-secularising minds, what could have been the scope of vocational training with no vocational opportunity?

These statistics in themselves may show an increase of religious observance and religiosity, but again not necessarily a reduction of the secular space. Nevertheless, if we accept Pratt's study on secularisation of the mind, the reverse process of de-secularisation of the mind is also possible.

At various times, Turkish citizens were surveyed by scholars on whether they longed for a state based on Islamic Law. Heper tabulated the survey responses as follows:[735]

Years	Affirmative Responses (%)
1986	0.7
1995	19.9
1996	26.7
1998	19.8
1999	21.0
2002	16.4
2006	8.9

Table 3

In 1996, when the RP did well in both municipal and parliamentary elections, an increase in the percentage of respondents longing for a country based on Sharia law is noticeable. Yet, as Heper notes:

---

733. *Ibid.*, p. 41.
734. *Ibid.* p. 42.
735. Metin Heper, "Does Secularism Face a Serious Threat in Turkey?" Berna Turam (ed.), *Secular State and Religious Society*, New York, 2012, p. 86. Bearing in mind Metin Heper's Kemalist credentials and likelihood of balance the original sources were checked and proved to be accurate.

When the respondents were asked whether men should be allowed to marry up to four wives, the affirmative response rate dropped from 21 percent to 7 percent, and when they were asked whether women who commit adultery should be stoned to death, the affirmative response rate plummeted to less than 2 percent.[736]

In a similar survey, in 2004 Ali Çarkoğlu asked respondents if they supported specific traditional Shari'a rules. 85% of respondents did not approve of polygamy; 78.5% did not approve of Shari'a divorce procedures; and 81.4% did not approve of Shari'a inheritance procedures. Even more importantly, in all three cases the large majority of those who did favor Shari'a governance rejected the actual Shari'a rule itself. In other words, only a tiny fraction of the Turkish electorate (who overwhelmingly self-identify as Muslim) are in favor of actual premodern Shari'a social arrangements; the vast majority of their coreligionists reject them outright. This indicates a widespread disapproval of premodern Shari'a-based social norms that holds whether the person is religious or not.[737]

Respondents' misconceptions about Sharia and what it entails if it is fully implemented, dictated their answers. Consequently, these figures do not give us a clear picture other than noticing long term trends in relation to the desire of a more Islamic way of life in Turkey. This can be interpreted as a nostalgia for the pre-Republican past. Paradoxically, as the percentage of those in favour of an Islamic way of life increased during the RP rule, the opposite occurred under the early years of AKP rule.

These markers outlined above may be difficult to measure objectively but they do give us an indication about the way Turkish society was progressing. Taylor approached this issue of secularisation philosophically. Taylor's study on the immanent frame is one framework through which to assess secularisation. Wayne Hankey points out that Taylor's study, outlined in *A Secular Age*, has restricted geographical and historical extent: "Taylor reminds us that secularism in north-western Protestant Europe and its dependencies, especially as it turns hostile to religion and becomes atheistic, is a product of reform movements within Christianity".[738]

Despite the argument for restricted application outside Protestant societies, these concepts could indeed be applicable to Turkey, if not to other

736. *Ibid.*, p. 87.
737. Philip Dorroll, 'Shari'a and the Secular in Modern Turkey', *Contemporary Islam*, No. 11, 2007, p. 132.
738. Wayne Hankey, "The Contemporary Debate about Secular and Sacred in Judaism, Christianity and Islam" in Wayne Hankey and Nicholas Hatt (Eds.), *Changing our Mind on Secularization*, Charlottetown, Prince Edward Island, 2009, p. 15.

Muslim majority countries. An early twentieth century Islamic thinker - Prime Minister between 1915 and 1917 - Said Halim Pasha, believed that the "Muslim mentality" was "falsified" and "dazzled by the material prosperity and power of Western society":

> a growing number of Muslim "intellectuals" take pleasure in regarding this position of the West, the object of their boundless admiration, as a miraculous result of the principle of a national sovereignty. Having got that principle adopted in some Muslim countries for form's sake only, for its operation has remained entirely artificial - they would wish the Shari'at to cease to be the source of inspiration and the criterion of Muslim rulers.[739]

The implication is that even before the establishment of the Republic and the process of secularisation undertaken, Muslim intellectuals assessed their environment through a western framework (the immanent frame), which Halil Pasha lamented. The Islamic discourse over the course of the Republic changed and adapted to the socio-political environment of its time. Hakkı Gürkaş noted this metamorphosis after the 1950s especially as

> a result of the democratization in politics and liberalization in economy, Islamist movements appeared and contested both the nominal Islam and the secular elite. The Islamist movements trained their own elite . . . to counter the secular elite. However, the new elite began to acquire the same cultural capital as the republican elites through secular education, parliamentary politics, and participation in public sphere.[740]

In many ways, the idea of the secularists and the intellectual elites performing on different planes was no longer applicable. The early Islamist intellectuals who operated in the early Republican period, such as Akseki and Nursî, were essentially products of the Ottoman environment, whereas the newly Islamic intellectuals were raised within the parameters, however imperfect, established by Mustafa Kemal. Despite their view; they were products of the Republic. Göle noted that the

> new Islamist intellectuals, both men and women, are quite distinct from the earlier Islamist thinkers in Turkey. They use modern Turkish language, refer to Western thinkers, discuss issues such as post-modernism, participate in public debates with secular intellectuals, and master Western foreign languages. Although in their writings, Islamist

---

739. Halim Pasha, Said. 'The Reform of Muslim Society', *Islamic Studies*, Vol. 47, No. 3, Autumn 2008, p. 384.
740. Hakki Gurkas, "Turkish Secular Muslim Identity on Display in Europe", in Gabriele Marranci (Ed.), *Muslim Societies and the Challenge of Secularization*, Heidelberg London New York, 2010, p. 124.

intellectuals seek to define an alternative Islamic identity and society, in their social profiles, their writing and communication styles, and their use of the mass media, they have a lot in common with the secular intellectuals.[741]

In other words, these new intellectuals, for instance Ali Bulaç, İsmet Özel, Abdurrahman Dilipak, could not readily be dismissed as *gerici*. Indeed, İsmet Özel was a former Marxist. They expressed themselves within a secular framework. This is especially pronounced with the Gülenist network, which created new educational opportunities and kept producing new intellectuals who expressed themselves in the language of the secularists. Their discernible aim was to deconstruct the secular and reconstruct a new hybrid system, in which the secular is no longer the dominant form, but the two modes operate concurrently.

Struggle between Islamists and Secularists in the 1980s

While the Islamisation was becoming a reality under the watch and encouragement of the military, there were always expressed concerns about the threat of *irtica*. When the military was still in power, a report was commissioned by the MGK and prepared by Korgeneral (Lieutenant General) Nevzal Bolugiray. Bolugiray admitted to the existence of the report four years later, in a period where concerns about *irtica* were reported by the opposition parties, representing the Kemalist Republican view. The MGK held a meeting and told Özal its concerns. Özal was not convinced that such danger existed, or perhaps he was not personally concerned, though even Diyanet was of the opinion that there was such risk.[742] Diyanet was in control of Sunni Islam and would not want volatile elements in its fold, which could have altered the *status quo*.

It is quite baffling at first glance that a political system infiltrated by tarikats and cemaats, with its tacit support, at the same time expressed concern about the dangers of *irtica*. Kenan Evren kept worrying about *irtica*, as reported in the press of the time,[743] while he oversaw the dismantling of measures designed to keep society secular and the state laic. The explanation of this apparent contradiction lies on the view of the Kemalists and

---

741. Nilüfer Göle, 'Secularism and Islamism in Turkey: The Making of Elites and Counter-Elites', *Middle East Journal*, Vol. 51, No. 1, Winter 1997, p. 56.

742. 'Diyanet, Özal'ı yalanlıyor, irtica tehlikesi vardir', [Diyanet refutes Özal, there is danger of reaction], *Milliyet*, 27 January 1987.

743. 'Herkes uyanık olsun' [Everyone should be vigilant], *Milliyet*, 29 September 1985.

Evren that still saw a controlled, state shaped Sunni Islam and versions of Islam outside the state-controlled space. By bringing marginalised Islam into the fold, the state had an opportunity to extend its penetration, or so it was hoped.

Thus, as well as re-defining Kemalism, neo-Kemalism, to make it more compatible with the growing Islamic influence in politics and civic life, they also redefined laicism, neo-laicism, we may call it. This new laicism was of reduced content and it only fulfilled the purpose of still keeping an artificial and ever moving dividing line, excluding only extremist elements. The only reason for the elite (the military, the judiciary, public service upper management) to stay in power was to differentiate themselves from the masses. The "neo-laicism", was a useful ideological tool to convince themselves of the need to stay in power to safe-guard Kemalist principles.

Occasionally, when the religious formations strayed out the acceptable circle of "soft Islam", the state remembered the tarikat prohibition law. In 1986, 18 Nakshibendi of the Khalidi branch were tried by the DGM for acting contrary to the law prohibiting dervish lodges. This law was remembered only when the activity did not fit into the tolerated range. In this particular instance, the charges were that the group's aim was to establish Sharia Law and that they were connected to the Saudi Arab Rabitat-ü Âlem-i İslam[744] (Rabitat al-Alam al-Islami), the Muslim World League, which propagates Wahabism/Salafism.[745] No doubt, the group's foreign connection accounted for their arrest.

In January 1987, over 100 cadets were arrested and expelled from the Military Academy, as members of Hezbollah.[746] The militant/violent Islam was obviously the unacceptable form of Islam. Moreover, the infiltration of military schools by Islamists could have spelt an end to the domination of this key institution by the Kemalists. Eventually they lost this institution in the purges of the aftermath of the attempted coup in 2016, but at the time they were still able to manoeuvre to protect their province.

Traditionally, the differences between the secularists and the Islamists are seen as a huge, insurmountable gap, as pointed out. Not all scholars agree on the nature of the conflict between the secularists and the Islamists.

---

744. '18 Nakşibendi DGM de yargılanacak', [18 Nakshibendi will be tried in the State Security Court], *Milliyet*, 12 June 1986, pp. 1 and 9.

745. Massimo Introvigne notes that Wahabism is a wester construct and that the Saudis prefer the term Salafism to refer to their version of Islam; Massimo Introvigne. "Turkish Religious Market(s): A View Based on Religious Economy Theory" in Yavuz, Hakan M. (ed.), *The Emergence of a New Turkey*, Salt Lake City, 2006, p. 29.

746. Σταύρος Λυγερός, 'Πώς κυριάρχησε το πολιτικό Ισλάμ στην Τουρκία', [How political Islam prevailed in Turkey], *Καθημερινή*, 10 November 2002.

For instance, Philip Dorroll argued that

> the history of Islam in modern Turkey is not so much a history of an ideological war between religious and secular individuals, but rather a struggle to define the exact boundaries of the religious and the secular: the supposed conflict between "religious" and "secular(ist)" ideas in Turkey may be better described as a debate over the definition of secularity itself. A concept of the secular is implied in both Kemalist political secularism and Islamic modernism, and these two interact in ways that contribute to each other's formation.[747]

The terms "soft" or "unofficial Islam" have been used to describe the appearance of political Islam. Yet, the idea of Islam manifesting in different forms was not necessarily shared by the Islamists. Erbakan himself, a person that benefited from the new approach, in his book *Davam*, defining the right Islam, wrote:

> Lately as thought pollution, such terms as modern Muslim, moderate Muslim, light Islam, modernity are being used. With these terms they are trying to protestantise Islam. . . . Islam is Islam.[748]

Thus, the first Islamist Prime Minister was suggesting that there are no different forms within Islam. Erbakan went on to explain that you cannot add or subtract anything from Islam, as it is perfect. In the same book, he also argued: "Islam means, science, modernisation, social justice and just order. . . . progress and modernisation is an attribute of original Islam."[749]

Şahin Filiz attributes these contradictions to confusion among the Islamists and argues that such concepts as "modernisation" and continuous progress did not exist in Islam and were added by the political Islamists as tools in their opposition against the West. Filiz argues that political Islam, which uses western concepts to define itself, in opposition to the West, is essentially a modernist movement. Filiz also calls this movement "neo-orientalist conservatism", which aims to take technology from the West but stay away from its culture.[750] Incidentally, this was Kısakürek's point of view. In essence, both camps, the Kemalists and the Islamists, modified their positions embracing and espousing contradictory positions for the sake of political and economic power.

There is, however, much antagonistic scholarship in Turkey on this subject. For instance, much like the categorisation of Muslims as sincere

747. Dorroll, *op. cit.*, p. 125.
748. Şahin Filiz. *Tarikat, Cemaat, Kadın*, İstanbul, 2016, p. 17.
749. *Ibid.*, p. 17.
750. *Ibid.*, pp. 17, 23-24.

or otherwise, as discussed in the previous chapter, Islamic scholar İhsan Süreyya Sırma also classified laicists as "sincere" and otherwise. He put the percentage of sincere laicists as 10% of all laicists. This was pure conjecture on his part as no survey is cited to support this claim. Sırma described the "insincere" laicists as self-interested (*menfaatçı*) and he outlined further groups as those that were religious (*dine bağlı*) and those that found it expedient to be seen as Muslims. Sırma doubted the sincerity of the laicists in the same way some laicists doubted the sincerity of the beliefs of some Muslims. Sırma uses the term "bigoted laicist" (*bağnaz laik*) just like the Kemalists used the same epithet to describe a category of pious Muslims.[751] In sum, some Islamists responded in kind.

Laicism was not only the preserve of the Republican Party, most public functionaries, the military and the judicial elite. The capitalist class represented by TÜSIAD also expressed its concerns about the increasing Islamisation of public life and education. TÜSIAD prepared a comprehensive report in 1990, entitled Education in Turkey (*Türkiye'de Eğitim*).

The report suggested that the country had more *İmam-Hatip* graduates than were needed and proposed that the Middle School section of *İmam-Hatip* be abolished and these schools be open to pupils who finish the elementary eight-year education first. TÜSIAD was also concerned that these schools were becoming general education institutions and asked the government to restrict entry of graduates of these schools to universities, other than to the Faculties of Divinity.[752] The government of the day implemented most of the changes. The *İmam-hatip* schools continued to be an issue and frequent changes reflected the difficulties in reconciling laicism with interference in religious education.

The incendiary issues of headscarves for women became apparent in the 1980s as a symbolic but significant battle marker between the secular minded and the Islamists. Göle noted in 1997, that

> [t]he veiling of women has emerged as the most visible symbol of the Islamization of the Turkish life-world. Islamist politics clearly define the role of the individual in the community, and the central issue has become the control of women's sexuality and the social separation of the sexes. But, in addition to that, Islamists have imposed beards for men, and taboos on promiscuity, homosexuality, alcohol consumption, and defined new moralist practices and the semiology of the Islamic way of life.[753]

751. İhsan Süreyya Sırma, *Alaturka Demokrasi Alaturka Laiklik*, İstanbul, 1997, pp. 81-82.
752. Akgül, *op. cit.*, pp. 275-76.
753. Göle, 'Secularism and Islamism in Turkey: The Making of Elites and Counter-Elites', p. 53.

Emergence of a Muslim community "for itself"

In the years following Erbakan's forced resignation and until 2002 when for the first time an Islamist party won election outright, the Kemalists tried to purge the Islamic elements from government to arrest the declining laicisation and secularity. It was too late; the process they instigated in 1980 could not be wound back: it had its own momentum. Also, the Muslim community transformed itself from being "in itself" to being "for itself". Gramsci's Marxian concept of a class "in itself" and "for itself" is a useful one. A class "in itself" shares awareness of some common conditions and grievances against the ruling class, whereas members of a class "for itself" eventually develop an awareness of themselves as forming a social class opposed to the ruling class.

A Muslim community is a community "in itself" by virtue of sharing common tradition, rituals and set of beliefs. But a Muslim community "for itself" expresses its opposition to the regime and thus it becomes a social movement not just a faith community operating in the private sphere. As Emel Taştekin notes "[a]fter the radical secularism of the Kemalists strictly ruled out a faith-based politics in Turkey, Nursi 'concluded that the rejuvenation of Islamic consciousness had to be carried out not on the state level but on the level of individuals'".[754] This transformation was to be built from the ground up.

I have modified Gramsci's concept in that both versions of the *class* understanding involve a lower class defining itself *against the ruling class* - class "in-itself" is a response to external oppressive conditions; whereas a class "for-itself" builds on this response, to develop a coherent sense of its own class consciousness. The privatised Islam of a Muslim community "in itself" is, in fact, a response to exogenous conditions, with privatisation and concentration on tradition being the means of coping with the hostile external environment.

In Gramsci, the transformation from "in itself" to "for itself" is indicated especially by the development of its own organic, as opposed to traditional intellectuals. Traditional intellectuals reproduce state ideology. In the Turkish context tarikat or cemaat leaders such Fethullah Gülen can be regarded as organic intellectuals in Gramsci's conception. When their supported ideology becomes dominant, organic intellectuals can become "traditional" to protect the new *status quo*.

It could be argued that, in the 1980s with the development of intellec-

---

754. Emel Taştekin, 'Secular Trauma and Religious Myth', *Monograf*, No. 1, January 2014, p. 82.

tuals (though not necessarily all organic intellectuals), the Muslim subaltern became an Islamic movement, a Muslim community "for itself". This subaltern produced counter elites, especially as the economic education and political opportunities increased for them to develop an alternative view of the world.

In Turkey, secularisation, as a process, generally decreased the presence of Islam in the public sphere. This did not mean the total absence of Islamic symbols but a reduction (for instance the absence of praying in public). De-secularisation is the opposing process and was caused by the neo-Kemalists, just as the early Kemalists undertook the secularisation process. Atay calls this emerging hybrid form post-modern secularism.[755]

I am mindful of the trend in scholarship to label new social and political phenomena as post-modern to describe the current trends in western societies. Nevertheless, whether or not the term is applicable to Turkey, it is evident that a different form of the secular is observable; a hybrid perhaps more suitable for a country where the pious Muslims constitute a good part of the society. As Nursi had argued the secular and Islam could co-exist. The term "post-secular" is increasingly used to describe this phenomenon, but the "post" suggests the end of something (the secular), which is not the case in Turkey. The secular has survived in some form and Jürgen Habermas uses the term "post-secular" to acknowledge this reality. In a paper presented at the Istanbul Seminar in June 2008, Habermas argued that in a "post-secular" society "religion maintains a public influence and relevance, while the secularistic certainty that religion will disappear worldwide in the course of modernization is losing ground."[756] Christian Bryan Bustamante noted that "Habermas' post-secularism is not a matter of objective reality, but of public perception and individual subjectivity."[757]

The inherently amorphous term post-secular is not entirely satisfactory, and it does not accurately reflect Habermas' view. Evidently, a new terminology is needed to describe the nature of current society in Turkey.

755. Atay, *op. cit.*, p. 74.
756. Jürgen Habermas, A "post-secular" society - what does that mean?, 16 September 2008, https://www.resetdoc.org/story/a-post-secular-society-what-does-that-mean/, [Accessed on 8 May 2020].
757. Christian Bryan Bustamante, "From Secularism to Post-Secularism", *Scientia*, June 2014, p. 9.

Conclusion

Drawing from a set of analyses about the relationship between religion and politics, this chapter demonstrated that the experience of prolongued opposition to the regime fostered the growth of a political consciousness on the part of the emerging Muslim community, becoming a community "for itself". This in turn forced the Kemalists to find a way to accomodate the Muslim community "for itself" in order maintain their hold of power. The elite Kemalists and the Islamists found a way to reconcile their seemingly irreconcilable differences, to form an alliance against perceived third-party threats (Kurds, extreme left).

This alliance was not a straightforward affair and there were periods when the military acted against the Islamists in government (in 1997), but it was too late. It was only a matter of time before the Islamist cohort realised that they could take over government in a Muslim-majority country. There is no great variation in the majority scholarly work about the period, except the Kemalist and the Islamists scholars prefer to describe this period as a period of two opposing forces. My argument has shown, however, that this oppositional framing exaggerates the difference; an exaggeration that serves ideological ends on both sides. A more accurate picture emerges in that the gap between the Kemalists and the Islamists are minimised. This contributes to my overall argument about the relationship between religion and politics by demonstrating that the Kemalists and the Islamists operated in a field which combined both ideological forces.

The end of Erbakan's short lived prime-ministership and the soft-coup in 1997 was meant to usher in another new period to address the de-secularisation and return government to the Kemalist parties. That did not occur despite the "exponential increase in the already ubiquitous images of Atatürk in late 1990s".[758] Atatürkism eschewed proto-Kemalism in the process.

The neo-Kemalist regime hung on for a few more years. In the meantime, the Gülenist cemaat was working more effectively than the Nakshibendi organisation building a frame, which was to bring the AKP to power. The Gülenist network already established in the 1980s, continued to grow exponentially consolidating its position in civic life in Turkey and abroad through educational institutions. In Turkey, the network included the "Light Houses" (Işık Evleri), infiltration of the army and the police, as well as educational institutions.

---

758. Özyürek, *op. cit.*, p. 93.

In the next chapter, I explore Gülen's movement, ostensibly a spiritual and educational endeavour, but in reality, a force seeking political mobilisation and influence. The review of the Gülenist network will advance the overall argument by demonstrating the interrelatedness of the categories of "religion" and "politics" in its operation. They function primarily as a political machinery, rather than solely being elements of education and pastoral care.

CHAPTER 7:
THE GÜLEN MOVEMENT

Introduction

Fethullah Gülen is an enigmatic and charismatic figure who oversaw the building of an empire consisting, at its height, of hundreds of educational institutions at all levels, media (both print and television) and other organisations. His movement refers to itself as *Hizmet* (Service), which is the main vehicle of the network, but in general by others as the Gülen's or the Gülenist Movement, or even simply the Gülenists. Gülen greatly influenced political processes and was instrumental in catapulting the AKP into power. To come to this position as king maker, Gülen worked patiently and methodically over 40 years to establish a network of influence and patronage. His movement is also called a cemaat and he presides over it as its Imam. Thus, as well as being a cemaat preoccupied with the interpretation of Islam and being involved in Islamic affairs, the Gülenists represent a social movement incorporating educational activities, social services and even inter-faith dialogue.

Studies related to Gülen and his movement range from the most negative to "hagiographic" depictions.[759] He at once is accused of intending to take over government "and turn it into a religious-based state", "being a CIA operative", an agent of some foreign country (perhaps China), a subversive funded by Saudi Arabia, or even a functionary of the papacy (a 'secret cardinal')".[760] Researcher Faik Bulut accuses him of being Sharia-minded, anti-Semitic but also connected to Israel, part of the Papal mission, and even linked to the Unification Church of the Unites States (pejoratively known as the "Moonies").[761] Gülen stirs up strong convictions both negative and positive:

> Even though Gülen attracts support from a great number of people, he is a controversial figure for others. For radical Islamists, he is too "soft" on Christians and Jews and not Muslim enough because he prizes a moral life more highly than ritualistic prayer that does not change

---

759. For instance for a very critical view see Bulut, Faik, *Kim Bu Fethullah Gülen*, İstanbul, 2016. For an admiring and uncritical study see Helen Rose Ebaugh, *The Gülen Movement*, Dordrecht Heidelberg London New York, 2010.
760. James C. Harrington, *Wrestling with Free Speech, Religious Freedom, and Democracy in Turkey*, Lanham, Maryland, 2011, p. 15.
761. Bulut, *op. cit.*, pp. 164 and 254-56.

a person's character. For neo-nationalists, he is a threat to the secularist nature of the Turkish republic and has a secret agenda to steer the nation toward Shari'a law or even an Islamic theocracy, although Gülen consistently says there is no turning away from democracy in the country.[762]

As the wide network of Gülen has engulfed many scholars, both Turkish and westerners alike (primarily US) through various programs, a researcher needs to be cautious in evaluating the information. The following chapter utilises both sympathetic and antagonistic sources. Most of the hostile research before the 2016 coup attempt comes from Kemalist sources, but as well as liberal secularists who were concerned about the reach of Gülen's network and suspicious of his ultimate goal.

The antagonistic, downright hostile, sources cloud the terrain with unsupported allegations. Although there is no doubt Gülen sought to influence Turkish society and politics, he demonstrated an admirable persistence in building education networks. As the Gülenist organisation helped the current Islamist president, Recep Tayyip Erdoğan, to come to power, both the Lightists' and Gülen's organisation and their involvement in politics is central to the discussion in this study of the interplay between "religion" and "politics".

Gülen as Nurcu

Gülen's cemaat is a branch of Nursî's cemaat, despite Gülen's efforts to disassociate himself from Nursî. It is not difficult to identify the reasons for Gülen seeking to distance himself from Said Nursî. The state relentlessly pursued Nursî and his followers. Nursî faced courts several times and was exiled internally. Consequently, it was a cautious step for Gülen to deny any links to Nursî, fearing that the same fate awaited him; at the very least, he sought to escape the scrutiny to which Nursî was subjected. Nevertheless, it is undeniable that his movement is one of the neo-Nurcu movements that were formed after the death of Nursî. Other post-Nur movements have never managed to match the scale and scope of Gülen's operation.

In 1971, when Gülen was indicted by the İzmir Martial Law Command Military Court, together with Nursî's solicitor, unlike other defendants, he

---

762. James C. Harrington, *Wrestling with Free Speech, Religious Freedom, and Democracy in Turkey*, Lanham, Maryland, 2011, p. 9.

stated that he was not Lightist. According to the court records Gülen said: "other than being a Muslim I am not a member of Lightism or any other movement".[763] Yet, there is much evidence that connects the Nurcu with the Gülenist organisation. As Holton and Lopez noted:

> Gülen's own formative influences derive from the Nurcu movement in Turkey. Sheikh Sa'id-i Kurdi (aka Sa'id-i Nursî, 1878–1960) was a Sunni Muslim in the Sufi tradition, whose 'reading circles' crystalized into a resistance movement against Kemal Ataturk's modernization process but yet nevertheless viewed itself as nationalistic and forward-looking. Nursî demanded that the new post-WW I Turkish republic be based on Islamic principles and ruled by Islamic Law (shariah). Gülen was his student and follower.[764]

This connection is emphasised in certain Turkish sources as well, referring to the Gülen movement as a "Neo-Nur movement" and pointing out to the association of the Gülenist with the Nurcu movement, and that the Gülen movement itself was inspired by Nursî's writings and teachings.[765]

Gülen used Nursî's educational and philosophical ideas and partly his organizational model, especially in the form of *Dersanes* (reading circles), to build his own network. However, there are significant differences between the two movements. According to Yavuz:

> Although Gülen's movement derived its conceptual framework and ideas from Nursî's writings, Gülen leads a different form of movement, one that is more praxis oriented and seeks to transform society and institutions by expanding its circles of sympathizers and supporters.[766]

Nursî was primarily interested in Quranic exegesis and wanted to transform society by persuasion rather than violent means. Yavuz noted in 2003 that Gülen also stressed the use of persuasion rather than confrontation. However, in the most recent publication edited by Yavuz and Bayram Balcı, in the context of the coup attempt of July 2016, it is pointed out that the Gülen movement sought confrontation with the AKP. The conclusion of the scholars that contributed to this volume is that the Gülenists in the

---

763. For instance, Abdülkadir Selvi, 'Fetullah Gülen: Ben Nurcu değilim', ['Fetullah Gülen: I am not Lightist'], *Yeni Safak*, 19 May 2015, http://www.yenisafak.com/yazarlar/abdulkadirselvi/fetullah-Gülen--ben-nurcu-degilim-2010876, [Accessed on 31 August 2017].

764. Christopher Holton and Clare Lopez, *The Gülen Movement*, Jihad Reader Series, Vol. 8, Washington D.C., 2015, p. 11.

765. Tuğrul Keskin, "Market Oriented Post-Islamism in Turkey" in Berna Turam, *Secular State and Religious Society*, New York, 2012, p. 123.

766. M. Hakan Yavuz, "Islam in the Public Sphere" in Yavuz, M. Hakan and Esposito, John L. *Turkish Islam and the Secular State*, Syracuse, 2003, p. 3.

military organised the coup, which ultimately failed.[767] Accordingly, attention has to be paid to these claims. Fundamentally, infiltration of the police, army and even judiciary indicates an organisation that seeks power, while the broad message of the movement seems to be emphasis on service and adherence to secularism, modernity, education and inter-faith dialogue.

Just like Nursî, Gülen also had his share of brushes with the law for activities that were deemed contradictory to laicism. He has been tried several times, spent six months in prison between 1970 and 1971; he was even internally exiled to Sinop. Eventually he left for the U.S. in 1999, never to return. His departure from Turkey did not end the Gülen chapter in the Republic's history. His organisation continued to function successfully in various fields, even with Gülen away from the power base of the movement.

Gülen's network

Gülen has many critics and enemies in Turkey but it was the break with the AKP that paved the way for the dramatic escalation of hostilities between the two entities. "Beginning in 2012, they started to fall out with each other. The conservative AKP government and the Gülenists began to engage in a silent 'civil war', although much of their conflict remained somewhat hidden from public view."[768] Hostility towards Gülen and his movement increased after the attempted coup of 15 July 2016. The AKP, the government and the media took to referring to the movement as FETÖ (*Fethullah Terör Örgütü*/Fethullah Terrorist Organisation). In contemporary Turkey, after the failed coup in 2016, even a tenuous connection to the Gülen movement is fraught with potential arrest.

Before the dispute and the dismantling of the network in Turkey, Gülen's expansive network included education institutions across 170 countries, both in Muslim majority countries but also countries where Turkish and Muslim Diaspora minorities can be found. As Aslı Aydıntanbaş notes,

> the movement was able to boast of having over 1,000 "Turkish schools" spread across 170 countries from the United States to Bangladesh to Uganda....Wherever Muslims lived, Gülenists and Gülen schools existed - with the exception of Saudi Arabia and Iran, which never allowed them. They were the modern-day version of Protestant missionaries who heeded a call for public duty to spread

---

767. Yavuz M. Hakan and Bayram Balcı, "The Gülen Momement and the Coup", in Yavuz M. Hakan and Bayram Balcı, *Turkey's July 15th Coup*, Salt Lake City, 2018, p. 12.
768. *Asli Aydıntaşbaş*, 'The Good, the Bad, And the Gülenists: The role of the Gülen movement in Turkey's coup attempt, European Council on Foreign Relations, September 2016, p. 2.

Evidently, Gülen established a sphere of influence beyond Turkey's borders. This influence was very useful for politicians such as Özal in the 1980s, who saw it as an opportunity to tap into the network to extend Turkish influence in the Turkic Republics of Central Asia and beyond. Özal's ambitions for expanding Turkey's territories and sphere of influence, and his economic vision of expanding commercial ventures abroad, brought him closer to Fethullah Gülen. In turn, Gülen used proximity to political power circles to expand his network, especially educational institutions, which reached even the far-flung countries of the world, including Australia.

Sociologist Berna Turam, who visited Gülen's schools in the Turkic Republics, noted that "[t]hey show videotapes of the Kazak, Kirghiz and Turkmen kids singing the Turkish anthem. This creates an emotionally charged atmosphere, which often leads to tears and ecstatic applause in the audience."[770] These activities aimed to replace Russia as the dominant power in that region using linguistic/kinship affinity and creating emotional attachment.

Gülen's network as agents of politics and infiltration: facts and fiction

It is hard to separate facts from fiction when it comes to Gülen and the Gülenists. The body of literature available is voluminous but deeply contradictory. Gülen is described as both progressive and conservative and his agency both hierarchical and loosely structured. The outermost cycle consists of more loosely defined allies, supporters and recruits, and the inner circle is the operational core that defines a course of action in state institutions.[771] The inner circle is more hierarchical than the outer cycle.

It was expected that the AKP would categorise the movement with some pejorative epithet such as FETÖ, after the failed coup in 2016, but we can also see former sympathisers such as Hakan Yavuz doing the same. In an outstanding study of the movement in 2013 Yavuz described Gülen as "the outcome of . . . religious enlightenment in Turkey".[772] In 2018, Yavuz

769. *Ibid.*, pp. 2-3.
770. Berna Turam, *Between Islam and the State*, Stanford, California, 2007, p. 59.
771. Aydıntaşbaş, *op. cit.*p. 3.
772. M. Hakan Yavuz, *Toward an Islamic Enlightenment*, Oxford, 2013, p. 66.

co-edited a volume in which the contributing scholars pointed to the net-work as the likely culprit.[773] Furthermore, in an interview with the Islamist *Daily Sabah*, Yavuz called the Gülenist Movement FETÖ, using the language of the current regime.[774]

Gülen has been careful not to express opinions on party politics. He described politics as "the art of managing a nation's affairs in ways that please God and people"[775] and built a remarkable mechanism permeating into different fields beyond education and service, acting as a future state. The point is that Gülen wanted to influence public opinion and he therefore was involved in politics through numerous media outlets. He also formed an alliance with the AKP for mutual gain: for Gülen extending influence, for the AKP attaining government.

Gülen is reported to have said that even if the Archangel Gabriel formed a party, he would not follow him. He said this in the context of not supporting Erbakan. He was criticized by Islamist circles for uttering such words, not so much because of his opposition to Erbakan, but on the grounds of his comments about the Archangel Gabriel. He was in effect saying he would not follow Allah's angels who were higher than the prophet in the pantheon.[776] This is brought up here for two reasons: firstly, that Gülen's every word has been subject to scrutiny and even an off-hand remark could and did cause controversy. Secondly, this is one of the examples of Gülen talking against political involvement. However, it is hard to see his movement not being involved in politics despite his protestations to this effect.

There is no doubt that political influence was part of his vision. This does not mean that Gülen sought a political office: by his own admission, in a moment of candour, to do so would have been below his station.[777] However, Gülen and his agency have always been lobbying politicians and Gülen co-operated with many, lending his support, in terms of the voter base he controlled, and in return asking for support to expand his ever-growing (until 2016) empire.

There are many aspects to the Gülenist network. Gülen established a formidable network inside Turkey consisting of *Işıklar Evleri* (Light Houses), *Dersanes*, Dormitories and Schools. Through *Işıklar Evleri*, operating very similarly to Mormon Missionary Houses, they recruited members to the ever-expanding organisation. A major aspect of the organisation was

773. M. Hakan Yavuz and Bayram Balcı, *op. cit., passim.*
774. 'Fight against FETÖ needs national involvement', *Daily Sabah*, 10 July 2017.
775. *Pearls, op. cit.,* p. 87.
776. Oral Çalışlar and Tolga Çelik, *Erbakan, Fetullah Kavgası,* İstanbul, 2000, p. 120.
777. https://www.youtube.com/watch?v=InSoXdrh-0c [Accessed on 9 June 2019].

the successful infiltration of the police and the military, through a carefully envisaged strategy; though this is vehemently denied by both Gülen and sympathisers.

The Turkish public was informed of these allegations of infiltration, primarily to the police intelligence and colleges, by investigative journalist Ahmet Şık's book *The Imam's Army* (*İmamın Ordusu*) and former police superintendent Hanefi Avcı's semi-autobiographical account *Haliç'te Yaşayan Simonlar* (*Devotee Residents of Haliç*). They were both arrested and imprisoned; in the case of Hanefi Avcı, on what seemed to be trumped up charges. This happened while the AKP was in power. Şık went to prison before the book was published, though the manuscript was released on the internet.[778]

Infiltration of the police and the army is not compatible with an organisation that purports to be interested only in education, interfaith dialogue and generally, in Islamic exegesis. Şık, subsequently a parliamentary member of the mainly Kurdish HDP and eventually Workers' Party of Turkey (*Türkiye İşçi Partisi*, TİP), was also briefly arrested in 2016, this time as an alleged Gülenist. In the sometimes-surreal world of Turkish politics the AKP regime charged as a Gülenist the very person who pointed out about Gülen's plan to take over strategic positions in the administration of the Republic.[779]

There is no reason to doubt the sincerity of Gülen's emphasis on education and service. At the same time, the network was not established solely to provide education and service but to establish a parallel or future state. Some of the sympathetic western scholars dismissed or avoided discussing the allegations of efforts of the network to infiltrate key positions in the Republic's power circles. These allegations cannot be easily written-off, given the weight of evidence.

The ultimate aim of the movement seems to have been political influence and control. The network assisted Erdoğan/AKP to come to power and when the rift between the two widened, sought to take over, using the army and the police, which it seemed to have infiltrated to some extent. One way of explaining the movement's involvement in such mechanisms is by looking at its different stages of evolution. Yavuz notes that the movement started as a "pietistic community", transformed to becoming a powerful movement (*Hareket*) and finally a structure parallel to the gov-

---

778. See Hanefi Avcı, *Haliç'te Yaşayan Simonlar*, Ankara, 2017; Ahmet Şık, *İmamın Ordusu*, İstanbul, 2017.
779. Ahmet Şık, *İtham Ediyorum*, İstanbul, 2018, p. 159.

ernment. Thus, eventually the cemaat became a "power obsessed" movement,[780] partaking in the fields of both religion and politics.

Taqiyya or plain old duplicity?

Turam, who conducted field research and visited many Gülen-funded venues, makes a distinction between "window sites" and the private realm of the movement. Needless to say, the window sites spread a message that is acceptable to an external audience. For instance,

> [w]hile most sites in Turkey accommodate public discussions on laicism, the window sites in the United States consist predominantly of interfaith and faith-provoking activities and seminars on dialogue between civilizations. Not surprisingly, the latter nurture a peaceful atmosphere between various religious traditions and groups - especially Christianity, Islam and Judaism - as a solution to the global terror most feared by the United States.[781]

In her fieldwork, Turam found considerable differences in attitude between the window sites and the private realm in relation to their approach to Mustafa Kemal Atatürk as well: the tributes to Atatürk in designated spaces displaying Atatürk memorabilia and related symbols did not translate to the private sphere. Thus, there were two conflicting parallel realities. However, it is to be noted that Turam was allowed unfettered access to the network activities in Central Asia.

Turam's research points to *taqiyya* (dissimulation) practices, which led to conspiracy theories. *Taqiyya* is a loaded term and it is an allegation that has followed the Gülen movement for a long time. Tamer Balcı and Christopher L. Miller note that the practice of *taqiyya* emerged in the eighth century in the Shia Muslim community to avoid persecution by the Ummayad Empire, and that "it applied only to Shi'a and not to the Sunnis".[782] In reality, this precautionary dissimulation was practised up to the twentieth century by Ghulat Shiites and was not confined to the eighth century.[783] Whether the Gülenists practise, despite being Sunni, this *modus operandi* or not, the allegations cannot easily be dismissed and need to be explored.

There are many conspiracy theories about Gülen in addition to those

---

780. Yavuz, "The Three Stages of the Gülen movement: From Pietitic Weeping Movement to Power-Obsessed Structure" in Yavuz and Balcı, *op. cit.*, pp. 20-45.
781. Turam, *Between Islam and the State*, p. 59.
782. Tamer Balcı, *op. cit.*, p. 11.
783. Matti Moosa, *Extremist Shiites*, Syracuse, New York, 1987, pp. 4, 37, 189, 410 and 412.

mentioned above, alleging that he is reforming Islam as a Western project to turn it into a form acceptable to the West. The most incredible claim is that he is a Secret Vatican Cardinal (*in pectore*). In essence, if we tally all the accusations and claims against Gülen, the movement is both in favour of Sharia Law and at the same time a Trojan horse for the Christian West. The claims that Gülen somehow represents Christianity ignore his genuine Islamist credentials, his connection to Nursî, Nursî's influence on Gülen, his training as imam in his younger days and his fervent sermons, which can be found on *YouTube*. The problem with conspiracy theories is that they cannot be disproved to the proponent; any explanation is simply negated by adding the interlocutor to the scope of the conspiracy.

An example of the allegations of the duplicity of the movement can be found in the large number of US diplomatic cables published through *Wikileaks*. Substantial numbers of documents relate to Gülen and his network.

> they are everywhere in Turkish society, including the strongest bastion of Kemalism - the military. [Leftist Taraf journalist Yasemin] Congar [Çongar] told us military leadership is increasingly concerned with the Gülen Moverment,s [sic] infiltration of the higher ranks of the armed forces, and are keen to continually purge Gülenists from their ranks. One tactic for ferreting them out is to hold a pool party where military officers are expected to bring their wives, thus exposing the pious women who refuse to wear a swimsuit to the detriment of their husbands' careers. Congar [Çongar], however, noted Gülen supporters have begun to act in a secular manner to protect their identities. For example, while the secularists' wives attend pool parties with one-piece suits, Gülenist,s [sic] wives will wear more revealing two-piece swimsuits. She also mentioned stories of pious officers stocking their house and trash with alcohol bottles to fool the ever vigilant inspectors seeking to root out non-secular officers.[784]

Multiple hypotheses can be discerned from this quotation. The source of the story is Yasemin Çongar, a journalist who was later charged with obtaining secret state records. The journalist must have relied on an insider source for this information, if it is true. It could have been fabricated by her source or even by herself to defame Gülen and his network. If that is the case, it raises the issue of the reliability of this type of information even if they form part of U.S. diplomatic cables. If we entertain the possibility of the story being true, then there are different implications. Primarily

---

784. *WikiLeaks*, Public Library of US Diplomacy, Canonical ID: 09ISTANBUL351_a, Subject: Diyanet in a changing Turkey, 14 September 2009.

the ethics of the Kemalist officers to push what they suspected to be pious women, to expose themselves in this manner, is of questionable conduct. The burden once again fell on women to demonstrate either piety or devotion to Kemal by choosing the appropriate attire. In itself, even if true, it is not evidence of infiltration, since all that it indicates is suspicion of infiltration.

This practice does not have to be called *taqiyya*. Many agencies, whether political parties, commercial entities, or government departments, publish one view but they privately hold another. In other words, we can divorce this duplicitous practice from any religious connotation by not calling it *taqiyya*. Evidently, Turam's research shows that the duality in the operation of the organisation is the Gülenists' *modus operandi*. Once we divorce the practice from *taqiyya* and all the connotations that the term entails, a view of an organisation emerges which is interested in influencing the social and political process. This vision is not necessarily to turn Turkey into a Sharia state, but still reflect Gülen's eclectic, varied and contradictory views.

Gülen himself used this tactic when it suited him. Under oath in the American court in 2001, in a hearing related to allegations made against him by the State Security Court of Turkey, he was questioned by the U.S. public prosecutor. When asked by the public prosecutor, Repetto, whether he was a member of any organisation, Gülen said no. He gave a negative response to the additional question on whether he was the leader of an organisation: "I have no business with any organization.

I have never been in the management or leadership of any organization", which was patently not true, unless one engages in dubious rationalisation. Finally, when Repetto insistently asked him whether an organisation was established on his behalf, Gülen still said no, all the while he was at the apex of a conglomerate.[785] In the same hearing, he also denied any involvement in the establishment and running of any educational institution.

It must be said that this is a method Nursî never used. Nursî stood up in court and defended and espoused his principles. Gülen is betrayed by his own words:

> In a famous sermon from the late 1990s, Gülen advised his followers to continue living incognito 'inside the veins of the state' until enough power had been amassed: You must move in the veins of the system, without anyone noticing your existence, until you reach all the power centres. . . . You must wait until such time as you have gotten all the state power, until you have brought to your side all the power of the constitutional institutions in Turkey. . . . Until that

785. Nusret Senem, *Fethullah Gülenín Konuşmaları ve Pensilvanya İfadesi*, İstanbul, 2012, p. 91.

time, any step taken would be too early, like breaking an egg without waiting the full 40 days for it to hatch.[786]

The key to understanding the Gülen movement lies with the movement's multiple messages to reach and satisfy multiple audiences. In other words, the movement tried to be all things to all people to expand their circle of influence.

Gülenists and Kemalism

Adem Çaylak and Güliz Dinç compared Kemalism and Gülenism, which are in their words "seemingly incompatible", and came to the conclusion that they share the following principles: (i) sacralization of modern knowledge, science and education; (ii) militarism and centrism; (iii) statism and corporatism, and; (iv) ethnic nationalism and Turkism.[787] In articulating these principles Kemalism uses "profane and secular language" while, the latter's language is spiritual and religious.[788]

To Çaylak and Dinç, using Gramsci's concept of hegemony, both ideologies represent capitalist hegemony. However, while "secular" Kemalism is "coercive", what they call "religionist" Kemalism, i.e. Gülenism, is "consensual". While Kemalism sometimes used force to penetrate society, Gülenism used religious language "to gain consent of the dominated classes".[789] Despite the use of religious discourse, Çaylak and Dinç regard Gülenism as secular and regard Kemalism and Gülenism as "coming from the same paradigm and a blend of Turko-Islamic imperial tradition and Western positivist modernity."[790]

In this interesting study the differences between the two ideologies are minimized and Gülenism builds on Kemalism to further expand the hegemony. It can be said that while both ideologies are étatist and Gülen is interested, just as Mustafa Kemal was, in controlling the state, Gülen managed to establish a network of voluntary participation.

Çaylak and Dinç's study suggests that Gülenism is an extension of Kemalism; at the very least the movement utilises ideas derived from the

---

786. Aydıntaşbaş, p.4, translated by Aydıntaşbaş based on a video found at YouTube: "Fethullah Gülen – Devlete Sızma", YouTube, 10 April 2014, https://www.youtube.com/watch?v=VZtJTt2lNJY (This clip is no longer available).
787. Adem Çaylak and Güliz Dinç, 'Gülenism as "Religionist" Kemalism', *Insight Turkey*, January 2017, p. 182.
788. Çaylak and Dinç, p. 184.
789. *Ibid.*, p. 182.
790. *Ibid.*, p. 184.

same pool. Gülen's view of nationalism, a core principle of Kemalism, is not so different to the neo-Kemalist version or Millî Görüş Movement's synthesis of nationalism with Islam:

> On defining the term "nation," Gülen calls on people to rediscover their cultural past which was embodied within Islam and the Ottoman past. Gülen states that the reimagination of the cultural content of Turkish nation will lead Islamic groups to construct the political nation as Muslim, Ottoman, and Turkish. Based on the revival of the cultural past of the Turkish Muslim community, Gülen formulates his own version of national identity as Muslim, Ottoman, and Turkish. Nevertheless, this definition creates some fears among Kemalists (those who advocate the secular Turkish state founded by Mustafa Kemal Atatürk) that reviving the past would lead to religious republicanism. Gülen intends to mingle the religious community and national community.[791]

Progressive?

Undoubtedly, in his corpus Gülen has expounded some "progressive" ideas. In fact, Balcı and Miller describe the Gülen movement as "a progressive religious movement".[792] However, there are many aspects to the movement which cannot be described as "progressive"; these ideas can easily be found in his writings. Gülen's view on gender relations reflect the same conservative values as Nursî:

> Today, the issue of gender has reached the point where some people refuse to recognize the very real differences between men and women and claim that they are alike and equal in all respects. Implementing these views has resulted in the "modern" lifestyle of women working outside the home, trying to "become men," and thus losing their own identity. Family life has eroded, for children are sent to daycare centers or boarding schools as parents are too busy, as "individuals," to take proper care of them. This violence against nature and culture has destroyed the home as a place of balance between authority and love, as a focus of security and peace.[793]

Despite this, there is a tendency to portray Gülen as more "progressive" than his "conservative" followers, but as Tore Fougner argues, this claim

---

791. Çıngıllıoğlu, p. 61.
792. In Tamer Balcı and Christopher L. Miller, "The Gülen Hizmet Movement: A Cautionary Tale" in Tamer Balcı and Christopher L. Miller (ed.), The Gülen Hizmet Movement, Newcastle upon Tyne, 2012, p. 2.
793. M. Fethullah Gülen, *Questions and Answers about Islam*, Vol. 1, 2000, pp. 89-90.

"does not stand up to a closer scrutiny of his writings".[794] Fougner further argues that:

> gender relations within the Gülen movement are fraught with patriarchy – this, with reference to the practice of strict gender segregation, the tendency for wives and daughters to be confined to the private sphere, and the absence of women in leadership positions – it is common among scholars to argue that Gülen himself has 'progressive' views on women and gender relations.[795]

Having studied Gülen's writing on gender relations and his views on women Fougner concluded that Gülen sees "that a woman's role is first and foremost limited to home-making and social breeding".[796] There is ample evidence in Gülen's extensive writings to reach this conclusion. Despite that, there has been an effort by some scholars, some of whom were cited here, to portray Gülen not only as a champion of women's rights, but also progressive, modern and secular.

Turam's research shed light on practices that cannot be described as such: in contrast to the mixing of men and women in the public sites, activities in the private and communal sites displayed consistent gender segregation.[797] On gender segregation, Tuğrul Keskin also notes that:

> in the Dersanes, men and women are completely segregated and they meet at different locations. From the outside, while the Gülen movement may represent a more 'modern' interpretation of Islam, from an insider perspective, the movement does not operate differently from any other Islamic movement.[798]

Another criticism levelled at Gülenism is about the gender roles in his schools:

> [Yeşim Arat] states, 'Although the schools provide excellent secular education, students are gently guided into the pious culture of the group, particularly through dormitory life. They are, thus, led to accept more orthodox religious understandings of gender roles and interests'.[799]

The school curriculum satisfies the demand by the secularists but privately the students are steered towards a particular way of life. The pub-

794. Tore Fougner, 'Fethullah Gülen's understanding of women's rights in Islam: a critical reappraisal', *Turkish Studies*, Vol. 18, No. 2, p. 255.
795. *Ibid.*, p. 252.
796. *Ibid.*, p. 260.
797. Turam, *Between Islam and the State*, p. 60.
798. Tuğrul Keskin, "Market Oriented Post-Islamism in Turkey" in Berna Turam, *Secular State and Religious Society*, p. 135.
799. Yesim Arat quoted in Salih Çıngıllıoğlu, *The Gülen Movement*, Cham, 2017, p. 71.

lic message to wider audience is divergent from the message to a specific audience in private. Consistently this has been the approach used by the Movement.

Gülen may not be "reactionary" (to use the Kemalists' favoured term of estrangement), anti-secular or anti-modern, but there are limitations in his perception and applications of all these principles. For instance, Gülen disapproves of the "Western" practice of children being placed in day-care centres and nurseries, because only a mother can "provide the compassion that a child needs the most."[800] Nurseries, day-care and after-school centres are necessities of the "modern" condition. As frequently, I argue in this study, there is a tendency by many scholars studying Nursî and Gülen and their espousal of modernism to equate modernism with technological advancement. Modernism, always hard to define, includes, however, in my estimation, the display of certain attitudes to social issues including gender roles and relations.

The issue of the "headscarf" was the pet hate of the Kemalist guard. By taking this stand, which was more than likely against the majority opinion of his cemaat, Gülen promoted the view point of the state. In another instances, Gülen delivered sermons through which he displayed a respect for human life, irrespective of religion, ethnicity or nationality. During the Gulf War Gülen gave a speech and said that "he cried for the Israeli babies" during the bombardment of Israel by Iraq. This talk shocked both his base and wider Islamist circles. Erbakan's RP was angry with him and *Milli Gazete* criticised Fethullah Gülen harshly.[801]

Gülen as secularist and modernist

Despite many court actions, Gülen has never expressed openly any thoughts against secularisation and has been a fervent proponent of "modernism", a constituent part of the ideology of secularism as conceived in Turkey. The problem is that given the Movement's *modus operandi* and the track record, regarding infiltration in the army and the police, it is hard to assess the veracity of Gülen's views on secularism. It is often pointed out by scholars that Gülen is against neither modernism nor secularism. Salih Cıngıllıoğlu notes that:

[r]ather than negating or challenging the modernization processes, Gülen seeks to demonstrate the way in which a properly conceived

---

800. Fougner, *op. cit.*, p. 260.
801. *Ibid.*, p. 94.

Muslim project affirms and furthers the most crucial ends of modernity, such as the formation of conscious actors who are armed with both religious and secular knowledge. According to Özdalga, modernity is an efficient means for Gülen to establish a renewed Islamic consciousness and a Muslim presence in the new public sphere. In other words, Gülen's ideas and actions revitalize the possibility of being both modern and Muslim at the same time.[802]

It can well be argued that modernism is not incompatible with Islam as practised in Turkey. In the presence of Kemalism and the Kemalist ideas about modernism and secularism, Gülen sought to find ways to reconcile the different tendencies of his movement with modernism and secularism, though some of the ideas he has expressed do not seem compatible with this effort:

> Even non-Muslim, Western scholars, who often are hostile to Islam, acknowledge that Jews, Christians, and other non-Muslims ruled by Muslims generally enjoyed much greater economic prosperity, dignity, and prestige, and had far more freedoms than under non-Islamic rule - even that of their own co-religionists. Nor did this situation change significantly in the Western world until a thorough-going secularization diminished the importance of religious beliefs, rites, and solidarity. Intolerant states did not become legally tolerant so much as legally indifferent.[803]

Gülen in this excerpt seems to promote secularisation in the West and the diminishing of religious, i.e. Christian beliefs, but not advocating the same for Turkey or other Muslim majority countries. Helen Rose Ebaugh, who is sympathetic to the movement, accentuates the movement's secularist credentials and plays down the obvious Islamist orientation of the movement:

> Mr. Gülen encouraged his listeners to invest in private secular elite high schools where he hoped to combine Islamic morals with secular knowledge. These schools are based on a secular curriculum approved by the state and use English for instruction. The only Islam that is formally taught in the schools is the hour that is allowed by the state for religious instruction in comparative religions with the textbook selected by the state.[804]

In contrast, Turam expands on this aspect of the movement:

802. Cıngıllıoğlu, *op. cit.*, p. 61.
803. M. Fethullah Gülen, *Questions and Answers about Islam*, p. 24.
804. Ebaugh, *op. cit.*, p. 30.

When the followers of the Gülen movement opened science schools and taught a secular curriculum, for example, they made sure that boarding was obligatory. This was their access to the private lives of the students, through which they socialized them not only into Islamic ways of life but also into discipline. The private sphere has not only included extracurricular activities in schools, but most of the charity work and fund-raising have also taken place in the private lives of social actors. Despite the multi-sited nature of Islamic revival, the deep interest in public Islam has rendered civil society and the public sphere as almost interchangeable terms in the Islamic context.[805]

Thus, while in the public sphere the secular aspect is promoted, in the private sphere an Islamic way of life is encouraged. This is not necessarily anti-secular behaviour; it is compatible with the Kemalist notions of the separation of public and private sphere, in which the public space is to remain free of any overt displays of Islam. What sort of secularism is Gülen's Movement espousing? Ahmet T. Kuru's separation of "passive" and "assertive" secularism is useful to decipher this vision. In Kuru's paradigm "assertive secularism" means in the public domain, the state supports only the expression of a secular worldview, and formally excludes religion and religious symbols from that domain. "Passive secularism" favoured by Pro-Islamic conservatives is the American model, according to which the state permits the expression of religion in the public domain." Kuru goes on to conclude that "[i]n short, what Turkey has witnessed over the last decade is no longer a tussle between secularism and Islamism, but between two brands of secularism".[806]

Who are the "assertive secularists" in Kuru's hypothesis? Kuru lists them as "the CHP, military generals, majority of the high court members, and major media outlets. . . .TÜSİAD".[807] In Kuru's list, after the purges that followed the 2016 attempted coup only the CHP and the *Cumhuriyet* newspaper remained assertive secularists. TÜSİAD found it more expedient to co-exist with the AKP and should no longer be counted in this column. In any case, these terms are second order definitions. It is unlikely that a secular person would classify themselves as assertive or passive. These categories come to life in scholarly inquiry. Certainly, the desired parameters of each secularist are different but these broad categories are useful.

---

805. Turam, Berna (ed.), *Secular State and Religious Society: Two Forces in Play in Turkey,* Pallgrave Macmillan, NewYork, 2012, p. 26.

806. Ahmet T. Kuru, "Changing Perspectives on Islamism and Secularism in Turkey: The Gülen Movement and the AKP Party" in International Conference Proceedings, *Muslim World in Transition: Contributions of the Gülen Movement,* London, 2007, p. 140.

807. *Ibid.,* p. 141.

Gülen started as a preacher at a young age and he was able to build a reputation to stir emotions. His charisma is beyond question. Çalışlar and Çelik note that one of the methods he employed was to assign some people in the audience to cry and encourage these emotions among the audience. No doubt he had a vision, but the precise nature of this vision is debatable. It is hidden under the clutter of the plethora of writing and the sheer size and multi-faceted nature of his organisation.

Harrington argues that Gülen's goal is for Turkey to return to traditional life. But what is traditional life? More to the point, traditional life of which point in the Republic's history or even the Ottoman Empire's history? Traditional life in the cities of western Turkey or eastern Turkey's regions and villages? Traditional Sunni, Kurdish or Alevi life? Could it be that, just like the Kemalists, who had "Nostalgia for the Modern", in the words of Özyürek, Gülen also yearns for a utopian ideal of the nostalgic past?

There is not sufficient evidence, despite many allegations, that Gülen's vision and intention was to turn the country into a state ruled by Sharia law, in the same way as Saudi Arabia and contemporary Iran are. At the same time, I think his modernism and progressiveness has been exaggerated by sympathetic scholars and advocates. In general, his emphasis on education and some of the goals of the movement, even if not entirely genuine, puts him in a modernist camp. However, this modernism is not necessarily western style, nor does it have to be.

Kuru notes that a group of social scientists launched a theoretical debate in the late 1990s on "multiple modernities" and "Islamic modernity" to challenge modernism, although they have not defined these terms.[808] In his 1958 study on traditional societies, Daniel Lerner quotes a Jordanian *qadi* who noted the ambivalence of Middle East elites, who want modernity but also to keep their Arab Muslim traditions:

> the Qodi admitted that he feels restrained by the conventional Muslim norms which his followers expect him to uphold. His personal dilemma involves those public choices between Mecca and mechanization which are crucial for the Middle East elites.[809]

This dilemma was simplified to represent modernity as technological advancement. Technology has been adapted in the Middle East even in countries such as Saudi Arabia, while maintaining local traditions. One

---

808. Ahmet Kuru, "Fethullah Gülen's Search for a Middle Way Between Modernity and Muslim Tradition" in Yavuz and Esposito, *op. cit.*, p. 115.
809. Daniel Lerner, *The Passing of Traditional Society*, London, 1958, p. 349.

is not an impediment to the other, as the experience of Japan has shown, combining modernity with tradition. Kuru postulates that Gülen himself searched for a middle way to combine Islam with modernity (Progress and Conservation of Tradition). Gülen rejected *medreses* in favour of modern schools, which nevertheless incorporated Islamic Knowledge. Some western modes of thought see history in linear form but Gülen argued that "[h]istory pursues cyclical ways even though it results in progress, and thereby it has a kind of spiral path";[810] historical progress incorporating tradition.

Modernism in Turkey is not necessarily a trait exclusive to Kemalism. Gülen ultimately extracted modernism from Kemalism, which is no longer the exclusive domain of the Kemalist secularists, but also married it to Islam, so it is no longer to be solely the domain of the West.

The Gülen movement is a mélange of conservative as well as a sort of modern thinking, a type of secularism, a genuine emphasis on education and service (*Hizmet*) but also an ambitious project to influence Turkey, Islam in other countries, especially in the Turkic Republics but also Christian-Muslim relations in the West, including Australia. The movement has multiple aims and it strives to present itself as "heterogenous", not monolithic with a single purpose.[811] In the earlier years, preceding the inter-faith dialogue phase of the movement, Gülen expressed anti-western feelings. In the editorial of the October 1980 issue of his magazine *Sızıntı*, directly following the coup d'état, Fethullah Gülen described Anatolia as "the final guard" against the [corrupt] mentality of the crusaders, the Jesuits and also against the poison of lust, alcohol and Western philosophies and ideologies.[812]

Gülenists and the failed coup

On 15 July 2016 a coup was attempted in Turkey. This was not successful for many reasons, including operational failures on the part of the *putschists* and the public backlash. Erdoğan quickly credited Gülen with the attempt. The coup attempt could have involved either the Kemalist, the Gülenist officers or both. There is simply no other force capable of taking

810. Kuru, "Fethullah Gülen's Search for a Middle Way Between Modernity and Muslim Tradition" in Yavuz and Esposito, *op. cit.*, p. 125.
811. Ercan Karakoyun, Director of the Gülen movement in Germany, interview with Tim Sebastian, 28 September 2016 edition of Conflict Zone, *Deutsche Welle*, https://www.dw.com/en/ercan-karakoyun-on-conflict-zone/av-35917426 [Accessed on 30 May 2019].
812. Günter Seufert, 'Is the Fethullah Gülen Movement Overstretching Itself?', *SWP Research Paper*, Berlin, 2014, p. 8.

such a brazen act.[813] There is also the issue of whether Gülen was involved personally in the organisation of the coup, if it is accepted that the coup was attempted by sympathisers. It is too early to write the definitive history of the attempted coup, though Hakan Yavuz and Bayram Balcı's publication entitled *Turkey's July 15th Coup* points towards Gülen, as cited above.

There is enough evidence linking followers of Gülen to the coup but evidence pointing to Fethullah Gülen himself remains scant.[814] Dani Rodrik, a Harvard economist, expert on the judicial power of the Gülen movement noted that

> [t]he Gülen movement is a highly hierarchical organization. People who have followed it closely over the years (such as Hanefi Avci or Rusen Cakir) report that very few important decisions take place without Gülen's blessing. There is certainly no tradition of autonomous, independent decision-making or dissent in the movement. It would be surprising if Gülenist officers had planned this on their own, without seeking at least the assent of their spiritual leader."[815]

This comes back to the issue of whether Gülen's organisation follows a rigid chain of command. Whether or not Gülen, Gülen's movement or sympathizers were involved in the coup, the charges and accusations by the government and their relentless pursuit of everyone they deem to be Gülenist, has once again changed the political landscape of the country.

Conclusion

Marie-Elisabeth Maigre, in an international conference about Gülen, noted that, in the 1980s and 1990s, the relationship between the Gülen movement and the Islamist RP were rather cold. "Erbakan ... even accused Gülen of accepting government support to threaten Refah." Maigre added that

---

813. Some commentators, such as Ahmet Nesin who lives in exile, interviewed former Turkish officers who escaped to Europe, is not convinced that the Gülenists were the leaders of the attempted coup. His view is that this congregation was already controlling Turkey; they had nothing to gain from this venture (Ergun Babahan. 'Ahmet Nesin: "15 Temmuz darbe girişiminin liderliği Cemaat'te değil!"', [Ahmet Nesin: the leader of the coup attempt was not the Congregation], *Ahval*, 23 February 2019).
814. Aydıntaşbaş, *op. cit.*, p. 1.
815. Dani Rodrik, "Is Fethullah Gülen behind Turkey's coup? (with update)", Dani Rodrik's weblog, 23 July 2016.

[c]onsidered as an elitist movement, the Gülen movement had 'little recognition in rural and working-class areas' . . . while Refah had developed since the 60s as a result of the support of the voters from the eastern and central Anatolian towns since the 1960s. Therefore, the two groups attracted different publics and send [sic] out different messages, one asking for the compromise with the secular system and the other proposing a rupture with the Kemalist principles.[816]

There are a number of issues packed in this paragraph: the relationship between the Millî Görüş Movement and the Gülen Movement, the relationship between Gülen and the Kemalists, and ostensibly the different support bases of the two parties. In general, Fethullah Gülen supported centre-right parties. In the 1983 elections Gülen supported the *Milliyetçi Demokrasi Partisi*. Çalışlar and Çelik note the philosophy of the movement was to side with the powerful.[817] At that stage it was expected the MDP would win the elections. Then Gülen switched to Özal's ANAP and continued with Çiller's DYP, rather than the more Islamist oriented Millî Görüş parties. The view that Erbakan's RP represented a rupture with Kemalism is only partially true. Early on Erbakan was definitely anti-Kemalist, as we have seen in Chapter 6.1, but later he compromised and his party embraced some secularists as well.

The Gülen movement can be characterized as a political Islamist organisation, in many respects no different from the Millî Görüş Movement. Yet, the Gülen movement made enormous efforts to reduce the gap between it and the Kemalists - when the Kemalists still had influence and still steered the Republic's course. At the same time, as they incorporated essentially a conservative cemaat, the Movement needed to keep a balance between secularism, modernism, inter-faith dialogue, education philosophy, his brand of neo-Nurcu Islamism and the tendency to seek power and influence.

The Gülen network's involvement in politics, whether directly or indirectly, and their once existing alliance with the AKP, show the difficulty in separating the categories of religion and politics in Turkey. The boundaries between the two categories, if any, are permeable. It is not clear at all whether Gülen himself has been *primarily* interested in spiritual enlightenment or political influence, or both; or indeed whether he sees them as inseparable facets of the same mission. Yet, Gülen's movement cannot dissociate itself from the reality of its involvement in politics. The sympa-

816. Marie-Elisabeth Maigre, "The Influence of the Gülen Movement in the Emergence of a Turkish Cultural Third Way" in *Muslim World in Transition: Contributions of the Gülen Movement*, pp. 38-39.
817. Çalışlar and Çelik, *op. cit.*, p. 46.

thetic studies, both Western and Turkish, present him as a person interested in education, social change, inter-faith dialogue and, for the Turkish context, secularism and modernism. Yet, it is evident that he and his ever-expanding network sought to influence Turkish public opinion and politics, through centre-right parties first and then the AKP in later years.

The Milli Görüş Movement was a springboard for such politicians as Abdullah Gül and Erdoğan, when Milli Görüş completed its cycle. In parallel, the Gülen movement grew, taking advantage of post-junta flexibility of Islamism. When the AKP was formed with Gül and Erdoğan at the helm, it was beneficial for Gülen's network, already strong and widespread, to have an alliance with the upcoming force. It was also beneficial for the AKP to have such an influential ally. The AKP called itself Muslim Democrats, in the mould of Christian Democrats. This was in line with Gülen's efforts to present a moderate, democratic, secular and spiritual movement. It was a reasonable proposition at the time but proved, eventually, to be false.

Goldenberg's theory of religions as vestigial states or in this case "future states" is an appropriate analytical tool that was used to interpret the reality of the Gülen movement. The state ceded to the movement social, educational and cultural functions which however was not sufficient for the Gülenists' ambition. They worked to establish a parallel state, which when it became antagonistic fell out of favour with the current regime.

Here, I am using Goldenberg's theory to help us understand the Gülen movement. The fact that they act like a once-and-future state helps us understand their fusion of religion and politics. While they professed to be interested, and were heavily involved in inter-faith dialogue, educational development and service, they were also building networks of power. Gülen as an imam of a cemaat is head of a religious organisation, which has expanded into many fields of activity beyond what could be considered "religious". The difficulty in separating their "religious" activities from other social, education and "political" activities demonstrates the close and, in most instances, inseparable relationship between religion and politics. Many of his sermons show that Gülen tried to give one message to his followers and a different one to those outside the *cemaat* (secularists, westerners, state elites). There are discrepancies between what they say to those outside their circle and what they tried to achieve in practice, which obscures the relationship between "religion" and "politics".

The next chapter examines the relationship between religion and politics under the AKP. I will demonstrate that the AKP, which used Gülen's network to its advantage, reduced any remaining distance between politics and Islam at an increasing rate. It will also be shown that a de-secularisation process was undertaken by increasing the visibility of Islam in public life. It will be argued that despite this process the secular continue to exist, albeit in conjunction with visible Islam.

CHAPTER 8:
JUSTICE AND DEVELOPMENT PARTY (AKP) IN POWER: THE FOURTH REPUBLIC

Introduction

The history of Mustafa Kemal and Kemalist ideology has been largely written. As AKP and President Recep T. Erdoğan continue to dominate Turkish politics, the history of Erdoğan and Erdoğanism is yet to be written. As we have seen, the transformation of Turkey from an aspiring secular country to a society where Islam dominates the public sphere was initiated in the 1980s. Until the arrival of Erdoğan in the political scene, the "secularist"/"laicist" military and politicians slowly introduced changes to undermine the laic and secular edifice they professed to defend, and facilitated the entrance of the Islamists into politics and government. In turn, the Islamists slowly dominated the political and civic landscape and they incorporated themselves into the system. Gülen's network facilitated this process.

By 2018 Erdoğan shaped Turkish politics in a way that no other politician since Mustafa Kemal Atatürk managed to do. Since 2002, Erdoğan had gradually established himself as a hegemon and set to retransform Turkish society. By all accounts, Erdoğan and the AKP have made a deep mark in the history of Turkish Republic. A key new idea posited in this chapter is that the AKP and Erdoğan have changed Turkish society sufficiently to herald another stage in the Republic's history: the Fourth Republic.

Different scholars argue that Turkey is now secular, non-secular, post-secular, post-Kemalist, Islamist-oriented and even post-Islamist. As there is no doubt that Turkey has been transformed during the AKP rule, a number of themes, *inter alia* the role of Diyanet, the headscarf controversy and nationalism, need to be explored to assess the validity of claims by different scholars as to the nature of Turkish society. My contention is that we cannot unequivocally declare in favour of any of these descriptors, as they are all deficient in some way. We need to articulate a new kind of terminology to capture the contemporary nature of Turkish society and so I propose to canvass a different terminology: practical secularity.

Another point that needs to be explored is the gap between the "secularists" and the "Islamists", which is often portrayed as insurmountable. This was discussed in the previous chapter, but it needs to be revisited in the context of the advent of the AKP and its Islamist orientation. White notes that

> [a]t one level Turkish society appears to be divided into secular and Muslim positions whose proponents are circling the wagons and demanding ideological and behavioural purity from their members. But neither term – secular or Muslim – does justice to the variety of possible positions and their sometimes surprising combinations.[818]

Genesis of the AKP

Erdoğan and the AKP did not emerge out of a vacuum; they were the result of the steady increase of the Islamist presence in politics, public administration and civic life. The AKP surfaced to rely on the new edifice to which a number of politicians and formations contributed: Erbakan, Millî Görüş, the Nakshibendi and Gülen.

The genesis of the AKP lies with Millî Görüş and both Erdoğan and Abdullah Gül, co-founders of the AKP, honed their skills in politics as members of the RP. After the closure of the RP, Millî Görüş established *Fazilet Partisi* (The Virtue Party/FP) in 2001, which was also banned by the establishment. Before it was closed two tendencies were formed within it: *Yenilikçiler* and *Gelenekçiler* (Reformists or Traditionalists).

Keyman and Gümüşçü note that *Yenilikçiler*, or "moderate Islamists" as they call them, formed an alliance with MUSIAD (Independent Industrialists and Businessmen Association), which represented smaller provincial businesses "in contradistinction to TUSIAD . . . which represented big business in Istanbul . . . The 'rising business class' wanted to conduct business with the West and they did not favour Welfare's increasing anti-Western rhetoric". MUSIAD cannot be described as pro-Western, in the sense that they appreciated western values, but they sought "to combine Islam with Western economic rationality".[819] They thus started as a pragmatic group, which wanted to avoid excessive ideological expressions.

The so-called *Yenilikçiler* under the leadership of Gül and Erdoğan went their way, while Millî Görüş formed yet another party: *Saadet Partisi* (The Felicity Party/SP). As Selman Yılmaz from the Divinity Faculty of Ankara University explains, the *Traditionalists* did not want to stray from the original Millî Görüş principles, while *Yenilikçiler* thought that flexibility

---

818. White, *op. cit.*, p. 10.
819. E. Fuat Keyman and Sebnem Gumuscu, *Democracy, Identity, and Foreign Policy in Turkey*, Basingstoke, 2014, p. 32.

should be shown by adapting to the times.[820] Sociologist Edibe Sözen wrote in 2006 that "The JDP [AKP] represented the liberal wing of the Islamic movement".[821]

As separated itself from Millî Görüş, the nucleus that formed the AKP also entered into an alliance with Gülen and his network. The Gülen movement with its network was one of the vehicles of socio-political attitude change that generated the victory of the AKP in 2002. The voters were fed up with the parties of the old regime, which by then included Erbakan as well. Most parties did not differ much from one another and were engulfed in economic scandals. They were pursuing old and tired policies and bickering with one another, even if they occupied the same political space. Part of the AKP's acronym, *Adalet ve Kalkınma*, forms the word AK, that is "white", symbolic of a corruption free party; a blank canvass, so to speak. In time this blank canvas was filled with economic scandals, corruption and authoritarian rule, but at the time presented a credible alternative option for the voters.

When the AKP won power in 2002, Erdoğan himself was not able to assume the Prime Ministership, due to a ban imposed on him for reciting part of a poem in a public meeting. Speaking to a crowd in the southeastern Turkish province of Siirt the previous year, Erdoğan had delivered the following lines, which offended the establishment: "The mosques are our barracks, the domes our helmets, the minarets our bayonets, and the faithful our soldiers."[822] The poem was considered to constitute a threat to the secular state, though it was not under any ban and it was composed by Mehmet Âkif Ersoy. Ersoy, considered a Turkish nationalist, was the writer of the Turkish national anthem and a member of the elite *100 Great Turks* (*Yüz Türk Büyüğü*) list constructed by the Kemalists.[823] Despite the nationalist credentials of the poet, reciting a couplet in a gathering was what attracted the ire of the regime, and

> [o]n 12 April 1998, Erdoğan was found guilty of attempting to mobilize people for an Islamic state. When his sentence ended a few months after the victory of the AKP, he was invited to come back to the Party and became the Prime Minister of Turkey on 13 March 2003.[824]

---

820. Selman Yılmaz, 'Milli Görüş Hareketi: Toplumsal Hareketlerde Çerçeve Değişimi Etkisi', İnsan ve Toplum Bilimleri Araştırmaları Dergisi, Vol. 5, No. 4, p. 1165.
821. Edibe Sözen, "Gender Politics of the JDP", Yavuz, M. Hakan. (Ed.). *The Emergence of a New Turkey*, Salt Lake City, 2006. p. 263.
822. Cagaptay, *The New Sultan*. p. 4.
823. The system which elevated Ersoy to this position overlooked his Islamic tendencies.
824. Turam p. 4.

Erdoğan spent a few months in prison but as Çağaptay noted, it "actually empowered him by casting him as a martyr. That, in return, boosted his appeal among the country's conservative constituencies. Ironically, the attempts of Turkey's secularist system to undermine him, in the end, helped him".[825] The Islamist movement was an avalanche that could not be stopped, and it was the Kemalist military that put it in motion.

The Kemalists misread the situation, believing it to be temporary, just like Erbakan's brief interlude as Prime Minister. They had found a way to remove Erbakan; they could do it again, if necessary. In the meantime, they started agitating about both Erdoğan and Gül's wives (Emine Hanım and Hayrünissa Hanım) for wearing a headscarf. Emine Erdoğan and Hayrünissa Gül were not allowed to attend Presidential functions in the Presidential Palace in Çankaya, as the headscarf prohibition was in operation. The Kemalists remembered the red line again. One can imagine that Erdoğan had a plan to tackle the issue, but it was not yet the right time. Though his party won the elections comfortably and despite all the influences of Islamic minded politicians in government since the 1980s, the Kemalists were still controlling key institutions: the army, military schools, the Constitutional Court, the Court of Cassation *etc.*

The Gülenists helped the government gradually rid the state institutions and the military of the Kemalists and the secularists who had run a "deep state" within Turkey for many years. The operation to remove the Kemalists involved much machination – at times resorting to mind-boggling conspiracies and show trials with fabricated evidence against them (*Ergenekon* and *Balyoz*).[826] The Kemalist "deep state" had set the boundaries on what political reforms were acceptable and overthrown civilian governments that failed to comply. Together, the Gülenists and the AKP, went a long way towards eliminating this threat. But, in time, the Gülenists became a "deep state" themselves, threatening the AKP's increasing dominance; one deep state replaced another.[827] This was also a vestigial state.

Erdoğan I, II, III

In the early period of his rule there was much good will towards Erdoğan:

825. Cagaptay, *The New Sultan*, p. 4.
826. Dani Rodrick, 'Ergenekon and sledgehammer: Building or undermining the rule of law?', *Turkish Policy Quarterly*, Vol. 10, No. 1, pp. 99-109.
827. Aydıntaşbaş, *op. cit.*, p. 2.

Since coming to power, the AKP government has broken a host of twentieth-century taboos: Both non-Muslim and Alevi minorities have been allowed to open institutions and maintain their properties. The government agreed to negotiate on divided Cyprus. An international scholarly conference to discuss the 1915 Armenian massacres received government support.[828]

Even a large proportion of the Christian minorities seemed to have voted for Erdoğan; editors of both the Armenian weekly *Agos* and Greek daily *Apoyevmatini* (Απογευματινή), claimed that in the 2007 election most Armenians and Greeks backed the AKP:

> A dramatic manifestation of the more nuanced attitude of Christian minorities toward the AKP was the support for the AKP of the Armenian patriarch, Mesrob II Mutafyan. Speaking to the German weekly Der Spiegel, the patriarch claimed the Armenian community would prefer the AKP to the CHP because the AKP's approach to minorities is coherent and less nationalistic.[829]

The beginning was promising and encouraging, but the AKP eventually resorted to authoritarian rule. Much like Said Nursî referring to his life as three distinct stages (Said I, II and III), we can also separate three stages in Erdoğan's years in power. Erdoğan I promised much and delivered to his main constituency, and, the case can be made that he also delivered beyond his immediate constituency. For instance, as Aslı Bâli pointed out, through the 12 September 2010 referendum on constitutional amendments Erdoğan I liberalised and reversed the 1982 military drafted constitution, including moves to:

> empower civilian courts while reducing the jurisdiction of military courts; strengthen gender equality and protections for children, the elderly, veterans and the disabled; improve privacy rights and access to government records; expand collective bargaining rights; afford individuals standing to bring constitutional challenges; and remove immunities long afforded to those responsible for the 1980 military coup.[830]

Akça *et al.* note that even some leftist circles have given credit to Erdoğan of this period for "managing to make the military step back momentarily".[831] Erdoğan I also allowed for restoration of churches, which was

---

828. White, *op. cit.*, pp. 49-50.
829. Rabasa, *op. cit.*, p. 67.
830. Quoted in Christopher Houston, 'Thwarted agency and the strange afterlife of Islamism in militant laicism in Turkey', *Contemporary Islam*, Vol. 7, No. 3, September 2013, p. 340.
831. İsmet Akça et al. (eds.) *Turkey Reframed*, London, 2014, p. 2.

an anathema to the nationalist Kemalists, but Erdoğan II (the transitional period), gradually became increasingly authoritarian and intolerant of alternative views - emulating the Kemalists before him. The Third Erdoğan clearly manifested himself in the aftermath of the attempted coup by disregarding the rule of law and democracy, removing public servants, judges, teachers, academics, closing down schools and also accelerating the pace of de-secularisation.

De-secularisation, in the case of Turkey, is a process which increases the presence of Islamic symbolism and discourse in the public life. Syaza Shukri and Ishtiaq Hossain noted that Erdoğan's main focus has been "religion, which made up 30.9% of the quotes attributed to him".[832] This process manifested itself in many ways. The "headscarf" issue was one such issue, given that for both the Kemalists and the Islamists it was a symbol standing for their ideology: "The dominant religion-related issue brought up by the AKP leaders was found to be the headscarf issue, which made up 14.9% of the quotes collected from the period between 2002 and 2017".[833]

The Headscarf Question

The headscarf has been a subject of contention for several decades between the Islamists and the secularists. The term "headscarf", or "veil" as often translated, does not sufficiently account for the full spectrum of headwear for women in Turkey. Given the rich tapestry of traditions that make up the Turkish culture, the influence of external traditions and the interference of both the Kemalists and the Islamists on the style of headscarf, it is not possible to talk about it as if it were a single identifiable item of universal style. There is a range of headgear for women that comes within the scope of the headscarf debate, such as *başörtüsü* and *eşarp*. It is not to these types of headscarf but to *çarşaf* and *türban* that the secularists objected strongly. Heper noted that

> [t]he secularists view the çarşaf as an Islamic outfit and not a modern one, and consequently they are dead set against it. However, since women wearing the çarşaf often stay out of the neighborhoods where most of the secularists reside, work, and otherwise are present this outfit is less controversial than the turban. The headscarf (başörtüsü/eşarp/Yemeni), does only cover part of the hair but the turban covers

832. Syaza Shukri and Ishtiaq Hossain. 'Political discourse and Islam: Role of rhetoric in Turkey', *Journal of Social, Political, and Economic Studies*. Vol. 42, No. 2, Summer 2017. p. 163.
833. *Ibid.*, p. 163.

all hair, the neck, and sometimes the shoulders, too. The secularists take this type of cover as a symbol of political Islam and are opposed to turbaned women (as well as those wearing the çarşaf) entering the "public sphere" . . .[834]

In the early Kemalist narrative, tesettür (veiling or covering of women) was not considered to be a Turkic custom and such types of veil as the çarşaf and peçe were introduced to the Turkish culture after Islam. It was even suggested by Ottoman history researcher Mehmet Zeki Pakalın that the çarşaf was introduced as late as in the post-Tanzımat era, when the number of visitors to Mecca for the annual pilgrimage (hac/hajj) increased. It appears that in the nineteenth century (1870 or 1889) the yaşmak, ferece and çarşaf were prohibited by law. Whether this law was implemented is questionable, noted Sarısaman Sadık, but evidently this issue, i.e. tesettür, did not preoccupy the Kemalists only and it was debated in the Ottoman period. The journal Ictihad argued in 1908 that tesettür was a problem "preventing women from participating in social, cultural and economic life" and expressed the view that freedom from veiling was the liberation of women. On the other side of the spectrum, the conservative Sebiluresad writers argued that tesettür was not a hindrance to women's participation in public life and objected to any changes.[835]

Mustafa Kemal's views on the subject varied. In 1923, he suggested that veiling should be simplified to alleviate distress of women but not to the extent that would contradict adab (spiritual manners). In the same year, he suggested that the veil should be simplified to allow women to participate in economic and social life together with men. In 1925, in the context of the Hat Law he also expressed the view that it was not appropriate for Turkish women to cover their eyes and faces.[836] While Mustafa Kemal's language became more radical in relation to the issue, as his grip on power tightened and he encouraged women to remove their veils, there was no attempt to legislate on this matter.

Though originally in the government narrative the veil was connected to the Islamic tradition, as noted above, in 1928 attempts were made to separate the veil both from Islam and the Turkish culture, stating that çarşaf and peçe passed on to the Turks from Greeks, Armenians and Persians and

834. Heper, Metin, "Does Secularism Face a Serious Threat in Turkey?" in Berna Turam, *Secular State and Religious Society*, p. 85.
835. Sarısaman Sadık, 'Cumhuriyetin ilk yıllarında Kadın Kıyafeti Meselesi', *Atatürk Yolu*, Vol. 6, No. 21, 1998, pp. 97-99.
836. *Ibid.*, pp. 100-01.

stressing that in Prophet Muhammad's time women did not use the veil.[837] The argument in both cases was that tesettür was not an "authentic" Turkic tradition but ηατ it was introduced.

As it can be surmised, the narrative changed over time to convince the Turkish public to change their habitual attire. No legislation was enacted to ban the headscarf, but in 1926 some overzealous local authorities, such as the Tirebolu Municipality and Trabzon Province Assembly, prohibited the wearing of the veil within their areas of control. In Trabzon this resulted in women not going out, which affected the economic life of the city.[838] In other words, the prohibition brought about the opposite result from what was intended.

Mustafa Kemal's private secretary, Soyak, recounted in his memoirs that Kemal was not in favour of using legislation to force women to remove the veil and use modern clothing: "it is not good to use force; the outcome will not be good". He hoped that this issue would be tackled through education. When the Afghan King Amânullâh Khân visited Turkey in 1927, he told him about his plans to change the dress code for women in Afghanistan; Mustafa Kemal advised him to be cautious on this matter. Later, when Mustafa Kemal found out that Amânullâh lost his crown, he attributed this to his haste in legislating about women's dress.[839]

Early republicans invested some effort to discourage women from wearing the headscarf, but the state eventually decided to pursue modernisation in clothing primarily through men's attire. Zeynep Kezer, from Newcastle University, noted that

[w]hereas the republican law banned the use of distinctive clothes and accessories that invoked religious allegiances in men, contrary to popular belief it did not require women to take off their veils. Instead republican policies tried to appeal to women's sense of fashion and played up the (upwardly mobile) class associations that came with a Westernized appearance.[840]

The headscarf issue as it re-emerged represents the shifting plane from men's clothing to women's clothing. As we have seen in Chapter 4, the Hat Law was imposed through the use of persuasion and violence, in the early years of the republic; the state outlawed the fez worn by men and any clothing that could be regarded as tarikat-wear, to coin a phrase. It also prohibited clerics from wearing their temple attire in public. Gradually the attitude

---

837. *Ibid.*, p. 102.
838. *Ibid.*, p. 103.
839. Soyak, *op. cit.*, p. 78.
840. Zeynep Kezer, *Building Modern Turkey*, 214.

shifted back to women's clothing and especially the headgear.

The veil had remained an important issue of contention for both the secularists and the Islamists. Its significance as a battleground for these two forces cannot be underestimated. As Şebnem Cansun from İstanbul Sabahattin Zaim University summarised:

> The headscarf question is one of the most debated issues in Turkey, because "head covering receives increasing legitimacy" and is related to the place of religion in Turkish society. The republican elite want to restrict this religious practice to the private sphere perceiving its presence in the public sphere as a symbol of political Islam and "the visible expression of (…) the (re)Islamization of Turkish society". Liberals argue that it is not fair to limit religious preferences to the private sphere. The logic of their defense is that freedom of dress is part of one's fundamental rights.[841]

The arguments put forward by liberals were also used by the Islamists pushing for veiling of women, as a matter of freedom of choice. Presenting the issue as women's choice ignores the effect of the patriarchal culture in which pressure is born upon women to behave and dress in a certain way. At the same time, it is important not to exaggerate the impact of patriarchalism and disregard individual women's preference to use a headscarf.

Olivier Roy argued that the headscarf can be regarded as a religious marker or not at all, as its function is not fixed to one field. As "religious marker" it becomes very potent:

> The religious marker: this is the sign, the action, the name, the heading that endorses the sacredness of an object, area or person: halal, kosher, blessings, rites, unction. This marker is moveable: a sacred song can be consumed in a profane manner, an ordinary dish can be blessed, a McDonald's can be halal, a headscarf can either be religious or a fashion statement.[842]

The headscarf can also combine these attributes. What Roy describes as "religious marker" can also be taken as a marker of tradition. Yael Navaro-Yashin describes the veil "as the most important good brought to the marketplace by Muslim businessmen in Turkey". Navaro-Yashin notes that veil merchants marketed the product as a symbol of the past, i.e. Ottoman

---

841. Şebnem Cansun, 'The Headscarf question in Turkey: The Examples of the AKP and CHP', The *Journal of Academic Social Science* Studies, Vol. 6, No. 8, October 2013, p. 125.
842. Olivier Roy, *Holy Ignorance*, Oxford, 2013, p. 30.

past, which the Republic altered.[843] Here the Republican period is treated as a rupture in the long tradition of veiling women. Thus, even as a commodity the headscarf can evidently accommodate a deeper meaning and context, including as a carrier of tradition.

In general, in Turkey this item of clothing was seen as "religious marker" by both the Kemalist and the Islamist camps, both associating the headscarf with Islam. The early Republican efforts to disassociate the veil from the Turkic culture and Islam failed to persuade and the headscarf continued to be seen as a mark of Islamic tradition by both the Islamists and the secularists.

In terms of party politics the issue has been seen as mainly a matter of contestation between Millî Görüş parties - later the AKP - and the CHP. It is often forgotten that the mainly pro-Kurdish HDP (or its previous iterations) is also secularist and in fact much more liberal on many social issues than the CHP. For instance, in the 2018 parliament the CHP elected 14 women MPs, while the HDP had 19, even though the latter had fewer members over all in the parliament. Also the first openly gay parliamentary candidate ran for office through the HDP in 2015.

The CHP continues to be the party of the Kemalist secularists, including Alevis, while Kurdish accommodates non-Kemalist leftist Turks and Kurds, minorities, as well as Kurdish nationalists. They tended not to be mentioned in any debates in the headscarf debate, primarily because the party focuses on other issues, considered to be more vital for their cause/s. Thus the debate historically from the secularist perspective was dominated by the CHP, or for a period when the CHP was closed down in the 1980s, by its off-shoots SODEP and DSP.[844] The far right MHP played a peripheral and ambiguous role in this debate.

Some incidents related to women wearing the headscarf were recorded in the 1960s and 1970s,[845] though the matter largely remained dormant until the coup of 1980. After the coup the issue flared up, when some universities, for instance Selçuk University, imposed a ban on headscarves on campus.[846] In 1981, a government Dress Code Regulation effectively con-

843. Yael Navaro-Yashin, "The Market for Identities: Secularism, Islamism, Commodities" in Deniz Kandiyoti & Ayse Saktanber, *Fragments of Culture*, London, New York, p. 225.
844. *Sosyal Demokrat Partisi* (Social Democratic Party) and *Demokratik Sol Partisi* (Democratic Left Party)
845.Respectively.
Fatma Benli, *1964-2011 Türkiye'de ve Dünyada Başörtüsü Yasağı Kronolojisi*, İstanbul, 2011, p. 11.
846. *Kamu Kurum ve Kuruluşlarında Çalışan Personelin Kılık Kıyafetine Dair Yönetmelik*

stituted a headscarf ban on students and teachers in schools. Although the regulation did not mention "headscarf", it did state that girls' hair should be 'uncovered' (açık and örtülmeyecek).

In 1982, Turkey moved to ban headscarves worn in all universities, both public and private, as well as in government offices, through another dress code regulation.[847] Toprak and Uslu noted that while a ban was contemplated on the headscarf in universities, a committee including the Prime Minister, Özal, convinced Kenan Evren that the headscarf should be used in universities in a uniform and orderly manner, rather than in different shapes, forms and colours. The group also succeeded in getting the approval of the army generals by persuading them that the headscarf was a part of fashion in countries such as Italy, as proved by the pictures in fashion magazines.[848] In other words, ANAP, seeing the military's resolve, looked for a way to diffuse the situation. Özal tried to rescue the matter from the military and control the nature of the impending ban on headscarves. To this end, Çınar contends that a new style of türban was invented by the Higher Education Council (Yüksek Öğrenim Kurumu, YÖK) to avoid the politically Islamic connotations, ironically turning it into an Islamist symbol:[849]

> The turban [türban] was described in a way that could be differentiated from the traditional headscarf which did not cover all of the hair in the front and in the back, and the ear lobes . . . YÖK issued a decree in which the turban was stipulated as a modern clothing item, and students were allowed to wear it in universities.[850]

Just as the fez, which was introduced as an item marking modernisation, then became a symbol of reaction in the eyes of the Kemalists, the turban also followed a similar path. Introduced as an item of supposed modernisation, it was taken up by practising Muslims and then, in Kemalist eyes, it became a symbol of backwardness. As Arnal and McCutcheon pointed out, any object can become sacred;[851] the process is arbitrary and subject to transformation. In this case the actual fez was not regarded as

(Regulation regarding the Dress Code of Staff working in Public Service Agencies), Benli, p. 12.

847. Vojdik, op. cit., p. 661.

848. Metin Toprak and Nasuh Uslu, The Headscarf Controversy in Turkey, MPRA Paper No. 16052, 22. November 2008, p. 47.

849. Çınar cited in Hilal Ozcetin, 'Breaking the Silence': The Religious Muslim Women's Movement in Turkey, Journal of International Women's Studies, Volume 11, 2009, p. 111.

850. Ozcetin, op. cit., p. 110.

851. Arnal and McCutcheon, op. cit., p.21.

sacred in a way that Prophet Muhammad's relics are regarded, but as a symbol.

In his talks Kenan Evren emphasised that the turban, which was worn in a uniform style, was more modern and simple and only the turban could be used by university students to cover their heads. President of YÖK Doğramacı stated that students procured notes from shops for university lecturers and authorities, certifying that this type of headscarf was a turban.

In this bizarre situation the state, universities and politicians invested considerable energy into defining and manipulating definitions of headscarf to satisfy both the secularists and the Islamists alike. Individual universities imposed bans on students wearing it, with no uniform approach, but the military refrained from forcing legislation against it until the soft-coup of 1997. In that year, as well as removing Erbakan from power, the generals also banned any type of headscarf in universities. The military intervened again 10 years later to prevent the candidate for the presidency, Gül, from being elected to the largely - at the time - ceremonial role, *inter alia*, on the ground of his wife wearing a headscarf, making the issue central to the debate about secularism.

Ali Çarkoğlu and Binnaz Toprak, who conducted research on the headscarf issue in 2007, noted that the issue was not one that preoccupied the Turkish people. Most people were concerned with unemployment, cost of living, terrorism/national security/southeastern Turkey/the Kurdish issue, education and economic instability/crisis. Only 3.7% of the respondents pointed out the "headscarf/turban" as an important issue. In contrast,

> [b]oth 'secular' and 'Islamist' sectors have deemed the 'turban' issue as one of the most serious problems Turkey has ever encountered. The secular sector has asserted that the turban is not a type of traditional covering but a political symbol; that this issue was carried into the country's agenda by Islamist parties; that the covering of women reflects the longing of political Islam for a Shari'ah state; and that all of these developments have resulted in an increase in the number of women wearing a turban. Conversely, the Islamist sector claims that covering is related to one's religious belief and/or identity; that it is not used as a political symbol; that banning covered students from obtaining higher education is a breach of human rights; and that finding a solution to this issue is one of the most significant problems of Turkey.[852]

Thus, according to Çarkoğlu and Toprak, the significance of the issue

---

852. Ali Çarkoğlu and Binnaz Toprak, *Religion, Society and Politics in a Changing Turkey*, trans. Çigdem Aksoy Fromm, İstanbul, 2007, p. 26.

has been exaggerated for different reasons by both camps. They also noted that, between 1999 and 2007, the number of women who wore a "headcover / headscarf / *Yemeni*" increased in rural areas, and decreased in cities. The number of women who wore turbans or *çarşaf* decreased both in rural and urban regions. Aggregated, the use of all types of headscarf was at 61.36%.[853]

In another survey conducted on behalf of the *Milliyet* newspaper in 2007, the percentage of women wearing headscarf was identified as 69.4, without making a distinction on the type of headscarf. It also identified that the percentage of women wearing a turban increased from 3.5% to 16%. The newspaper attributed the increase in the past five years to the AKP's rule.[854] Over 5,000 people were surveyed but Aynur İlyasoğlu, from Marmara University, doubted the results. İlyasoğlu contended that this was a media manipulation rather than a scientific study and that the *Milliyet* newspaper was using women as a pretext to push for "laicism" (*laiklik*).[855]

The headscarf, as many scholars pointed out, has little to do with the desire of many women to wear this particular item. It became a symbol representing political Islam and a battleground between the Islamists and the Kemalist establishment. With the AKP coming to power, the debate intensified. Particularly after the government's proposal to amend the Constitution to abolish the ban on the headscarf at the universities in 2008, the conflict on the headscarf and secularism in Turkey came to a head.[856]

There is much literature on the headscarf and while this issue effects women, historically it has largely been debated by men. This has changed in contemporary times with female scholars, Turkish and Western conducting research, both but also intellectuals emerging in Turkey who define themselves as feminist Muslims. According to the Islamist writer, Yıldız Ramazanoğlu, the start of the questioning of modernization and tradition by the 1978 generation paved the way for the emergence of Islamist women, who see the scarf (i.e. turban) as a symbol of being a servant of God (Allah) rather than as being subordinate to male-dominated systems.[857]

In the same vein, Valorie K. Vojdik noted that

[w]hile many Western and indeed some Kemalist feminist scholars portray Turkish women as passive victims compelled to cover by a patriarchal religion or political movement, Gole and other Turkish schol-

853. *Ibid.*, p. 27.
854. 'Türbanlı sayısı 4 yılda 4 kat arttı', [The number of headscarf wearing women increased fourfold], *Gazetevatan*, 4 December 2007.
855.*Biamag Cumartesi*, 29 September 2018.
856. Ozcetin, *op. cit.*, p. 111.
857. Sözen, *op. cit.*, p. 271.

ars have focused on the diversity of veiling practices among women based on their membership in different social and economic classes, their regional origin, and their religious commitments. Their research suggests that a certain group of women - young, urban, and typically the daughters of migrants from rural areas - deliberately embraced the choice to cover, challenging the secular elites as a political matter.[858]

As Meyda Yeğenoğlu notes "[a]lthough the headscarf appears to be an item of individual preference, it has also become translated into the lexicon of a major political battle".[859] Certainly, the headscarf represented a significant part of the political struggle for many, including Erdoğan. In 2007, the AKP start taking measures to lift the ban, starting from universities; it appointed a new president for the YÖK, who circulated a directive to rectors to announce the end of the ban. The democratisation package in 2013 was the second step in which the Dress Code Regulation was modified to allow headscarfed women in the public service. In the same year female MPs were also allowed to wear the headscarf in the parliament.[860]

To achieve his aim Erdoğan used a well-tested method of disseminating falsehoods to dominate the narrative. For instance, he propagated in his public speeches a story about a young, veiled mother who was set upon by about eighty topless hooligans who also urinated on her, supposedly as retribution for her religious and political views overtly expressed through her choice of clothes.[861] Eventually, in 2017, as Erdoğan's power increased and the Kemalist light was flickering, the AKP succeeded in lifting any remaining restrictions on the headscarf, thus settling the issue for the foreseeable future.

As it dominates public life, the AKP managed to reverse the process of secularisation. A study conducted on behalf of Diyanet in 2014 reported that 71.6% of women "covered their heads in public".[862] Even 34.9% of women who declared themselves not be pious at all covered their heads in public,[863] which may be taken as a sign of pressure on women to conform, though this is not to deny that for some women it is a matter of personal

858. Valorie K. Vojdik, 'Politics of the Headscarf in Turkey: Masculinities, Feminism, and the Construction of Collective Identities', *Harvard Journal of Law & Gender*, Vol. 33, No. 1, 2010, 664.
859. Meyda Yeğenoğlu, "Clash of secularity and religiosity" in Jack Barbalet *et al* (Eds.) *Religion and the State*, London, New York, Delhi, 2011, p. 233.
860. 'Türkiye'de başörtüsü yasağı: Nasıl başladı, nasıl çözüldü?'[The headscarf ban in Turkey: how it started, how was it resolved], *Al Jazeera Turk*, 30 December 2013.
861. Zeynep Kezer, *Building Modern Turkey*, Pittsburgh, 2015, p. 288 footnote 7.
862. Diyanet İşleri Başkanlığı, *Türkiye'de Dinî Hayat Araştırması*, Ankara 2014, p. 103.
863. *Ibid.*, p. 102.

choice. The visibility of more headscarved women in the public space and state institutions marks the deep transformation that Turkey is experiencing, through which the religious discourse dominates and what traditionally has been described as secular society retreats.

A Pew Research Centre/Michigan University survey conducted in 2013 across seven Muslim majority countries asked respondents what style of headdress was appropriate for women in public. No respondent in Turkey selected the *burqa*, which is not a Turkish tradition, and only 2% selected *niqab (peçe)*. In total 68% selected a type of head covering as appropriate, while 32% chose no cover at all. These numbers are commensurate with Diyanet statistics, with the qualification that the Pew study surveyed attitudes across genders and not actual usage.[864]

The ubiquitous Diyanet weighed in on the issue and surprisingly this time its president Bardakoğlu refused to recommend to Muslim women to wear the headscarf, emphasizing that it is not a formal requirement of the religion. This was surprising because after 28 February 1997 (known as "28 February process"), Diyanet came to disagree with the Kemalist establishment on the headscarf issue. During that period, extreme pressure was applied to Diyanet, but it did not compromise on the headscarf and issued a fetva about the headscarf being the command of Allah.[865]

Yet, with the AKP in government, Bardakoğlu took a different stand from the AKP. This was a rare divergence with the AKP. Predictably, Bardakoğlu was replaced shortly thereafter by Mehmet Görmez, who has been clearly more pliant toward the AKP leadership's wishes."[866] This study has established that Diyanet has been a successful state tool in the control of Sunni Islam, particularly Hanefi jurisprudence in Turkey. With the advent of neo-Kemalism, and later of the AKP, Diyanet's role was to be enhanced even further.

The AKP, Diyanet and the Alevis

The reach of the agency was extended in the 1980s. Whereas, up to that point, Diyanet's access had been limited to Turkey's Muslims, after

---

864. Rich Morin, Q&A with author of U. Mich. study on preferred dress for women in Muslim countries, https://www.pewresearch.org/fact-tank/2014/01/14/qa-with-author-of-u-mich-study-on-preferred-dress-for-women-in-muslim-countries/, January 14, 2014.

865. İhsan Yılmaz, *op. cit.*, p. 74.

866. Svante Cornell, 'The Rise of Diyanet: the Politicization of Turkey's Directorate of Religious Affairs', *The Turkey Analyst*, 9 October, 2015.

the coup it expanded its activities into countries with Turkish immigrant populations. Since the early 1980's Diyanet has sent imams to Europe to counterbalance the influence of other Islamic communities, such as the Salafists/Wahhabists supported by Saudi Arabia, on Turkish Muslims, and to maintain their loyalty to the Turkish state.[867] Furthermore, in this period Diyanet has become a defender of the Turkish-Islam synthesis, which combined nationalism with Islam.[868] The state used Islam as a way to mobilise and nationalise its own citizens. In the meantime, it wanted to control the Turkey-originated "religious market" in those countries that involved *Millî Görüş*, *Süleymancılar* and others.

By the time the AKP came to power, it found a formidable organisation with a network of imams across the world. The AKP enlarged the scope even further and increased staff numbers of the agency to manage and mobilise the diaspora. There are strong, well-founded, suspicions that Turkey is using its imams in Europe as a spy network, especially keen on reporting on Gülen sympathizers, since the dissolution of their alliance. Many European countries have taken action to expel or not provide visas to Diyanet imams due to their activities beyond pastoral care.[869] In 2017, German authorities investigated 19 imams alleged to have acted on the orders of Turkish diplomatic posts to spy on Gülen.[870]

The Diyanet juggernaut widened its scope to include "issuing *halal* certificates for food products, managing a television station, issuing *fetvas* on demand, a hotline service that provides Islamic guidance on everyday matters, which "encourages callers to harmonize their daily lives with the principles of Islam".[871] To manage the span of the increased activities, the agency grew in size exponentially under the AKP; over 117,000 staff are employed by Diyanet in Turkey and in 40 countries. In 2002, when the AKP came to power the total number of Diyanet staff was 74,433.[872]

Reportedly, its 2017 budget was higher than the money allocated to 11

867. Istar Gozaydin and Ahmet Erdi Ozturk, 'The Management of Religion in Turkey', London, November 2014.

868. İhsan Yılmaz. *op. cit.*, p. 72.

869. For instance, 'Austria to shut down mosques, expel foreign-funded imams', Reuters, 8 June 2018, https://www.reuters.com/article/us-austria-politics-islam/austria-to-shut-down-mosques-expel-foreign-funded-imams-idUSKCN1J40X1, [Accessed on 15 July 2019].

870. Chase Winter, 'German intelligence mulls putting largest Turkish-Islamic group under surveillance', *Deutsche Welle*, 21 September 2018.

871. Svante Cornell, 'The Rise of Diyanet: the Politicization of Turkey's Directorate of Religious Affairs', *The Turkey Analyst*, 9 October, 2015.

872. Samuel W. Watters, 'Developments in AKP Policy Toward Religion and Homogeneity', *German Law Journal*, Vol. 19, No. 02, 2018, p. 364.

other Turkish ministries put together.[873] This disproportional budget allocation demonstrates the importance assigned to Islamic matters in the AKP government. In 2008 Diyanet oversaw 86,760 mosques in Turkey and more than 2,000 abroad:

> The Diyanet also provides religious education for imams and supports the construction and maintenance of mosques, not just for Turkish Muslims but for all Muslims in countries where it operates. Provided, of course, that they are Sunni. The agency, which follows mainstream Hanafi Sunni Islam, is indifferent to the diversity of Islam in Turkey. Though it has been criticised by other Islamic sects, the Diyanet continues to impose Sunni views on the diaspora and Muslim communities abroad.[874]

Banu Şenay who researched Diyanet activities in Australia, noted their anti-Kurdish political mobilization, involving inter alia, collection of money from Australian Turks for Turkish soldiers killed by the "Kurdish guerillas", as well as conducting rituals such as holding funeral prayers in absentia for the Turkish soldiers killed. These activities served to maintain a discourse of martyrdom and seek to instill in citizens certain affective moods and capacities which is what nationalism is all about.[875]

Diyanet was also involved in the government's propaganda when the Turkish army entered into Syria, in 2018, through the Operations Euphrates Shield and Olive Branch. It played a significant role in these operations. Diyanet boasted that it prepared 30 videos in Arabic, distributed Qur'ans to Kurds and used its entire means to ensure the success of the operations.[876] In its report, Diyanet listed building and renovation of mosques and other places where Quranic courses were held, education, identification and appointment of religious personnel, visits to the area and publications, as the activities carried out in Syria. Its crude language and thinly veiled references to the Kurds as "terrorists with blood on their hands"[877] leaves little doubt that, under the AKP, there is coalescence of Diyanet Islam and militant version of nationalism.

---

873. '2017 bütçesi Erdoğan ve Diyanet'e yaradı', [The 1917 budget benefited Erdoğan and Diyanet], *Birgün*, 26 December 2016.
874. 'Does Turkey use 'spying imams' to assert its powers abroad?', *The Conversation*, 4 April 2017, theconversation.com/does-turkey-use-spying-imams-to-assert-its-powers-abroad-75643 [Accessed on 28 August 2018].
875. Banu Şenay, *Beyond Turkey's Borders*, London, New York, 2012, p. 142.
876. *Diyanet Haber*, 'Diyanet, Fırat Kalkanı ve Zeytin Dalı Harekatı'nda Etkin Rol Oynadı', 13 September 2018 [Accessed on 3 June 2019].
877. Diyanet İşleri Başkanlığı, *Suriye Fırat Kalkanı ve Zeytin Dalı Faaliyet Raporu*, Ankara, 2018, p. 16.

In its many years of operations, Diyanet's scope kept expanding to embrace many activities that would normally be beyond its originally envisaged role. At some stage the government considered granting jurisdiction over some Syriac Orthodox (Assyrian) churches to Diyanet, but this plan was abandoned.[878] While Diyanet's remarkable network asserts the authority of Sunni Islam, it continues to ignore the Alevis and their worship places, cemevleri.

Any student of Turkish politics and history would eventually discover the tension between Sunni and Alevi communities. Sometimes this tension culminated in violent pogroms against Alevis (Maraş, 1978; Çorum, 1980; Sivas, 1993; Gaziosmanpaşa, 1995). Given the general Sunni hostility to their belief systems - real or imagined - Alevis have long supported the Republic and its secular/laic policies, hoping that the state could counter the fundamentalist edges of Sunni Islam.[879]

As has been discussed in Chapter 4.0, Kemal's system brought some relief to the Alevis, who were in favour of secularism, but he still treated them as outsiders, since he did not allow for Alevis to be part of Diyanet. Also, Tunceli was attacked in 1937-38 by the Republican Army and atrocities were committed against Kurds, including Kızılbaş Kurds and Zaza, who live in the province called Dersim by Kurds. These atrocities were formally recognised by Erdoğan's government.[880] Consequently, the views of the Kurdish Alevis are not the same as those of Turkish Alevis. The enduring admiration of Mustafa Kemal as Atatürk among the Turkish Alevis is evident. However, their vision of him is idealised and lacks historicity.

The picture below, taken in 2016, depicts an Alevi prayer session in a cemevi. On the walls the pictures of Ali (as imagined and idealised by Alevis), Mustafa Kemal Atatürk and Hacı Bektaş, are prominently displayed. It is also noteworthy that the Alevis seem to be conducting namaz (salah). Though this may not necessarily take the same form as the Sunni namaz, nevertheless, it contradicts the premise that the Alevis do not pray this way at all.[881] On the other hand, even if some Alevis conduct namaz similarly to Sunnis, unlike the Sunnis, men and women pray together and some women are not wearing headscarves or hijab. One should be careful

878. Sevgi Adak, 'Turkish secularism revisited', *The Middle East in London*, Vol. 13, No. 5, October-November 2017, p. 11.

879. Shankland, 'Maps and the Alevis', p. 1-2.

880. Racho Donef, "*Sayfo* and Denialism" in David Gaunt *et al*, (eds), *Let Them Not Return*, New York, Oxford, 2017, p. 216.

881. Cited in İsmail Beşikçi, Alevilerde Kafa Karışıklığı, 23 December 2012, http://gomanweb.org/GOMANWEB2/koseli_demokrasi/ismail_besikci.htm [Accessed on 2 February 2018].

not to generalise from this picture, but similar pictures depicting similar scenes from different cemevi can be found on the Internet. Atatürk is always prominently displayed.

Image 6: An Alevi prayer session in a cemevi[882]

The only safe conclusion that can be ascertained from this picture is the prominent role of Ali and Hacı Bektaş in some cemevis and the endurance of Mustafa Kemal as Atatürk in Alevi consciousness and their emotional connection to his image to the point of deification. Shankland notes:

> The loyalty that the Alevis feel towards Atatürk can hardly be exaggerated. They regard him as a number of things: the founder of the nation and protector from religious persecution, the man who rescued them from foreign rule, who revealed scientific *enlightenment* and modernity to a sometimes reluctant population, and enabled Anatolian, Turkish civilisation to emerge once more after centuries of Arab and Koranic-dominated interpretations of history.[883]

As Diyanet, which interprets and shapes Sunni Islam, does not recognise *cemevis*, it is left to cultural institutions such as ABF, CEM Vakfı, Pîr Sultan Abdal Kültür Derneği and Ehl-i Beyt Vakfı to carry out the work that Diyanet does not.

The agency consistently continues to be a Hanefi Sunni Islam, management project, also excluding the Shafis (both Turks and mainly Kurds) and the Nusayris (Alawites). As Şenay noted "the mosques and other religious

---

882. http://www.pirha.net/alevilik-islam-midir-13279.html [Accessed on 2 February 2018].
883. Shankland, *The Alevis in Turkey*, p. 21.

services provided by Diyanet solely benefited Sunni Turks".[884] The AKP continued the tradition of excluding the Alevis, not being able to bring itself to recognise Alevism, Alevi worship places and its *dedelik* institution. The AKP looked for ways to placate Alevis without introducing real change in the way Diyanet operates *vis-a-vis* Alevis. In one such effort a *cami-cemevi* (mosque-cemhouse) building project, a compound including both a mosque and a cemevi, was announced; this was clearly an experiment. It was announced as part of "democratization package" in 2013 but was immediately denounced by the Alevi organisations as an assimilation project:

> We believe that the aim is to reduce Alevism to Sunni tarikats, as conceived in Sharia Islam, the cemevis to Sunni lodges, as conceived in Sharia Islam, and the dedes to the rank of public servants.[885]

The project was eventually shelved, being labelled as a Gülenist initiative,[886] though it was envisaged when the AKP and Gülen were allies and it was announced as a government project. Faruk Çelik, the Minister of Work and Social Security, presided over the laying of the foundation ceremony, yet the AKP disassociated itself from the project[887] and accused Gülen's network of trying to infiltrate the Alevi community.[888]

While the integration of cemevleri through mosques was abandoned, it appears that the AKP has invented a new concept, that of worship centres, labelling them *irfan evleri* or *irfan merkezleri* (wisdom houses, centres). There was an attempt to label these new constructs as "traditional". It was a newly invented tradition to be sure, but it appears that with this new concept of *irfan evleri*, the AKP is trying to create a parallel tradition with *cemevleri* and then equate the two systems and recognise them officially - or at least this is the fear of some Alevi organisations. It is hard to establish what exactly these "irfan evleri" were supposed to be. The former Prime Minister Davutoğlu described them as "traditional", but as Alevi journalist

884. Şenay, *op. cit.*, p. 135.
885. 'Alevi örgütlerinden ortak açıklama: Cami-cemevi projesi kabul edilemez', *sol haberler*, 10 September 2013, http://haber.sol.org.tr/devlet-ve-siyaset/alevi-orgut-lerinden-ortak-aciklama-cami-cemevi-projesi-kabul-edilemez-haberi-79400 [Accessed on 12 September 2018].
886. 'Cami-cemevi projesi tarih oldu', *Cumhuriyet*, 7 March 2018.
887. 'Faruk Çelik, 'Cami-cemevi birbirlerinin rakibi değil kardeşidir', İhlas *Haber Ajansı*, 8 September 2013, http://www.iha.com.tr/haber-faruk-celik-cami-cemevi-birbirleri-nin-rakibi-degil-kardesidir-297894/ [Accessed on 12 September 2018].
888. https://www.sabah.com.tr/gundem/2018/03/08/fetonun-cami-cemevi-proje-si-davasinda-flas-ifadeler [Accessed on 12 September 2018].

Rıza Aydın notes there are no records of such places in the Ottoman Empire or Anatolia.[889]

Alevis were concerned that some sort of equivalence with cemevleri will be established in order to blur the lines between *irfan evleri* and *cemevleri* to assimilate the Alevis. Aydın describes this new initiative as Machiavellian and believes that the state will recruit collaborating *dedes* and turn them into a vehicle for the AKP. *Cumhuriyet* journalist Tayfun Atay contends that these centres seem to be tarikat lodges under a different name.[890] The prohibition of the Law of Religious Orders is still in operation, although the tarikats are operating freely. This new concept may have also been a ploy to re-establish tarikat lodges as centres of wisdom and incorporate them into Diyanet. At the same time, the *cemevleri* may also be incorporated to Diyanet as part of a two-pronged approach. Thus, Diyanet can expand even further and become not only centre of management of Sunni Hanefi Islam, but also of Sufism and Alevism. If this occurs, Diyanet may become a pluralist organisation, controlling and managing not only Hanefi Sunni but also Alevi institutions and Sufism. By bringing to the fold traditions outside the state sanctioned space, the expanse and control of Diyanet can expand even further; to the monopolization of the Sunni Islam it can transform to compete in the Alevism market against Alevi agencies.

As Abdülkadir Yeler notes, amongst Alevis there can be observed a number of tendencies in relation the role of Diyanet. One group of Alevi agencies and *wakfs* (Pîr Sultan Abdal Dernekleri, Hacı Bektaş Veli Dernekleri, Semah Kültür Vakfı ve Şah Kulu Sultan Dergahı) prefers that Diyanet is abolished all together. Cem Vakfı and other groups working with it hold the view that Diyanet should be restructured in a way that would allow for Alevi representation. There is also the view that there should be an Alevi faith presidency, to be autonomous but under financial tutelage of the state and the budget to be allocated according to Sunni/Alevi population ratio.[891]

The irony is that the Alevis have been lobbying for a long time to become officially recognised, but official recognition is likely to come at the

889. Rıza Aydın, AKP Hükümetinin İrfan Evleri, [AKP's Wisdom Houses], https://yalansz.wordpress.com/2016/01/28/akp-hukumetinin-irfan-evleri/, [Accessed on 7 September 2018].

890. Tayfun Atay, '"İrfan Merkezleri" ne iş?!", [What sort of business are these Wisdom Centres?!], *Cumhuriyet*, 27 January 2016.

891. Abdülkadir Yeler, "Aleviliğin Kurumsallaşma Süreci", *Geçmişten Günümüze Alevilik I. Uluslararası Sempozyumu*, Vol. 2, Bingöl, 2014, p. 180.

expense of the independence of Alevism. If Alevism is to be recognised by Diyanet as either distinct religious category or as an Islamic sect, the *dedelik* institution will need to be incorporated into the system, and *dedes* would be subject to official scrutiny and instructions on sermons through circulars. It must be pointed out, however, that the AKP has been in power since 2002 and incorporating the Alevis to Diyanet has not been a priority. Although there are Alevi MPs elected to parliament through the AKP, the party remains Sunni dominated and primarily representing the Sunni point of view. Alevis, at least the Turkish Alevis, are seen as CHP voters and secularists and therefore the AKP so far has not seen a great political benefit in investing in this community. Diyanet offices continue to be the mouthpiece of Sunnism, using any means at its disposal to spread its message.

One significant function of Diyanet is the control of the *hutbes* (sermon) delivered after the Friday noon prayers in all mosques. Traditionally these *hutbes* were delivered by local imams, with no effective control from Diyanet. The Kemalist military was responsible for the change in the practice of delivery of sermons. Thijl Sunier *et al* note that after the soft-coup of 1997, given the concerns at the time regarding the spread of political Islam and Islamism, the military requested that the sermons

> be controlled by the central administration of Diyanet. These hutbes were being prepared by a hutbe commission, functioning within the Higher Council of Religious Affairs. Afterwards, the hutbes were sent to the imams through the Diyanet Gazetesi (a monthly journal). However, this very centralised procedure of controlling the content of Friday sermons was relaxed in 2006, when the task of preparing the hutbes was transferred to hutbe commissions within regional mufti offices.[892]

Thus, after the AKP came to power, efforts were made to decentralise the function of the *hutbes*. Nevertheless, as Umut Korkut and Hande Eslen-Ziya note, there is a process in place through which Diyanet continues to control the outcome and leaves local "imams only with relatively small powers" in relation "to *hutbe* language".[893] In effect, despite decentralisation of sermons, Diyanet maintains significant editorial control.

Some of the sermons delivered under Diyanet's tutelage indicate the direction the AKP is taking in transforming Turkey. Early in 2018 a sermon

892. Thijl Sunier *et al*, 'Diyanet: The Turkish Directorate for Religious Affairs in a changing environment', Utrecht University, Amsterdam, January 2011, p. 52.
893. Umut Korkut and Hande Eslen-Ziya, *Politics and Gender Identity in Turkey*, New York, 2018, p. 39.

was delivered in a mosque in Hoorn, under the jurisdiction of Diyanet, which the Dutch government claimed it was a "jihad" sermon in support of Turkey's operation in Afrin. The Dutch newspaper *De Telegraaf* asserted that the same sermon was delivered in mosques in Turkey.[894] Indeed, the text of the sermon can be found on the Diyanet site, which states that "the engagement of a believer in armed struggle for belief, existence, homeland, patience, and freedom, is the highest level of jihad".[895]

The sermon went on to state that *Jihad* is not about arming oneself to kill innocent people for the sake of it and condemns those who committed crimes in the names of Islam. Nevertheless, the jihad in the sermon does not seem to be about the 'Greater Jihad', which is a spiritual journey, but the 'Lesser Jihad', which is an armed struggle to expand the House of Islam (Dar al-Islam) . The fact that such a sermon is delivered in mosques outside the country suggests that Diyanet is very brazen in pushing an Islamist (as opposed to Islamic) agenda.

As Çağaptay notes:

> [d]uring the first two days of the operation [in Afrin], which began on Jan. 20, the government's Directorate of Religious Affairs ordered all of Turkey's nearly 90,000 mosques to broadcast the 'Al-Fath' verse from the Koran – 'the prayer of conquest' - through the loudspeakers on their minarets. Mainstreaming jihad, which sanctions violence against those who 'offend Islam', is a crucial step in draping the sheath of sharia over a society.[896]

Cornell argues that from 2010 onwards after Ali Bardakoğlu's tenure Diyanet became a political instrument. Yet, it can also be argued that Diyanet was established to become a political instrument in the first place, as it was envisaged as an agency of control. However, Diyanet was never involved in party political matters and stayed out of favoring particular parties. This has changed under the AKP. For instance, "before the 2015 parliamentary election, a number of imams urged their flock not to vote for "certain parties" but for "Muslims", which in effect meant the AKP or Saadet Partisi.[897] In its new role Diyanet participated in public discourse preoccupying itself with matters related to both the categories of "religion"

894. Yusuf Özkan, 'Hollanda'dan Diyanet'in 'Cihat hutbesi'ne inceleme', *BBC Turkish*, 17 February 2018.
895. https://www.diyanet.gov.tr/tr-TR/Kurumsal/Detay/11302/cuma-hutbesi-cihd-al-lah-yolunda-canla-ve-malla-mucadele [Accessed on 29 August 2018].
896. Soner Cagaptay, 'In long-secular Turkey, sharia is gradually taking over', *Washington Post*, 16 February 2018,
897. Svante Cornell, 'The Rise of Diyanet: the Politicization of Turkey's Directorate of Religious Affairs', *The Turkey Analyst*, 9 October, 2015, n.p.

and "politics", mimicking Erdoğan's and the AKP's practice of same. Mehmet Görmez the former President of Diyanet,

> publicly called the Pope 'immoral' over his stance on the Armenian genocide. Görmez also weighed in on the Hagia Sophia mosque, which was turned into a museum in the early years of the Republic – stating that 'Hagia Sophia is not a church, not a museum, but the sanctuary of Mehmet the Conqueror and all Muslims'. He has also called for the 'liberation of the Al-Aqsa Mosque' and said that there is 'no difference between Israel and ISIS' in terms of the religious doctrines that led to the creation of their respective state entities.[898]

These statements demonstrate that Diyanet is not only a political tool, but it has also become specifically an AKP-tool:

> The head of Diyanet had previously reported to a minister, but Erdogan has raised the status of the directorate's new leader, Ali Erbas, to that of a de facto vice president. Erbas now regularly attends major public events at Erdogan's side, blessing everything from Istanbul's third bridge across the Bosporus to Turkey's campaign against Kurdish militia in Syria.[899]

In the process, AKP ideology replaced Kemalist ideology and hegemony and enabled Diyanet to free itself from secular scrutiny. Unquestionably, in the AKP Diyanet found a like-minded ally. While under the Kemalists the agency showed some restraint, under the AKP's tendencies to express itself through Islamic discourse and also Erdoğan's tendency to see himself as a leader of the Islamic world,[900] allowed Diyanet to become a powerful agency and even express views which normally would have been the purview of Department of Foreign Affairs.

Diyanet is increasingly delving into every facet of civil life, interpreting rules for daily life through Islamic law. In one of the cases, it caused significant controversy related to the age of consent for marriage. Although, via a Friday sermon Diyanet stated that "Forcing children into marriage can have no religious or scientific legitimacy", this was a response to allegations that it in fact supported "the marriage of girls as young as nine." This allegation was based on a statement on Diyanet's website contained in the *Dictionary of Religious Terms*, which stated that "girls go through puberty at the age of nine and boys at the age of 12", adding that "those who have

---

898. *Ibid.*, n.p.
899. Soner Cagaptay, 'In long-secular Turkey, sharia is gradually taking over', *Washington Post*, 16 February 2018.
900. Donef, 'Does Turkey want to become member of the European Union', *Platform for Peace and Justice*, 8 July 2018.

gone through puberty may marry."[901]

Diyanet removed this item, which angered the secularists, from their website. Perhaps the AKP was trying to measure the strength of any opposition if it were to make changes to the civil law. The AKP tried in 2004 to make adultery a crime, which was only decriminalised in 1996, but abandoned it on the strength of criticism from both within and outside the country. At that point, Erdoğan was not as powerful and was still concerned about the military's stance. Recently, he re-iterated that Turkey should criminalise adultery.[902]

Criminalisation of adultery does not necessarily mean introduction of Sharia Law; after all, Erdoğan is not suggesting stoning transgressors, nor does there seem to be great public demand for it; but it means Erdoğan leaves no stone unturned in his quest to transform Turkish society to make it congruent with his ideology. In this quest the headscarf issue was handled but there are other aspects of public and private life which the AKP also tries/tried to influence, gender segregation being such an issue.

The AKP and Gender Segregation

While the headscarf received enormous attention both in Turkey and abroad, it is gender segregation, articulated in Turkish as *Haremlik/Selamlık*, that may accelerate the de-secularisation process. Although, at this stage, it is still very limited in its application, this type of segregation is practised mainly in mosques and in some households. A 2014 study conducted on behalf of Diyanet found that 27.4% of the population preferred to always revert to *Haremlik/Selamlık* when there were visitors in the household; 32.1% reported they preferred gender segregation in households sometimes only, thus bringing the aggregated total to 59.5%, if this study is to be relied upon.[903] The practice started becoming the norm in the AKP rallies, including in major cities such as Istanbul.[904]

Other than AKP rallies, there have been other occasions such as in

901. 'No religious or scientific legitimacy in forcing children into marriage: Turkey's top religious body', *Hurriyet Daily News*, 5 January 2018, http://www.hurriyetdailynews.com/no-religious-or-scientific-legitimacy-in-forcing-children-into-marriage-turkeys-top-religious-body-125303 [Accessed on 30 January 2018].

902. Jason Rezalan, 'Turkey's Erdogan wants to make adultery a crime', *The Washington Post*, 28 February 2018.

903. Diyanet İşleri Başkanlığı, *Türkiye'de Dinî Hayat Araştırması*, p. 201.

904. 'Erdoğan'ın karşısında Harem-Selamlık ayırdılar', *oda tv*, 15 April 2018, https://odatv.com/erdoganin-karsisinda-harem-selamlik-ayirdilar--15041816.html [Accessed on 13 August 2018].

municipality meetings (for instance in Ipsala, Edirne)[905] and also in schools where the practice has been observed. A school canteen in Kartal, Istanbul, seemed to have separate counters for boys and girls, according to the *Birgün Daily*.[906] Another picture about the same school in a different publication, also claiming gender separation, showed a picture of children not segregated at the canteen, despite there being two separate counters. In their defence the Kartal Cevizli Middle School principal stated that there is no physical barrier between the counters and that it was established because of requests from parents of female students.[907]

Iren Özgür notes that

> [m]ost Imam Hatip Schools in Turkey practice some form of gender segregation. It is commonly understood among religiously conservative Turks that the Qu'ran and sünnet [Sunnah] emphasizes the need to minimize instances that may lead to improper and unlawful interaction between men and women.[908]

Özgür's comments suggest that gender segregation, as practised in Turkey, is a religious requirement, rather than, say, at least in the school environment, an affirmative action. The Gülen Movement also practised some form of gender segregation, but argued that it was for pedagogical reasons rather than a religious tenet. Caroline Tee argues that gender segregation is a requirement of a conservative conception of Islam.[909] However, it is wrong to see gender segregation always as a religious practice emanating from Islam. There are Women's Health Centres (*Kadın Sağlığı Merkezleri*) to cater for specific health issues affecting women, as well as historic Christian Missionary Schools, such as Notre Dame de Sion for female students only. Furthermore, the Greek community also operated five gender segregated high schools, until the dwindling numbers forced them to merge them into two cross-gender high schools.

Nevertheless, Erdoğan seems to intend expanding gender segregation in many fields, including universities. He suggests that there would be advantages in segregated education system and cites Japan as a model. "Erdogan and the leadership of the AKP, his Islamic-conservative governing

905. Belediyede haremlik selamlık toplantı tepki çekti, *A24*, 3 April 2018, https://www.a24.com.tr/belediyede-haremlik-selamlik-toplanti-tepki-cekti-haberi-40122435h.html?h=52 [Accessed on 13 August 2018].

906. Gender segregation at a public school in Turkey', *Birgun Daily*, 16 September 2017.

907. https://www.artigercek.com/haberler/devlet-okulunda-harem-selamlik-kantin [Accessed on 13 August 2018].

908. Iren Özgür, *Islamic Schools in Modern Turkey*, Cambridge, 2012, p. 90.

909. Caroline Tee, *The Gülen Movement in Turkey*, London and New York, 2016.

party, argue that gender segregation in educational institutions would improve female students' performance". Political scientist Fatmagül Berktay disagrees with this proposition and comments that "there's no logic to this reasoning. If you look at the grades of girls at elementary school, you'll see that their school performance is better than ever - although they're being taught alongside boys."[910]

Though there is some increasing evidence of a push for gender segregation in various spheres (e.g. transport), these examples are sporadic and isolated. On the other hand, gender segregation in AKP rallies is systematic. Whether or not this practice will apply through government policy to other aspects of *la vie quotidienne* remains to be seen. Clearly, this is not a widespread practice in public, or at least there is no sufficient data at this stage to trace any pattern and draw reliable conclusions. Yet, as the AKP's and Erdoğan's discourse has increasingly become Islamic, the argument can be made that gender segregation will remain on their agenda.

The issues highlighted above were included in order to trace any elements of de-secularisation and Islamisation, but there are a myriad of other aspects of public and private life, not all of which can be reviewed comprehensively to assess the extent of de-secularisation and Islamisation. Nevertheless, all the indications are that from 1980s Turkey went through a transformation, re-transformation to be exact, to reverse some of the early Republican reforms. This re-transformation intensified under Erdoğan II and III is significant enough to mark it as the Fourth Republic.

The Fourth Republic: Sharia law, de-secularisation or plain old authoritarianism?

There is a cornucopia of literature on the Islamisation of Turkey and secularism. More recent studies comment on Erdoğan and his increasingly authoritarian style. Many secularists fear that Erdoğan is introducing Sharia Law by stealth. Certainly, the AKP have introduced many anti-secular measures since 2002, which contributes to the Islamisation of public life; for instance, all new schools are now required to build prayer rooms.[911] Whether the building of prayer rooms amounts to de-secularisation depends on one's definition of secular. If secular is about stamping

---

910. Burcu Karakas, 'Turkey's Erdogan pushes for gender segregation in universities', 8 July 2019, https://www.dw.com/en/turkeys-erdogan-pushes-for-gender-segregation-in-universities/a-49508416 [Accessed on 2 February 2020].
911. Soner Cagaptay, 'In long-secular Turkey, sharia is gradually taking over', *op. cit.*

out religion, then building prayer rooms could be viewed as markers of de-secularisation, but not if they are about facilitation of religious choice. After all, in Australia universities and many government buildings have prayer rooms to facilitate religious practice. However, Turkish schools did not have this facility before the AKP came to power and they are seeing, by both the Kemalists and the leftist secularists, as part of the expansion of the realm of Islam in the public domain. In other words, irrespective whether they are markers of de-secularisation in the scholar's mind they are seen as markers of de-secularisation by those concerned that the secular public space gives way to visible Islam.

Although attendance in prayer rooms is not compulsory, as Çağaptay notes

> Ministry of Education has been pressuring citizens to conform to conservative Islamic practices in public schools. . . . Recently, for instance, a local education official in Istanbul demanded that teachers bring pupils to attend morning prayers at local mosques.[912]

It should also be noted that prayer rooms are gender segregated, replicating the traditional norms of mosque prayer practices. It may well be argued that many of the incremental changes pointed out above in themselves are not sufficient to eliminate the secular, but taken as a whole a pattern emerges of a de-secularisation process.

Furthermore, one of the reversals of laic/secular measures found in the civil code is the ability to perform marriages only via municipalities. Gradually this ability was given to *muhtars*, muftis and eventually to imams. Thus, a fundamental laic practice of affirming marriages through an administrative process has been weakened.

This right which has been given to Sunni imams has not been extended to Christian, Jewish clergy, or the Alevi dedelik institution, for that matter. The right to officiate at weddings was granted to Christian and Jewish minorities through the Lausanne Agreement. The government pressured the minorities to give up this right in 1925. The Jewish community was first to waive this right, then the Armenians and eventually, the Greeks "after much resistance also, complied because Greek community leaders and journalists were arrested and were not released without a 'resignation' to the fact".[913]

While it was an illegal act to force community and church leaders to sign away rights enshrined into an international agreement, Turkey had

---

912. *Loc. cit.*
913. Baskın Oran, Turkey should take a lesson from Greece, *Ahval*, 15 December 2017.

signed barely a year earlier, the restriction to register marriages applied to all religious groups. It can be said that the Kemalists who were not concerned about minority rights, on this occasion, were motivated by laicism/secularism rather than nationalism. After more than 90 years, when granting the right to imams to register marriages, the AKP ignored minorities. Thus the AKP, while against many aspects of Kemalism, still practises policies of discrimination established in the early Republic years and pursued throughout its history.

The Kemalists put a system in place to modernise/westernise Turkey, and ostensibly de-Islamise the public space. The system they put in place they labelled as laic, but it pertained to both laicism and secularism. As far as laicism is concerned, that is to say the removal of the state in involvement of religious affairs, it failed. However, a clarification has to be made: laicism *failed* insofar as a stated objective of the Republic. Kemal and his cohort defined laicism in part as separation of religion and politics. While this was the discourse, in practice the policy was to subdue and control Islam, which is not laicism. The competing concepts were lumped together under the guise of laicism so that the state had a unified narrative. Both the stated and concealed aims were treated as if there were a cohesive single objective.

The cognate concept, i.e. secularism, that is to say the absence of Islam in the public sphere, to the extent that is possible in a country where traditional norms are significant, is multi-layered and significantly more complex than laicism. Secularism constituted the dominant narrative until the AKP's gradual transformation of the Turkish society. This period marking AKP rule has been labelled "post-secular" by many scholars. Others are not convinced this is the case. Edip Asaf Bekaroğlu from Bilkent University argues that up to 2002 it was assertive or authoritarian secularism that was dominant and that since the AKP rose to power "inclusive (or conservative/"passive") secularism in line with the Anglo-American model" has been implemented. In any case, Bekaroğlu argues the strict separation of state and religion is only a myth even in Western democracies.[914]

Certainly, Turkey has shifted to a different kind of secularity. The reality is that the public domain is slowly being overtaken by Islamic symbolism. Perhaps "restricted secularity" is a more apt description. This "post-secular" world, as depicted by many scholars, is not "non-secular"; it combines elements of both. We can also call it "practical secularity" to divorce it from the utopia of the ideology of secularism.

---

914. Edip Asaf Bekaroğlu, 'Post-Secular Turkey?: Justice and Development Party Governments and Updating the Secular Contract', İnsan ve Toplum, Vol. 5, No. 9, 2015, p. 118.

This new kind of secularity, by whatever name, is less secular measured by the interference of religious discourse and practices in the public domain (segregation in AKP rallies, expansion of Diyanet's role, removal of evolution from the secondary education curriculum *etc.*):

> the AKP's majoritarian understanding of the national will and its capacity to control the state apparatus have pushed the party to be more daring in transforming the daily life in its own mirror image, in line with religious conservatism through such policies as the restrictive regulation on the sale and consumption of alcoholic beverages, anti-abortion regulations, promotion of childbirth and the injection of courses of religion into the educational system.[915]

A key measure, which is bound to speed up the process of de-secularisation of the mind is the removal of evolution from the high school curriculum in 2017, while adding the teaching of the concept of *jihad*.[916] While the space of the secular is evidently being reduced, it is not likely that it will be eradicated all together.

Hegemony and Islamism

There is another aspect of contemporary politics in play, which requires some attention: increasing authoritarian rule by a system fashioned to be one-person rule. Turam notes that Sami Zubaida convincingly argued that

> [f]ew Islamists are principled democrats. They are not unlike the great majority of political activists of all persuasions" in the Middle East region. The case of Turkey wonderfully illustrates that when the oppositional pious forces come to power in an authoritatively secular state, they seem to inherit and follow some of the undemocratic patterns of the secularist elite.[917]

Turam's point, citing Zubaida, is that the Islamists in Turkey adopted and adapted to these patterns to suit their political agenda. Turam goes on to say that the "Islamism-secularism controversy disguises the challenge

915. İsmet Akça, "Hegemonic Projects in Post-1980 Turkey and the Changing Forms of Authoritarianism" in İsmet Akça et al. (eds.) Turkey Reframed, London, 2014, p. 45.
916. Harriet Agerholm, Turkey drops theory of evolution from national curriculum as children go back to school': Erdogan's regime trying 'to plague the brains of our little children,' says opposition MP, The Independent, 19 September 2017.
917. Turam, op. cit., p. 4.

of democratization".[918] Similarly, many scholars argued that secularism and Islamism dominated the agenda in Turkey, while the issue to focus on should have been the lack of democracy. Kemalism looked to the West to identify a model to secularise and modernise and ostensibly build a society fashioned after the West. Yet,

> [a]s Şerif Mardin pointed out 'the republic took over educational institutions and cultural practices (museums, painting and sculpture, secularism) from the West without realizing that these were just the tip of an iceberg of meanings, perceptions, and ontological positions'. It did not inherit concepts such as 'human rights, democracy, diversity, civil society'. That is to say, the Republican modernizers adopted the symbols ('such as hat instead of fez, Latin alphabet, Gregorian calendar, European numerals, and metric system') instead of concepts . . .[919]

Thus, Kemal ignored the most important components of the western model and went on to impose a system of hegemony. Since June 2018, new, highly centralised governance is in operation. This new governance arrangement, which required constitutional amendments, was voted in during a referendum in 2017, and the majority of the population gave consent to the changes. This is consistent with Gramsci's idea of hegemony, i.e., the acquiescence of the subjects to the hegemonic system. "Hegemony implies a willing agreement by people to be governed by principles, rules, and laws they believe operate in their best interests, even though in actual practice they may not."[920]

At the centre of this new centralised governance lies the Office of the Presidency, with powers that have not been seen since the days of Kemal. The system is tailored to match Erdoğan's ambitions:

> the new system empowers the president to appoint Cabinet ministers and vice presidents, while remaining at the helm of his party. In one of his most notable moves, Erdoğan merged the Treasury and the Finance Ministry, handing the post to his son-in-law Berat Albayrak. Major economic and financial institutions, including the central bank and public banks, were all attached to Albayrak's ministry . . . 12 of the 15 Constitutional Court judges are appointed by the president, with the remaining three left to parliament. All members of the Court of Appeals, three-fourths of the Council of State members and four members of the 13-member Judges and Prosecutors Board are directly selected by the president, in addition to the justice minister and the

---

918. *Ibid.*, p. 9.
919. Sena Karasipahi, *Muslims in Modern Turkey*, London & New York, 2009, p. 30.
920. James Lull, *Media, Communication and Culture*, New York, 1995, p. 34.

minister's undersecretary who sit on the board. The president also appoints the members of the Higher Education Board, which controls universities.[921]

To this asphyxiating domination of all power bases, the control of media can be added. Although Turkey is Islamising gradually, Erdoğan's aim is not to turn Turkey into a Sharia Law country, such as Iran and Saudi Arabia, where the criminal code is very harsh and unforgiving. Erdoğan is an authoritarian in the mould of Vladimir Putin and Mustafa Kemal; leaders who do not tolerate dissent and any opposition to their way of thinking:

> The AKP's authoritarian populism does not accept any social, political and even individual opposition or critic [sic] as legitimate. It rather blames them as being not part of the national will, being an attack to the national will, if not terrorist acts.[922]

Islamism is a convenient ideological and legitimising tool for Erdoğan to motivate the masses. Mustafa Kemal (Atatürk) used mainly nationalism to establish one-person rule, whereas Erdoğan uses mainly Islamism to castigate and will the dissenters into submission:

> In recent years, the government led by Recep Tayyip Erdoğan has been limiting individual freedoms, as well as sanctioning individuals who "insult Islam" or neglect Islamic practices. Since November 2017, the national police . . . has been monitoring online commentary on religion and suppressing freedom of expression when they find such commentary 'offensive to Islam'. . . . For example, world-renowned Turkish pianist Fazil Say has been prosecuted twice because of "provocative commentary" on Islam. His crime: making gentle fun of the Muslim call for prayer on Twitter.[923]

Kemalism pursued those who allegedly insulted Turkishness; Erdoğanism pursues also those that allegedly insult Islam. Nevertheless, a notable scholar and commentator, Baskın Oran, does not believe that the government ideology is Islamism any longer; he notes a shift in Erdogan's attitude:

> As Erdoğan has come to dominate Turkey's politics, his ego and hubris have overtaken the cause of Islamism. Therefore, in the context of Turkey today, instead of Islamism, it is more appropriate to talk about

921. Mustafa Sonmez, Turkey's economy struggles with the new political reality, *Al-monitor*, 6 August 2018.

922. Akça, *op. cit.*, p. 45.

923. Soner Cagaptay, 'In long-secular Turkey, sharia is gradually taking over', *Washington Post*, 16 February 2018.

Erdoğanism, which is little more than leadership cult, rather than a coherent ideology. Whether this is what Erdoğan always aimed for, or if he changed his mind along the way, moving from being a genuine Islamist to a conservative reformist and finally to an autocrat, is an issue of endless polemic in Turkey.[924]

Effectively, Oran argues that Turkey has entered a post-Islamist stage. Many would disagree with his statement, given that Erdoğan and the AKP have evidently and successfully managed to transform Turkish society into being less secular and more Islamic oriented. In the process he adopted an Islamic discourse to justify his actions. Even when Turkey faced an economic embargo from the United States, Erdoğan's response was typical: "if they have dollars, we have Allah". Invoking the supreme deity and drawing references from Islam to attack his adversaries is a standard tactic of Erdoğan's.

Oran is not alone in his hypothesis, Journalist and writer Mustafa Akyol makes an argument similar to Oran's. He also contends that Erdoğan's:

'New Turkey', if there is any, is not 'Islamism', as some Westerners seem to think. It is rather Erdoganism. The latter is a blend of Islamism, Turkish nationalism, anti-elite populism, moralism, nepotism and opportunism. It may even include, as we can now see, a rightly redefined dose of Ataturkism.[925]

It is far too early to call Turkey post-Islamist, the complex processes Turkey is undergoing include de-secularisation, Islamisation, hegemonisation and the spread of Turco-Islamic nationalism. Unquestionably, Erdoğan utilises nationalism as well as Kemalism/Atatürkism when it suits.

AKP Nationalism

Under the AKP's rule, Kemalism as an all-consuming ideology of the state and guidance for citizens' conduct has been diminished. Many of the Kemalist dominated institutions (army, courts) are now dominated by Islamist-leaning appointees. I describe this period as meta-Kemalism. As discussed in Chapter 2.4, there are different iterations of Kemalism. For instance, while cultural Kemalism (an ideology and movement protect-

924. Baskın Oran interviewed by Karabekir Akkoyunlu, "Kemalism and the Republican People's Party (CHP)" in Özyürek E., Özpınar G., Altındiş E. (eds), *Authoritarianism and Resistance in Turkey*, Cham, 2019, p. 15.

925. Mustafa Akyol, Why Erdogan now embraces Ataturk, https://demokratiki-kypros.org/2017/11/21/why-erdogan-now-embraces-ataturk/, [Accessed on 24 September 2018]

ing laicism, rationalism and fundamentalist cultural reformism) is on the wane, the nationalist aspect of Kemalism has been taken up by Erdoğan and the AKP. While the language of Erdoğan tends to be peppered with religious overtones, frequent references to Allah and the Crusades, political Kemalism has not disappeared completely, but its content has been reduced in government narrative. Political Kemalism can be described as authoritarian, with the desire to shape and control most aspects of both public and private life. Erdoğan replaced Kemal in this hegemonic system, by emulating Kemal.

Atatürkism, defined as a personality cult in this study, is now generally confined to CHP circles and is mainly expressed through the Cumhuriyet newspaper and a few remaining non-AKP controlled, mostly on-line media outlets such as Oda TV and the Birgun Daily and social media. But Erdoğan is not averse to using whatever means available to enable him to retain and extend power. In 2017, he even seemed to have discovered Atatürkism and attended the annual ceremony commemorating Atatürk's death. Akyol suggests there is a degree of cynicism in Erdoğan's embrace of Atatürk and the coverage of "the pro-Erdogan media ... which now constitutes the overwhelming majority of the Turkish media",

> have shown only half-hearted interest in Nov. 10 commemorations before came out this time with huge tributes to Ataturk, marking an unmistakable difference in tone. Members of Erdogan's ruling Justice and Development Party (AKP) expressed an unexpected admiration for Ataturk in their public messages. The local branches of the AKP organized free bus trips to Anitkabir and announced them with posters in urban centers. And most importantly, Erdogan himself, who had conspicuously skipped some previous Nov. 10 commemorations, led the ceremonies at Anitkabir.[926]

Akyol believes the only reason for this approach was the impending, at the time, presidential elections. Erdoğan needed to win more than 50 per cent of the vote to be elected in the first round to the office of presidency. Every vote counted. He also needed to court the far-right vote. Thus, Erdoğan adopted "pseudo-Kemalism" in the hope of expanding his electoral base.

In his speeches, Erdoğan often emphasizes martyrdom and jihad, while using symbolism established by Kemal. Narratives related to the Turkish soldier, glorified as *Mehmetçik* (Little Mehmet).[927] Sometimes this is very crude, for instance:

---

926. Mustafa Akyol, Why Erdogan now embraces Ataturk, *op. cit.*
927. Similar to the British nickname for common soldiers "Tommy".

Turkish President Recep Tayyip Erdogan has come under criticism for telling a small girl dressed in a military uniform that she would be honored if she were "martyred" for Turkey. Erdogan spotted 6-year-old Amine Tiras weeping and saluting while the president [was] delivering a speech at his ruling party's congress in the city of Kahramanmaras on Saturday, and had her brought on stage. After trying to comfort the girl by kissing her on both cheeks, Erdogan told the crowd: "She has the Turkish flag in her pocket. If she becomes a martyr, God willing, this flag will be draped on her."[928]

The AKP came to power presenting itself as moderate Muslim party or "Muslim Democrats". Its first steps were tentative, being mindful of the military. As it consolidated its vote base, the AKP started abandoning its "moderate" or "democrat" component. In 2005, through Abdullah Gül, expressed his sentiment that

> [w]hile attaching importance to religion as a social value, we do not think it right to conduct politics through religion, to attempt to transform government ideologically by using religion, or to resort to organisational activities based on religious symbols. To make religion an instrument of politics and to adopt exclusive approaches to politics in the name of religion harms not only political pluralism but also religion itself.[929]

Conclusion

Erdoğan did not abide by these principles expressed by Gül. After all, in the context of Turkish politics not even Mustafa Kemal avoided making Islam an instrument of politics, as demonstrated in earlier chapters. Erdoğan followed the pattern in a more intense fashion, continuing to see Islam as an instrument of politics, blending Islamism with nationalism and causing Turkey to undergo a transformation. This transformation is not complete. States are not static organisms, we can only speculate as to what form will emerge as Erdoğan continues to rule in an authoritarian style. "[H]egemony is not a 'given' and permanent state of affairs, but it has to be actively won and secured; it can also be lost".[930] In the short term, Turkey remains a complex society in which the scope of secularity has been re-

---

928. https://www.timesofisrael.com/erdogan-under-fire-for-wishing-martyrdom-on-crying-6-year-old-girl/ [Accessed on 11 October 2018]
929. Recep Tayyip Erdoğan, "Conservative Democracy and the Globalisation of Freedom" in Yavuz, M. Hakan. (Ed.). *The Emergence of a New Turkey*, p. 336.
930. Stuart Hall, 1985, quoted in Lull, *op. cit.*, p. 35.

duced, but it has not disappeared and Islam plays a most significant role in shaping the polity and society. In this process, the boundaries between the categories of "religion" and "politics" are proving to be porous.

CHAPTER 9: EPILOGUE

Ertit, reviewing several qualitative and quantitative indicators, including the number of mosques in Turkey, argues that contrary to claims, Islamisation has not occurred. Ertit labels this as a failure of Erdoğan and the AKP: they intended to Islamise the country, but their efforts were fruitless. Ertit lists a number of criteria he assessed to support his argument:

> praying rates have decreased, extramarital sexual relationship has become prevalent, the number of mosques per person has decreased, the belief in virginity is a point of honour for fewer people, people's clothes have become more flatteringly formfitting and more attractive, including women's head-scarves; secular experts rather than religious officials are being sought for help concerning problems in daily life, homosexuality has become more socially acceptable[,] visible, traditional family structures has [sic] been shattered.[931]

Ertit states that the number of mosques was 57,060 in 1985 and rose to 87,381 in early 2017. This equated to 53% increase, while the population increase during the same period was 57%. Ertit arrived at the conclusion that the number of mosques per person has decreased slightly.[932] However, this is not a very significant decrease and it would be premature to draw the conclusion that the Islamisation project has failed, *inter alia*, based on the number of extant mosques.

Even more recent statistics suggest that the number of mosques in Turkey reached 90,000 in 2018. The number of mosques still deemed "insufficient" by the President of Diyanet Ali Erbaş, increased by 15 percent in 11 years and exceeded the annual population growth rate of 13.5 per thousand.[933] Mosque building stalled for a brief period, but evidently, the AKP intends to continue to increase the number to keep up with population growth, or exceed it, whether or not there is actual demand for it.

The building of the mosques is also an issue of town planning, availability of space, suitability of location. Eventually, within a short period of time, the number of mosques caught up and exceeded population growth. The excessive building of mosques reflects the ideology of the establishment. The different statistical methods used and comparison with different

---

931. Volkan Ertit. 'God is dying in Turkey as Well', *Open Theology*, Volume 4, No. 1, 2018, p. 192.
932. *Ibid.*, p. 195.
933. *Loc. cit.*

years will inevitably skew the results, but considering that in the first years of the CHP rule mosques were neglected (see Chapter 5.1), at the very least, we may be entitled to adduce that the AKP intends to keep building mosques, not only for consumption of religious services, but also as a tool to de-secularise minds. This mentality is articulated by Erbaş who asserted that

> [m]osques are not only places for prayer. They are places where children in the neighborhood receive religious education from an early age. Therefore, no neighborhood in any city should remain without a mosque".[934]

The rate of attendance at mosques has also been a study area by both Diyanet and outside researchers. Diyanet, which has a vested interest in exaggerating the numbers of pious citizens, claimed that, in 2014, 42.5% of the survey respondents always went to the mosque, 16.9% never went to the mosque and added that 92.5% of the population always prayed.[935] Yet a Pew Research Centre study in co-operation with Michigan University, which ran surveys in seven Muslim-majority countries around the same period, found that only 42% of respondents prayed often, 21% of respondents in Turkey did not go to the mosque at all and 38% went very rarely.[936] Ertit also argued that the praying rates declined, as well as the rate of mosque attendance, citing a number of studies including by the Open Study Society Foundation.[937]

In his 2014 study, Ertit suggested that secularisation did not mean to become irreligious or to lose faith[938], yet his more recent study used reduced mosque attendance as one of the indications that "God is dying in Turkey as well" - as he provocatively puts it. In this study it has already been suggested that lack of attendance or conversely increase in attendance of religious institutions are not sufficient markers of secularisation/de-secularisation. Casanova suggests the decline of religious beliefs and practices as one of the three components of the secularisation process, but people can practise outside the mosque or can attend a mosque out of peer pressure and not be a genuine believer.

---

934. Mustafa Mert Bildircin, Cami sayisindaki artis nufus artis hizini gecti, https://www.birgun.net/haber-detay/cami-sayisindaki-artis-nufus-artis-hizini-gecti-198305.html, 12 June 2019.
935. Diyanet İşleri Başkanlığı, *Türkiye'de dinî hayat araştırması*, Ankara, 2014.
936. 'The World's Muslims: Unity and Diversity: Chapter 2: Religious Commitment', https://www.pewforum.org/2012/08/09/the-worlds-muslims-unity-and-diversity-2-religious-commitment/, 9 August 2012.
937. Ertit. 'God is dying in Turkey as Well', p. 195.
938. Ertit, 'Birbirinin Yerine Kullanılan İki Farklı Kavram, p. 108.

These statistics are brought up here to demonstrate that from fundamentally different angles, Diyanet and Ertit use them to support divergent points of view. However, I am using a different definition of secularity, i.e. absence of Islam in public life, rather than about demographics, e.g. religious practice. Accordingly, praying is perfectly compatible with the secular, but the issue of mosque building (public activity) is more significant than the question of who is actually using them (private practice).

While the rate of attendance of mosques and praying may have declined, as various surveys suggests, there was a sharp increase in the number of *Umrah* performances, which can be taken as a sign of piety, but also of increase of wealth and consumer power.[939] There are other markers that can be used to assess the degree of secularisation/de-secularisation or Islamisation/de-Islamisation. For instance, the support for Sharia Law was at its highest in 1996, according to surveys cited in Chapter 6.1. The Pew study in 2013 found that in Turkey support for Sharia was only at 12%. Compared with 1996, there was little difference in support of harsh Islamic law in Turkey, though some were using religious law in family and property disputes.[940] These figures support Ertit's study of the AKP's failed Islamisation project, even if the number of mosques does not.

Mustafa Aydın from Kadir Has University conducted a study in 2017 to canvass community views on current issues. One key question asked in the survey was whether, in the view of the participants, Turkey was pious (*dindar*) or laic (secular); 51% of those that described themselves as pious thought that Turkey was laic, while 32.9% of the Republican/Kemalists category thought Turkey was laic. In the estimation of only 20% of those who described themselves as socialist, Turkey was laic. In other words, the stronger the secularist ideology the more pessimistic their outlook of the nature of Turkish society. Conversely, the higher proportion of the pious segment of the population thought that the state was secular.[941] The conclusion that can be derived from these responses is that the view of the nature of Turkish society is defined by the ideology and experience of the person. In other words, it is based on perception of the individual rather than any objectively defined criteria as Habermas postulated. It turns out, one per-

939. https://www.dogrulukpayi.com/bulten/turkiye-de-cami-sayisi-hizla-artiyor-an-cak-nufus-kadar-hizli; Umrah is the requirement to visit Mecca.

940. The World's Muslims: Religion, Politics and Society, https://www.pewforum.org/2013/04/30/the-worlds-muslims-religion-politics-society-overview/, 30 April 2013.

941. Mustafa Aydın et al, 'Türkiye Sosyal-Siyasal Eğilimler Araştırması', Center for Turkish Studies, Kadir Has Üniversitesi, 31 January 2018, p. 83.

son's laic/secular society is another person's pious society. This supports the argument that the secular and the non-secular co-habit.

Aydın's overall conclusion was that in Turkey the conservative, pious and nationalist base was growing. He calculated this mass as 60% of the population and identified the AKP and the MHP voter base as having similar *Weltanschauung*.[942] This is an artificial distinction and deficient, as Aydın does not include the "Cumhuriyetçi/Kemalist" (Republican/Kemalist) cohort in the conservative, nationalist category. If we include a proportion of "Cumhuriyetçi/Kemalist" excluding perhaps the majority of Alevis, noting that Alevis can also be "paranoid nationalists"[943] as the leader of the CHP Kılıçdaroğlu demonstrates,[944] there is even a large percentage of the population that converge into a nationalist/conservative category.

In assessing the 2018 election campaign for presidential elections, Reşat Kasaba noted that

> with the exception of the Kurdish party – the parties that are running for the parliament have competed with each other to showcase their nationalist and religious credentials. Most of them have formed alliances to boost each other's chances. But they have all rejected any form of cooperation with the pro-Kurdish People's Democracy Party, HDP.
>
> As for Islam, none of the candidates are promising a return to the strict secularism of the early 20th century. Even Muharrem Ince, the presidential candidate of the Republican People's Party that was founded by Ataturk, enthusiastically flaunts his religious beliefs in his rallies. In fact, his unexpected success in the polls is attributed, in part, to his embrace of Islam.[945]

Thus, the differences between parties and voters, the "secularists" and the "Islamists", were not so pronounced in the campaign. As noted earlier, Erdoğan I approached national issues from a wider perspective, but Erdoğan III changed his position, for instance, on the Cyprus issue and the

---

942. Salom, 'Prof. Mustafa Aydın: "Türkiye'de muhafazakâr, dindar ve milliyetçi taban büyüyor"', http://www.salom.com.tr/arsiv/haber-102227 prof_mustafa_aydin_turkiyede_muhafazakr_dindar_ve_milliyetci_taban_buyuyor.html [Accessed on 23 June 2019].

943. A term coined by Ghasan Hage, *Against Paranoid Nationalism*, Pluto Press Australia, Sydney, 2003.

944. See R Donef, 'War cries emanating from Turkey', *Platform for Peace and Justice*, 27 March 2018.

945. Resat Kasaba, Nationalism and piety dominate Turkey's election, 23 June 2013, http://theconversation.com/nationalism-and-piety-dominate-turkeys-election-98609 [Accessed on 15 July 2019]. İnce also joined worshippers in the first mass prayer outside the newly re-converted Mosque of Hagia Sophia on 24 July 2020.

Armenian massacres (Genocide) and came to reflect the standard Kemal-ist-Nationalist thinking.[946] As White argued "[b]oth secularists and "conscious" Muslims share a belief that to be Turkish means to be Muslims, and that Turkish Islam is better form of Islam.[947] At its inception the Republic constructed an identity in which both the nationalist and Islamic elements were constituent parts. The emphasis was on nationalism and considerable efforts were made to Turkify the Islamic element. Though the ideology of the state shifted with the Fourth Republic, nationalism remained an important element, augmented by Islamic imagery.

Dichotomies and Convergences

Chapter 2.1 established that the sacred and the profane are not necessarily two different spheres. The fluidity of these concepts has already been pointed out. Much like many social constructs, this dichotomy cannot account for all the permutations encountered in societies.

White interprets the sacred in the Turkish situation rather differently. White stretches the concept of the sacred to apply to phenomena beyond what traditionally was seen as a "religious" sphere. The reverence and dedication to Mustafa Kemal Atatürk, the often repeated utterances of his as though being imbued with a transcendental quality, led White to conclude that

> [r]eligion . . . can be secularised (individualised, privatized) while the secular sphere becomes sacralised as profane images are imbued with attributes of the sacred, and religious meaning and legitimacy can extend to new practices.[948]

White goes on to say that "Kemalist secularism has taken on aspects of the sacred".[949] In Kemalist discourse, Anatolian earth is sacred and busts and statutes of Atatürk mark sacred territory, just as the tombs of Sufi saints did. Moreover, his final resting place, *Anıtkabir*, is sacred in a country where tombs were closed as a sign of backwardness. Furthermore, the

946. 'Cumhurbaşkanı Erdoğan: Kıbrıs'ta aynı adımı atmaktan tereddüt etmeyiz', [President Erdoğan: We will not hesitate taking the same steps in Cyprus, *Haberler*, 20 July 2019, https://www.haberler.com/son-dakika-cumhurbaskani-erdogan-dogu-ak-deniz-12262846-haberi/ [Accessed on 23 July 2019]; and, https://ahvalnews.com/armenian-genocide/erdogan-accuses-west-hypocrisy-over-armenian-geno-cide-claims.
947. White, *op. cit.*, p. 19.
948. *Ibid.*, pp. 4-5.
949. *Ibid.*, p. 6.

treatment of his discourse by the Kemalists almost has the quality of "hierophany" as described by Eliade.[950] As Bozarslan puts it

> Sunni Islam was (and remains) at the heart the Republic of Turkey, and in complementarity with the Kemalism that is projected into the future as an ideology of substitution to religion. Certainly, as early as 1927, Mustafa Kemal's discourse was presented by the Turkish press as the sacred book of Muslims and Mustafa Kemal as the God-Prophet of the Turks. Similarly, the posterity of Kemalism was ensured by its transformation into a transcendental system, with its sacred symbols, starting with the mausoleum of Atatürk.[951]

Evidently, White is not the only researcher to point out these contradictions in the application of the sacred and the profane. For instance, Meyda Yeğenoğlu also points to the patterns that emerged in Turkey in the defence of secularism, which can be described as sacralisation:

> Secular sentiments, ceremonial and ritualistic practices and symbols are being deployed, such as attending to Atatürk's mausoleum, excessive use of the Turkish flag, and the use of the slogan 'Turkey will remain secular' on almost every occasion ... Such expressions can be understand [sic] as a process of sacralization and transcendentalization of the principles of secularism.[952]

Bozarslan also notes that the concept of public space as an ideological tool, in the sense of being the "domain of the state", is fairly recent, dating from the mid-1990s:

> Thus, women wearing headscarves [were] prohibited from entering schools and universities, and from participating in official receptions. The wives of many ministers, starting with that of the Prime Minister, [were] not admitted to receptions organised by the army or the presidency of the Republic.[953]

The Nakshibendi Sheikh Mahmut Hoca, as described on Chapter 6.0, was asking women to refrain from certain activities and virtually withdraw from the public space. The consequences of the Kemalist views, as outlined by Bozarslan, are similar, varying only in their scope. Essentially, both views were in favour of restricting public space for headscarved women, although from diametrically opposed ideologies.

---

950. Eliade, *op. cit.*, p. 11.
951. Hamit Bozarslan. 'La laïcité en Turquie'. *Matériaux pour l'histoire de notre temps*, n°78, 2005, p. 48.
952. Meyda Yeğenoğlu, 'The sacralisation of secularism in Turkey', *Radical Philosophy*, No. 145, September/October 2007, p. 4.
953. Bozarslan, *op. cit.*, p. 42.

White contends that confrontation in Turkey should not be secularism versus religion, as these terms are generally understood,

> but might better be described as struggles over blasphemy of the sacred, with secularists and the pious fighting over the designation of what is sacred, what is intrinsic to tradition and inviolable, and what lies outside the boundaries of identity sacralised by tradition.[954]

Özyürek approaches the problematic from a different perspective. She argues that the state ideology and imagery in Turkey became "privatized". This privatisation Özyürek sees as a result of the Kemalist elite (political, intellectual, military) but also citizens' support. To defend their ideology, they carried "symbols, practices and emotional affiliation with the state outside the conventional and public boundaries".[955] Today this privatisation of symbolism expresses itself through social media such as *Facebook*, with proliferation of Mustafa Kemal Atatürk related postings, thus making private sentiments public.

The Kemalist tendency to control Islam has been discussed in this study at numerous points; yet there is another aspect, which the Kemalists dismissed as superstition: religious healers. This form could not be controlled by the state and survived. The Diyanet study also claimed that 11.7% of respondents still practice lead casting to ward off evil spirits (kurşun dökmek).[956] Religious healers were not organised like tarikats or cemaats and so able to be shut down, as they practised individually in the margins and in the "private" sphere. Though this aspect of healing which Dole calls "Exilic Forms of Religious Life" and "Islam Without Movement"[957], was not the ideal form of Islam for the Kemalists, it did not pose any threat to the regime.

The Turkish state, whether Kemalist or post-Kemalist, is only threatened by religious movements when they display state-like characteristics; as long as they remain disorganised or informal, the state is content to let them flourish. Goldenberg's concept of religions as vestigial states, which currently existing states need to control, is applicable here. Even the AKP could not tolerate the Gülenist network, when its organisational capabilities reached a level where it could compete for power, i.e. act as future state. This distinction between "religion" that makes the state nervous and

---

954. White, *op. cit.*, p. 5.
955. Esra Özyürek, *Nostalgia for the Modern*, Durham and London, 2006, pp. 3-4.
956. Diyanet Diyanet İşleri Başkanlığı, *Türkiye'de dinî hayat araştırması*, p. xxxiii; the practice of melting lead and pouring it into cold water over the head of a sick person on order to break an evil spirit.
957. Dole, *op. cit.*, p. 13.

"religion" that does not, supports many of the contradictions I pointed out throughout the study in aid of my arguments about laicism and secularisation.

One of the most intriguing examples of "religious healing", if it can be called that at all, is the case of Zöhre Ana (Mother Zöhre) as recounted by Dole. Paradoxes and ironies abound in this account. Zöhre Ana was regarded as a "living saint" (*evliya*) and religious healer.[958] This is not entirely unusual in the Turkish context. What is unusual about Zöhre Ana, is that she was an Alevi and a secularist who draws inspiration from Atatürk for her healing practice through *nefes* ("breath"). Dole notes "she is regarded as the inheritor of Atatürk's spirit (*ruh*) and a person through whom Atatürk was once again able to speak".[959]

Furthermore, in Zöhre Ana's *nefesler* it is claimed that "Mustafa Kemal Atatürk, Turkey's arch-secularist and modernist founder, had similarly inherited Ali's *ruh* and was, consequently, an *evliya*.[960] Zöhre Ana's case is difficult to reconcile with the prevailing orthodoxies about the nature of the secular form. What is regarded as profane becomes the sacred in this account, in line with White's analysis.

Evidently, the dichotomies of public/private, sacred/profane, secular/religion do not sufficiently account for all socio-political conditions, at least not in the case of Turkey, subject to this study. There are grey areas, which allow scholars to explore the terrain, interpret and re-interpret the new realities. Nilüfer Göle notes that

> despite the political polarization between the religious and the secular, the wall of separation between the two becomes more and more porous; mutual borrowings and cross-fertilizations blur the rigid distinctions. Hence it is difficult to speak of clear-cut distinctions between the projects of the secular and the Islamic.[961]

Göle describes Erdoğan as a "passive secularist" and notes that he

> declared that he could view himself as 'a secular individual' in upholding the secular characteristic of the state, while eschewing the Kemalist secularism geared to colonize every aspect of everyday life.[962]

In this process, Erdoğan strengthened the commemoration of the Conquest of Constantinople (İstanbul'un Fethi) in 1453, instead of the found-

---

958. *Ibid.*, p. 1. Süheyla Höke (Zöhre Ana) passed away in 2020.
959. *Ibid.*, p. 2.
960. *Ibid.*, p. 104.
961. Nilüfer Göle, *Islam and Secularity*, Durham and London, 2015, p. 62.
962. *Ibid.*, p. 14.

ing of the Republic and introduced the Holy Birth Week to mark the birth of Prophet Mohammed. Another aspect of Goldenberg's theory which explains Erdoğan's strategy is about how actually-existing states draw on vestigial states (religions) to mystify and endorse their origins.

> Allusion to God as a distant yet grander sovereign force bestows gravitas on non-vestigial states as a justification for the violence in their power and serves as a mystified and glorified reference to former governing systems they portray themselves as having rightfully succeeded.[963]

Erdoğan has shown tendencies to colonise every aspect of life through an Islamic/traditional perspective (to replace the Kemalist perspective). In a way, Erdoğan's personal views on modesty and way of life are slowly being codified. For instance, Erdoğan does not consume alcohol, so restrictions were introduced on the sale of alcohol; his wife wears a headscarf, so he abolished any restrictions pertaining to the headscarf. As Lull notes the "ruling elites . . . perpetuate their power, wealth, and status [by popularizing] their own philosophy, culture and morality".[964] The Kemalists did it before, the new elite is emulating them.

---

963. Goldenberg, *op. cit.*, p. 284.
964. Lull, *op. cit.*, p. 33.

CHAPTER 10: CONCLUSION

Primarily, this study examined the deep entanglements between religion and politics in modern Turkey. Its analysis has shown that, just like anywhere else, the boundaries between religion and politics are porous and hard to draw. While many scholars theorised about this interpretation, this study, being particularly about the Turkish Republic, has verified this interpretation and found it to be also applicable to Turkey. Furthermore, my study has added Turkish data to the existing body of theory. In doing so, I have identified particular circumstances under which the currently-existing state feels the need to try to control potential rival systems, by designating them as "religion" and implementing mechanisms to either suppress or co-opt them.

I have used Goldenberg's concept of religions as vestigial or once-and-future states to demonstrate that it is the Turkish state's perception of such tendencies on the part of Muslim and non-Muslim traditions that brings out the Turkish state's impulse to either suppress or co-opt them. I have shown that broad impulse to be consistent across both the laicist and Islamist phases of Turkish nationalism.

The second problematic this study examined was laicism. However, as pointed out in the introductory chapters, a distinction has to be made between laicism and secularism. The Republicans used the term *laiklik* (laicism) to describe both separation of state and religion, religion and politics but also elimination of religion, ostensibly Islam, from the public space. I have argued that in order to evaluate the success of these stated aims, we needed to separate laicism, which is about the way the state mechanism operates, from secularism, which is an ideology to change processes in society to achieve a particular outcome: secularity.

That laicism did not work has been a consistent contention in this study. I pointed out the flaws and contradictions in the way laicism has been put to practice in Turkey by political actors. Neither the separation of religion and state, nor of religion and politics, was particularly successful in Turkey. However, I have also argued throughout this study that laicism was a flawed idea in the first place because separating religion and state is arguably theoretically impossible. Regardless, Kemalist Republican tried to impose laicism on a newly formed country after a tumultuous period of over a decade, on a conservative, rural based and largely illiterate population. As Asad noted,

Winnifred Sullivan has . . . argued that the legal discourse of a secular state operates in ways that are contrary to the general sense of 'secularism' as a political doctrine: complete separation from and strict neutrality toward all 'religions' turn out to be neither a good nor a bad thing but impossible.965

Laicism as a political arrangement requires a state institution to keep equal distance from all groups, irrespective of their religious affiliation. In Turkey, this principle was espoused but not put into practice. The state treated Sufi tarikats, cemaats and Alevis as marginal. The Kemalist Republicans tolerated a controlled version of Sunnism, which turned it into a *de facto* state religion, and through a variety of strategies dealt with other religious affiliations. The tarikats, and the cemaats for that matter, eventually returned to influence party politics. The Alevis remained marginal, still looking for salvation through their supporting of the CHP, the party responsible for positioning them there in the first place.

Alevism has been a difficult issue for the state to manage, since the state promoted Sunnism as the dominant form of worship. The initial willingness to incorporate the Alevis into the system dissipated when the state opted for a standardized, Turkified Sunni version of Islam, as the preferred form of worship. The Republic had too many contradictory aims: laicisation with control of Islam, de-Arabisation of Sunni Islam but with its imposition as one of the core elements of the constructed Turkish identity. State efforts concentrated on controlling Islam through its long arm, Diyanet. Control and separation were conflicting aims.

The Kemalist Republicans adopted a peculiar approach to Islam. On the one hand they ferociously attacked institutional aspects of Islam, including the tarikats and local cultural manifestations, which they deemed Islamic; on the other hand, they excluded non-Muslims from the public service and actively discriminated against them. The Kemalists had little tolerance for diversity whether ethnic, linguistic or religious. Their hegemonic approach required homogenisation. Non-Turks were not welcome in the Republic; Kurds were denied their identity altogether. The Turkish state was to be a Muslim Turkish state with Sunnism being the dominant form, despite the antagonism the elite Republicans showed towards the Muslim masses. Through physical extermination and other exclusionary measures, the numbers of non-Muslim minorities eroded. But the Muslim element, which formed part of the Turkish iden-

---

965. Asad, 'Thinking about the secular body, pain, and liberal politics', p. 660.

311

tity, also needed to be reformed, standardised, controlled by the state and confined to the private space.

The examination of secularism as an ideology and secularisation as a process proved to be a more taxing task than laicism. I speculated that a question to explore was whether a Muslim society (a country in which the majority of the people are Muslims) can be secular, when Islam at its inception was both a temporal as well as a spiritual system and the Ottoman Caliphate did not have clear-cut boundaries between the "political" and "religious" activities.

In other Muslim majority countries secularisation was forced, for instance in Afghanistan (both under Amânullâh Khân and the Soviet era), in Iran under Shah and in Egypt in intermittent periods. Countries such as Syria, Iraq and Algeria also experimented with secularity as a political project. In all these cases secularism was an ideology held by the elites and secularism was imposed from above, sometimes with brutal force. There was no popular demand for secularisation.[966] It was an imported ideology. Secularism in Turkey in the 1920s required political will as mass support was lacking. This political will for the imposition of secularity was abundant in the first years of the Republic.

As cited in Chapter 2.1, Norris and Inglehart argued that "[w]e simply do not have the massive longitudinal database that would be required to demonstrate beyond any doubt whether secularization is or is not taking place. In its absence, no single approach can be absolutely conclusive, and the results will always remain open to challenge."[967] They meant secularisation as it emerged and developed in the West. In the case of Turkey, we have nearly 100 years of experience and much data. Evaluating Turkey's experience, I conclude that secularity is not incongruent with Islam, or at least Turkish Islam. To be sure, with the changing of political actors in the post-2002 period, secularism/secularity has come under concerted attack by the new hegemonic powers. Nevertheless, while the secular space has evidently retreated, Islam has not annihilated it but forced it to co-habitation with evident tensions. This tension between the two modes was also present in the first years of the Republic when the state rhetoric strongly supported secularism as the dominant form in the public space.

While the boundaries between the categories of religion and politics are not solid, another divide also proved to be permeable. There has been

---

966. In Iran there seems to be a nucleus movement which is seeking to end theocracy and replace it with a secular system. This is a grass-roots movement, but it remains to be seen whether it will be successful.
967. Norris and Inglehart, *op. cit.*, p. 36.

a continuous convergence of nationalisms and Islamism. Until the emergence of the Millî Görüş Parties, the parties competed in the Kemalist/Nationalist market for votes. As the system opened up to competition from Islamic parties, it gradually incorporated Islamic discourse. This is not to deny that there are differences between the secularists and the Islamists. Secularism and Islamism are spectrums of ideology; there are pronounced differences between opposite extreme ends of the spectrum, nihilist secularists on one side and violent/militant Islamists on the other. A transformation took place to convert Turkey from an aspiring secular country to a hybrid form that necessitates a new kind of terminology to describe more accurately the current reality.

I canvassed a number of terms utilised in contemporary scholarship, while attempting to describe the change in the nature of secularity in Turkey, as conceived originally and as it developed in the Fourth Republic. In the Fourth Republic, the AKP ideology replaced aspects of Kemalist ideology, especially related to laicism/secularism, but not Kemalism's Turkic-nationalistic dimension.

I have also argued that although this ideology was primarily Islamist, it is not Sharia-driven. In any case, a strict Sharia law society in which the secular does not exist is very rare. The most extreme manifestations were imposed by such pseudo states as the Taliban's Afghanistan and the so-called Islamic Caliphate. If we discount these dystopias, there are many variations of the implementation of Sharia in the Islamic world.

In Turkey, no intention is noticeable to extend the influence of Islam in public life to that extent, nor is there popular support for such a course. However, the state is actively pursuing the de-secularisation of minds. Though there is no appetite for Sharia, there is appetite for the de-secularisation of minds. Secularisation of mind was undertaken by the Republicans, but the process is being reversed. A key element in this process is religious education, which gradually expanded, starting from the post-Kemal era, and kept expanding to a point of slowly undermining evolutionary theories and explaining the world through references to Islam.

The Fourth Republic is a place where Islam is de-privatised, to borrow Casanova's expression,[968] Kemalism subsumed into an Islamo-nationalist discourse and Kemal fetishised as Atatürk. Secularism is no longer the dominant ideology, but secularity is an accepted condition, with no signs from government to eliminate it but plenty of signs of reducing its extent. Secularity and Islam co-exist in public life.

---

968. Yeğenoğlu, *op. cit.*, p. 225: Following Casanova's thinking, it is possible to talk about a process of "deprivatization" of Islam in Turkey since the 1980.

In terms of ideology, we can call this "pragmatic secularism", as the term passive secularist suggests that the AKP and Erdoğan accept secularity as is. Yet, it has been argued that they actively worked to challenge secularist ideology and secularity, through a number of ways. Pragmatic secularism recognises the role of Islam and local traditions in Turkey. Consequently, Turkish society can be described as practical-secular.

Cox postulated that we no longer think in terms of the "supernatural" and certainly the early Republicans, as positivists, embarked upon their projects to impose this view. This process of secularisation of minds and any progress towards that goal was stalled and even reversed. To use Taylor's terminology, the immanent frame is not the dominant form. Through Diyanet's ever expanding role and the AKP's efforts as described in Chapter 6.3, the changing nature of school education and Erdoğan's theological language in the public square have marked the increasing domination of Islamic discourse over other discourses.

As argued, despite the erosion in the secular space, the domination of religious rules is not absolute, but the state actively supports Islamisation. This can also be called re-traditionalisation as nostalgia for the pre-Republican days colours and restricts the AKP's and Erdoğan's drive towards technological advancement, urbanisation and modernisation of the built environment.

The Kemalist historiography examined here has lost its influence and its monopoly of interpretation of Turkish Republic's history. There are now more narratives competing to explain the Republic's trajectory: Kemalist, non-Kemalist, various Islamists. As the taboos withered away and more research material became available, a more balanced narrative of the early Republic was able to be reconstructed. This study has contributed to this reconstruction.

Having exploited the religious sentiments of the population between 1920 and 1923, the Republicans embarked upon a laicisation/secularisation project. The laicisation/secularisation project required the construction of distinction between religion and politics, the secular and the non-secular. This ideological position was maintained despite all the contradictions and inadequacies observed. Gradually, Kemalists started the process of deconstructing their ideological construct to accommodate the opposing Islamist forces. Eventually, with the Islamists coming to power, the deconstruction process was complete. The Republic came to a full circle.

POSTSCRIPT

My research and analysis in this study based on a doctoral thesis mainly covered the period between the establishment of the First Parliament in 1920 and the November 2018 elections in Turkey. In the intervening four years President Erdoğan increased his Islamisation efforts and involvement in armed conflicts outside Turkey (Libya, Syria, Nagorno-Karabakh and Yemen), as well as escalating disputes with Greece and Cyprus.[969] Erdoğan also continued to imprison journalists, academics, opposition politicians and others simply labelled as Gülenists. The situation remains dynamic and ever-changing, as it is characteristic of Turkish politics. However much it changed in the political scene in the past four years, it has not altered my findings about the interplay between religion and politics and the state of play in the de-secularisation process.

Some examples I can cite supports this conclusion. Erdoğan continued to interpret matters through an Islamic prism. For instance, he attacked unnamed and alleged stockpilers when shortages of many food items and goods appeared in 2021 by condemning them under his own interpretation of Islamic law: "Stockpiling is also *haram* [forbidden] in our religion".[970] On cue, Diyanet issued a fetva (*fatwa*) by declaring stockpiling as *haram* (sin).[971]

Another contention in this study has been the convergence of Islamists and secularist/laicist Republicans on the expression of nationalism. Opposition parties, other than the pro-Kurdish HDP, have been largely supportive of Turkey's incursion to Iraq and Syria and continuous threats to other neighbours, especially Greece. Opposition leader Kılıçdaroğlu set his attacks on Erdoğan aside to express his support to his imperialist tendencies.[972] This convergence has been a theme discussed in the study and the current state of play

---

969. Racho Donef, The Fourth Republic, Erdoğan IV, Neo-Ottomanism and Conversion of the Hagia Sophia Museum into a Mosque, *Platform for Peace and Justice*, 14 July 2020; Racho Donef, Is a Greco-Turkish War Inevitable?, *Platform for Peace and Justice*, 20 September 2020.

970. https://www.diyanethaber.com.tr/bilim-teknoloji/diyanet-haber-mobil-uygulama-lari-yayinlandi-h8707.html, [Accessed on 21 May 2023].

971. Abdulhakim Günaydın, Diyanetten "stokçuluk" fetvası, , *Independent* Turkish, 10 December 2021.

972. Tom Ellis, 'Dealing with Turkey's aggressive behaviour', *Ahval*, 10 June 2022.

in politics does not contradict this contention of the study. It is therefore worthy of note that the current Islam-nationalist actions promoted by President Erdoğan has been partly supported by the Republicans.[973]

Furthermore, another nationalist party İYİ Parti which emerged from a split in the nationalist party *par excellence* (MHP) in 2017, in its fourth anniversary congress adapted the slogan "Ömerin yolundayız", "We are on Caliph Umar's path" (ʿUmar ibn al-Khaṭṭāb, the second Rashidun Caliph). This way İYİ parti cements its position in the religio-nationalism market to compete for votes with likeminded parties.[974]

A few examples from 2022 indicate that the state continued not to abide by the rules set by the early Republicans in relation to laicism. For instance, nine imams who read *hutbes* in Kurdish were arrested. Part of the indictment alleged also that Shafi practices and rituals were performed and the imams went outside the official hutbes and framework for preaching. During the investigation they were told that "they acted against the Islamic religion".[975] Evidently Diyanet equates Islam to Sunnism and denies the legitimacy of other jurisprudence schools or theological interpretations.

Lastly, as *Nordic Monitor* demonstrated in 2022, with documentary evidence, the army red-flagged non-Muslim Officers:

> In one document, Capt. S.K. was identified as being of Greek descent with a minus sign in red next to his name, implying that his advancement in the ranks was not approved because of his non-Turkish ethnic background.[976]

In addition to favouritism at the expense of ethnic groups the army also discriminated on other grounds emulating Erdoğan's ideology:

> In another document Lt. O.E. was red flagged and received a negative mark because his entire family was said to consume alcohol.[977]

Not satisfied with conversion to mosque of Ayasofya Museum, Erdoğan also announced a *medrese* (religious school) attached to Ayasofya,

973. Turkey's main opposition CHP serves to legitimize Erdoğan's aggressive foreign policy, *Nordic Monitor*, 22 September 2020.
974. İYİ Parti'nin yeni sloganı: Ömer'in Yolu, *Serbestiyet*, 24 October 2021.
975. Kürtçe hutbe okuyan 9 imama tutuklama kararı ifade öncesi verildi, http://mezopotamyaajansi35.com/tum-haberler/content/view/140833, [Accessed on 23 May 2022].
976. Abdullah Bozkurt, Turkish army red flagged non-Muslim officers, profiled those with minority backgrounds, *Nordic Monitor*, 28 April 2022.
977. *Loc. cit.*

eliminating thereby any secular symbolism that may have remained with the image of the former museum/church.[978]

Finally, a recent survey found that more than 70 percent of the population want to live in a "secular-democratic" country and only 18.5 percent in a "conservative-authoritarian" country.[979] The survey did not ask whether people desired to live under Sharia law, and even if we discount the large number of people who vote for anti-democratic parties and yet expressing desire to live in a democratic environment, it is evident that the secularist ideology has not disappeared in Turkey and continues to co-exist with Islamism, as pointed out in the main corpus of my study. This is a continuous conflict which the secularist are losing yet there is no *dénouement*. Islam and the secular co-habitate. It is unlikely that the elections of 2023 will change this situation but they may change the socio-political context of the last 20 years if the opposition parties win the elections, bring to an end the second hegemony of the Turkish Republic and usher yet another era in its history.

---

978. 'Erdoğan inaugurates Ayasofya madrassa, two years after conversion of Mosque', *Ahval*, 15 April 22.
979. Over 70 pct of Turks want to live in democratic, secular country – survey, *Ahval*, 3 June 2022.

BIBLIOGRAPHY

Ahmad, Feroz. *İttihatçılıktan Kemalizme*, [From Ittihadism to Kemalism], Kaynak Yayınları, İstanbul, 1985.

Akça İsmet, Bekmen Ahmet and Barış, Alp Özden, (eds.) *Turkey Reframed:*Constituting Neoliberal Hegemony, Pluto Press, London, 2014.

Akdağ, Ömer. *Çok Partili Dönemin Başlarında CHP'nin Laiklik Politikası*: Konya Örneği, [The Laicity Policy of CHP in the Beginning of the Multy-party Period: The Konya Case], Çizgi Yayınları, Konya, 2012.

Akgül, Ahmet. *Erbakan'ın Farkı*, [Erbakan's Difference], Buğra Yayınları, İstanbul, 2013.

Akgündüz, Ahmed, *Tabular Yıkılıyor 2*, [Taboos are being demolished], Osmanlı Araştırmaları Vakfı, İstanbul, 2007.

Akseki, Ahmed Hamdi, *Askere Din Kitabı*, [Religious Book to the Soldier] Adapted to contemporary Turkish by Talât Koçyiğit, Diyanet İşleri Başkanlığı, Ankara, 1976.

Aksüt, Hamza. 'Erdoğan Çınar Skandalı', *Kızılbaş*, No. 9, June 2009.

Aktar, Ayhan *Varlık Vergisi ve 'Türkleştirme' Politikaları*, [The Wealth Tax and Policies of 'Turkification'], İletişim Yayınları, İstanbul, 2000.

Algar, Hamid. 'An introduction to Said Nursi', *Journal of Shi'a Islamic Studies*, Vol. 6, No. 3, Summer 2013, pp. 337-342.

Ali, Mehmet. 'Türkiye'de Toplumun dine ve dini değerlere bakışı', [Community approach to religion and religious values in Turkey], MAK Danışmanlık, Ankara, 2017.

Altaş, Nurullah, 'Türkiye'de Örgün Öğretimde Dinin Yeri', [The Place of Religion in Formal Education], *Marifet*, Vol. 2, no. 1, Spring 2002, pp. 219-229.

Altındal, Aytunç. *Laiklik*: Enigma'ya Dönüşen Paradigma, [Laicism: Paradigm turned into an Enigma], 2nd Edition, Anahtar Kitaplar Yayınevi, İstanbul 1994.

Altinordu, Ates. 'The Debate on "Neighborhood Pressure" in Turkey', *International Perspectives*, Vol. 37, No. 2, February 2009.

Amerikan Gizli Belgelerinde Türkiye'de İslamcı Akımlar, [Islamist Movements in Turkey in American Secret Documents], trans. Yılmaz Polat, Beyan Yayınları, İstanbul, 1990.

Anık, M. 'Two Axes Revolving Around the Discussions of Secularism in Turkey: Şerif Mardin and İsmail Kara', *insan & toplum*, Vol. 2, No. 4, 2012, pp. 9-34.

Arnal, William and McCutcheon, Russell T. *The Sacred is the Profane*: the Political Nature of "Religion", Oxford University Press, Oxford, 2013.

Aronoff, Myron J. "Introduction" in Aronoff, Myron J., (ed.), *Religion and Politics*, Transaction Books, New Brunswick and London, 1984.

Apaydın, Cem, 'Belgeler Işığında Tekke Zaviye ve Türbelerin Kapatılması Üzerine Bir Değerlendirme', [An Evaluation of the Closure of Lodges and Tombs in the Light of Documents], *Yakın Dönem Türkiye Araştırmaları*, Vol. 16, No. 32, 2017, pp. 149-171.

Asad, Talad. *Genealogies of Religion*: Discipline and Reasons of Power in Christianity and Islam, The John Hopkins University Press, Baltimore and London, 1993.

Asad Talal, "Reading a Modern Classic: W. C. Smith's *The Meaning and End of Religion*," *History of Religions*, Vol. 40, No. 3, 2001, pp. 205–22.

Asad Talal, *Formation of the Secular*: Christianity, Islam and Modernity, Stanford University Press, Stanford, California, 2003.

Asad, Talal. 'Thinking about the secular body, pain, and liberal politics', *Cultural Anthropology* Vol. 26, No. 4, 2011, pp. 657–75.

Atabaki, Touraj. (Ed.). *The State and the Subaltern*: Modernization, Society and the State in Turkey and Iran, I. B. Tauris, London, 2007.

Atay, Tayfun. *Parti, Cemaat, Tarikat*: 2000'ler Türkiye'sinin Dinbaz-Politik Seyir Defteri, [Party, Congregation, Sect: The Journal of Dinbaz Politics in Turkey in 2000s], Can Saat Yayınları, 2017.

Avcı, Hanefi. *Haliç'te Yaşayan Simonlar*, [Devotee Residents of Haliç], Angora Kitapları, Ankara, 2017.

Aydin, Necati, *Said Nursi and Science in Islam*: Character Building through Nursi's Mana-i harfi, Rutledge, Oxon, 2019.

Aydın, Rıza. AKP Hükümetinin İrfan Evleri, https://yalansz.wordpress.com/2016/01/28/akp-hukumetinin-irfan-evleri/.

Aydın, Mustafa *et al*, 'Türkiye Sosyal-Siyasal Eğilimler Araştırması', Center for Turkish Studies, Kadir Has Üniversitesi, 31 January 2018.

Aydıntaşbaş, Asli, 'The Good, the Bad, And the Gulenists: The role of the Gulen movement in Turkey's coup attempt', European Council on Foreign Relations, September 2016.

Aydoğan, Erdal. 'Üçüncü Umumi Müfettişliğinin Kurulması ve III. Umumî Müfettiş Tahsin Uzer'in Bazı Önemli Faaliyetleri, [The Establishment of the 3rd General Inspectorate and Some Important Activities of the 3rd Inspector Tahsin Uzer], *Atatürk Yolu*, May-November 2004, pp. 1-14.

Aysal, Necdet. 'Yönetsel Alanda Değişimler ve Devrim Hareketlerine Karşı Gerici Tepkiler "Serbest Cumhuriyet Fırkası - Menemen Olayı"', [Changes in Administrative Field and Backward Reaction to Revolutionary Movements - 'The Free Republican Party - The Menemen Incident'], Ankara Üniversitesi Türk İnkılâp Tarihi Enstitüsü, *Atatürk Yolu*, No. 44, 2009, pp. 581-625.

Ayubi, N, Nazih. *Political Islam*: Religion and Politics in the Arab World, Routledge, London and New York, 1991.

Azak, Umut. *Islam and Secularism in Turkey*: Kemalizm, Religion and the Nation State, I. B. Tauris, London, 2010.

Azman, Ayşe. 'Niyazi Berkes: Ulusçuluk-Devrimcilik Ekseninde Kemalist Çağdaşlaşma Modelinin İnşasi' [Niyazi Berkes: Construction of Kemalist Modernization Model on the Bases of Nationalism – Revolutionism], *Sosyoloji Dergisi*, Vol. 3, No. 17, 2008/2, pp. 31-47.

Babacan, Hasan and Mehmet Ali Karaman, *Said Nursi:* Siyaset ve Devlet, Altınpost Yayınları, Ankara, 2013.

Baer, Marc David. *The Dönme*: Jewish converts, Muslim Revolutionaries, and Secular Turks, Stanford University Press, Standford, California, 2010.

Bali, Rıfat N. II. Dünya Savaşında Gayrımüslimlerin Askerlik Serüveni: *Yirmi Kur'a Nafıa Askerleri*, [The military adventure of the non-Muslims in the II. World War: 20 Classes Public Works Soldiers], Kitabevi Yayınları, İstanbul, 2008.

Bali, Rıfat N. 'Cumhuriyet döneminde azınlık milletvekilleri', *Toplumsal Tarih*, No. 186, June 2009, pp. 60-64.

Bayrak, Mehmet. *Alevilik ve Kürtler*, ÖZ-GE Yayınları, Wuppertal, 1997.

Balcı, Tamer and Miller, Christopher L. (ed.), *The Gülen Hizmet Movement*: Circumspect Activism in Faith-Based Reform, Cambridge Scholars Publishing, Newcastle upon Tyne, 2012.

Baran, Zeyno. *Torn Country*: Turkey between Secularism and Islamism, Stanford, 2010.

Bareilles, Bertrand. *Le Drame Oriental*: D'Athènes a Angora, [The Oriental Drama: From Athens to Ankara], Éditions Bossard, Paris, 1923.

Bayrak, Mehmet. *Alevilik ve Kürtler*, [Alevism and the Kurds], ÖZGE Yayınları, Wuppertal, 1997.

Bekaroğlu, Edip Asaf. 'Post-Secular Turkey?: Justice and Development Party Governments and Updating the Secular Contract', *insan ve toplum*, Vol. 5, No. 9, 2015, pp. 103-122.

Benli, Fatma. 1964-2011 Türkiye'de ve Dünyada Başörtüsü Yasağı Kronolojisi, Mazlumder, İstanbul, 2011.

Bergunder, Michael. 'What is Religion? The Unexplained Subject Matter of Religious Studies', *Method and Theory in the Study of Religion* 26 (2014) 246-286.

Berkes, Niyazi. *The Development of Secularism in Turkey*, first published by McGill University Press, 1964, present edition in a facsimile edition by Hurst & Company, London, 1998.

Beşikçi, İsmail. *Türk Tarih Tezi ve Kürt Sorunu*, [Turkish History Thesis and the Kurdish question], Stockholm, 1986.

Beşikçi, İsmail. *Tunceli Kanunu (1935) ve Dersim Jenosidi*, [The Tunceli Law and the Genocide of Dersim], Belge Yayınları, İstanbul, 1990.

Beşikçi, İsmail. *Bilim-Resmi İdeoloji Devlet-Demokrasi ve Kürt Sorunu*, [Science – Official Ideology State-Democracy and the Kurdish Question], Alan Yayıncılık, İstanbul, 1990.

Beşikçi, İsmail, Alevilerde Kafa Karışıklığı, *Alevihaber*, 23 December 2012.

Bisku, Michael B. 'Atatürk's Legacy versus Religious Reassertion: Secularism and Islam in Modern Turkey', *Mediterranean Quarterly*, 3(4), September 1992, pp. 75-93.

Bora, Tanıl and Gültenkingil Murat, (Eds.) *Milliyetçilik*, [Nationalism], Modern Türkiye'de Siyasî Düşünce, Vol. 4, İletişim Yayınları, İstanbul, 2002.

Bora, Tanıl and Gültenkingil Murat, (Eds.) *İslamcılık*, [Islamism], Modern Türkiye'de Siyasî Düşünce, Vol. 6, 2nd Edition, İletişim Yayınları, İstanbul, 2005.

Bora, Tanıl and Gültenkingil Murat, (Eds) *Kemalizm*, [Kemalism], Modern Türkiye'de Siyasî Düşünce, Vol. 2, İletişim Yayınları, İstanbul, 2009.

Bora, Tanıl. 'Türk Milliyetçiliği Söyleminde Dersim', [Dersim in the Turkish Nationalist Discourse], *Tîroj*, Vol. 7, No. 47, December 2010, p. 14-8.

Bozarslan Hamit. 'La laïcité en Turquie'. *Matériaux pour l'histoire de notre temps*, n°78, 2005, pp. 42-49.

Brittain, Christopher Craig. 'The "Secular" as a Tragic Category: On Talal Asad', Religion and Representation, *Method & Theory in the Study of Religion*, Vol. 17, No. 2, 2005, pp. 149-165.

Buggein, Gretchen, 'Museum space and the experience of the sacred', *Material Religion*, Vol. 8, No. 1, pp. 30-51.

Bulut, Faik, *Kim Bu Fethullah Gülen*: Dünü-Bugünü-Hedefi, [Who is this Fethullah Gülen: Yesterday, Today, His Aim], Berfin Yayınları, İstanbul, 2016.

Bulut, Faik. *Ali'siz Alevilik*, Berfin Yayınları, İstanbul, 2011.

Bustamante, Christian Bryan. "From Secularism to Post-Secularism: Jürgen Habermas on Religion in a Secular State", *Scientia*, The Research Journal of the College of Arts & Sciences, June 2014, pp. 1-20.

Cansun, Şebnem. 'The Headscarf question in Turkey: The Examples of the AKP and CHP', The *Journal of Academic Social Science* Studies, Vol. 6, No. 8, October 2013, pp. 123-142.

Casanova, José. *Public Religions in the Modern World*, The University of Chicago Press, Chicago, 1994.

Casanova, José. 'Rethinking Secularization: A Global Comparative Perspective', The *Hedgehog* Review, Vol. 8, Spring & Summer 2006, pp. 7-12.

Caymaz, Birol. Türkiye Cumhuriyeti'nin kuruluş sürecinde laiklik tartışmaları, [Debate on laicism during the foundation of the Republic], unpublished monograph, n.p., 2006.

Cheetham, David. 'Ritualising the Secular? Interreligious meetings in the "Immanent Frame"', *The Heythrop Journal*, 15 February 2017, p. 7.

Cilasun Emrah, Yeni Paradigmanın Eşiğinde Beddiüzzaman Efsanesi ve Said Nursî, Tekin Yayınevi, İstanbul, 2018.

Cizre, Ümit. (ed.), *Secular and Islamic Politics in Turkey*: The making of the Justice and Development Party, Routledge, New York, 2008.

Cornell, Svante E., 'The Naqshbandi-Khalidi Order and Political Islam in Turkey', Hudson Institute, 3 September 2015.

Cornell, Svante. 'The Rise of Diyanet: the Politicization of Turkey's Directorate of Religious Affairs', *The Turkey Analyst*, 9 October, 2015.

Cox, Harvey. *The Secular City: Secularization and Urbanization in Theological Perspective*, Princeton University Press, Princeton and Oxford, 2013.

Cündioğlu, Dücane. *Türkçe Ku'ran ve Cumhuriyet İdeolojisi*, [Turkish Quran and the Republican Ideology], Kitabevi, İstanbul, 1998.

Çağatay, Neşet. *Türkiye de Gerici Eylemler:* (1923'den Buyana), [Backward Movement in Turkey (From 1923 Onwards)], Ankara Üniversitesi Basımevi, Ankara, 1972.

Çalışlar, Oral and Çelik, Tolga. *Erbakan, Fetullah Kavgası*, [Erbakan Fetullah Clash], Sıfır Noktası Yayınları, İstanbul, 2000.

Çakan, Işıl. *Türk Parlamento Tarihinde II. Meclis*, [The 2nd Assembly in the History of the Turkish Parliament], Çağdaş Yayınları, İstanbul, 1999.

Çarkoğlu, Ali and Toprak, Binnaz. *Religion, Society and Politics in a Changing Turkey*, trans. Çiğdem Aksoy Fromm, Tesev Publications, İstanbul, 2007.

Çarmikli, Eyup Sabri. Caught between Islam and the West: secularism in the Kemalist discourse, Unpublished PhD thesis, The University of Westminster. 2011.

Çaylak, Adem and Dinç, Güliz. 'Gülenism as "Religionist" Kemalism', *Insight Turkey*, January 2017, pp. 181-206.

Çetinoğlu, Sait and Cibran, Dara. 'Pontus Sorunu', [The Pontus Question], unpublished monograph, 2007.

Çetinoğlu, Ali Sait. *Varlık Vergisi 1942-1944*: Ekonomi ve Kültütel Jenosid, [The Wealth Tax 1942-44): Economic and Cultural Genocide], Belge Yayınları, İstanbul, 2009.

Çınar, Alev. *Modernity, Islam, and Secularism in Turkey:* Bodies, Places, and Time, University of Minnesota Press, Minneapolis, London, 2005.

Çınar, Erdoğan. *Aleviliğin Kökenleri*, [Origins of Alevism], Kalkedon, İstanbul, 2008.

Daniel, Kasomo. 'An examination of co-existence of religion and politics', *International Journal of Sociology and Anthropology*, Vol. 1, No. 7, November, 2009, pp. 124-131.

Demirel, Ahmet. *Birinci Meclis'te Muhalefet: İkinci Grup*, [Opposition in the First Parliament: The Second Group], İletişim Yayınları, İstanbul, 2015.

Diyanet İşleri Başkanlığı, *Türkiye'de Dinî Hayat Araştırması*, [Research on Religious Life in Turkey], Ankara, 2014.

Diyanet İşleri Başkanlığı, *Suriye Kalkanı ve Zeytin Dalı Faaliyet Raporu*, [Syria Shıled and Olive Branch Operation Report], Ankara, 2018.

Dole, Christopher. *Healing Secular Life*: Loss and Devotion in Modern Turkey, University of Pennsylvania Press, Philadelphia, 2012.

Donef, Racho. Identities in the Multicultural State: Four immigrant Populations from Turkey in Australia and Sweden, Unpublished Doctoral Thesis, Macquarie University, 1998.

Donef, Raço. '6-7 Eylül olayları 50 yıl sonra', [The 6-7 September incidents 50 years on], *Nsibin*, Stockholm, 2006.

Donef, Raço. Resmi Tarih ve Rumlar' [Official History and the Greeks] in Fikret Başkaya and *Sait Çetinoğlu* (Eds.) *Resmi Tarih tartışmaları 8*, Özgür Üniversite Yayınları, İstanbul, 2009, pp. 253-281.

Donef, Racho. "The Role of Teşkilat-ı Mahsusa (Special Organization) in the Genocide of 1915" in Tessa Hofmann, Matthias Bjørnlund and Vasileios Meichanetsidis, (Eds.) *Studies on the State Sponsored Campaign of Extermination of the Christians of Asia Minor (1912-1922) and Its Aftermath: History, Law, Memory*, *Aristide D. Caratzas, New York &* Athens, 2011, pp. 179-194.

Donef, Racho. Assyrians post-Nineveh: conflict, identity, fragmentation and survival: A study of Assyrogenous communities, Mesopotamia Series 1, Tatavla Publishing, Sydney, 2012.

Donef, Racho. *The Hakkâri Massacres*, Tatavla Publishing, Sydney, 2014.

Donef, Racho, *"Sayfo* and Denialism" in Gaunt, David, Atto, Naures & O. Barthoma, Soner, (Eds), *Let Them Not Return*, Berghahn, New York, Oxford, 2017, pp. 205-218.

Donef, Racho, 'War cries emanating from Turkey', Platform for Peace and Justice, 27 March 2018.

Donef, Racho. 'Does Turkey want to become member of the European Union', Platform for Peace and Justice, 8 July 2018.

Dorroll, Philip, 'Shari'a and the Secular in Modern Turkey', *Contemporary Islam*, No. 11, 2007, pp. 123-135.

Dr Rıza Nur'un Lozan Hatıraları, [Dr Nur's Lausanne Memoirs], Boğaziçi Yayınları, İstanbul, 1992.

Dressler, Markus, "Public-Private Distinctions, the Alevi Question, and the Headscarf: Turkish Secularism Revisited" in Linell E. Cadu and Hurd.

Elizabeth Shakman (Eds). *Comparative Secularisms in a Global Age*, Palgrave Macmillan, Basingstoke, 2010, pp. 121-41.

Dressler, Markus and Mandair, Arvind-Pal S. (eds.), *Secularism and Religion-Making*, Oxford University Press, Oxford, 2011.

Dressler, Marcus. *Writing Religion*: The making of Turkish Alevi Islam, Oxford University Press, Oxford, 2013.

Dressler, Marcus. 'Turkish politics of Doxa: Otherizing the Alevis as heterodox', *Philosophy and Social Criticism*, Vol. 41, Nos 4-5, pp. 445-451, May 2015; original manuscript published online, 31 January 2015.

Duran, Burhanettin. Transformation of Islamist Political Thought in Turkey from the Empire to the Early Republic (1908-1960): Necip Fazıl Kısakürek's Political Ideas, Unpublished Doctoral Thesis, Bilkent University. Ankara, 2001.

Duran, Burhanettin and Cemil Aydın, 'Competing Occidentalisms of Modern Islamist Thought: Necip Fazıl Kısakürek and Nurettin Topçu on Christianity', the West and Modernity', *The Muslim World*, Vol. 103, No. 4, 2013, pp. 489-500.

Durkheim Émile, *Elementary Forms of the Religious Life*, trans. Joseph Ward Swain, George Allen & Unwin Ltd., London, 1915.

Dündar, Fuat. *Modern Türkiye'nin Şifresi*: İttihat ve Terakkinin Etnislik Mühendisliği (1913-1918), [The Cipher of Modern Turkey: Ethnic Engineering of Union and Progress], İletişim Yayınları, Istanbul 2008.

Ebaugh, Helen Rose. *The Gülen Movement*: A Sociological Analysis of a Civic Movement Rooted in Moderate Islam, Springer, Dordrecht Heidelberg London New York, 2010.

Edib, Halidé. *Turkey Faces West*: A Turkish view of recent changes and their origin, Yale University Press, New Haven, 1930.

Edelma, Edel *et al*. *Turkey Transformed*: The Origins and Evolution of Authoritarianism and Islamization Under the AKP, Bipartisan Policy Center, Washington D.C., October 2015.

Eliade, Mircea. *The Sacred & the Profane*: The Nature of Religion, tr. Willard R Task, Harcourt, Brace & World Inc., New York, 1959.

Ellison, Grace. *An English Woman in Angora*, E.P. Dutton & Company, New York, 1923.

Eligür, Banu. *The Mobilization of Political Islam in Turkey*, Cambridge University Press, Cambridge, 2010.

Erdeha, Kamil, *Milli Mücadelede Vilayetler ve Valiler*, [The Prefectures and the Governors in the National Struggle], Remzi Kitabevi, İstanbul, 1975.

Erde, Gazi. 'Religious Services in Turkey: From the Office of *Şeyhülislām* to the *Diyanet*', *The Muslim World*, Vol. 98, No. 2-3, pp. 199-215.

Erol, Ayhan. 'Re-Imagining Identity: The Transformation of the Alevi Semah', *Middle Eastern Studies*, 46:3, 375-387.

Ertit, Volkan. 'Birbirinin Yerine Kullanılan İki Farklı Kavram': Sekülerleşme ve Laiklik, [Two Different Terems That Used Interchangeably: Secularization ans Laicité], *Akademik İncelemeler Dergisi*, Vol. 9, No. 1, 2014, pp. 103-122.

Ertit, Volkan. 'God is dying in Turkey as Well: Application of Secularisation Theory to a non-Christian Society', *Open Theology*, Volume 4, No. 1, 2018, pp. 192-211.

Ersanlı, Büşra. *İktidar ve Tarih*: Türkiye'de "Resmî Tarih Tezinin Oluşumu" (1929-1937), [Government and History: "The Formation of the Official History Thesis"], İletişim Yayınları, İstanbul, 2003.

Ertunç, Ahmet Cemil. TBMM Hükümeti Birinci Meclis (1920-1923) – 1, [TGNA Government First Parliament], http://ilimcephesi.com/tbmm-hukumeti-birinci-meclis-1920-1923-1/.

Es, Murat. "Alevis in *Cemevis*: Religion and Secularism in Turkey" in *Topographies of Faith*: Religion in Urban Spaces, Becci Irene, Burchardt Marian and Casanova José, Bill, Leiden and Boston, 2013, pp. 25-43.

European Stability Initiative, *Islamic Calvinists: Change and Conservatism in Central Anatolia*, Berlin, Brussels, Istanbul, 2005.

Eyüboğlu, İsmet Zeki. *İslam Dininden Ayrılan Cereyanlar*: Nakşibendilik, [Movements that separated from Islam: Nakshibendism], *Cumhuriyet Gazetesi*, n.p., 1998.

Farias, Miguel *et al.* 'Atheists on the Santiago Way: Examining Motivations to Go On Pilgrimage', *Sociology of Religion*, Vol. 80, No. 1, 9 January 2019, Pages 28–44.

Fitzgerald, Timothy. 'Religion is not a standalone category', *The Immanent Frame*, 29 October 2008, https://tif.ssrc.org/2008/10/29/religion-is-not-a-standalone-category/.

Fougner, Tore. 'Fethullah Gülen's understanding of women's rights in Islam: a critical reappraisal', *Turkish Studies*, Vol. 18, No. 2, 2016, pp. 251-277.

Φραγκούλης, Σ. Φράγκος. [Frangos S. Frangoulis], Ποια Τουρκία; Ποιοι Τούρκοι; [Which Turkey? Which Turks?], Εκδοτικός Οργανισμός Λιβάνη, Αθήνα (Athens), 2012.

Fernandez, Laura, 'El desarollo del Islamismo politico en Turquía: ¿Un modelo de democracia o un obstáculo para la adhesion al union europea?', [The development of Islamic politics in Turkey. A model of democracy or an obstacle to Accession to the European Union?], *Unisci Discussion Papers*, No. 9, October 2005, pp. 135-150.

Filiz, Şahin. *Tarikat, Cemaat, Kadın*: Neo-Oryantalizmín Kadın Üzerinden Egemenlik Arayışı ve Siyasal İslamcılık, [Order, Congregation, Women: the neo-Orientalism's quest for domination over women and political Islamism], Say Yayınları, İstanbul, 2016.

Friedlaender, Israel, 'The Heterodoxies of the Shiites in the Presentation of Ibn Ḥazm', *Journal of the American Oriental Society*, Vol. 28, 1907, pp. 1-80.

Garnett, Lucy M. J. *Mysticism and Magic in Turkey*: An account of the religious doctrines, monastic organization, and ecstatic powers of the Dervish Orders, Charles Scribner's Sons, New York, 1912.

Genelkurmay Belgelerinde Kürt İsyanları 1, [Kurdish Uprisings in General Staff Records 1], Kaynak Yayınları, İstanbul, 1992.

Goldenberg, Naomi. 'An Argument for Thinking of Religions as Vestigial States', 12 March 2012, https://criticalreligion.org/2012/03/12/an-argument-for-thinking-of-religions-as-vestigial-states.

Gorer, Geofrey. *Exploring English Character*, Criterion Books, New York, 1955.

Gozaydin, Istar and Ozturk, Ahmet Erdi. 'The Management of Religion in Turkey', *Turkey Institute*, London, November 2014.

Göle, Nilüfer. 'Secularism and Islamism in Turkey: The Making of Elites and Counter-Elites', *Middle East Journal*, Vol. 51, No. 1, Winter 1997, pp. 46-58.

Göle, Nilüfer. "İslam'ın Demokratik Hak Davası" in Yerasimos, Stéphane, (ed.) *Turkler*: Doğu ve Batı, İslam ve Laiklik, [The Turks: East and West, Islam and Laicism], original title *Les Turcs*, tr, Temel Keşoğlu, Doruk, Ankara, 2005, pp. 127-138.

Göle, Nilüfer. *Islam and* Secularity: The Future of Europe's Public Sphere, Duke University Press, Durham and London 2015.

Göldaş, İsmail. *Takrir-i Sükûn Görüşmeleri*, [Negotiations on the Law on the Maintenance and Reinforcement of Public Order], Belge Yayınları, İstanbul, 1997.

Gözaydın, İştar B, 'Diyanet and Politics', *The Muslim World*, 98(2-3), April 2008, pp. 216-27.

Gözaydın, İştar. 'Religion, Politics and the Politics of Religion in Turkey', Occasional Paper 121, *Liberal Institute*, 2013.

Gözler, Kemal. *Türk Anayasa Hukuku*, [Turkish Constitutional Law], Ekin Kitabevi Yayınları, Bursa, 2000.

Graham E. Fuller, *The Future of Political Islam*, Palgrave MacMillan, Basingstoke, 2004.

Gurkas, Hakki, "Turkish Secular Muslim Identity on Display in Europe" in Gabriele Marranci (Ed.), *Muslim Societies and the Challenge of Secularization*: An Interdisciplinary Approach, Springer Dordrecht, Heidelberg London New York, 2010, pp. 113-31.

Gülen, M. Fethullah, *Questions and Answers about Islam*, Vol. 1, feedbooks, 2000.

Günaydın Mehmet, 'Din Kültürü ve Ahlâk Eğitiminin İlköğretimde ve Liselerde Zorunlu Ders Olmasının Prof. Dr. Hüseyin Atay'ın Katkıları', [Dr. Hüseyin Atay's Contributions to Religious Culture and Moral Education as a Compulsory Lesson in Primary Education and High Schools], *Din Bilimleri Akademik Araştırma Dergisi*, Vol. IX, No. 1, pp. 287-304.

Gürbey, Sinem. 'Islam, Nation-State, and the military: A Discussion of Secularism in Turkey', *Comparative Studies of South Asia, Africa and the Middle East*, Vol. 29, no. 3, Duke University Press, 2009, pp. 371-380.

Habermas, Jürgen. A "post-secular" society - what does that mean?, 16 September 2008, https://www.resetdoc.org/story/a-post-secular-society-what-does-that-mean/.

Halim Pasha, Said. 'The Reform of Muslim Society', *Islamic Studies*, Vol. 47, No. 3 (Autumn 2008), pp. 379-404.

Hamrin-Dahl, Tina. 'The Alevi and Questions of Identity, Including Violence and Insider/Outsider Perspectives', Exercising Power: The Role of Religions in Concord and Conflict, *Scripta Instituti Donneriani Aboensis*, Vol. 19, 2006.

Hankey, Wayne. "The Contemporary Debate about Secular and Sacred in Judaism, Christianity and Islam" in Wayne Hankey and Nicholas Hatt, *Changing our Mind on Secularization*, St. Peter Publications Inc., Charlottetown, Prince Edward Island, 2009, pp. 11-40.

Harrington, James C. *Wrestling with Free Speech, Religious Freedom, and Democracy in Turkey*: The Political Trials and Times of Fethullah Gülen, University Press of America Inc, Lanham, Maryland, 2011.

Heper, Metin, "Does Secularism Face a Serious Threat in Turkey?" in Berna Turam, *Secular State and Religious Society*, pp. 79-94.

Holton, Christopher and Lopez, Cale. *The Gulen Movement*, Turkey's Islamic Supremacist Cult and its Contributions to the Civilization Jihad, Civilization Jihad Reader Series, Vol. 8, The Centre for Security Policy, Washington D.C., 2015.

Houston, Christopher. 'Thwarted agency and the strange afterlife of Islamism in militant laicism in Turkey', *Contemporary Islam*, Vol. 7, No. 3, September 2013, pp. 333-51.

Houston, Christopher, 'Kemalism and Beyond', The Oxford Handbook of Contemporary Middle-Eastern and North African History, September 2015, pp. 1-13.

Houston, Christopher. 'Politicizing place perception: a phemonology of urban activism in Istanbul', *Journal of the Royal Anthropological Institute*, Vol. 21, No. 4, 2015, pp. 720-738.

Houston, Chris. Shaping the City: Three Urban Events in Istanbul, *Idealkent*, Vol. 9, No. 24, 2018, pp. 342-363.

Ibrahim M. Zakyi, 'Said Nursi', *Cont Islam*, 2011, pp, 5:85–87.

Işıklı, Alpaslan. Said Nursi Fethullah Gülen ve "Laik" Sempatizanları, [Said Nursi Fethullah Gülen and its "Laic" Sympathisers], Mülkiyeliler Birliği Yayınları, Ankara, 1998.

International Conference Proceedings, *Muslim World in Transition: Contributions of the Gülen Movement*, Leeds Metropolitan University Press, London, 2007.

Introvigne, Massimo. 'Turkish Religious Market(s): A View Based on Religious Economy Theory' in Yavuz, Hakan M. (ed.), The Emergence of a New Turkey, The University of Utah Press, Salt Lake City, 2006, pp. 23-48.

İnan, Süleyman. Muhalefette Adnan Menderes, (1945-1950), [Menderes in opposition], unpublished Ph.D. thesis, Süleyman Demirel Üniversitesi, Isparta, 2012.

Işık, Hasan, "Muallim Cevdet'in Türk Eğitim Tarihindeki Yeri ve Derslerinde Yerel Tarih Uygulamaları", [The Place of Muallim Cevdet in Turkish Education History and His Local History Practices in His Courses], TUHED, Spring 2020, Vol. 9, No. 1, pp. 189-208.

Jenkins, Gareth. *Political Islam in Turkey*, Palgrave MacMillan, Basingstoke, 2008.

Kansu, Mazhar Müfit. *Erzurum'dan* Ölümüne *Kadar Atatürk ile Beraber,* [Together with Atatürk from Erzurum till his Death], Türk Tarih Kurumu Yayınları, Vol. 1, Ankara, 1986.

Kara, Hüseyin. 'Tek Parti Dönemi Din Politikası (1923-1946)', [The religion policy in the single party period], *Mehmet Akif Ersoy Üniversitesi Sosyal Bilimler Enstitüsü Dergisi,* Vol. 9, No. 19, January 2017, pp. 111-136.

Kara, Mustafa. *Tasavvuf ve Tarikatlar*, İletişim Yayınları, 2013.

Karabekir, Kazım. *İstiklal Harbimiz*, [Our Independence War], Volumes 1-5, Emre Yayınları, İstanbul, 1995.

Karakaya-Stump, Ayfer, 'Documents and Buyruk Manuscripts in the Private Archives of Alevi Dede Families', *British Journal of Middle Eastern Studies*, December 2010, Vol. 37, No. 3, p. 273-86.

Karasipahi, Sena. *Muslims in Modern Turkey*: Kemalism, Modernism and the Revolt of the Islamic Intellectuals, I. B. Tauris, London & New York, 2009.

Karpat, Kemal H. *Turkey's Politics*: The transition to a Multi-Party System, PUP, Princeton, New Jersey, 1959.

Keskin Tuğrul, "Market Oriented Post- Islamism in Turkey" in Berna Turam, *Secular State and Religious Society*, pp. 121-142.

Keyman E. Fuat and Sebnem Gumuscu, *Democracy, Identity, and Foreign Policy in Turkey*: Hegemony through Transformation, Palgrave Macmillan, Basingstoke, 2014.

Kezer Zeynep, *Building Modern Turkey*: State, Space, and Ideology in the Early Republic, University of Pittsburgh, Pittsburgh, 2015.

Kılıçdağı, Ohannes, 'Genelkurmay "Askere Din Kitabi Hazırlatmış"', [The Chief of General Staff Prepared a Book on Religion for Soldiers], *Agos*, 29 April 2016; http://www.agos.com.tr/tr/yazi/15171/genelkurmay-askere-din-kitabi-hazirlatmis.

Kısakürek, Necip Fazıl. *Yahudilik – Masonluk Dönmelik*, [Judaism – Masonism Donmeism] Senyıldız Matbaası, İstanbul, 2008.

Kıvılcım Yayınları, Kemalizm nedir?, [What is Kemalizm?], Unpublished monograph, n.p., n.d.

Kirli, Biray Kolluoglu, 'Forgetting the Smyrna Fire', *History Workshop Journal*, Oxford University Press, Issue 60, Autumn 2005, pp. 25-44.

Konuralp, Nuri Aydın. *Hatay´ın Kurtuluş ve Kurtarış Mücadelesi Tarihi*, [Liberation of Hatay and History of the Liberation Struggle], Hatay Postası Gazete ve Basımevi, İskenderun, 1970.

Korkut, Umut and Eslen-Ziya, Hande. *Politics and Gender Identity in Turkey*: Centralised Islam for Socio-Economic Control, Routledge, New York, 2018.

Köni, Hakan. 'Religion and Politics in Turkey: An Analysis of Turkish Secularism', *JLSS*, Vol 1, No. 2, July 2012, pp. 79-83.

Köse, Talha. 'Ideological or religious? Contending visions on the future of Alevi identity', *Identities*, Vol. 5. No. 19, October 2012, pp. 576-596.

Küçükaydın, Demir, *Tersinden Kemalizm (İsmail Beşikçi'nin Eleştirisi)*, [Kemalism from Reverse: Criticism of İsmail Beşikçi], Kitap Kurdu Araf Yayıncılık, Istanbul, 2004.

Laborde, Cécile. Three approaches to the study of religion, the immanent Frame, SSRC, https://tif.ssrc.org/2014/02/05/three-approaches-to-the-study-of-religion/, 5 February 2014.

Lagendijk, Joost. 'Turquía en la Encrucijada', [Turkey at the Crossroads], *Mediterráneo Económico*, No. 12, December 2007, pp. 243-53.

Lerner, Daniel. *The Passing of Traditional Society*, Free Press, London, 1958, p. 349.

Lewis, Bernard. 'The Question of Orientalism', *The New York Review of Books*, 24 June 1982.

Lewis, Geoffrey. *The Turkish Language Reform*: A Catastrophic Success, Oxford University Press, Oxford, 1999.

Locke, John. 'Letter Concerning Toleration', trans. William Popple, 1689.

Lull, James. *Media, Communication and Culture*: A Global Approach, Columbia University Press, New York, 1995.

Mango, Andrew. *Atatürk*: The Biography of the Founder of Modern Turkey, Overlook Press, New York, 2000.

Mardin, Şerif. "Religion and secularism in Turkey" in Ali Kazancigil and Ergun Özbudun (eds.) *Atatürk, founder of a Modern State*, C. Hurst, London, 1981.

Mardin, Şerif. *Türkiye'de Din ve Siyaset*: Makaleler III, [Religion and Politics in Turkey: Articles III], İletişim Yayınları, İstanbul, 1991.

Mardin, Şerif, 'The Just and the Unjust', *Daedalus*, Summer, 1991, pp.113-129.

Mardin, Serif, "The Nakshibendi Order of Turkey" in Martin E. Marty & R. Scott Appleby (eds.), *Fundamentalisms and the State*, University of Chicago Press, 1993, pp. 204-32.

Markham Ian S. and Suendam Birinci Pirim, *An Introduction to Said Nursi*: Life, Thought, and Writings, Ashgate, Surrey, 2011.

Martin Richard C. and Abbas Barzegar, (eds.), *Contested Perspectives on Political Islam*, Stanford University Press, Stanford, 2010.

Martens, Stefan, Being Alevi in Turkey: Discursive Unity and the Contestation of Communal Boundaries, 1980 – 2009, Unpublished Master's thesis, Simon Fraser University, 2005.

Massicard, Élise. *Alevi Hareketinin Siyasallaşması*, [The politicization of the Alevi Movement], translation of *L'autre Turquie*, [The Other Turkey], trans. Ali Berktay, İletişim Yayınları, İstanbul, 2007.

Massicard Elise, Alevism in the 1960s: Social Change and Mobilisation, *Isis*, 2005, pp. 109-135 [submitted to Hal Archives on 4 April 2013].

Minorsky, Wladimir. 'Notes Sur le Secte des Ahl-é Haqq', *Revue du Monde Musulman*, Vols. XL-XLI, September-December 1920.

Mirsepassi, Ali. *Political Islam, Iran, and The Enlightenment*: Philosophies of Hope and Despair, Cambridge University Press, Cambridge, 2011.

Moosa, Matti. *Extremist Shiites*: The Ghulat Sects, Syracuse University Press, Syracuse, New York, 1987.

Mumcu, Uğur. *Tarikat, Siyaset, Ticaret*, [Tarikat, Politics, Commerce], Tekin Yayınevi, Ankara, 1993.

Mumyakmaz, Alper. 'Elitlerin Yeni Yüzü, Islami Burjuvazi', [The New Face of Elites, Islamic Bourgeoisie], *Mustafa Kemal Üniversitesi Sosyal Bilimler Enstitüsü Dergisi*, Vol 11, No. 27, 2014, pp. 367-382.

Narli, Nilüfer, 'The Rise of the Islamist Movement in Turkey', *Middle East*, Vol. 3, No. 3, 1999, pp. 38-48.

Naskali, Emine Gürsoy. *Celal Bayar Arşivinden Serbest Fırka Anıları*, [The Free Party according to the memoirs from Celal Bayar's Archives], Doğan Kitap, İstanbul, 2015.

Navaro-Yashin, Yael. "The Market for Identities: Secularism, Islamism, Commodities" in Deniz Kandiyoti & Ayse Saktanber, *Fragments of Culture*: The Everyday of Modern Turkey, I.B. Tauris, London, New York, 2002, pp. 221-53.

Navaro-Yashin Yael, *Faces of the State: Secularism and Public Life in Turkey*, Princeton University Press, Princeton, 2002.

Nedim, Ahmed. *Ankara İstiklâl Mahkemesi Zabıtları – 1926*, [Transcripts of Ankara Independence Tribunal], İşaret Yayınları, İstanbul 1993.

Nongbri, Brent. *Before Religion*: A History of a Modern Concept, Yale University Press, New Haven and London, 2013.

Norris, Pippa and Inglehart, Ronald. *Sacred and Secular*: Religion and Politics Worldwide, Cambridge University Press, Cambridge, 2004.

Nursî, Bediüzzaman Said. *Emirdağ Lâhikası*, Sahdamar Yayınları, İstanbul, 2014.

Oran, Baskın, 'État et religion en Turquie', [The State and religion in Turkey], *multitudes altyazı*, Vol. 8, No. 9, October 2005, pp. 12-16.`

Oran, Baskın. Turkey should take a lesson from Greece, *Ahval*, 15 December 2017.

Ortaylı, İlber. 'Tarikatlar ve Tanzimat Dönemi Osmanlı Yönetimi'. *Ankara Üniversitesi Osmanlı Tarihi Araştırma ve Uygulama Merkezi Dergisi*, No. 6, 1995, pp. 281-287.

Ozcetin, Hilal. 'Breaking the Silence': The Religious Muslim Women's Movement in Turkey, *Journal of International Women's Studies*, Volume 11, 2009, p. 106-119.

Ökte, Faik. *Varlık Vergisi Faciası* [The Tragedy of the Turkish Capital-Tax], Nebioğlu Yayınları İstanbul, 1951.

Öndeş, Osman. *Vahdeddin'in Sırdaşı Avni Paşa Anlatıyor*, [Vahdeddin's confidant Avni Pasha Narrates], Milli Timaş, İstanbul, 2012.

Öngider, Seyfi. *Kuruluş ve Kurucu*, [Foundation and Founder], Aykırı Yayın, İstanbul, 2003.

Öz, Baki. *Çağdaşlaşma Açısından Tarikatlar ve Tekkelerin Kapatılma Olayı*, [The Closure of Orders and Lodges from the Perspective of Modernisation], Can Yayınları, İstanbul, 2004.

Öz, Eyüp, 'Yasak Bir Hafızayla Yüzleşmek: Menemen Olayı İrtica mı, Komplo mu?', [Facing a Forbidden Memory: The Menemen Incident, a Reaction, a conspiracy?], *İnsan ve Toplum Bilimleri Dergisi*, No 5, 2015, pp. 409–440.

Özdek, Çetin, *Türkiye'de Gerici Akımlar*, [Reactionary Movements in Turkey], Gerçek Yayınevi, İstanbul, 1968.

Özdoğa, Elizabeth. Modern Türkiye'de Örtüme Sorunu Resmi Laiklik ve Popüler İslam, [The issue of veiling in Modern Turkey, Official Laicism and Popular Islam], tr. Yavuz Alogan, Barmal Yayınevı, İstanbul, 1991.

Özgür, Iren, *Islamic Schools in Modern Turkey*: Faith Politics and Education, Cambridge University Press, Cambridge, 2012.

Özsaray, Mustafa. Arşiv Belgeleri Işığında Osmanlı'da Devlet Tekke ilişkileri (XIX. Yüzyıl), [State-Tekke Relationship in the Ottoman Empire in Light of Archival Documents], Unpublished Ph.D. Thesis, Fatih Sultan Mehmet Vakıf Universitesi, 2018.

Öztürk, Ünsal. '"mu rahipleri" (a)luvi miydi?' *Kızılbaş*, No. 9, June 2009.

Özyürek, Esra, *Nostalgia for the Modern*: State and Secularism and Everyday Politics in Turkey, Duke University Press, Durham and London, 2006.

Peçe, Halil. "Dinî Çeşitliliğin Artması: Dinî Grupları Sınıflandırma Sorunu Bağlamında Tarikat-Cemaat Ayrımı", *V. Türkiye Lisansüstü Çalışmalar Kongresi*, İstanbul, 2016.

Pekdemir, Melih. *Kemalistler Ülkesinde Cumhuriyet ve Diktatörlük*, [The Republic and Dictatorship in the Country of Kemalists], Vol. 2, Doruk Yayınları, İstanbul, 1997.

Pekdemir, Melih. *Kemalistler Ülkesinde Cumhuriyet ve Diktatörlük*, [The Republic and Dictatorship in the Country of Kemalists], Vol. 1, Su Yayınları, İstanbul, 1999.

Parla, Taha. *Ziya Gökalp, Kemalizm ve Turkiye'de Korporatizm*, [Kemalism and Corporatism in Turkey], İletişim Yayınları, 2nd Edition, 1993, İstanbul.

Parla, Taha and Davison, Andrew. *Corporatist ideology on Kemalist Turkey*: Progress or Order?, Syracuse University Press, Syracuse, New York, 2004.

Pongiluppi, Francesco. "La Turchia di Adnan Menderes: Il Demokrat Parti dalla Fondazione al Declino", [Adnan Menders' Turkey: the Democrat Party from Foundation to Decline], in E. Locci (ed.), *Volti della Politica*, [Faces of Politics], Bastogi Libri, Rome, 2015, pp. 109-129.

Pratt, Vernon. *Religion and Secularisation*, Palgrave Macmillan, London and Basingstoke, 1970.

Rabasa, Angel and Larrabee F. Stephen, *The Rise of Political Islam in Turkey*, Rand Corporation, Santa Monica, 2008.

Radloff, Wilhelm. *Türklük ve Şamanlık*, [Turkishness and Shamanism], tr. Ö. Andaç Uğurlu, A. Temir, T. Andaç, N. Uğurlu, Örgün Yayınevi, Istanbul, 2008.

Roy, Olivier. *Holy Ignorance*: When Religion and Culture Part Ways, trans. Trans. Ros Schwartz, Oxford University Press, Oxford, 2013.

Rustow, Dankwwart A., "Türkiye'de Islâm ve politika 1920 – 1955", [Islam and Politics in Turkey] in *Türkiye'de İslâm ve Laiklik*, İstanbul, 1995, p. 78.

Saf, Hacı Hasan. 'Türkiye'de Yükselen Siyasal İslam'ın Postmodern Nedenleri', [Postmodern Reasons of Political Islam Rising on Turkey], *Karadeniz Teknik Üniversitesi İletişim Araştırmaları Dergisi*, Vol. 3, No. 12, pp. 104-119.

Said, Edward W. *Orientalism*, Vintage Books, New York, 1979.

Said, Bobby S. *A Fundamental Fear*: Eurocentrism and the Emergence of Islamism, Zed Books Limited, London & New York. 1997.

Sadık Sarısaman, 'Cumhuriyetin ilk yıllarında Kadın Kıyafeti Meselesi', [The issue of women's dress in the first years of the Republic], Ankara Üniversitesi Türk İnkilap Tarih Enstitüsü, *Atatürk Yolu*, Vol. 6, No. 21, 1998, pp. 97-106.

Sarıkaya, M. Saffet, 'Dini Zihniyetimizin Oluşumunda Dini Tarikat ve Cemaatlerin Olumsuz İz Düşümleri', [Negative Trace of Religious Orders and Congregations in the Formation of Our Religious Mind] *Arayışlar*, Vol. 3, Nos. 5-6, 2001, pp. 45-60.

Satlow Michael L., 'Disappearing Categories: Using categories in the study of religion', *Method & Theory in the Study of Religion*, No. 17, 2005, pp. 287-298.

Satlow, Michael L. 'Defining Judaism: Accounting for "Religions" in the Study of Religion', *Journal of the American Academy of Religion*, Vol. 74, No. 4 (Dec., 2006), pp. 837-860.

Saymaz, İsmail. *Şehvetiye Tarıkatı*, İletişim Yayınları, İstanbul, 2019.

Senem, Nusret. Fethullah Gülenin Konuşmaları ve Pensilvanya İfadesi, Kaynak Yayınları, İstanbul, 2012.

Seufert Günter, 'Is the Fethullah Gülen Movement Overstretching Itself?: A Turkish Religious Community as a National and International Player', *SWP Research Paper*, Berlin, 2014.

Adak, Sevgi. 'Turkish secularism revisited', *The Middle East in London*, Vol. 13, No. 5, October-November 2017, pp. 11-12.

Shankland, David. *The Alevis in Turkey*: The emergence of a secular Islamic tradition, RoutledgeCurzon, London and New York, 2003.

Shankland, David. 'Maps and the Alevis: On the Ethnography of heterodox Islamic Groups'. *British Journal of Middle Eastern Studies*, December 2010, 37(3), 227-239.

Shindeldecker, John. Turkish Alevis today, https://alevi.dk/ENGELSK/Turkish_Alevis_Today.pdf

Şahin, Mustafa Gökhan. 'Said Nursi and the Nur Movement in Turkey', *Domes*, Vol. 20, No. 2, Fall 2011, p. 226-241.

Shukri, Syaza & Hossain, I. 'Political discourse and Islam: Role of rhetoric in Turkey'. *Journal of Social, Political, and Economic Studies*. Vol. 42, No. 2, Summer 2017. Pp. 157-179.

Silverstein, Brian. "Sufism and Modernity in Turkey: From the authenticity of experience to the practice of discipline" in Bruinessen, Martin Van and Howell, Julia Day (eds), *Sufism and the 'Modern' in Islam*, I. B. Tauris, London and New York, 2007.

Seufert, Günter. 'Is the Fethullah Gülen Movement Overstretching Itself?: A Turkish Religious Community as a National and International Player', *SWP Research Paper*, Berlin, 2014.

Smith Jonathan Z., *Imagining Religion:* From Babylon to Jonestown, University of Chicago Press, Chicago, 1982.

Sırma İhsan Süreyya, *Alaturka Demokrasi Alaturka Laiklik*, [A la Turca Democracy. A la Turca Laicity], Beyan, İstanbul, 1997.

Solberg, Anne Rose. *The Mahdi Wears Armani*: An Analysis of the Harun Yahya Enterprise, Södertörns Högskola doctoral dissertation published by the University of Gothenburg, Goteborg, 2013.

Soyak, Hasan Rıza, *Atatürk'ten Hatıralar*, [Memories from Atatürk], Vol. 1, Yapı ve Kredi Bankası, İstanbul, 1973.

Subaşı, Necdet. Öteki *Türkiye'de Din ve Modernleşme*, [Religion and Modernisation in Turkey], Vadi Yayınları, Ankara, 2003.

Sunier Thijl, Landman Nico, Linden, Heleen van der, Bilgili Nazlı, Bilgili Alper. 'Diyanet: The Turkish Directorate for Religious Affairs in a changing environment', Utrecht University, Amsterdam, January 2011.

Şahiner, Necmeddin Bediüzzaman Said Nursî'nin Kayıp Mezarının Sırrı, Elips Kitap, Ankara, 2012.

Şenay, Banu. *Beyond Turkey's Borders*: Long-Distance Kemalism, State Politics and the Turkish Diaspora, I. B. Tauris, London, New York, 2012.

Şenermen, Sedat. *Atatürk, İslam ve Laiklik*, [Atatürk, Islam and Laicism], Elmadağı Yayınları, İstanbul, 2015.

Şık, Ahmet. *İmamın Ordusu*, [Imam's Army], Kırmızı Kedi Yayınevi, İstanbul, 2017.

Şık, Ahmet. *İtham Ediyorum*, [I accuse], Kırmızı Kedi Yayınları, İstanbul, 2018.

Şur, Şükrü. 'Demokrat Parti ve Atatürk'ün üç ilkesi: Cumhuriyetçilik Laiklik ve Devletçilik (1950-1960), [Democrat Party and Atatürk's three principles: Republicanism, Laicism and Statism], Ankara Üniversitesi Türk İnkılâp Tarihi Enstitüsü, *Atatürk Yolu*, No. 176. Spring, 2015, pp. 147-176.

Taşkın, Yüksel. "12 Eylül Atatürkçülüğü ya da Bir Kemalist Restorasyon Teşebbüsü olarak 12 Eylül" [12 September Atatürkism or Kemalist Resotartion Attempt], in Tanıl Bora, Gültenkingil Murat, *Kemalizm*, Modern Türkiye'de Siyasî Düşünce, Vol. 2, İletişim Yayınları, İstanbul, 2009.

Taştekin, Emel. 'Secular Trauma and Religious Myth: The Case of Said Nursi Bediuzzaman's *Risale-i Nur*', *Monograf*, No. 1, January 2014, pp. 67-82.

Taylor, Charles, *A Secular Age*, The Belknap Press of Harvard University Press, Cambridge, Massachusetts, and London, 2007.

Taves, Ann. *Religious Experience Reconsidered*: A Building-Block Approach to the Study of Religion and Other Special Things, Princeton University Press, Princeton and Oxford, 2009.

T.B.M.M. Gizli Zabıtları, [Grand National Assembly of Turkey Secret Minutes], Vols. 1-4, İş Bankası Kültür Yayınları, İstanbul, 1999.

Tee, Caroline, *The* Gülen Movement in Turkey: The Politics of Islam and Modernity, I. B. Tauris, London and New York, 2016.

Tibi, Bassam. *Islam Between Culture and Politics*, Palgrave Basingstoke, 2001.

Toker, Metin. Demokrasimizin İsmet Paşa'lı Yılları (1944-1973): *DP Yokuş Aşağı (1954-1957)*, [The İsmet Pasha Years of Our Democracy (1944-1973): DP Downhill (1954-1957)], Bilgi Yayınevi, İstanbul, 1991.

Toprak Metin and Uslu Nasuh, The Headscarf Controversy in Turkey, MPRA Paper No. 16052, 22. November 2008.

Tosun, Necdet. "Nakşibendiyye" in Ceyhan, Semih. (ed.) *Türkiye'de Tarikatlar*: [New Religious Orders in Turkey], Tarih ve Kültür, İsam Yayınları, İstanbul, 2015, pp. 611-94.

Troxell, Ted. Belief in the Immanent Frame, Religion at the Margins, 6 November 2010, http://religionatthemargins.com/2010/11/belief-in-the-immanent-frame/.

Tunçay, Mete, *et al*. *Çağdaş Türkiye 1908 1980*, [Contemporary Turkey 1908-1980], Cem Yayınevi, İstanbul, 1989.

Turam, Berna. *Between Islam and the State*: The Politics of Engagement, Stanford University Press, Stanford, California, 2007.

Turam, Berna (ed.), *Secular State and Religious Society*: Two Forces in Play in Turkey, Pallgrave Macmillan, NewYork, 2012.

Türk Tarih Heyeti, *Türk Tarihinin Ana Hatları*, Devlet Matbaası, Ankara, 1930; reprint *Türk Tarihinin Ana Hatları*: Kemalist yönetimin resmî tarih tezi, 3rd Edition, [Outline of Turkish History: Kemalist regime's official history thesis], Kaynak Yayınları, İstanbul. 1999.

Türk, Resul, 'Türkiye'de Siyasal İslam'ın Örgütlenme Faaliyetleri', *Journal of The Academic Elegance*, Vol. 2, No. 3, 2015, pp. 99-131.

Türkiye'de İslâm ve Laiklik, [Laicism and Islam in Turkey], insan yayınları, İstanbul, 1995.

Ulusan, Şayan. "Atatürk Dönemi Din Uygulamaları (1923-1938)", [The Atatürk Period and Religious Practices], *Cappadocia Journal of History and Social Sciences*, Vol. 11, October 2018, pp. 306-320.

Vahide, Şükran. *Islam in Modern Turkey*: An intellectual Biography of Bediuzzaman Said Nursi, State University of New York Press, Albany, 2005.

Vieste, di Mauro, Promesse e tradimenti. Kurdistan terra divisa, [Promises and Betrayals: Kurdistan a divided land], n.p., n.p., 2008.

Voll, John Obert. 'Renewal and Reformation in the Mid-Twentieth Century: Bediuzaman Said Nursi and Religion in the 1950s', *The Muslim World*, Vol. LXXXIX, No. 3-4, July-October. 1999, pp. 245-259.

Vojdik, Valorie K, 'Politics of the Headscarf in Turkey: Masculinities, Feminism, and the Construction of Collective Identities', *Harvard Journal of Law & Gender*, Vol. 33, No. 1, 2010, 661-685.

Warhola, James W. and Egemen B. Bezici, 'Religion and State in Contemporary Turkey: Recent Developments in "Laiklik"', *Journal of Church and State and State*, Oxford University Press, November 2010, pp. 1-27.

Watters, Samuel W. 'Developments in AKP Policy Toward Religion and Homogeneity', *German Law Journal*, Vol. 19, No. 02, 2018, pp. 351-74.

White, Jenny. *Muslim Nationalism and the New Turks*, Princeton University Press, Princeton and Oxford, 2013.

White, Paul J. and Jongerden, Joost, *Turkey's Alevi Enigma*: A Comprehensive Overview, Brill, Leiden, 2003.

Weismann, Itzchak. *The Naqshbandiyya*: Orthodoxy and activism in a worldwide Sufi tradition, Routledge, New York, 2007.

Yanardağ, Ayşe, 'Tarikat ve Zaviye ve Türbelerin Kaldırılmasına Dair Devrim Kanunu ve Uygulamaları', [Revolution Law and Implementation Regarding the Removal of Orders, Zaviyes, Tombs], *I. Uluslar Arası Tarih ve Kültür Kongresi*, Gaziantep, 19-22 August 2017.

Yanmış, Mehmet. 'Post-modern Kabileler veya Cemaat-Tarikatlar', [Post-modern Tribes and Cemaats-Tarikat], Milliyet, 27 October 2016.

Yavuz, M. Hakan. *Islamic Political Identity in Turkey*, Oxford University Press, Oxford, 2003.

Yavuz, M. Hakan and Esposito, John L. *Turkish Islam and the Secular State*: The Gülen Movement, Syracuse University Press, Syracuse, 2003.

Yavuz, M. Hakan. (Ed.). *The Emergence of a New Turkey*: Democracy and the AK Parti, The University of Utah Press, Salt Lake City, 2006.

Yavuz, M. Hakan. *Secularism and Muslim Democracy in Turkey*, Cambridge Universty Press, 2009.

Yavuz, M. Hakan. *Toward an Islamic Enlightenment: The Gülen Movement*, Oxford University Press, Oxford, 2013.

Yavuz M. Hakan and Bayram Balcı, *Turkey's July 15th Coup*: What happened and Why, The University of Utah Press, Salt Lake City, 2018.

Yeler, Abdülkadir. "Aleviliğin Kurumsallaşma Süreci", Geçmişten Günümüze Alevilik I. Uluslararası Sempozyumu, [Alewism From Past To Present I. International Symposium], Vol. 2, Bingöl Üniversitesi Yayınları, Bingöl, 2014, pp. 166-88.

Yeşilada, Birol A. "The Refah Party Phenomenon in Turkey" in Birol A. Yeşilada (ed.) *Comparative Political Parties and Party Elites*, The University of Michigan Press, Michigan, 1999, pp. 123-150.

Yeğenoğlu, Meyda, 'The sacralization of secularism in Turkey', *Radical Philosophy*, No. 145, September/October 2007.

Yeğenoğlu, Meyda. "Clash of secularity and religiosity: the staging of secularism and Islam through the icons of Atatürk and the veil in Turkey" in Jack Barbalet *et al* (Eds.) *Religion and the State: A Comparative Sociology*, Anthem Press, London, New York, Delhi, 2011, pp. 225–244.

Yıldırım, Tercan and Şimşek, Ahmet. "'The Narrative of Religion' in the High School Textbooks of the Early Republican Period in Turkey", *Education and Science*, Vol. 40, No. 179, 2015, pp. 323-340.

Yildirim, Seval. "The Search for Shared Idioms: Contesting Views of Laiklik Before the Turkish Constitutional Court", Gabriele Marranci (Ed.), *Muslim Societies and the Challenge of Secularization*: An Interdisciplinary Approach, Springer Dordrecht, Heidelberg London New York, 2010, pp. 235-52.

Yıldız, Ahmet. *"Ne Mutlu Türküm Diyebilene"*: Türk Ulusal Kimliğinin Etno-Seküler Sınırları (1919-1938), [What happiness for those who are able to say they are Turks: The Etno-secular Boundaries of the Turkish National Identity], İletişim Yayınları, İstanbul, 2001.

Yıldız, Ayşe Nevin. 'Türkiye modernleşmesine bir muhalif basın olarak Büyük Doğu', [Büyük Doğu as opposition press to modernisation of Turkey], *İletişim Fakültesi Dergisi*, Vol. 0, No. 13, 2012, pp. 577-595.

Yılmaz, Hacı. 'Kâhire Bektâşî Dergâhı''nın son postnişîni Ahmed Sırrı Dedebaba'ya göre Bektâşîlik'. [Bektâshism according to Ahmed Sirri Dedebaba who is the last postnishin of Cairo Bektashism Dervish Lodge], *Journal of Human Sciences*, Vol. 14, No. 4, pp. 3310-3327.

Yılmaz, H. Kâmil. *Anahatlarıyla Tasavvuf ve Tarîkatlar*, [Outline of Mysticism and Tarikats], Ensar Neşriyat Kitapevi, İstanbul, 2004.

Yılmaz, İhsan. *Kemalizm'den Erdoğanizme*, [From Kemalism to Erdoğanism], Ufuk Yayınları, İstanbul, 2015.

Yılmaz, Selma. 'Milli Görüş Hareketi: Toplumsal Hareketlerde Çerçeve Değişimi Etkisi, [The Milli Görüş Hareketi Movement: Effect in Social Movements of Framework Change], *İnsan ve Toplum Bilimleri Araştırmaları Dergisi*, Vol. 5, No. 4, pp. 1164-1185.

Yılmazçelik, İbrahim and Erdoğan, Seher Kont. 'Alevilikte Dedelik Kurumu ve Mustafa Dede Örneği', [The Institution of Dede in Alevi Faith and the Example of Mustafa Dede], *Alevilik Araştırmaları Dergisi*, Vol. 2, No. 4, 2012, pp. 1-34.

Zarcone, Thierry, "La fabrication des saints sous la République turque", [The manufacture of saints under the Turkish Republic], in Mayeur-Jaouen, Catherine (ed.). Saints et héros du Moyen-Orient contemporain, [Saints and heroes of the contemporary Middle East], Maisonneuve & Larose, Paris, 2002.

Zarcone, Thierry, "Confrérisme, maraboutisme et culte des saints face au réformisme: Le cas de la Turquie d'Atatürk et de la Tunisie de Bourguiba", [Brotherhood, maraboutism and cult of saints facing reformism: the case of Atatürk's Turkey and Bourguiba's Tunisia], L'Harmattan, Paris, 2009, pp. 323-336.

Zarnett, David. "Edward Said and the West", *Democratiya*, Spring 2008.

Zelyut, Rıza. 'Tekke ve Zaviyeler Niçin Kapatıldı?', [Why were the Dervish Lodges Closed Down?], *Güneş gazetesi*. 25 May 2011.

Zürcher, Erik, *Turkey: A Modern History*, I. B. Tauris, 3rd Edition, London, 2004.

Zürcher, Erik, *The Young Turk Legacy and Nation Building*: From the Ottoman Empire to Atatürk's Legacy, I.B. Tauris, London, 2010, p. 144.

Journals
Bulletin périodique de la presse Turquie

Archives
Australian Archives
T.B.M.M. Celse Zabıtları
T.C. Resmi Gazete
Milli Güvenlik Konseyi Tutanak Dergisi
Wikileaks, Public Library of US Diplomacy

Party Programs
C.H.P. Kurultayı, 1947.
Cumhuriyetçi Köylü Partisi Seçim Bildirisi, 1965.
Güven Partisi Programı, 1967/
Demokrat Parti Programı, 1946.
Millî Nizam Partisi: program ve tüzük, Ankara, n.d.
Millî Selâmet Partisi, *Program ve Tüzük*, Ankara, n.d.
M.P. Millet Partisi Programı, Ankara, 1967.
Yeni Türkiye Partisi Tüzüğü ve Programı, 1967.

Newspapers
Ahval
Akşam
Al Jazeera Turk
Birgün
Cumhuriyet
Hürriyet
Le Populaire
Milliyet
Kurun
Kathimerini (Καθημερινή)
Radikal
Stargazete
The Independent
The Times
Ulus
Vakit
Vatan
Washington Post

www.ingramcontent.com/pod-product-compliance
Lightning Source LLC
Chambersburg PA
CBHW060039100426
42742CB00014B/2640